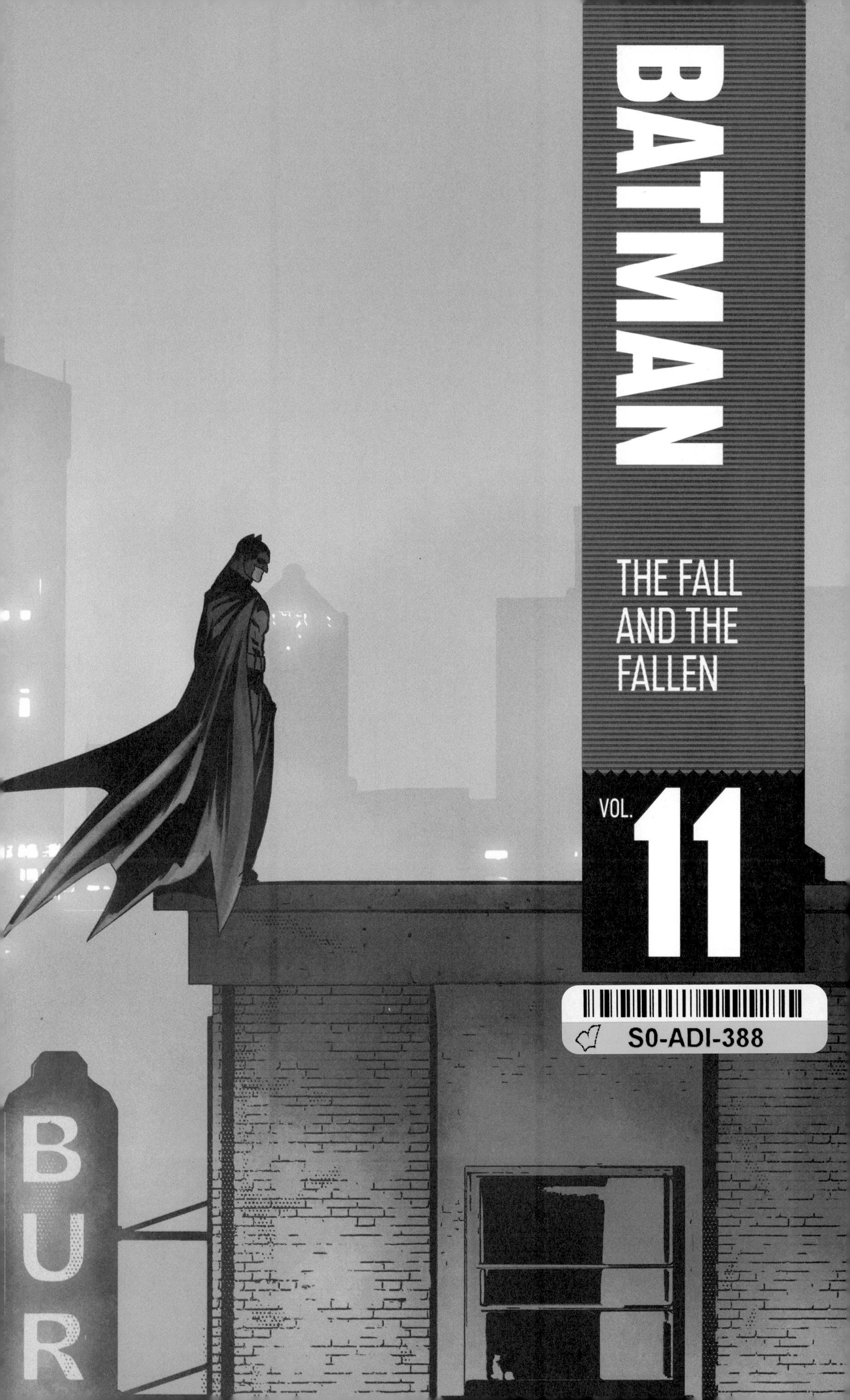
BATMAN
THE FALL AND THE FALLEN
VOL. 11
BUR

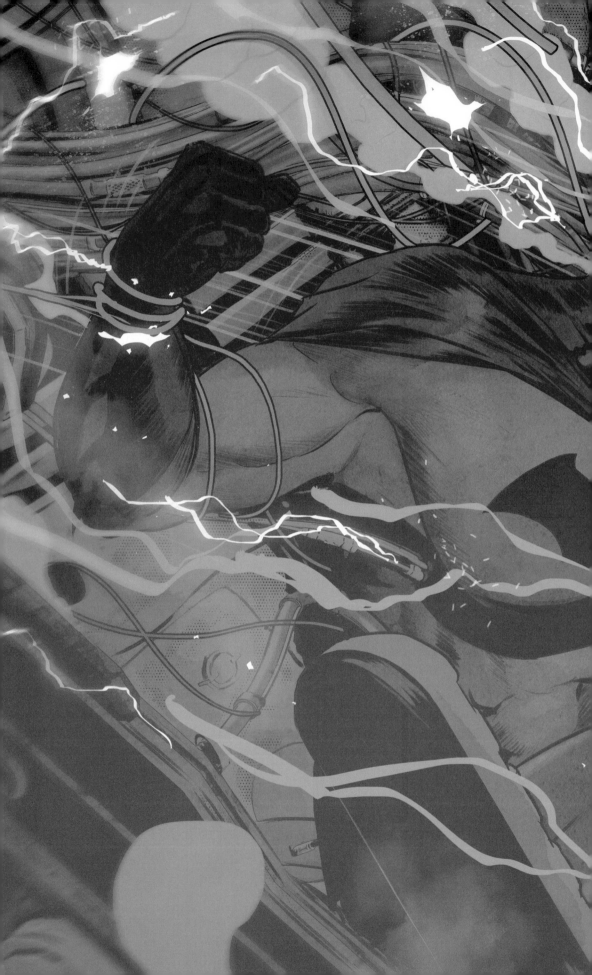

BATMAN
THE FALL AND THE FALLEN

writers
TOM KING
ANDY KUBERT
COLLIN KELLY
JACKSON LANZING
MAIRGHREAD SCOTT
STEVE ORLANDO
TIM SEELEY

artists
MIKEL JANÍN
JORGE FORNES
AMANCAY NAHUELPAN
CARLOS D'ANDA
GIUSEPPE CAMUNCOLI
CAM SMITH
EDUARDO RISSO
PATRICK GLEASON

colorists
JORDIE BELLAIRE
TRISH MULVIHILL
LUIS GUERRERO
TOMEU MOREY
DAVE STEWART
JOHN KALISZ

letterers
CLAYTON COWLES
STEVE WANDS
ANDWORLD DESIGN
JOHN WORKMAN
TOM NAPOLITANO

collection cover artists
ANDY KUBERT and BRAD ANDERSON

BATMAN created by BOB KANE with BILL FINGER

VOL. **11**

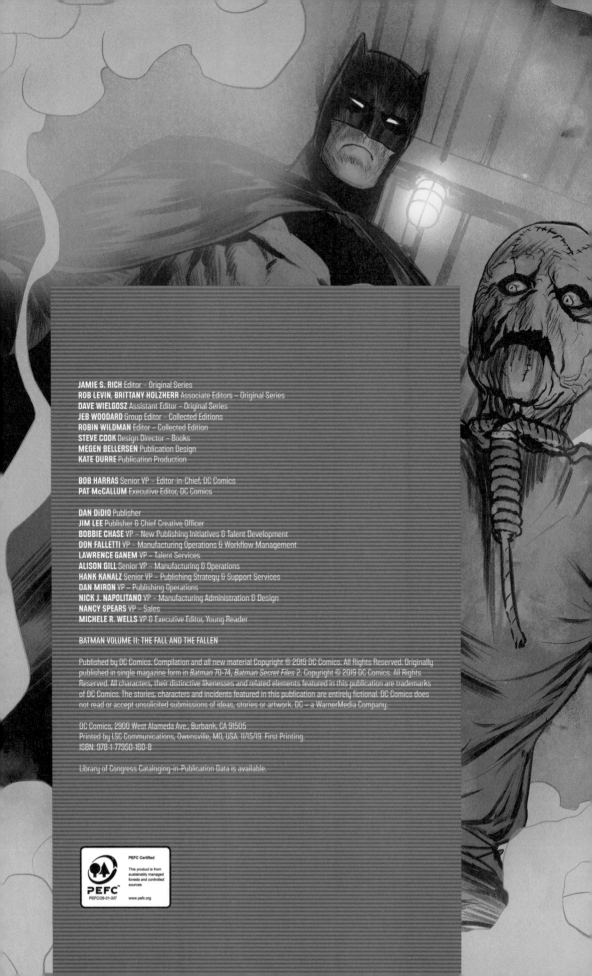

JAMIE S. RICH Editor – Original Series
ROB LEVIN, BRITTANY HOLZHERR Associate Editors – Original Series
DAVE WIELGOSZ Assistant Editor – Original Series
JEB WOODARD Group Editor – Collected Editions
ROBIN WILDMAN Editor – Collected Edition
STEVE COOK Design Director – Books
MEGEN BELLERSEN Publication Design
KATE DURRE Publication Production

BOB HARRAS Senior VP – Editor-in-Chief, DC Comics
PAT McCALLUM Executive Editor, DC Comics

DAN DiDIO Publisher
JIM LEE Publisher & Chief Creative Officer
BOBBIE CHASE VP – New Publishing Initiatives & Talent Development
DON FALLETTI VP – Manufacturing Operations & Workflow Management
LAWRENCE GANEM VP – Talent Services
ALISON GILL Senior VP – Manufacturing & Operations
HANK KANALZ Senior VP – Publishing Strategy & Support Services
DAN MIRON VP – Publishing Operations
NICK J. NAPOLITANO VP – Manufacturing Administration & Design
NANCY SPEARS VP – Sales
MICHELE R. WELLS VP & Executive Editor, Young Reader

BATMAN VOLUME 11: THE FALL AND THE FALLEN

DC Comics, 2900 West Alameda Ave., Burbank, CA 91505
Printed by LSC Communications, Owensville, MO, USA. 11/15/19. First Printing.
ISBN: 978-1-77950-160-8

Library of Congress Cataloging-in-Publication Data is available.

PEFC Certified
This product is from sustainably managed forests and controlled sources
PEFC
PEFC/29-31-337
www.pefc.org

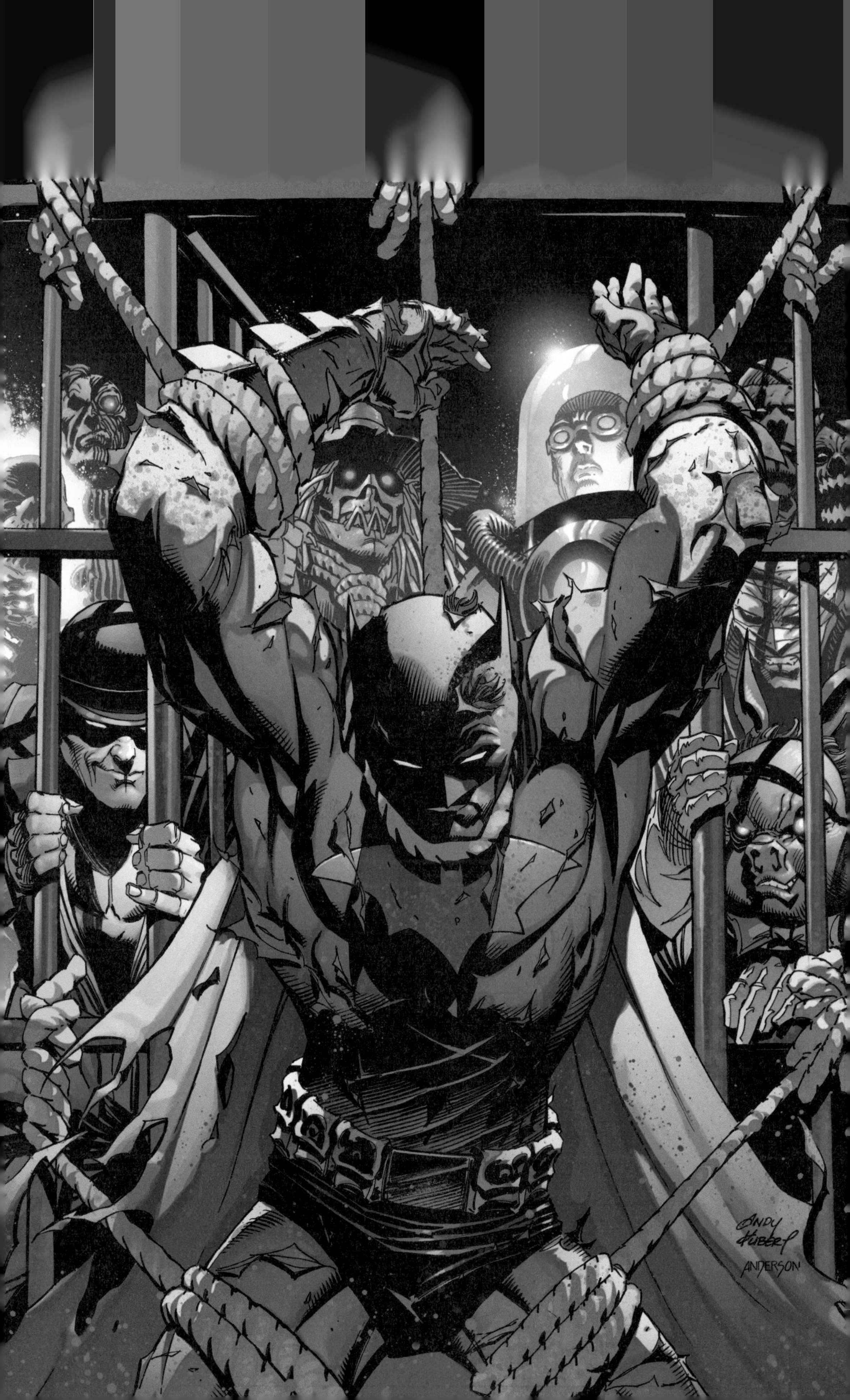
ANDY KUBERT
ANDERSON

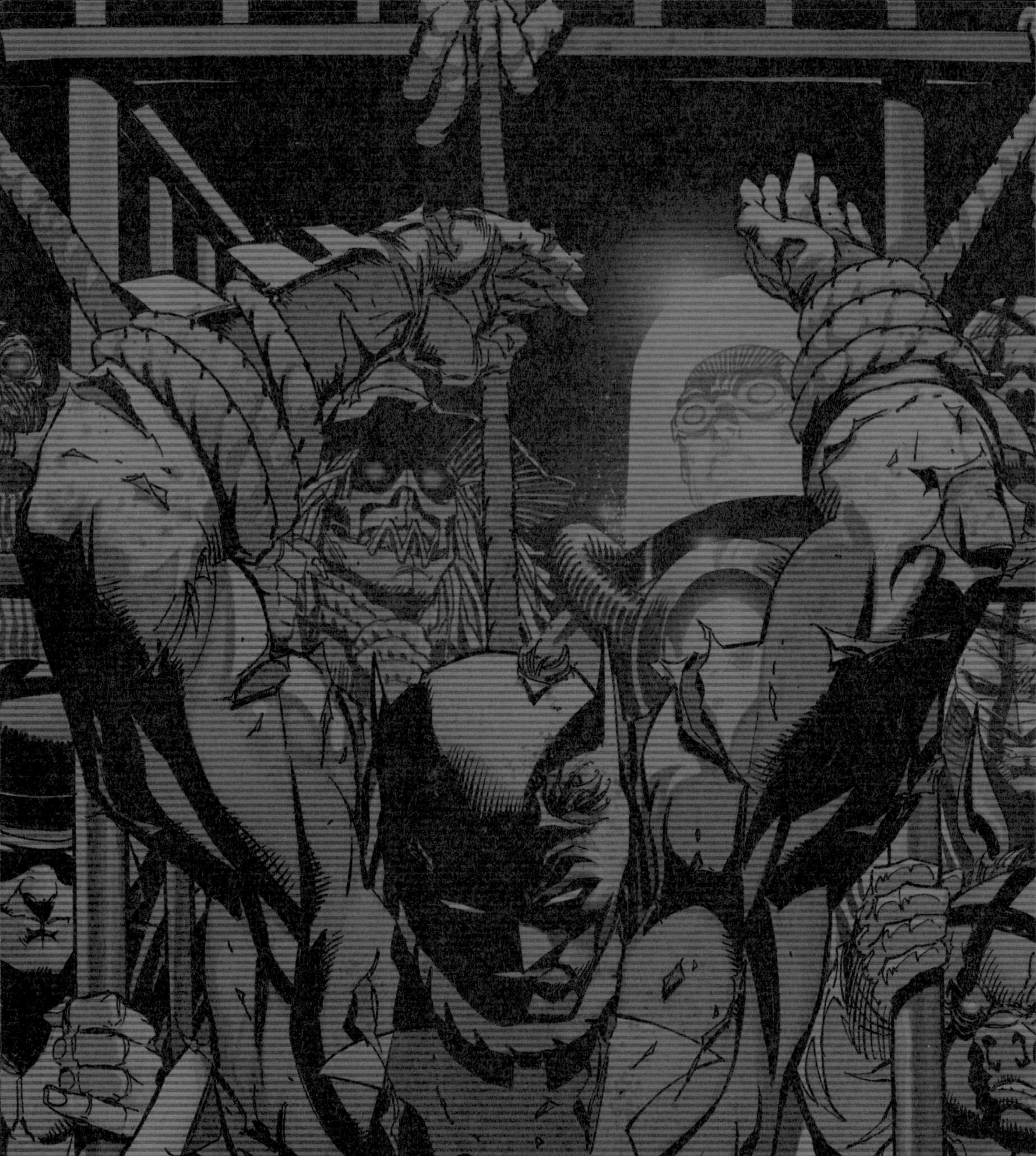

BATMAN
#70

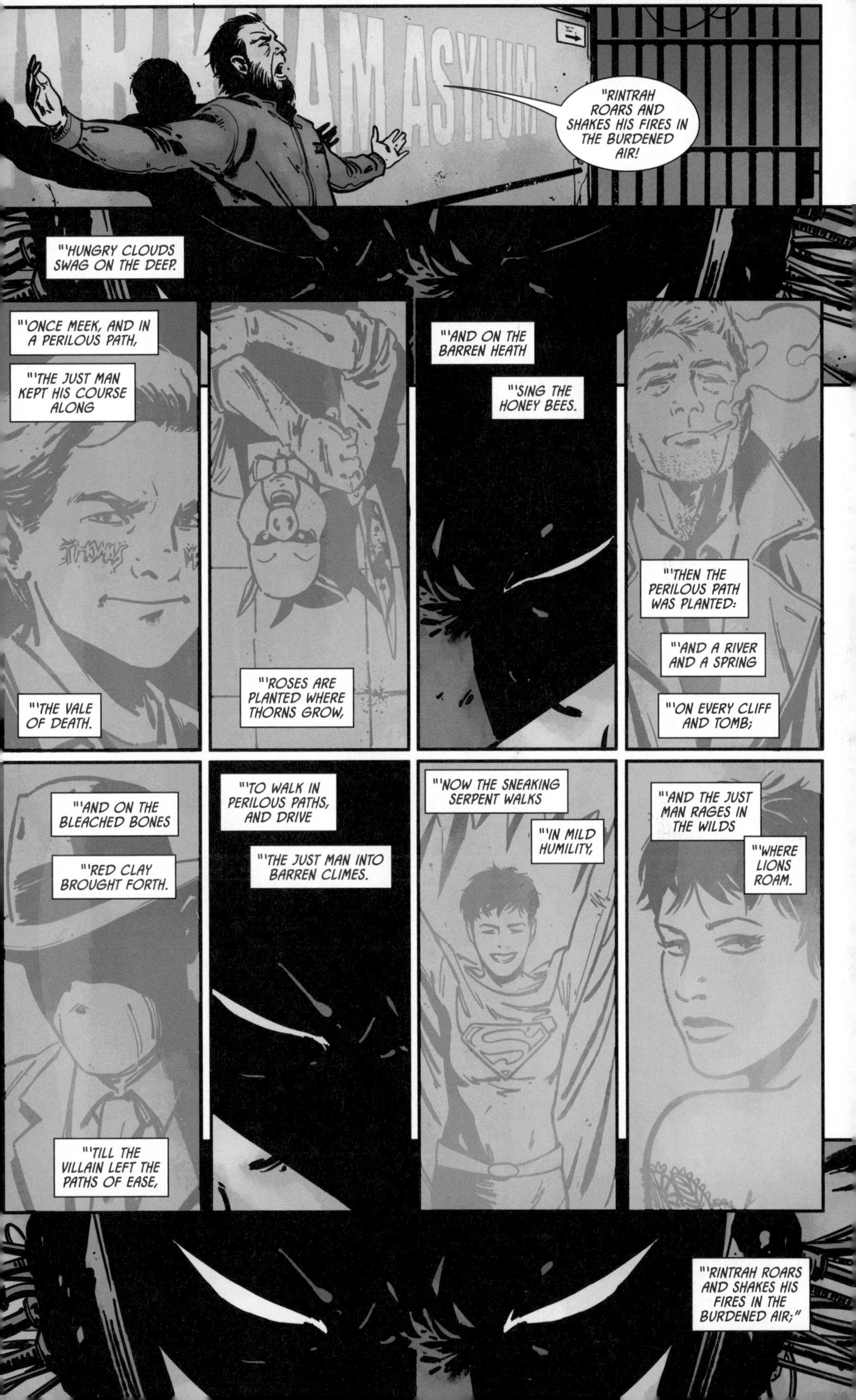
ARKHAM ASYLUM
"RINTRAH ROARS AND SHAKES HIS FIRES IN THE BURDENED AIR!
"'HUNGRY CLOUDS SWAG ON THE DEEP.
"'ONCE MEEK, AND IN A PERILOUS PATH,
"'THE JUST MAN KEPT HIS COURSE ALONG
"'THE VALE OF DEATH.
"'ROSES ARE PLANTED WHERE THORNS GROW,
"'AND ON THE BARREN HEATH
"'SING THE HONEY BEES.
"'THEN THE PERILOUS PATH WAS PLANTED:
"'AND A RIVER AND A SPRING
"'ON EVERY CLIFF AND TOMB;
"'AND ON THE BLEACHED BONES
"'RED CLAY BROUGHT FORTH.
"'TILL THE VILLAIN LEFT THE PATHS OF EASE,
"'TO WALK IN PERILOUS PATHS, AND DRIVE
"'THE JUST MAN INTO BARREN CLIMES.
"'NOW THE SNEAKING SERPENT WALKS
"'IN MILD HUMILITY,
"'AND THE JUST MAN RAGES IN THE WILDS
"'WHERE LIONS ROAM.
"'RINTRAH ROARS AND SHAKES HIS FIRES IN THE BURDENED AIR;"

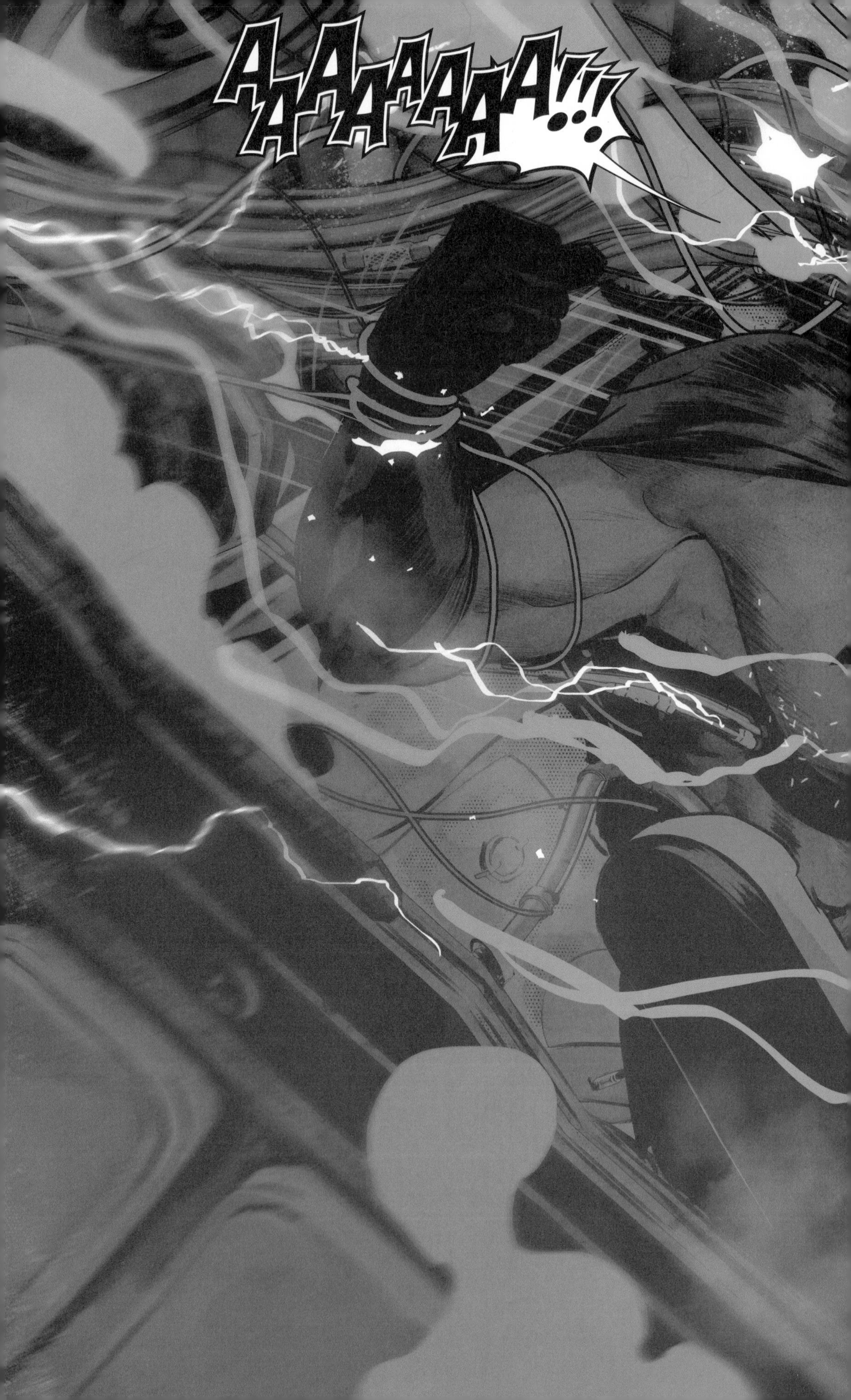
AAAAAAAA!!!

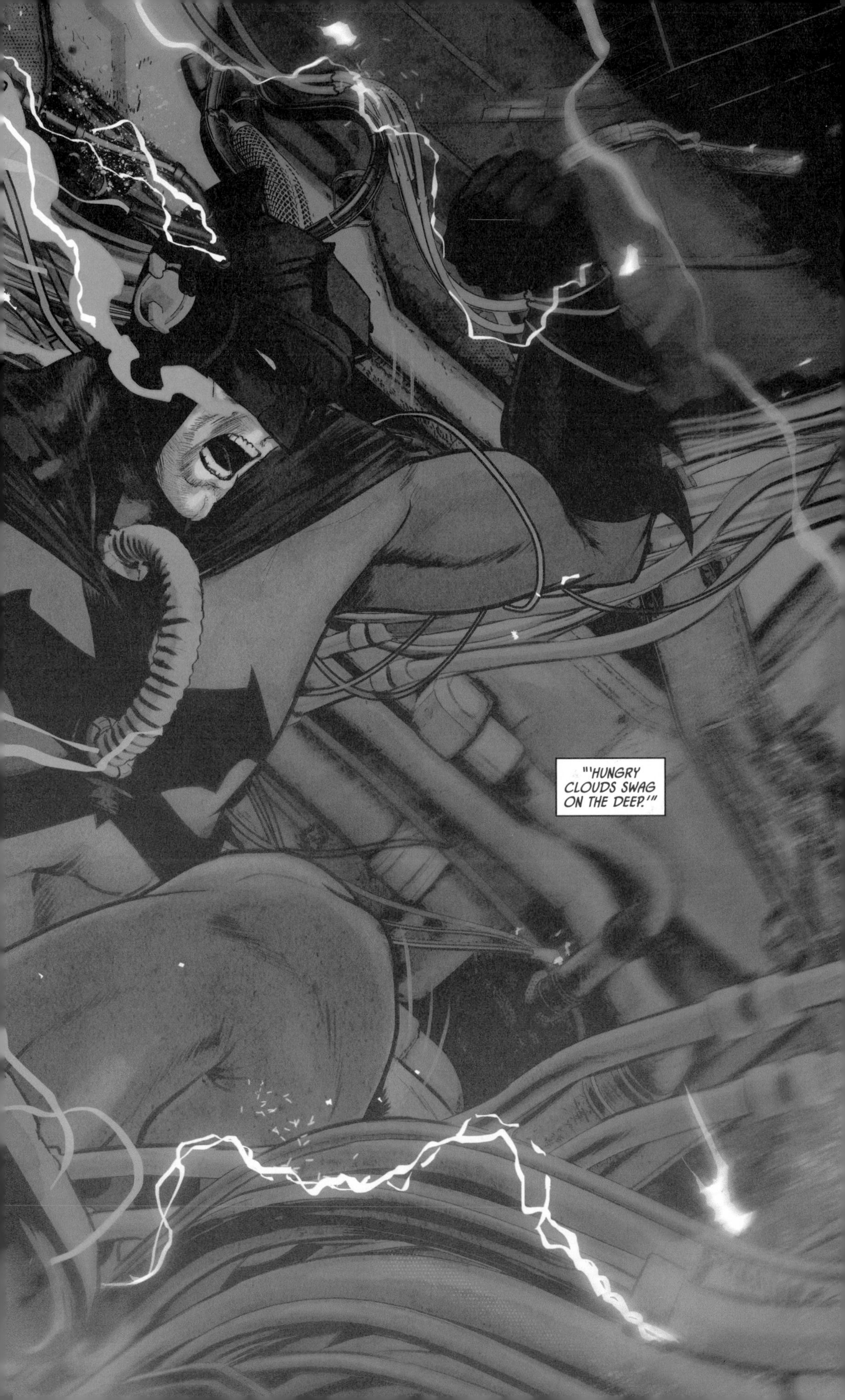
"'HUNGRY CLOUDS SWAG ON THE DEEP.'"

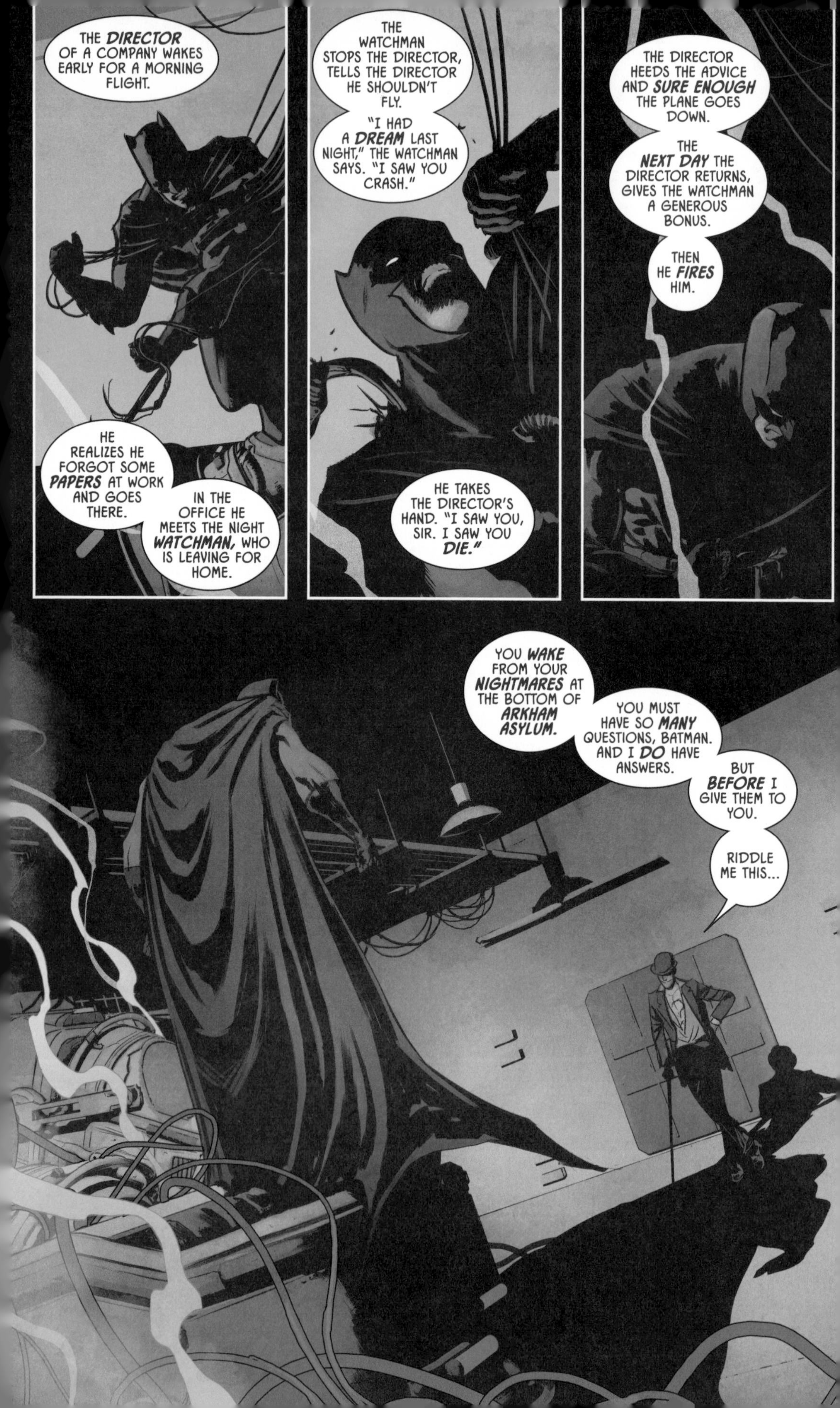
THE DIRECTOR OF A COMPANY WAKES EARLY FOR A MORNING FLIGHT.
HE REALIZES HE FORGOT SOME PAPERS AT WORK AND GOES THERE.
IN THE OFFICE HE MEETS THE NIGHT WATCHMAN, WHO IS LEAVING FOR HOME.
THE WATCHMAN STOPS THE DIRECTOR, TELLS THE DIRECTOR HE SHOULDN'T FLY.
"I HAD A DREAM LAST NIGHT," THE WATCHMAN SAYS. "I SAW YOU CRASH."
HE TAKES THE DIRECTOR'S HAND. "I SAW YOU, SIR. I SAW YOU DIE."
THE DIRECTOR HEEDS THE ADVICE AND SURE ENOUGH THE PLANE GOES DOWN.
THE NEXT DAY THE DIRECTOR RETURNS, GIVES THE WATCHMAN A GENEROUS BONUS.
THEN HE FIRES HIM.
YOU WAKE FROM YOUR NIGHTMARES AT THE BOTTOM OF ARKHAM ASYLUM.
YOU MUST HAVE SO MANY QUESTIONS, BATMAN. AND I DO HAVE ANSWERS.
BUT BEFORE I GIVE THEM TO YOU.
RIDDLE ME THIS...

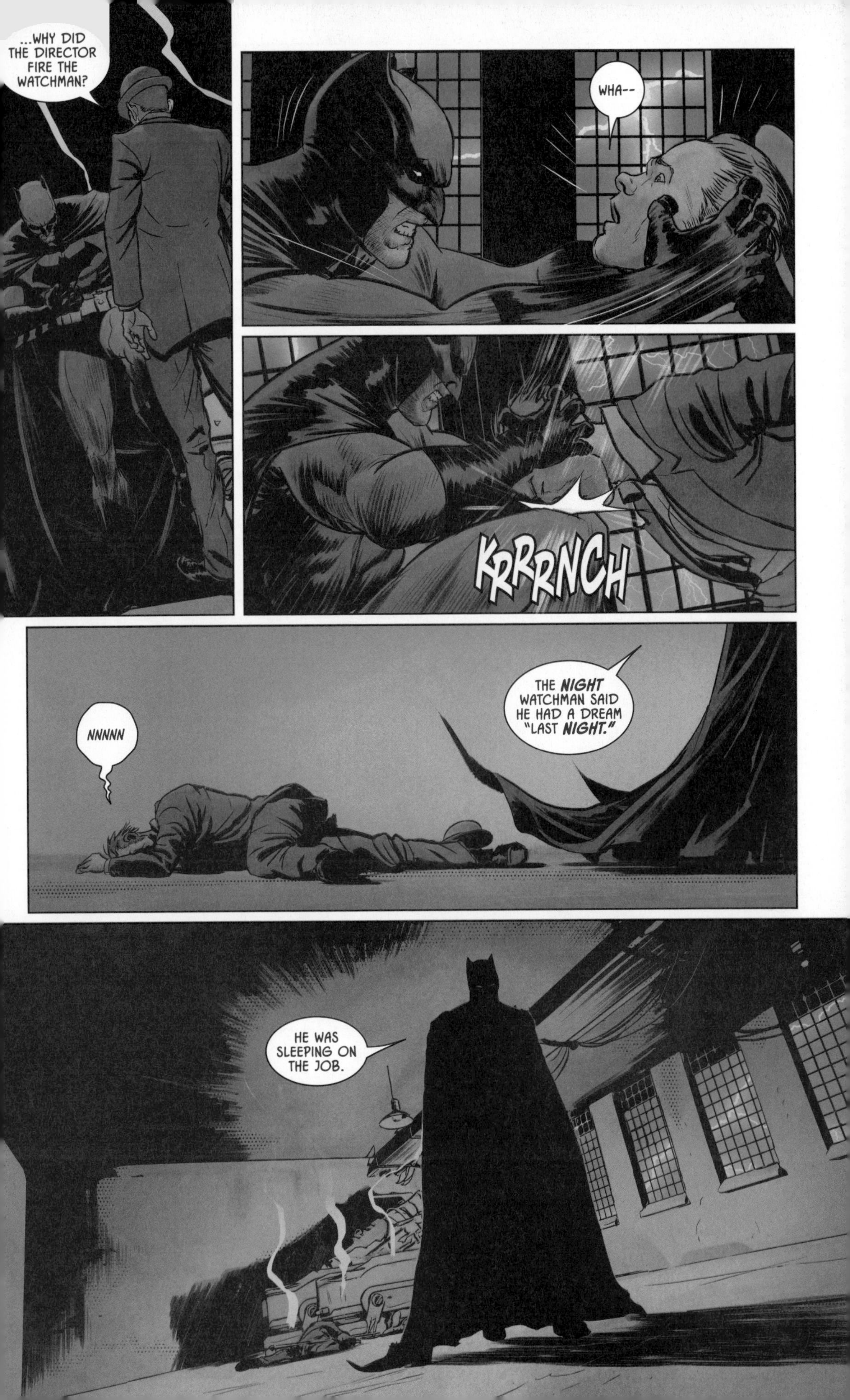
...WHY DID THE DIRECTOR FIRE THE WATCHMAN?
WHA--
KRRRNCH
NNNNN
THE **NIGHT** WATCHMAN SAID HE HAD A DREAM "LAST **NIGHT.**"
HE WAS SLEEPING ON THE JOB.

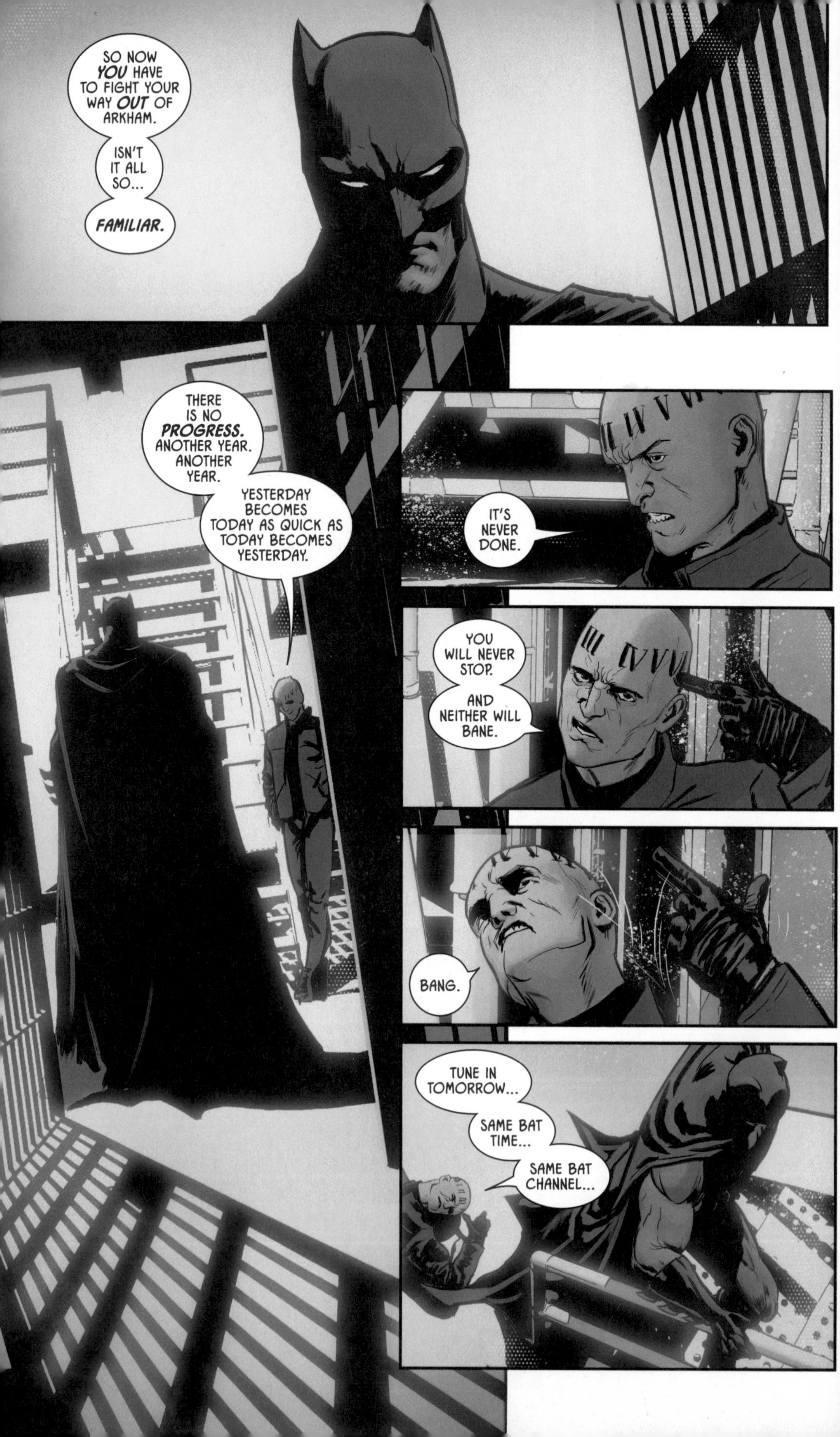
SO NOW *YOU* HAVE TO FIGHT YOUR WAY *OUT* OF ARKHAM.
ISN'T IT ALL SO...
FAMILIAR.
THERE IS NO *PROGRESS.* ANOTHER YEAR. ANOTHER YEAR.
YESTERDAY BECOMES TODAY AS QUICK AS TODAY BECOMES YESTERDAY.
IT'S NEVER DONE.
YOU WILL NEVER STOP.
AND NEITHER WILL BANE.
BANG.
TUNE IN TOMORROW...
SAME BAT TIME...
SAME BAT CHANNEL...

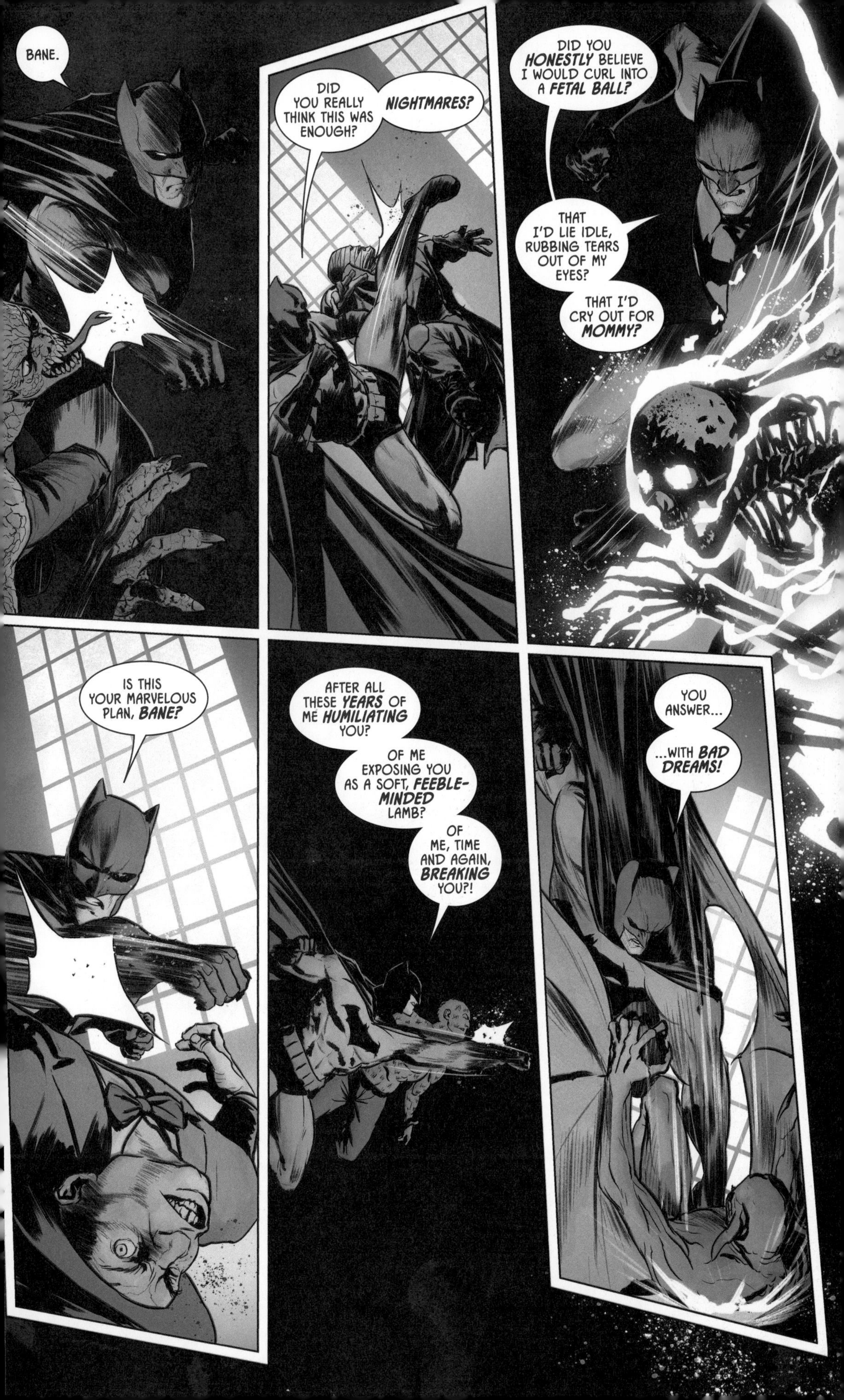
BANE.
DID YOU REALLY THINK THIS WAS ENOUGH?
NIGHTMARES?
DID YOU HONESTLY BELIEVE I WOULD CURL INTO A FETAL BALL?
THAT I'D LIE IDLE, RUBBING TEARS OUT OF MY EYES?
THAT I'D CRY OUT FOR MOMMY?
IS THIS YOUR MARVELOUS PLAN, BANE?
AFTER ALL THESE YEARS OF ME HUMILIATING YOU?
OF ME EXPOSING YOU AS A SOFT, FEEBLE-MINDED LAMB?
OF ME, TIME AND AGAIN, BREAKING YOU?!
YOU ANSWER...
...WITH BAD DREAMS!

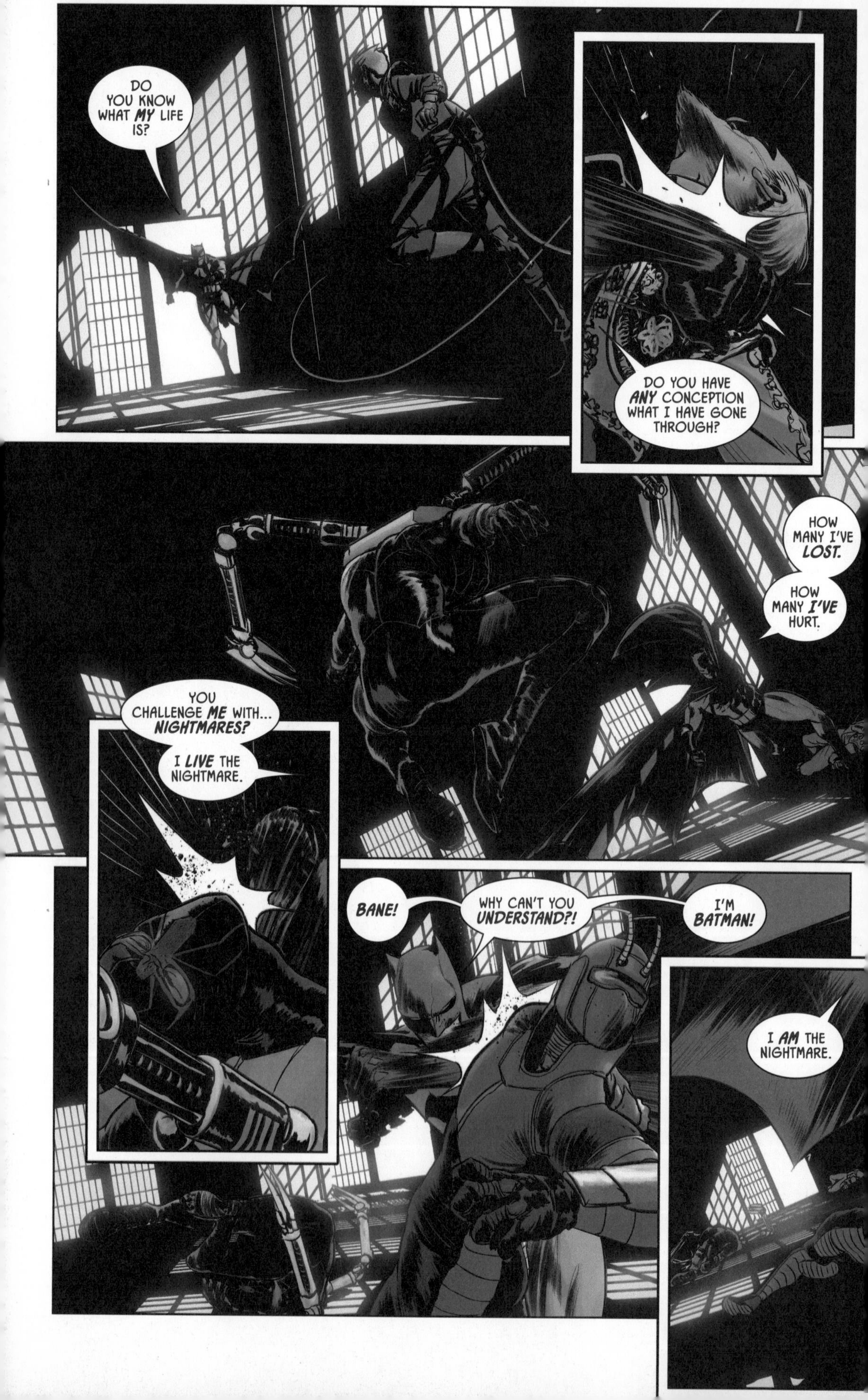
DO YOU KNOW WHAT MY LIFE IS?
DO YOU HAVE ANY CONCEPTION WHAT I HAVE GONE THROUGH?
HOW MANY I'VE LOST.
HOW MANY I'VE HURT.
YOU CHALLENGE ME WITH... NIGHTMARES?
I LIVE THE NIGHTMARE.
BANE!
WHY CAN'T YOU UNDERSTAND?!
I'M BATMAN!
I AM THE NIGHTMARE.

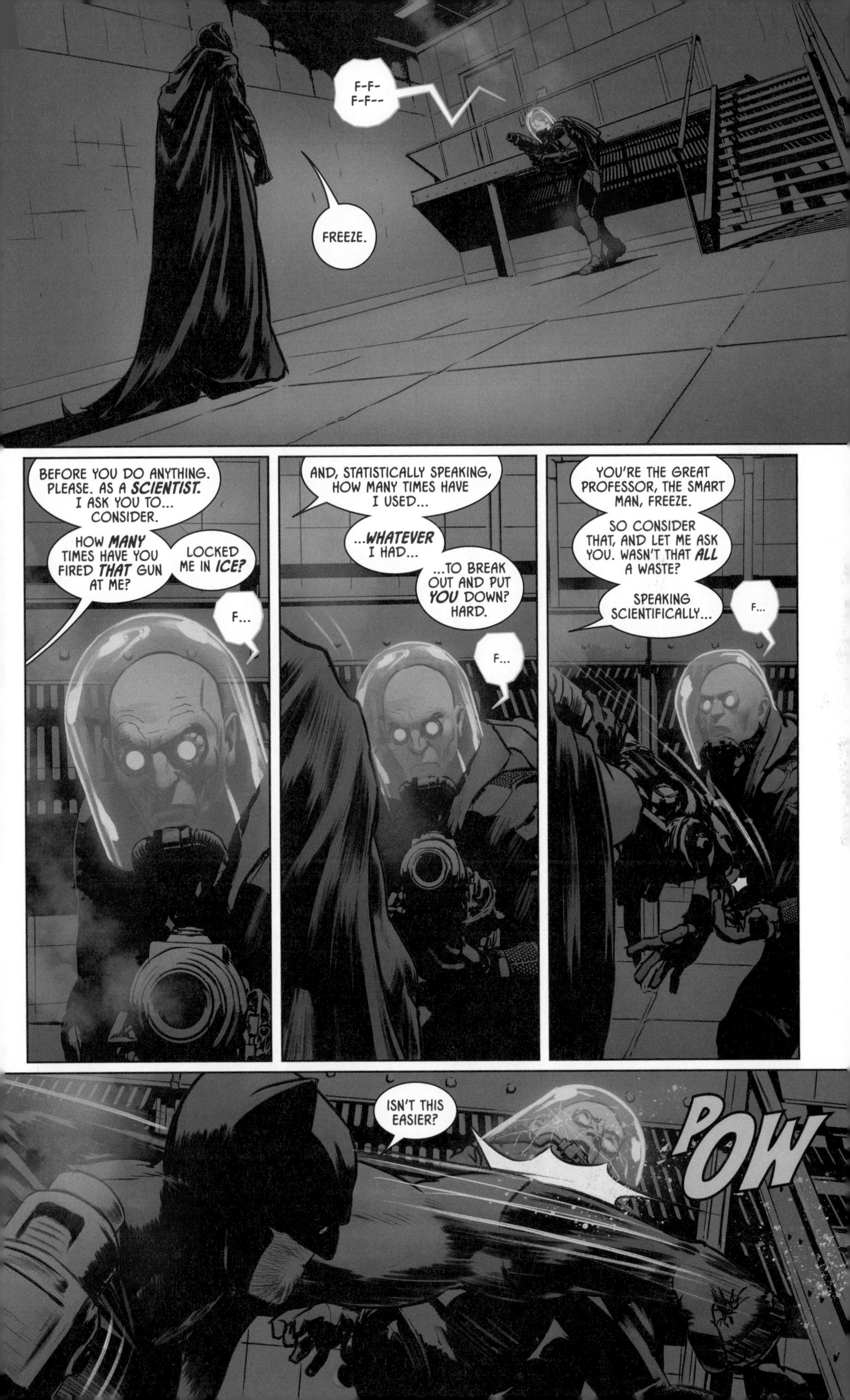
F-F-
F-F--
FREEZE.
BEFORE YOU DO ANYTHING. PLEASE. AS A SCIENTIST. I ASK YOU TO... CONSIDER.
HOW MANY TIMES HAVE YOU FIRED THAT GUN AT ME?
LOCKED ME IN ICE?
F...
AND, STATISTICALLY SPEAKING, HOW MANY TIMES HAVE I USED...
...WHATEVER I HAD...
...TO BREAK OUT AND PUT YOU DOWN? HARD.
F...
YOU'RE THE GREAT PROFESSOR, THE SMART MAN, FREEZE.
SO CONSIDER THAT, AND LET ME ASK YOU. WASN'T THAT ALL A WASTE?
SPEAKING SCIENTIFICALLY...
F...
ISN'T THIS EASIER?
POW

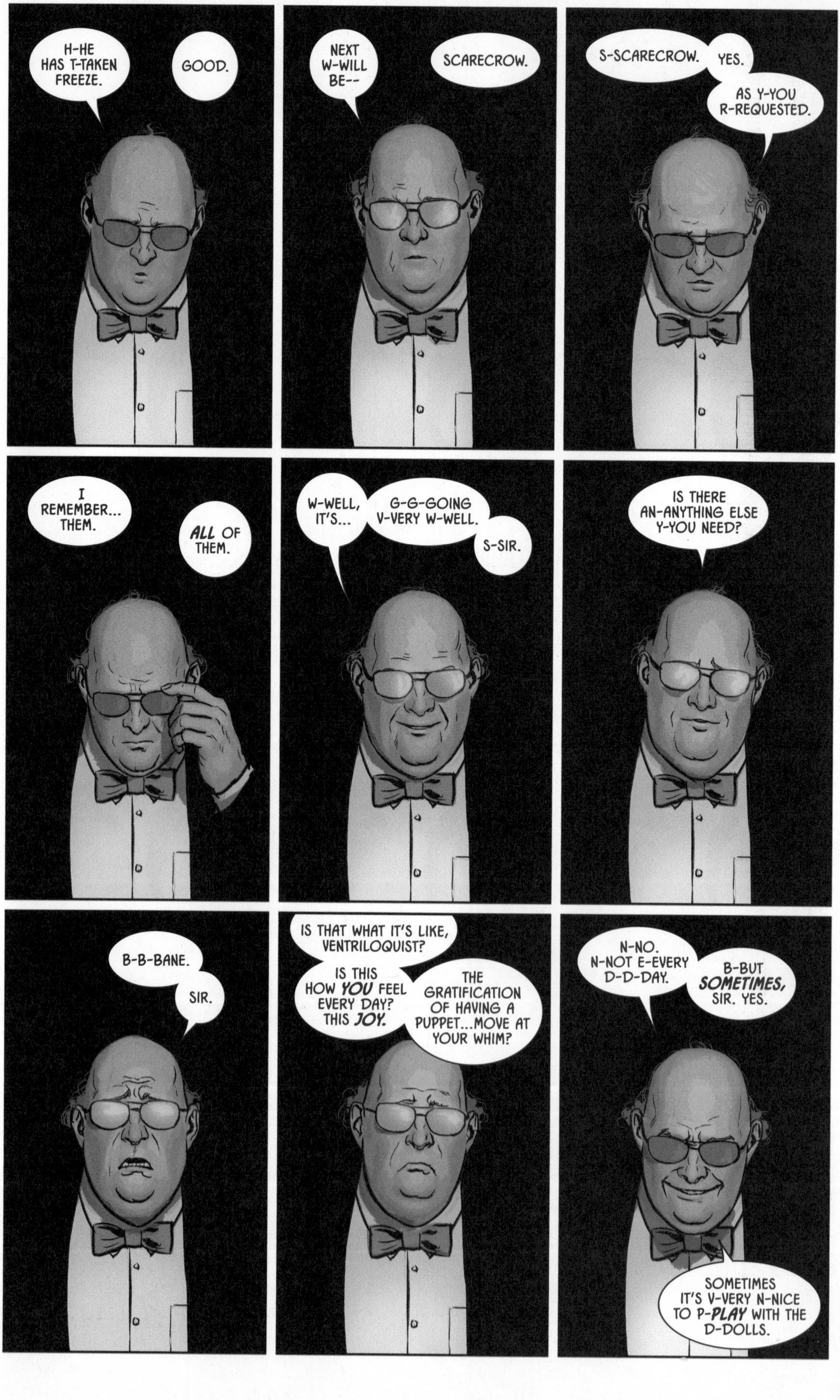
H-HE HAS T-TAKEN FREEZE.
GOOD.
NEXT W-WILL BE--
SCARECROW.
S-SCARECROW.
YES.
AS Y-YOU R-REQUESTED.
I REMEMBER... THEM.
ALL OF THEM.
W-WELL, IT'S...
G-G-GOING V-VERY W-WELL.
S-SIR.
IS THERE AN-ANYTHING ELSE Y-YOU NEED?
B-B-BANE.
SIR.
IS THAT WHAT IT'S LIKE, VENTRILOQUIST?
IS THIS HOW YOU FEEL EVERY DAY? THIS JOY.
THE GRATIFICATION OF HAVING A PUPPET...MOVE AT YOUR WHIM?
N-NO. N-NOT E-EVERY D-D-DAY.
B-BUT SOMETIMES, SIR. YES.
SOMETIMES IT'S V-VERY N-NICE TO P-PLAY WITH THE D-DOLLS.

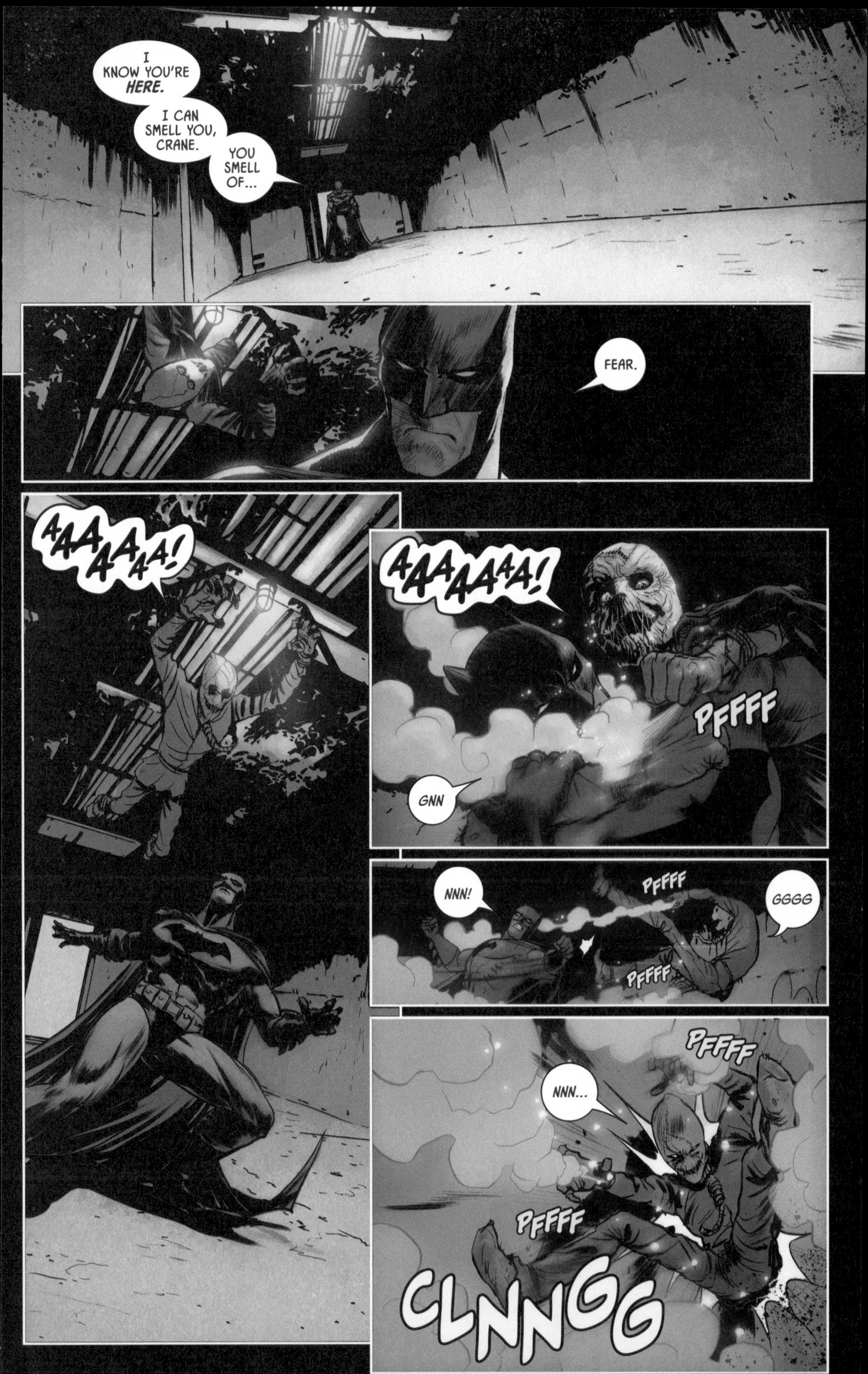

I KNOW YOU'RE *HERE.*
I CAN SMELL YOU, CRANE.
YOU SMELL OF...
FEAR.
AAAAAAA!
AAAAAAA!
PFFFF
GNN
NNN!
PFFFF
GGGG
PFFFF
PFFFF
NNN...
PFFFF
CLNNGG

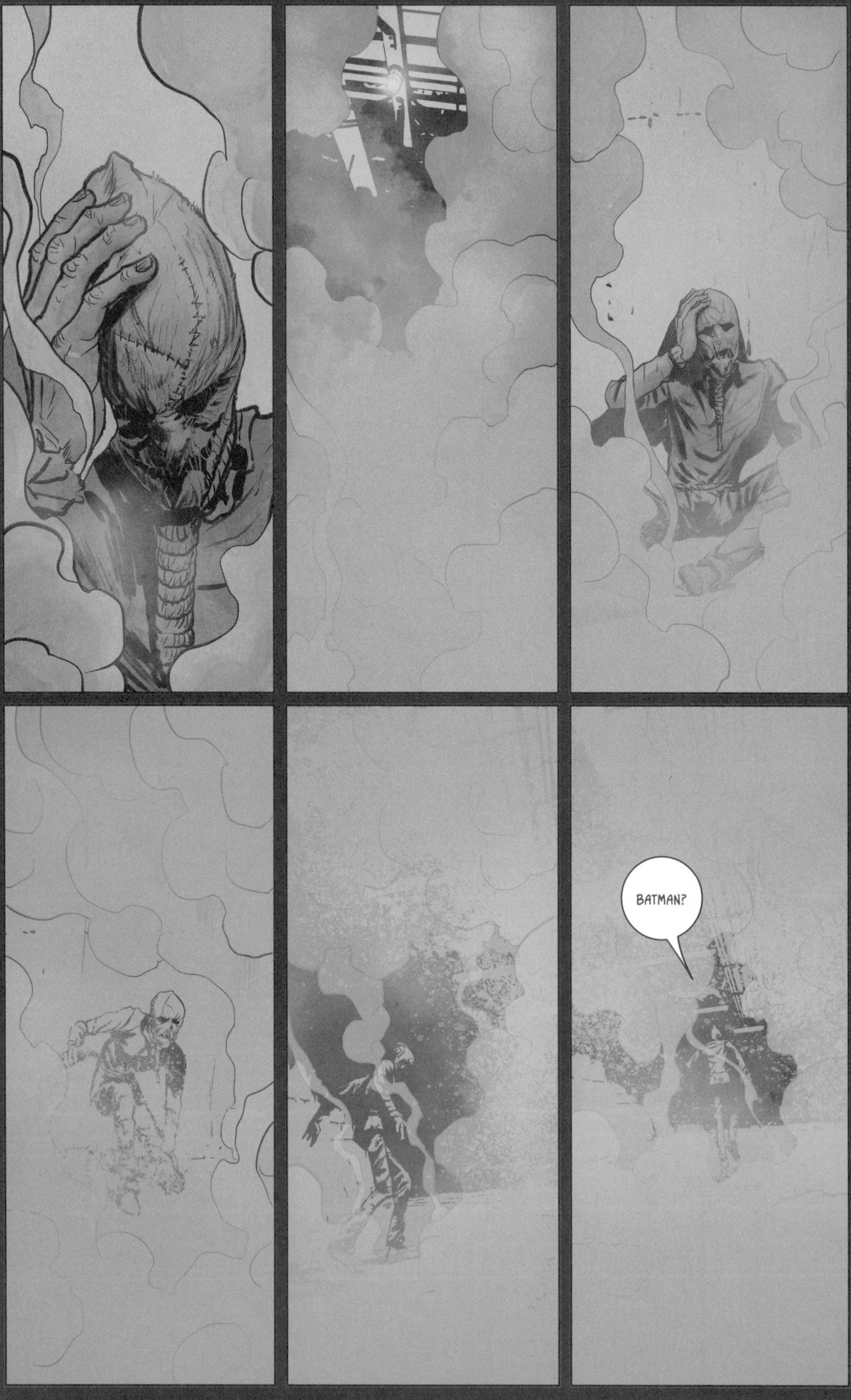
BATMAN?

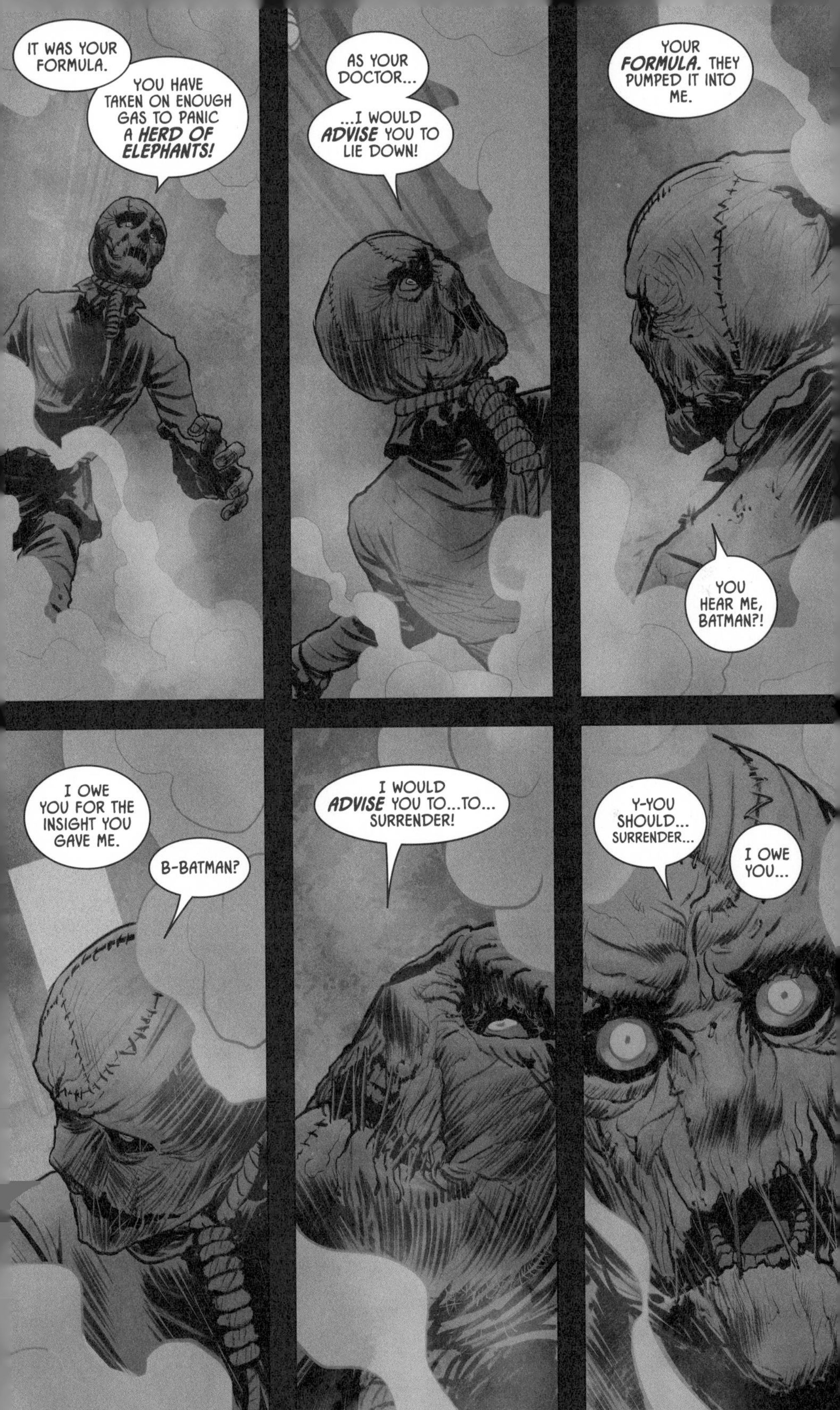
IT WAS YOUR FORMULA.
YOU HAVE TAKEN ON ENOUGH GAS TO PANIC A HERD OF ELEPHANTS!
AS YOUR DOCTOR...
...I WOULD ADVISE YOU TO LIE DOWN!
YOUR FORMULA. THEY PUMPED IT INTO ME.
YOU HEAR ME, BATMAN?!
I OWE YOU FOR THE INSIGHT YOU GAVE ME.
B-BATMAN?
I WOULD ADVISE YOU TO...TO... SURRENDER!
Y-YOU SHOULD... SURRENDER...
I OWE YOU...

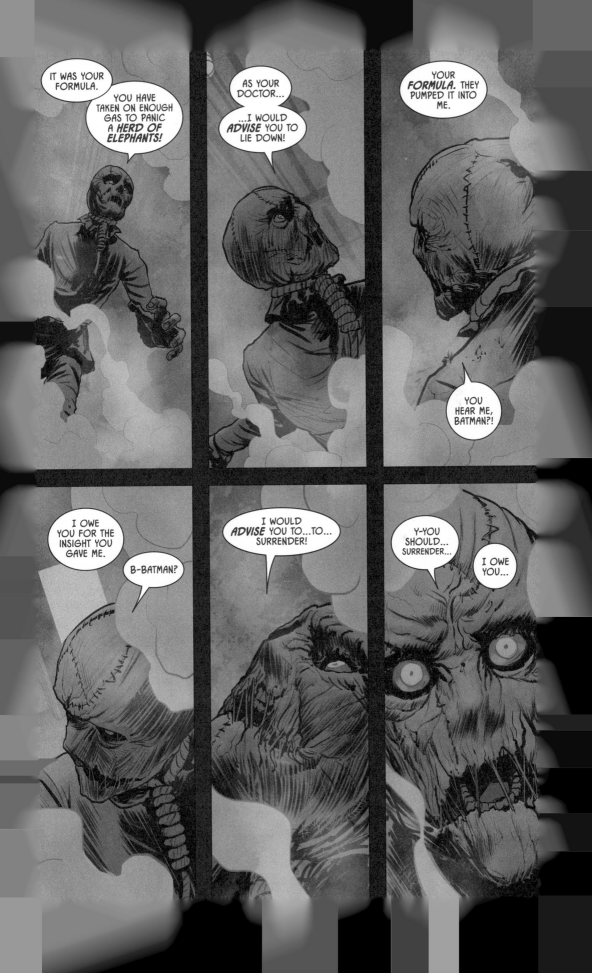

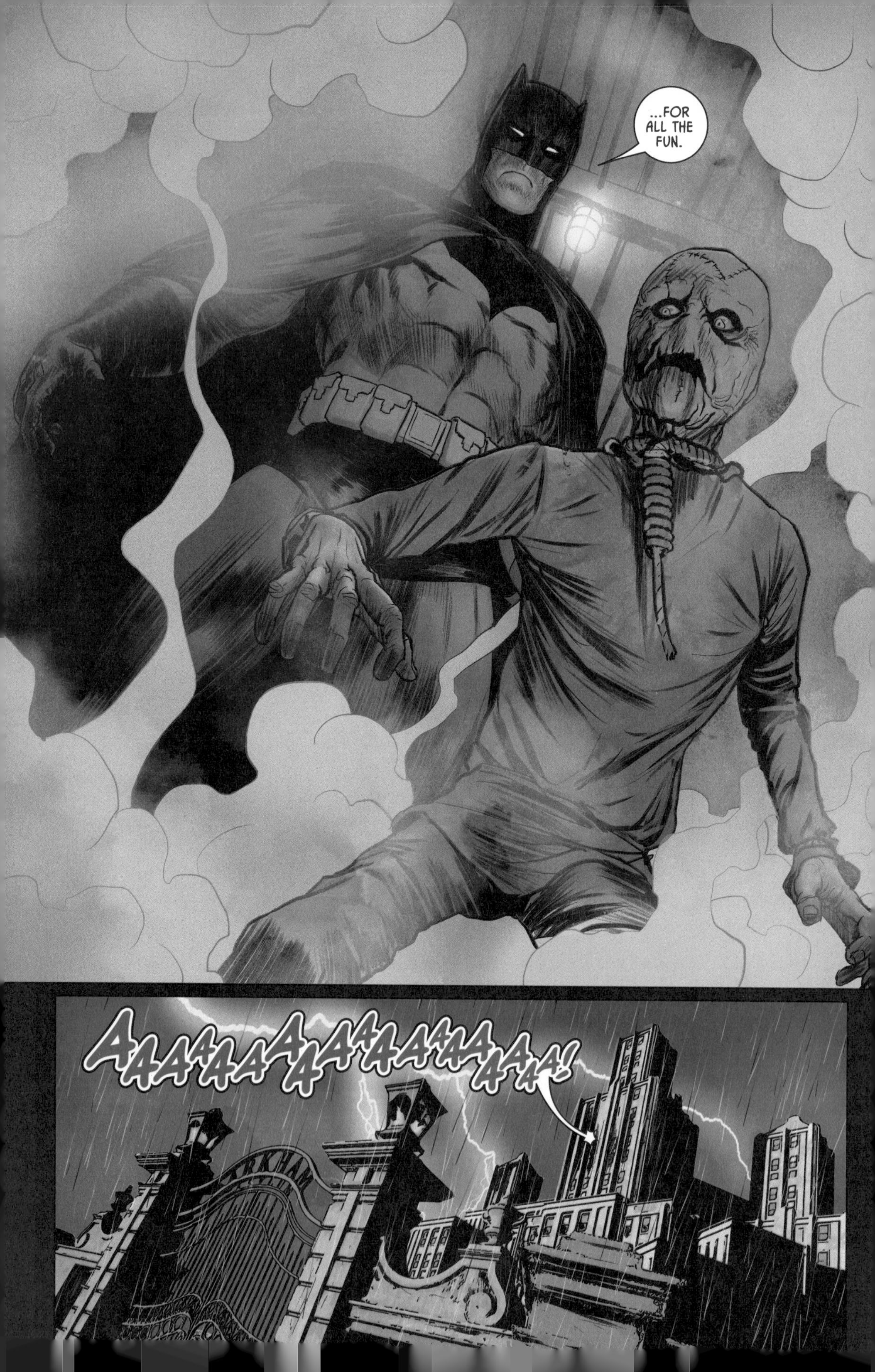
...FOR ALL THE FUN.
AAAAAAAAAAAAAAAAAAA!

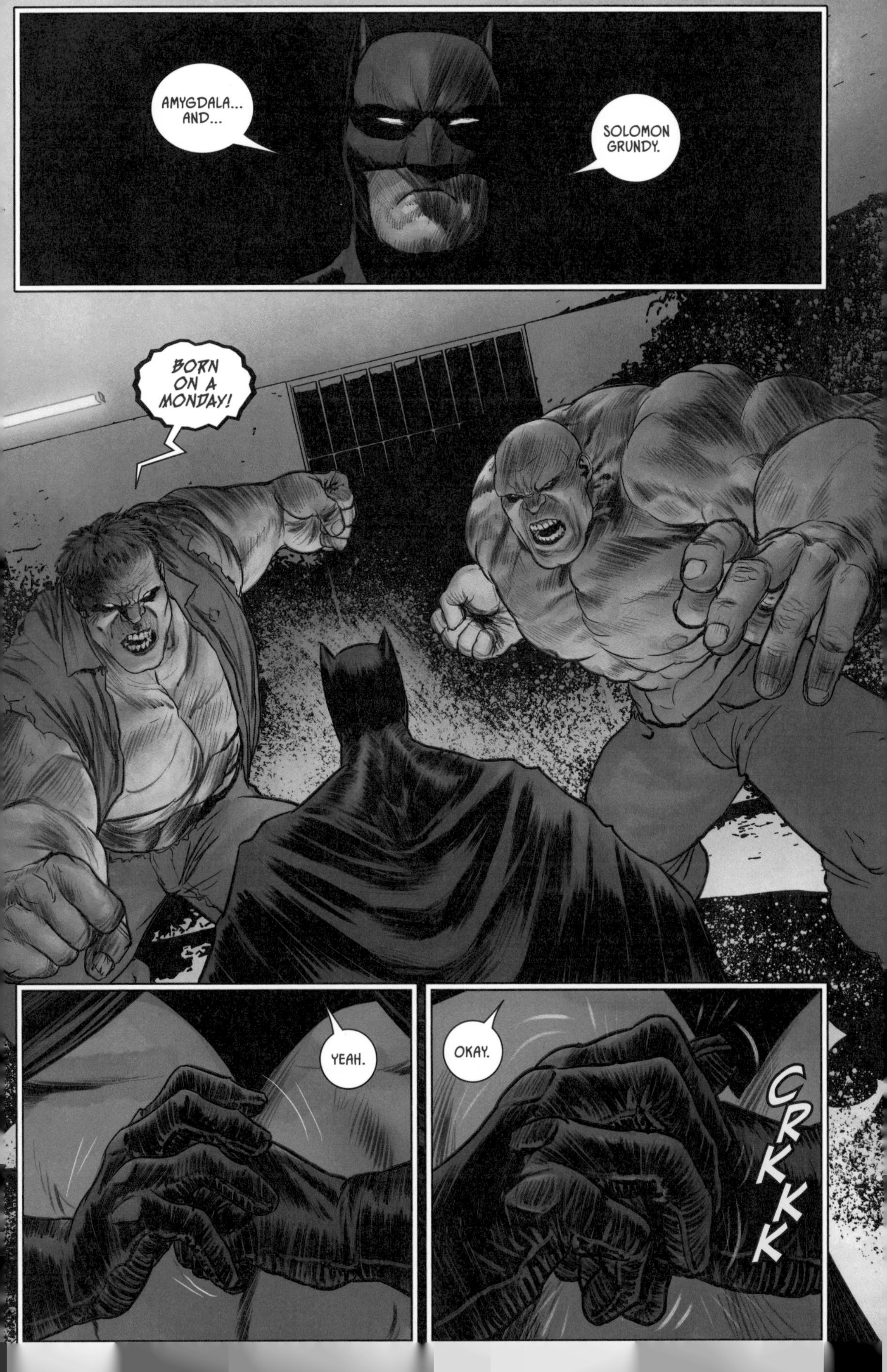
AMYGDALA... AND...
SOLOMON GRUNDY.
BORN ON A MONDAY!
YEAH.
OKAY.
CRKKK

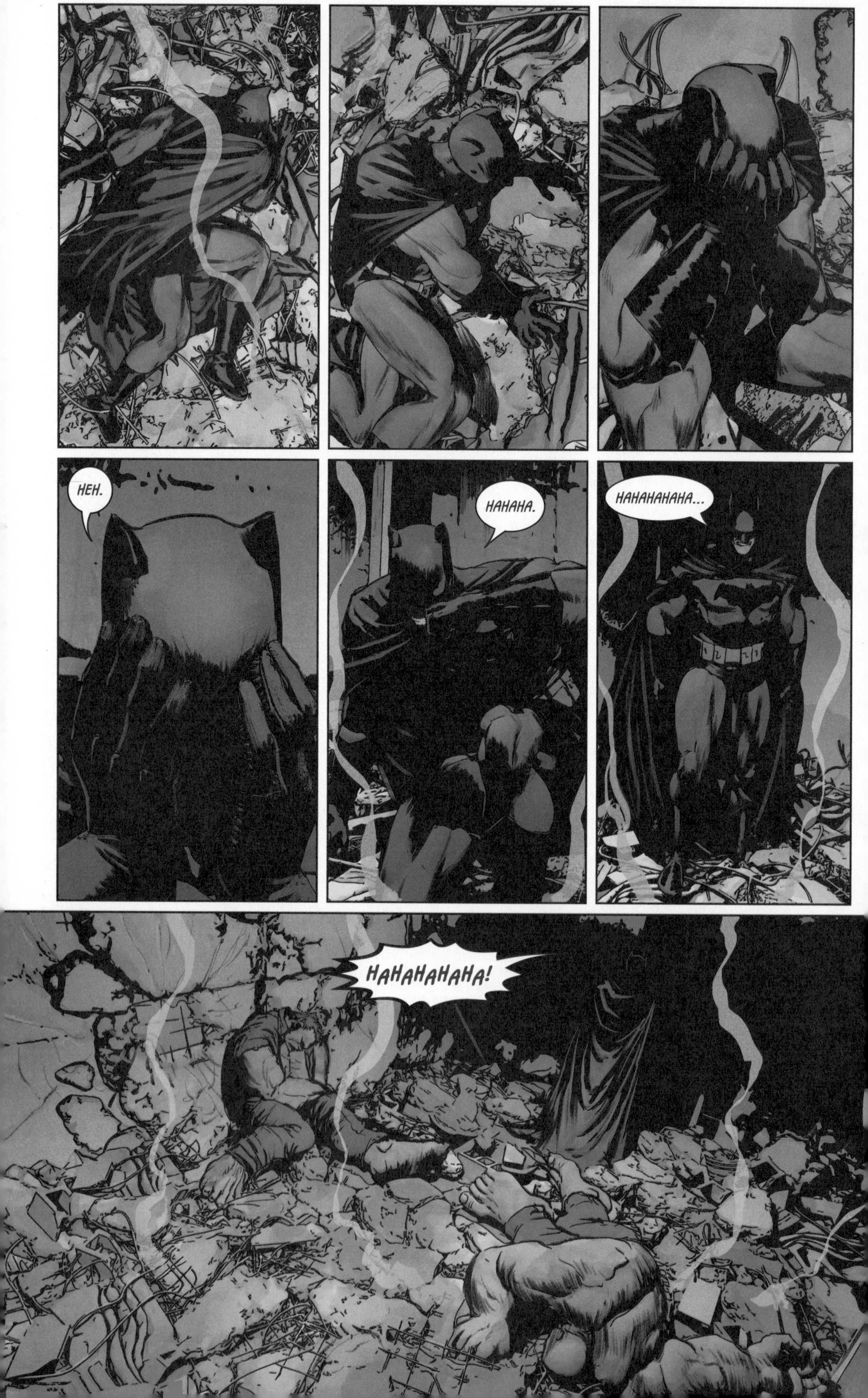

HEH.
HAHAHA.
HAHAHAHAHA...
HAHAHAHAHA!

PLEASE, NO MORE, NO, NO, BATMAN...I SURRENDER... PLEASE...

YOU ASININE, WORTHLESS, PATHETIC *NOTHING!* TOUCH ME AGAIN, AND I *KILL* YOU!

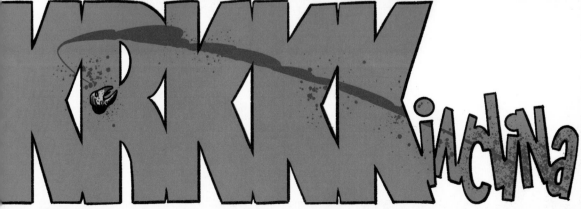

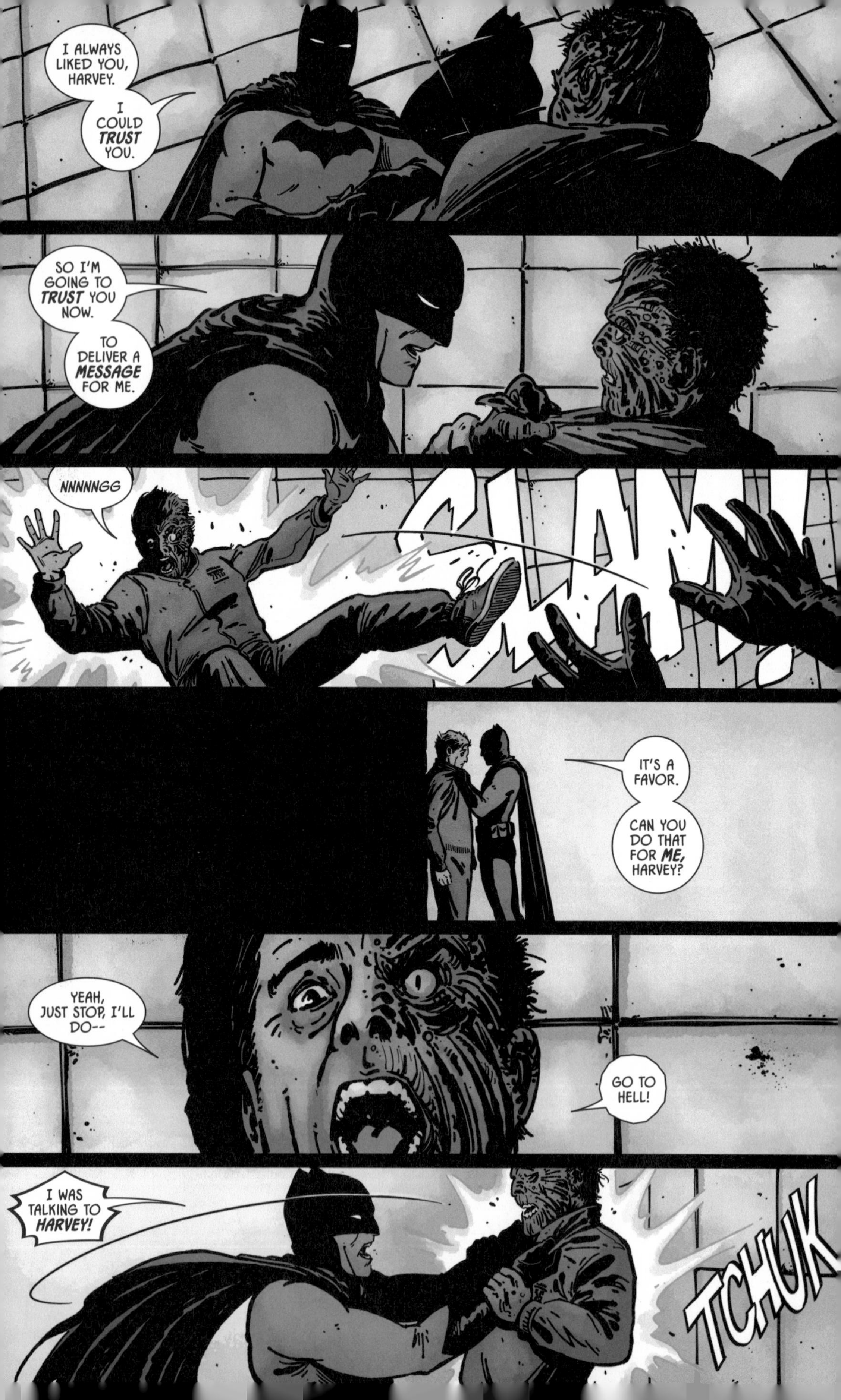

I ALWAYS LIKED YOU, HARVEY.
I COULD TRUST YOU.
SO I'M GOING TO TRUST YOU NOW.
TO DELIVER A MESSAGE FOR ME.
NNNNNGG
IT'S A FAVOR.
CAN YOU DO THAT FOR ME, HARVEY?
YEAH, JUST STOP, I'LL DO--
GO TO HELL!
I WAS TALKING TO HARVEY!
TCHUK

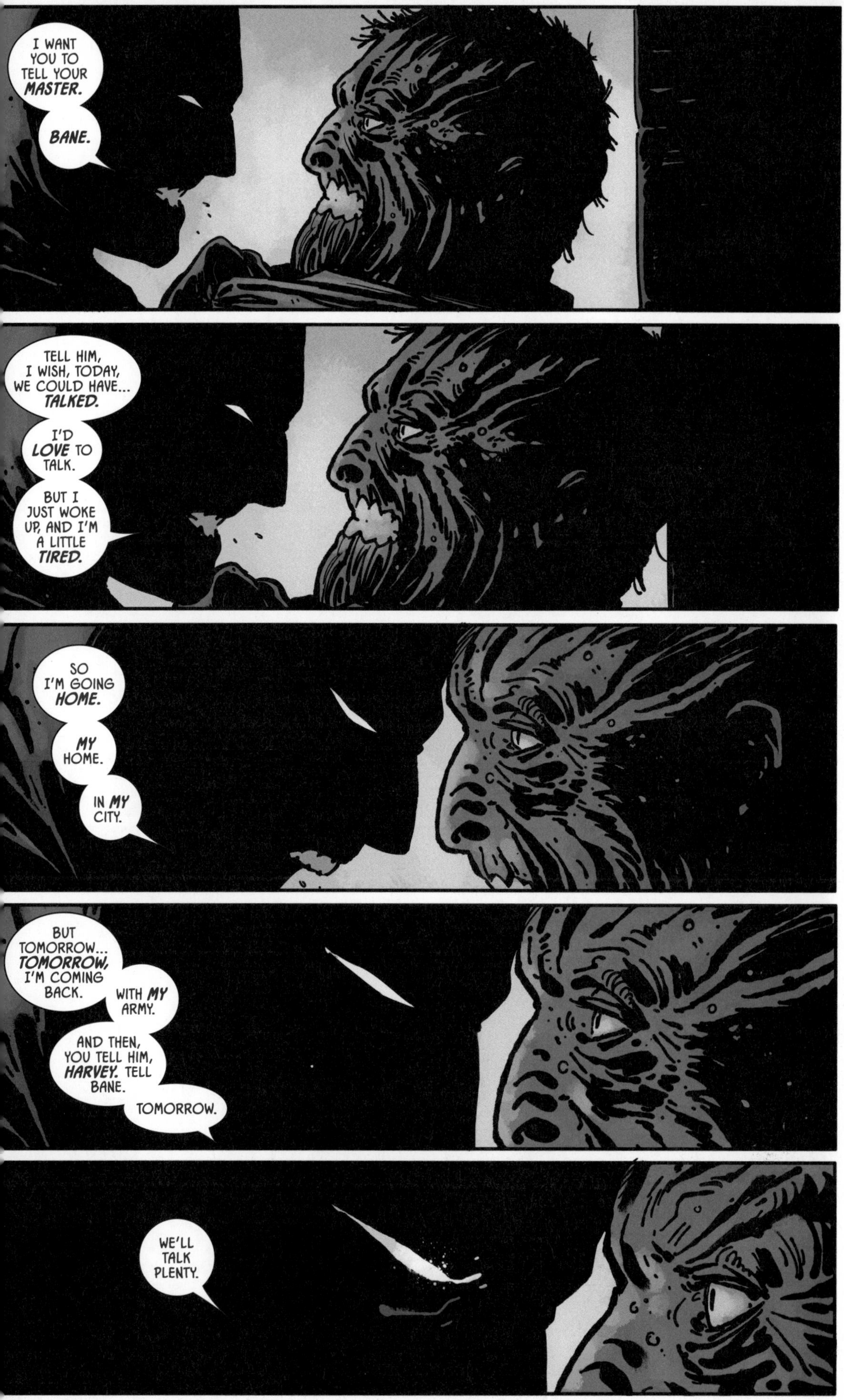
I WANT YOU TO TELL YOUR MASTER.
BANE.
TELL HIM, I WISH, TODAY, WE COULD HAVE... TALKED.
I'D LOVE TO TALK.
BUT I JUST WOKE UP, AND I'M A LITTLE TIRED.
SO I'M GOING HOME.
MY HOME.
IN MY CITY.
BUT TOMORROW... TOMORROW, I'M COMING BACK.
WITH MY ARMY.
AND THEN, YOU TELL HIM, HARVEY. TELL BANE.
TOMORROW.
WE'LL TALK PLENTY.

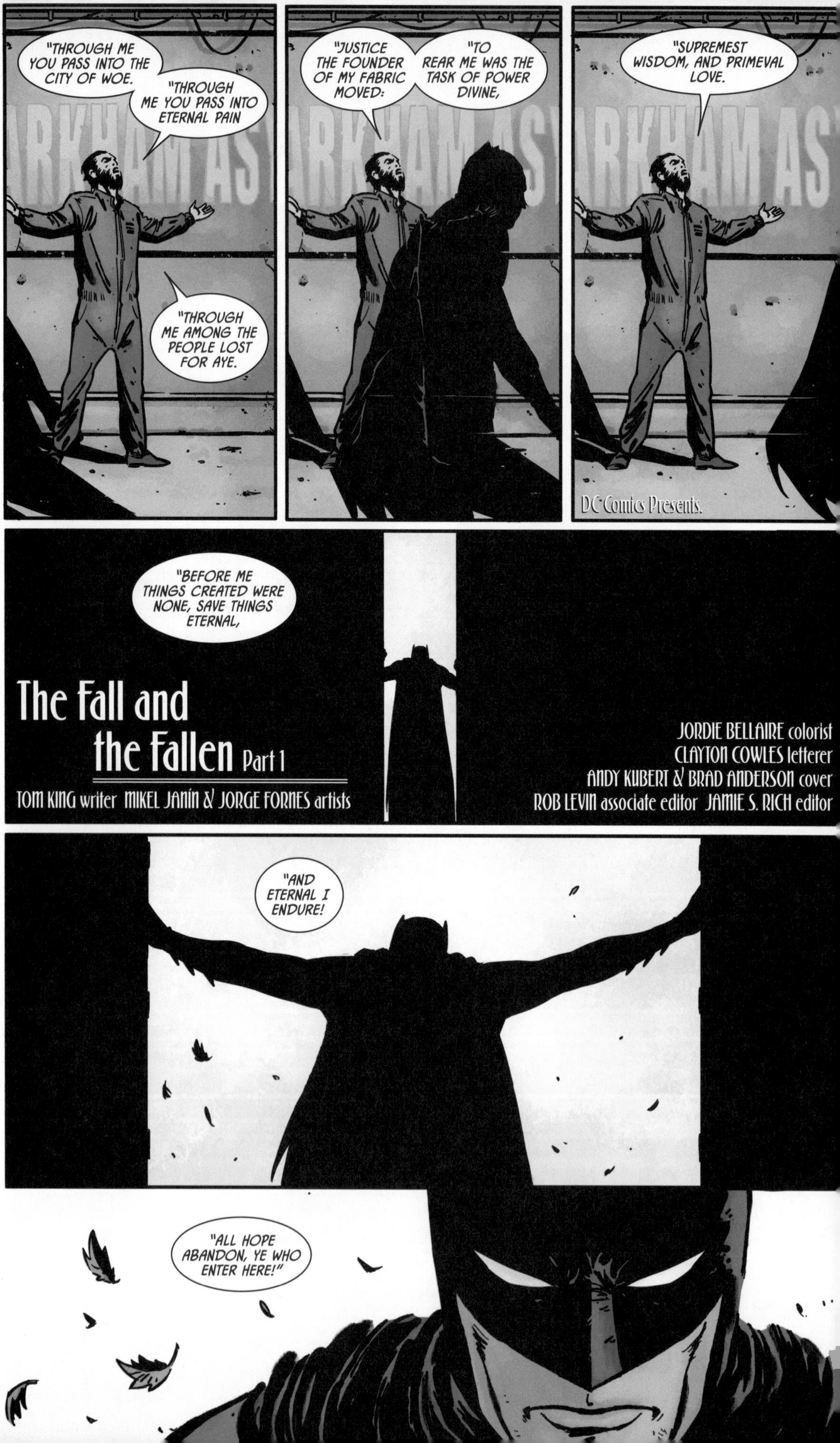
"THROUGH ME YOU PASS INTO THE CITY OF WOE.
"THROUGH ME YOU PASS INTO ETERNAL PAIN
"THROUGH ME AMONG THE PEOPLE LOST FOR AYE.
"JUSTICE THE FOUNDER OF MY FABRIC MOVED:
"TO REAR ME WAS THE TASK OF POWER DIVINE,
"SUPREMEST WISDOM, AND PRIMEVAL LOVE.
DC Comics Presents.
"BEFORE ME THINGS CREATED WERE NONE, SAVE THINGS ETERNAL,
The Fall and the Fallen Part 1
TOM KING writer MIKEL JANÍN & JORGE FORNES artists
JORDIE BELLAIRE colorist
CLAYTON COWLES letterer
ANDY KUBERT & BRAD ANDERSON cover
ROB LEVIN associate editor JAMIE S. RICH editor
"AND ETERNAL I ENDURE!
"ALL HOPE ABANDON, YE WHO ENTER HERE!"

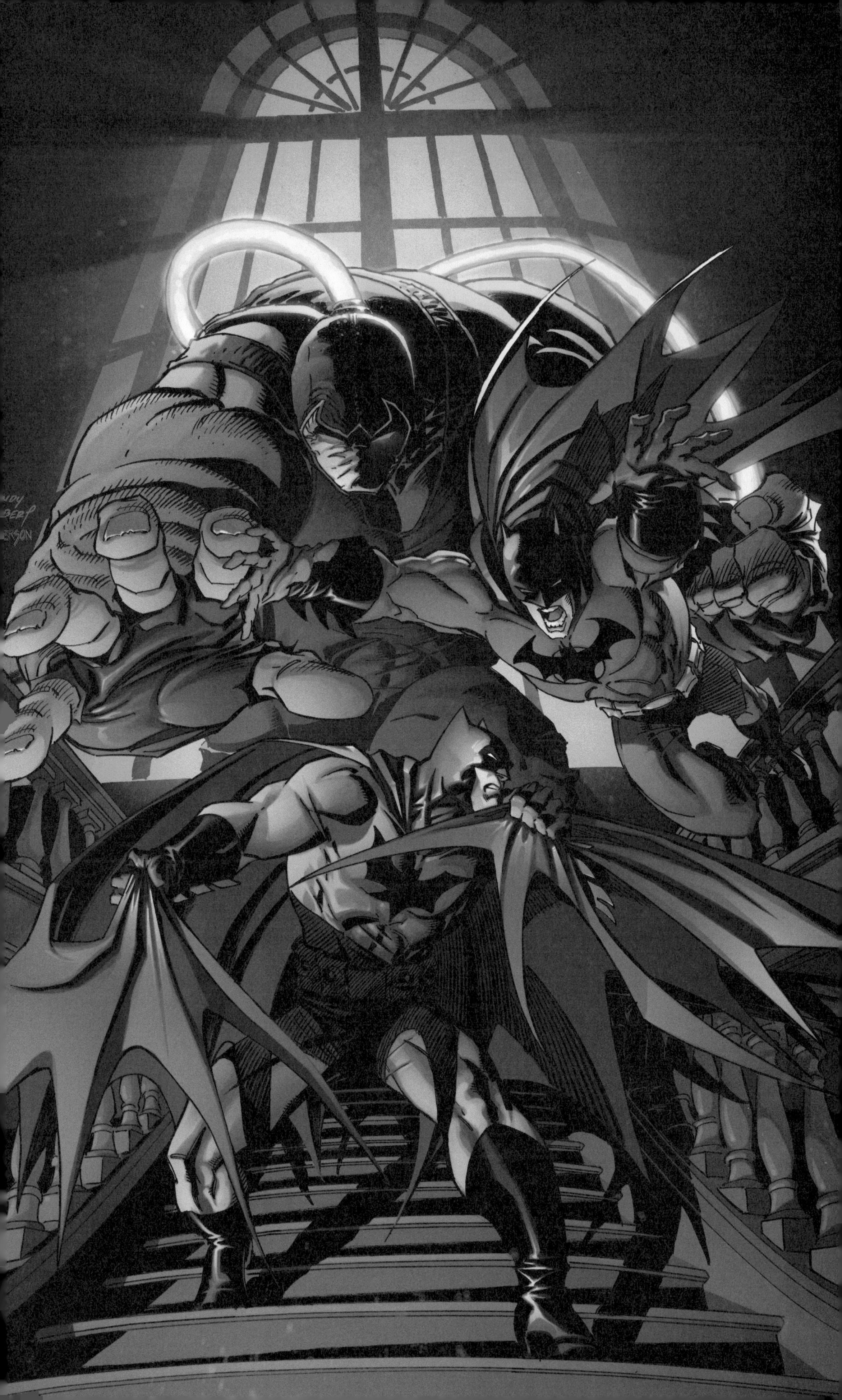

BATMAN
#71

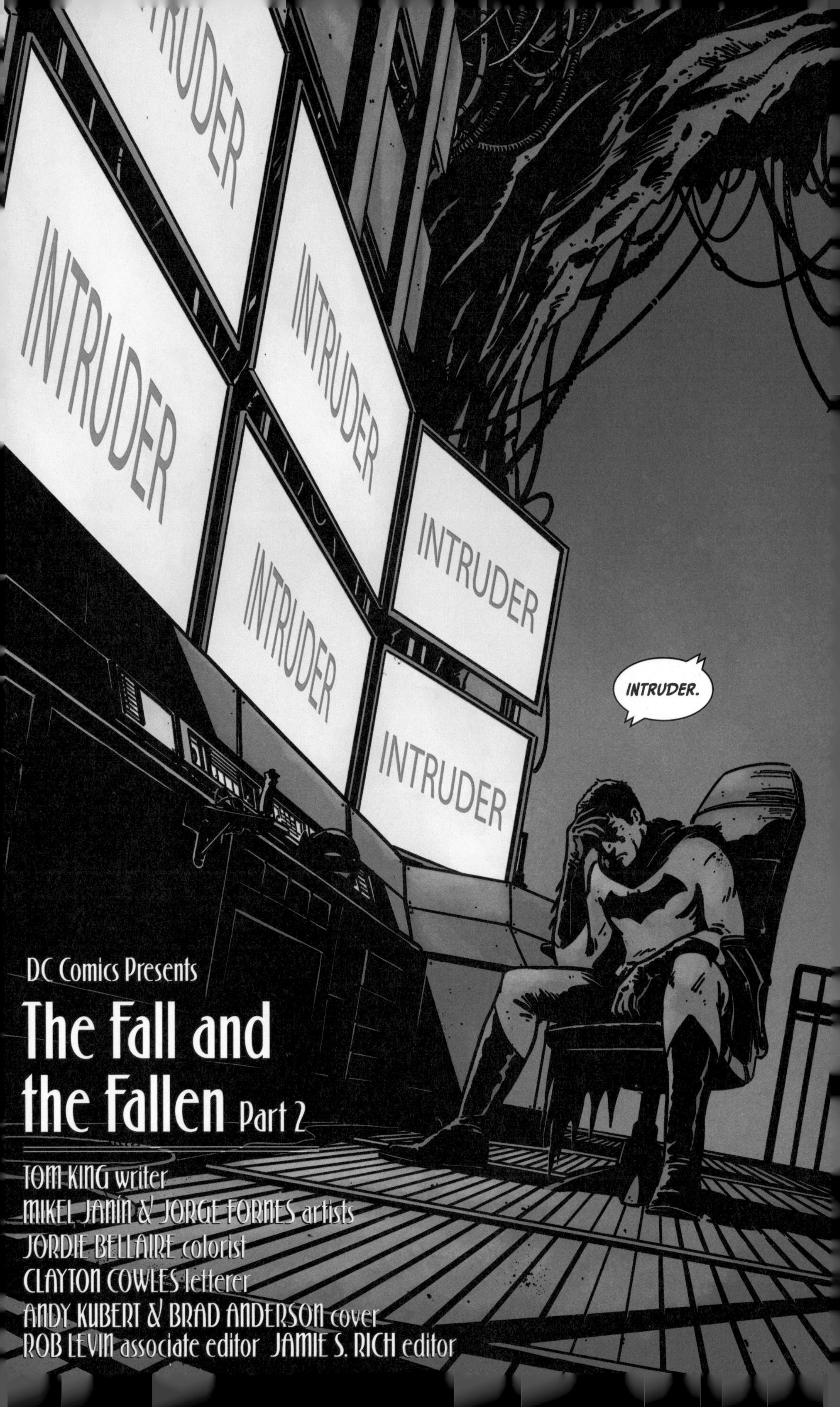
INTRUDER
INTRUDER
INTRUDER
INTRUDER
INTRUDER
INTRUDER.

DC Comics Presents

The Fall and the Fallen Part 2

TOM KING writer
MIKEL JANÍN & JORGE FORNES artists
JORDIE BELLAIRE colorist
CLAYTON COWLES letterer
ANDY KUBERT & BRAD ANDERSON cover
ROB LEVIN associate editor JAMIE S. RICH editor

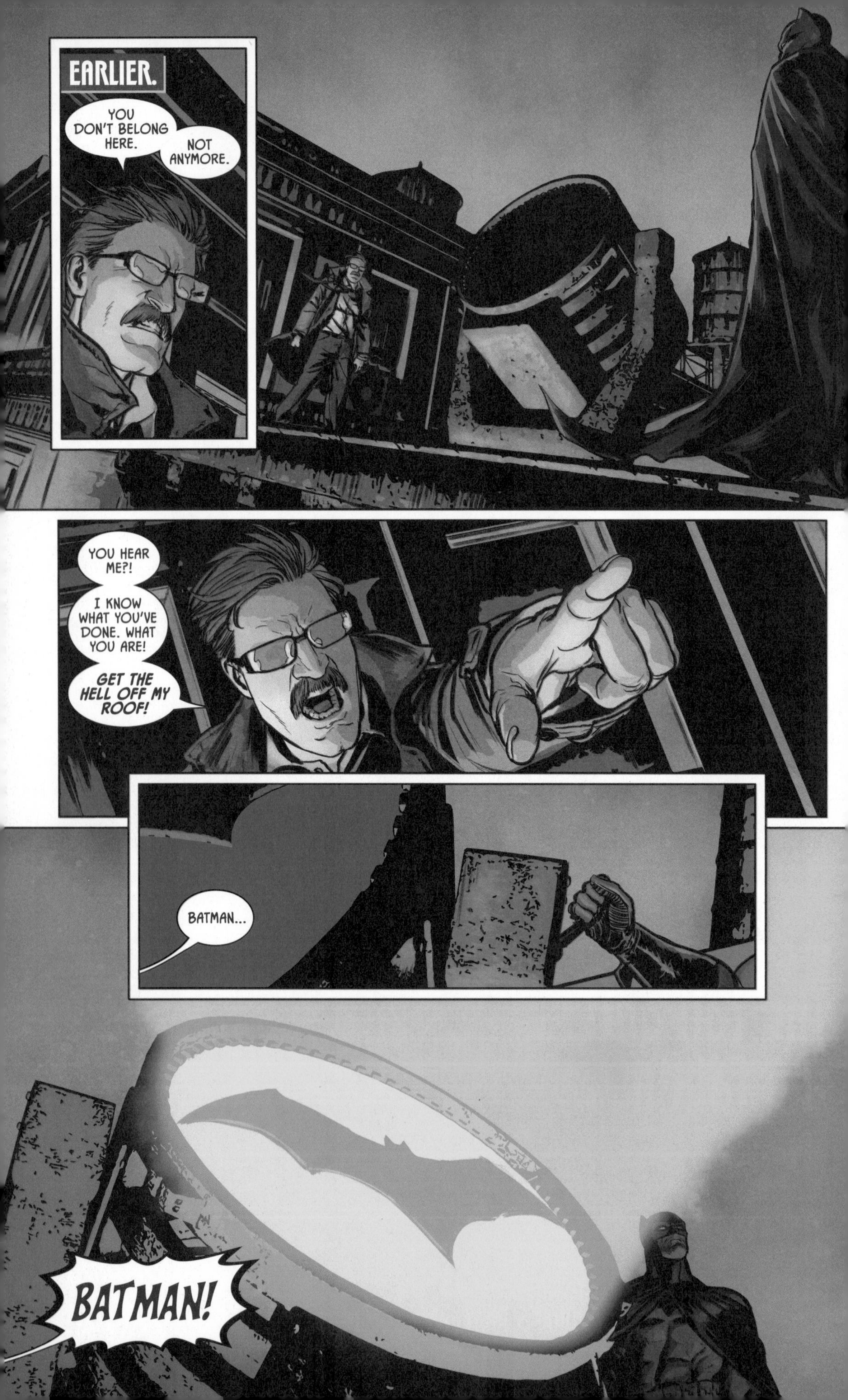
EARLIER.
YOU DON'T BELONG HERE.
NOT ANYMORE.
YOU HEAR ME?!
I KNOW WHAT YOU'VE DONE. WHAT YOU ARE!
GET THE HELL OFF MY ROOF!
BATMAN...
BATMAN!

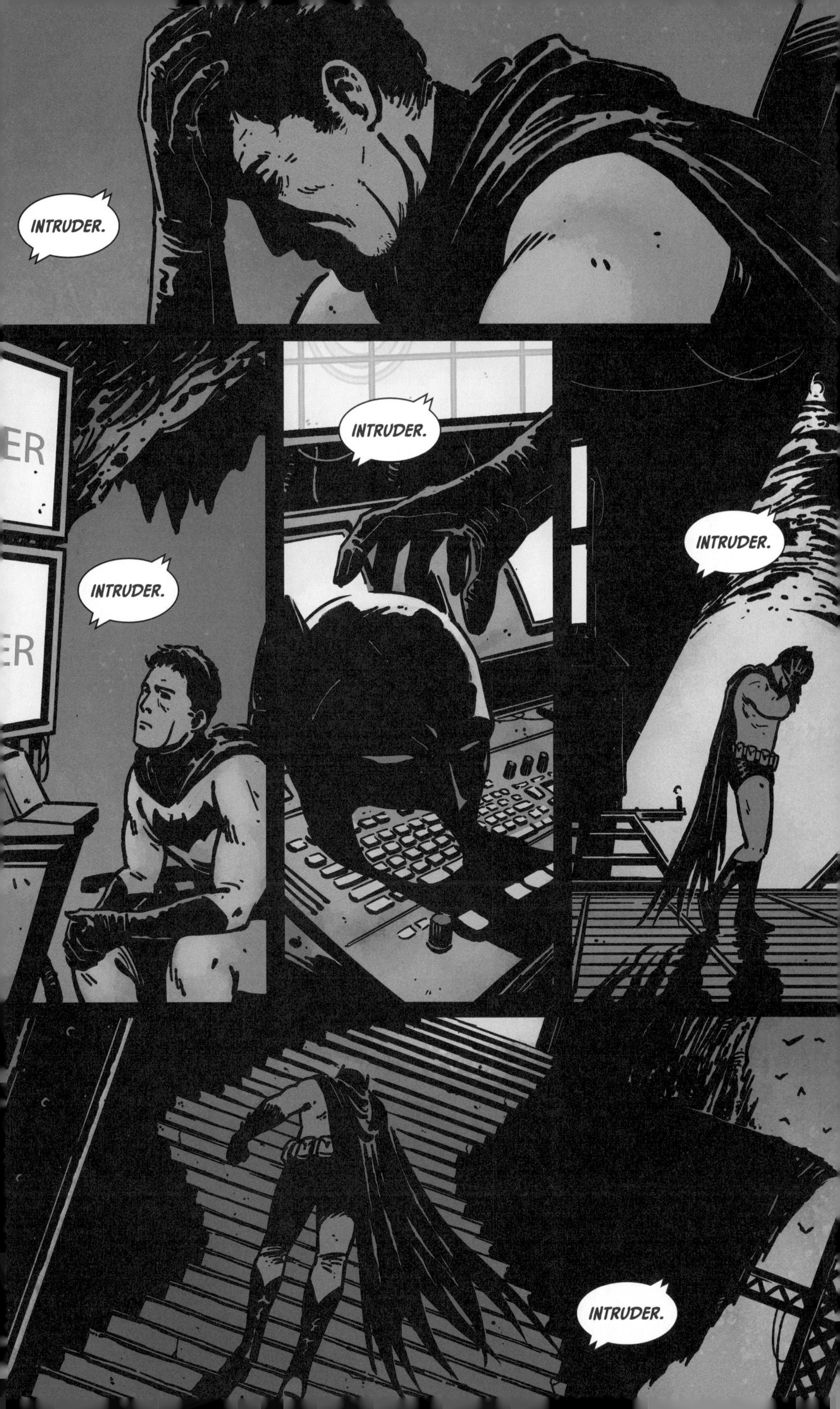
INTRUDER.
INTRUDER.
INTRUDER.
INTRUDER.
INTRUDER.

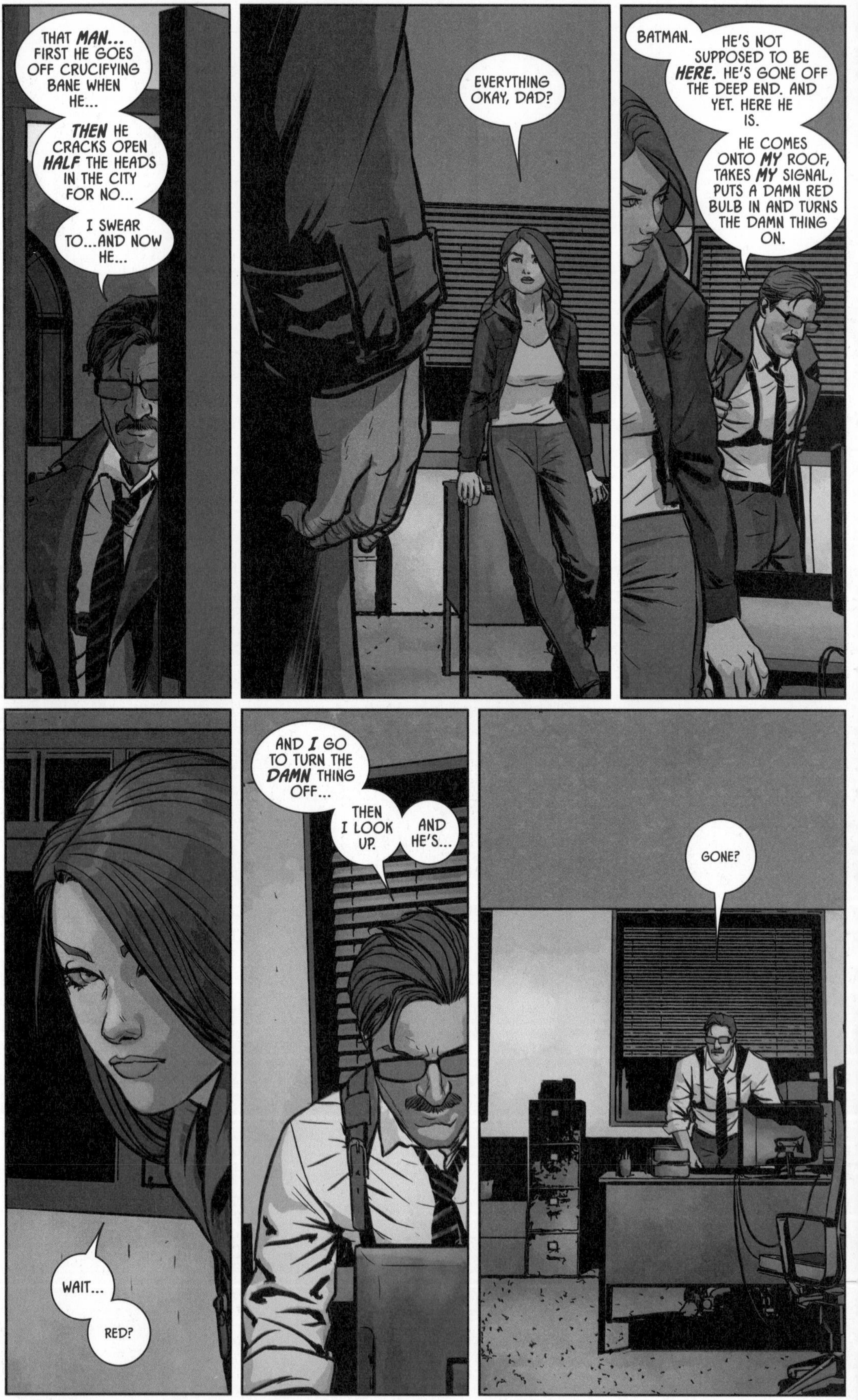

THAT MAN... FIRST HE GOES OFF CRUCIFYING BANE WHEN HE...
THEN HE CRACKS OPEN HALF THE HEADS IN THE CITY FOR NO...
I SWEAR TO...AND NOW HE...
EVERYTHING OKAY, DAD?
BATMAN.
HE'S NOT SUPPOSED TO BE HERE. HE'S GONE OFF THE DEEP END. AND YET. HERE HE IS.
HE COMES ONTO MY ROOF, TAKES MY SIGNAL, PUTS A DAMN RED BULB IN AND TURNS THE DAMN THING ON.
WAIT...
RED?
AND I GO TO TURN THE DAMN THING OFF...
THEN I LOOK UP.
AND HE'S...
GONE?

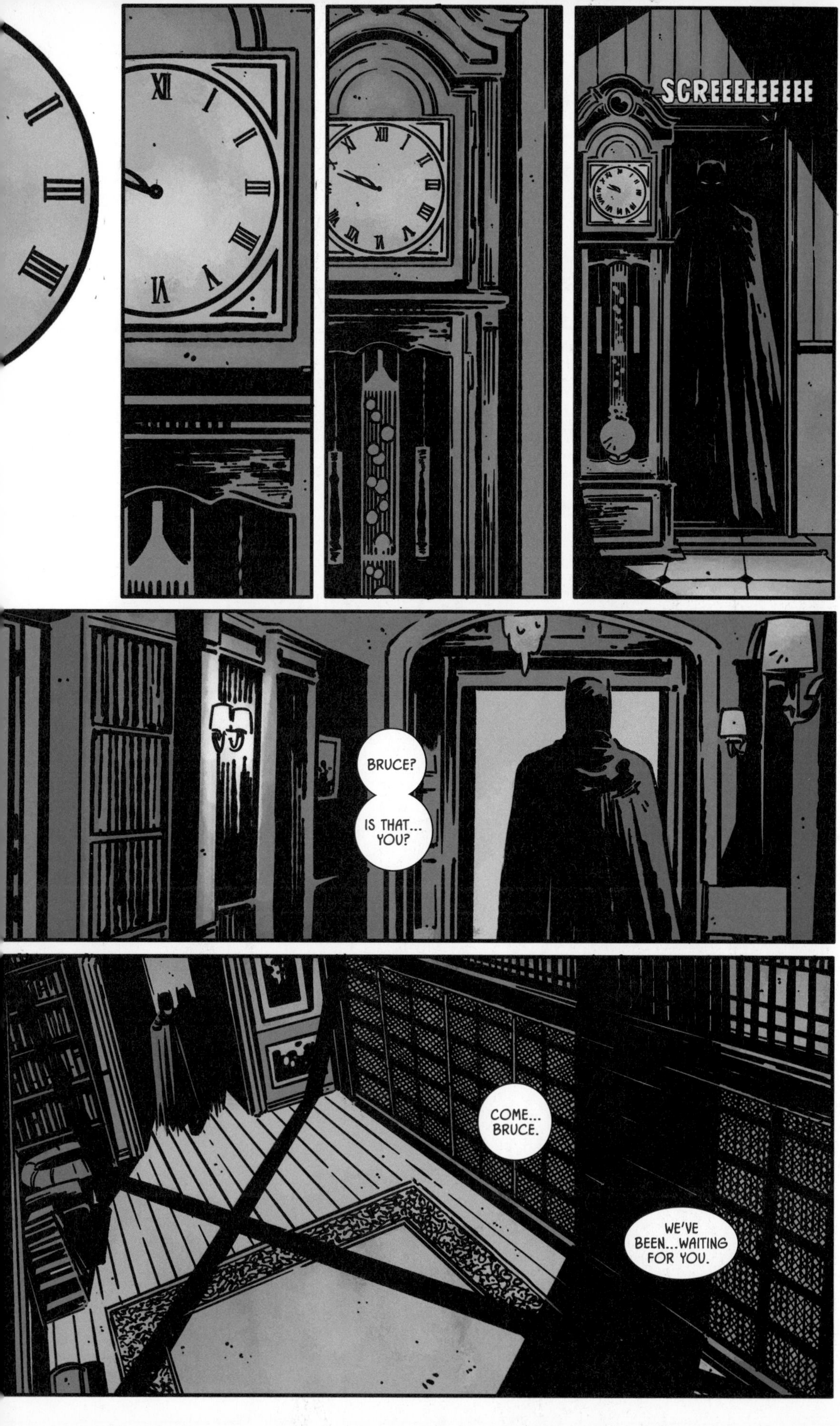
SCREEEEEEEEE
BRUCE?
IS THAT... YOU?
COME... BRUCE.
WE'VE BEEN...WAITING FOR YOU.

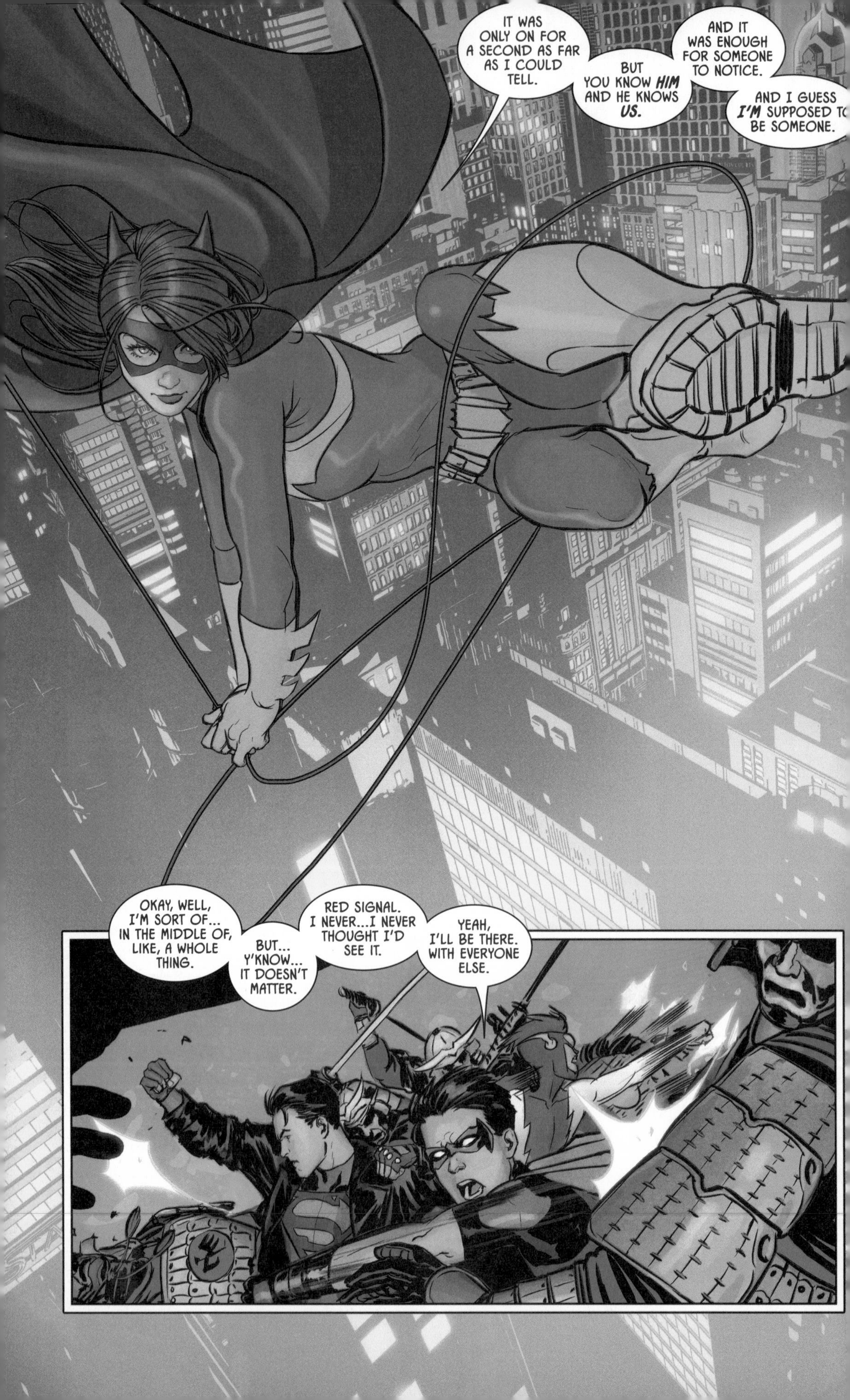
IT WAS ONLY ON FOR A SECOND AS FAR AS I COULD TELL.
BUT YOU KNOW HIM AND HE KNOWS US.
AND IT WAS ENOUGH FOR SOMEONE TO NOTICE.
AND I GUESS I'M SUPPOSED TO BE SOMEONE.
OKAY, WELL, I'M SORT OF... IN THE MIDDLE OF, LIKE, A WHOLE THING.
BUT... Y'KNOW... IT DOESN'T MATTER.
RED SIGNAL. I NEVER...I NEVER THOUGHT I'D SEE IT.
YEAH, I'LL BE THERE. WITH EVERYONE ELSE.

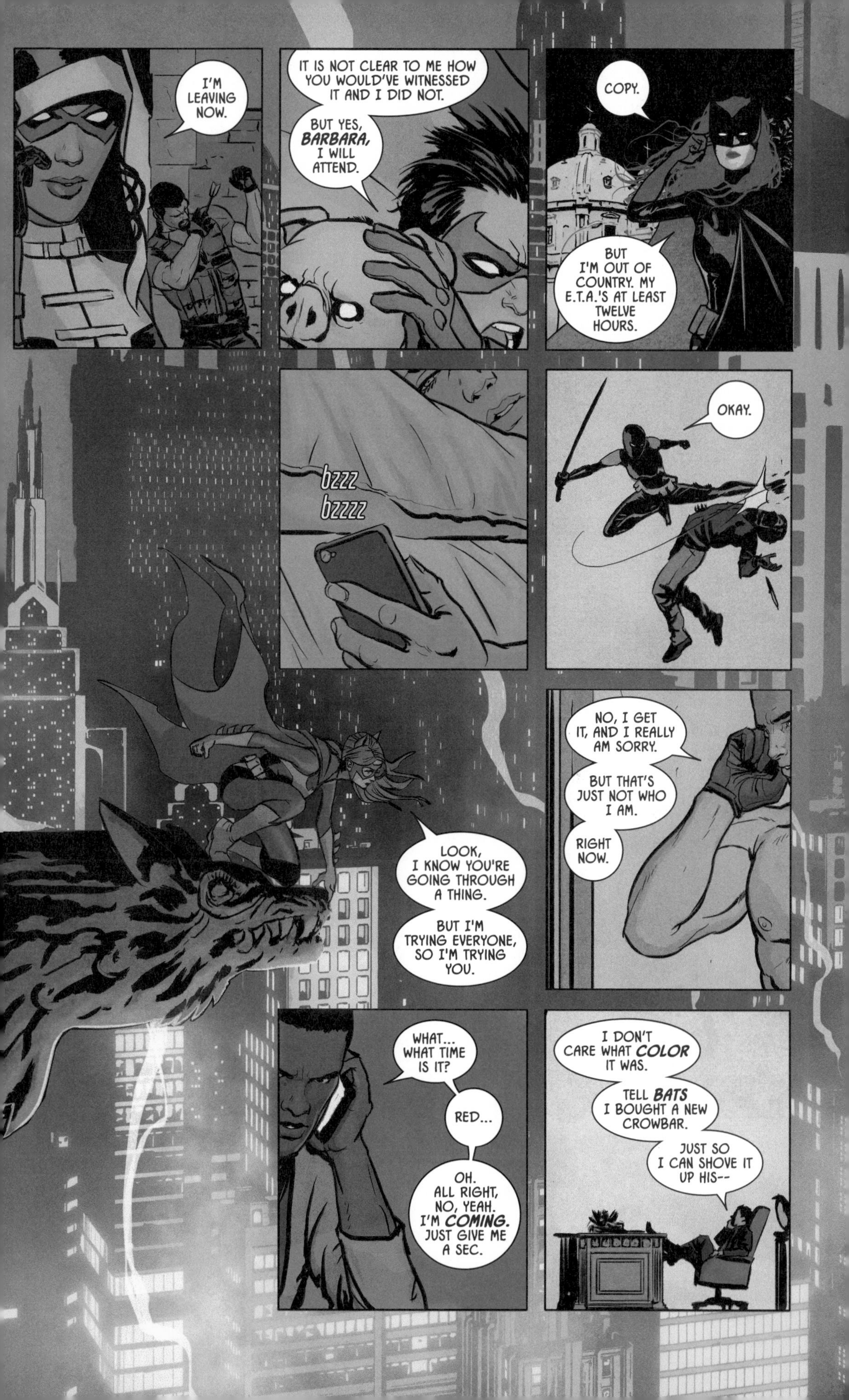
I'M LEAVING NOW.
IT IS NOT CLEAR TO ME HOW YOU WOULD'VE WITNESSED IT AND I DID NOT.
BUT YES, BARBARA, I WILL ATTEND.
COPY.
BUT I'M OUT OF COUNTRY. MY E.T.A.'S AT LEAST TWELVE HOURS.
bzzz
bzzzz
OKAY.
LOOK, I KNOW YOU'RE GOING THROUGH A THING.
BUT I'M TRYING EVERYONE, SO I'M TRYING YOU.
NO, I GET IT, AND I REALLY AM SORRY.
BUT THAT'S JUST NOT WHO I AM.
RIGHT NOW.
WHAT... WHAT TIME IS IT?
RED...
OH. ALL RIGHT, NO, YEAH. I'M COMING. JUST GIVE ME A SEC.
I DON'T CARE WHAT COLOR IT WAS.
TELL BATS I BOUGHT A NEW CROWBAR.
JUST SO I CAN SHOVE IT UP HIS--

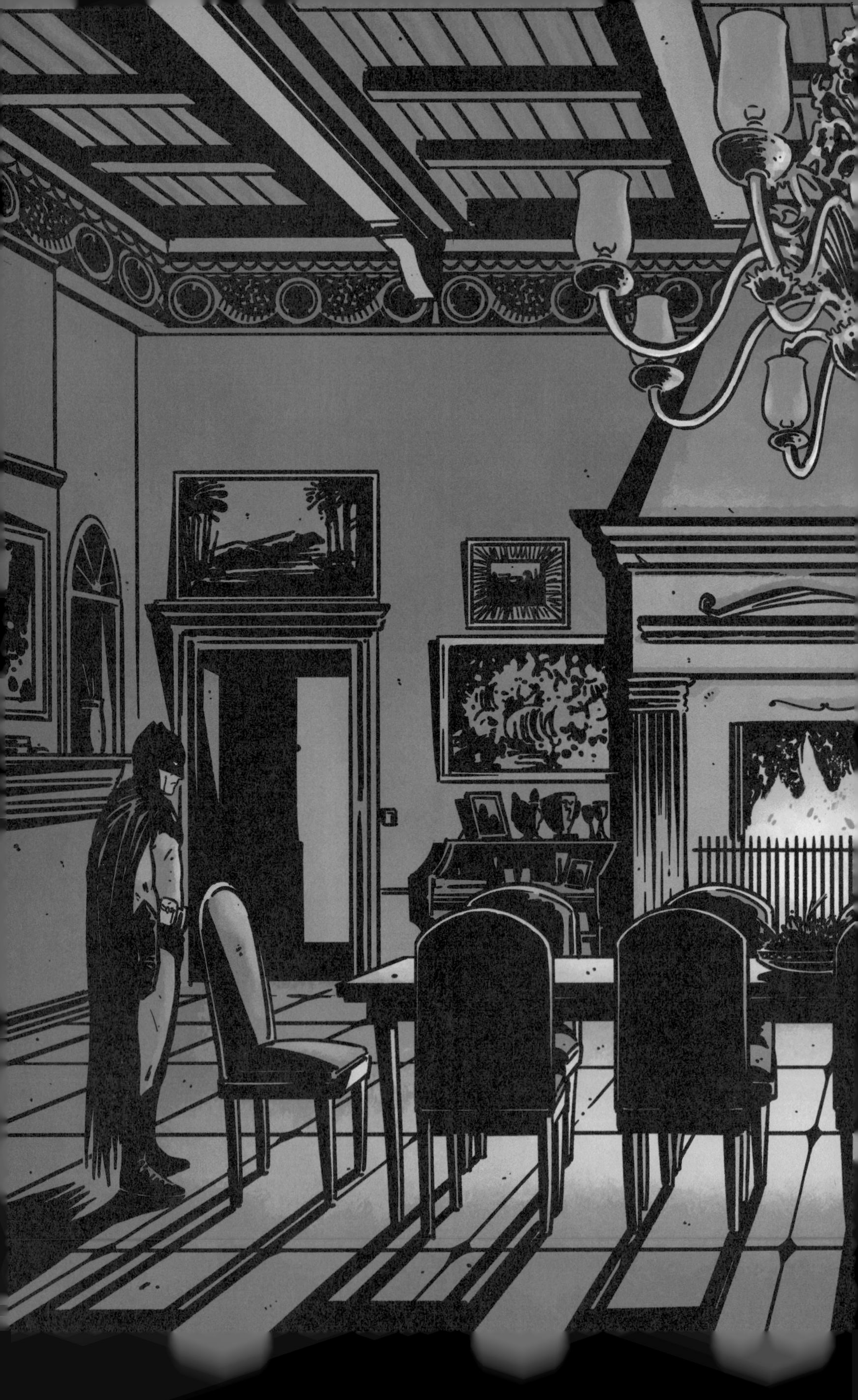

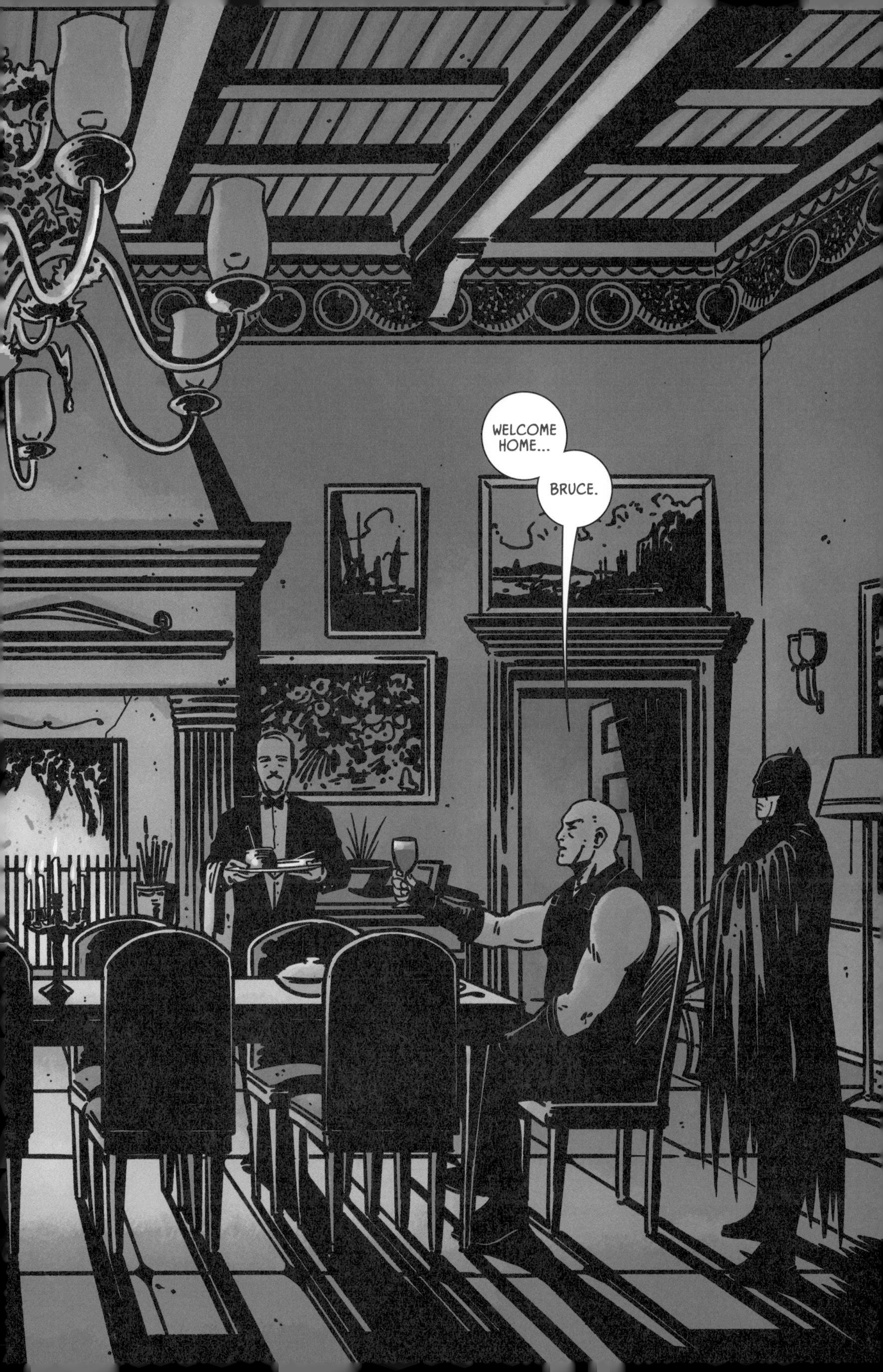
WELCOME HOME...
BRUCE.

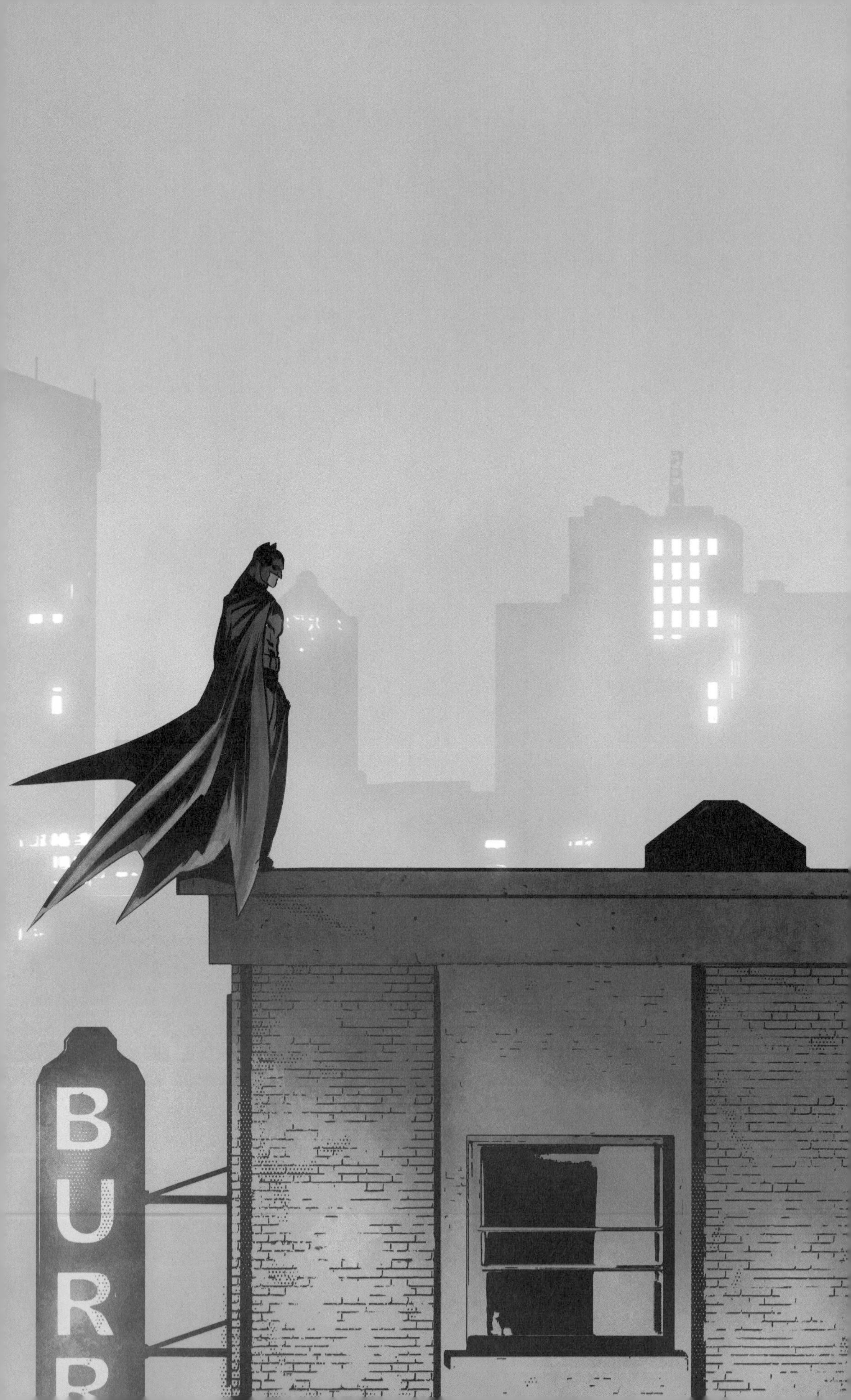
BUR

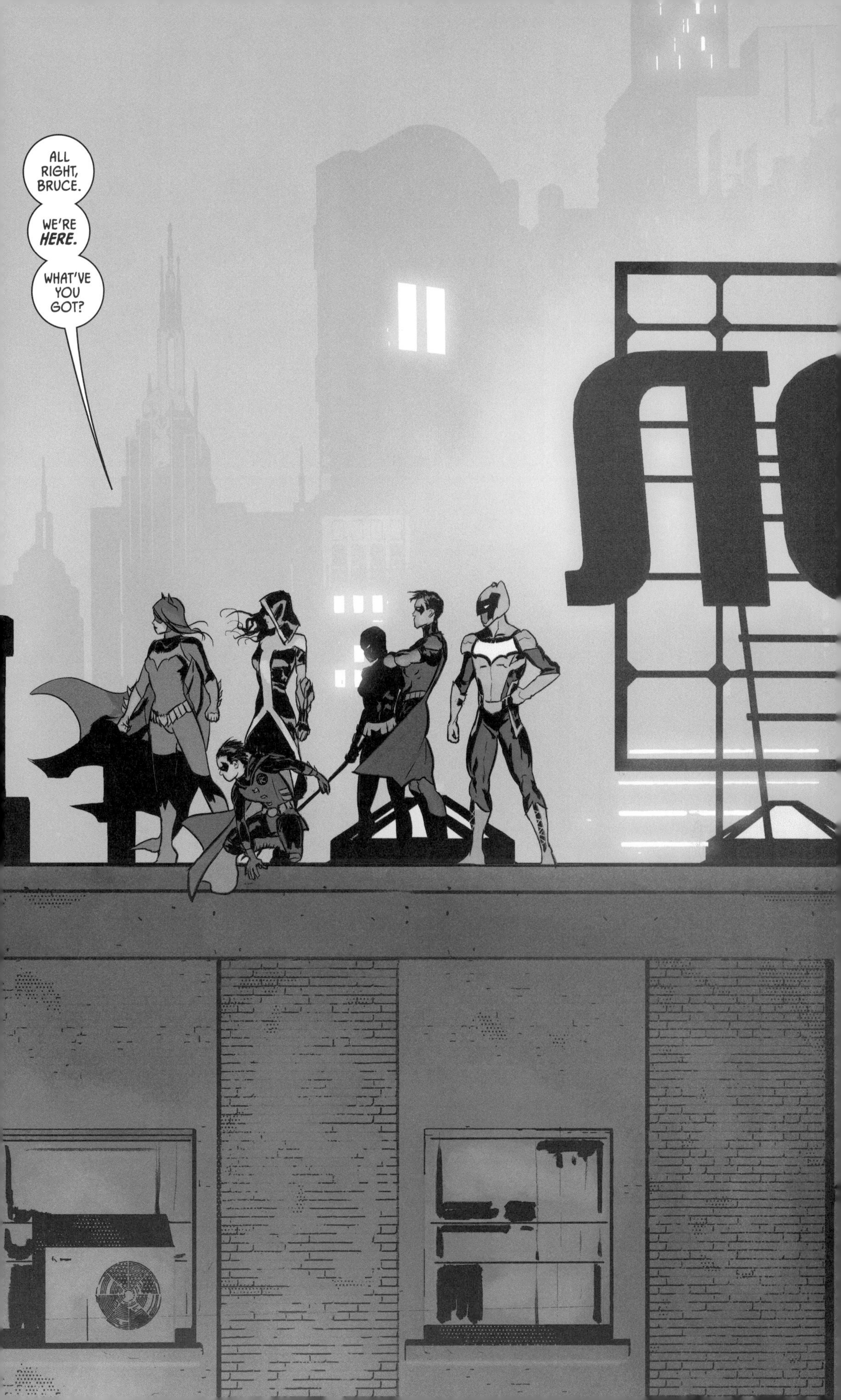
ALL RIGHT, BRUCE.
WE'RE **HERE.**
WHAT'VE YOU GOT?

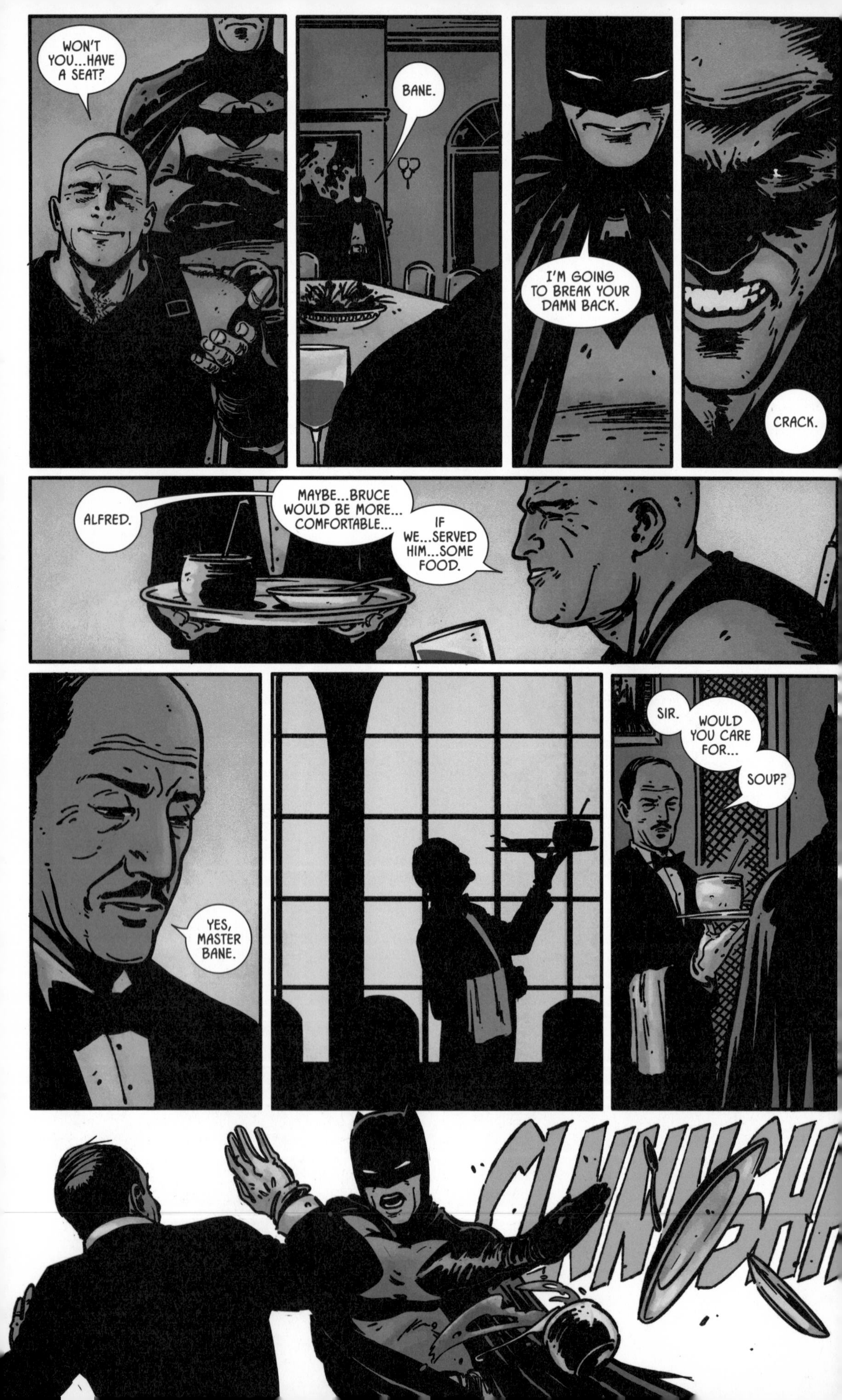
WON'T YOU...HAVE A SEAT?
BANE.
I'M GOING TO BREAK YOUR DAMN BACK.
CRACK.
ALFRED.
MAYBE...BRUCE WOULD BE MORE... COMFORTABLE...
IF WE...SERVED HIM...SOME FOOD.
YES, MASTER BANE.
SIR.
WOULD YOU CARE FOR...
SOUP?

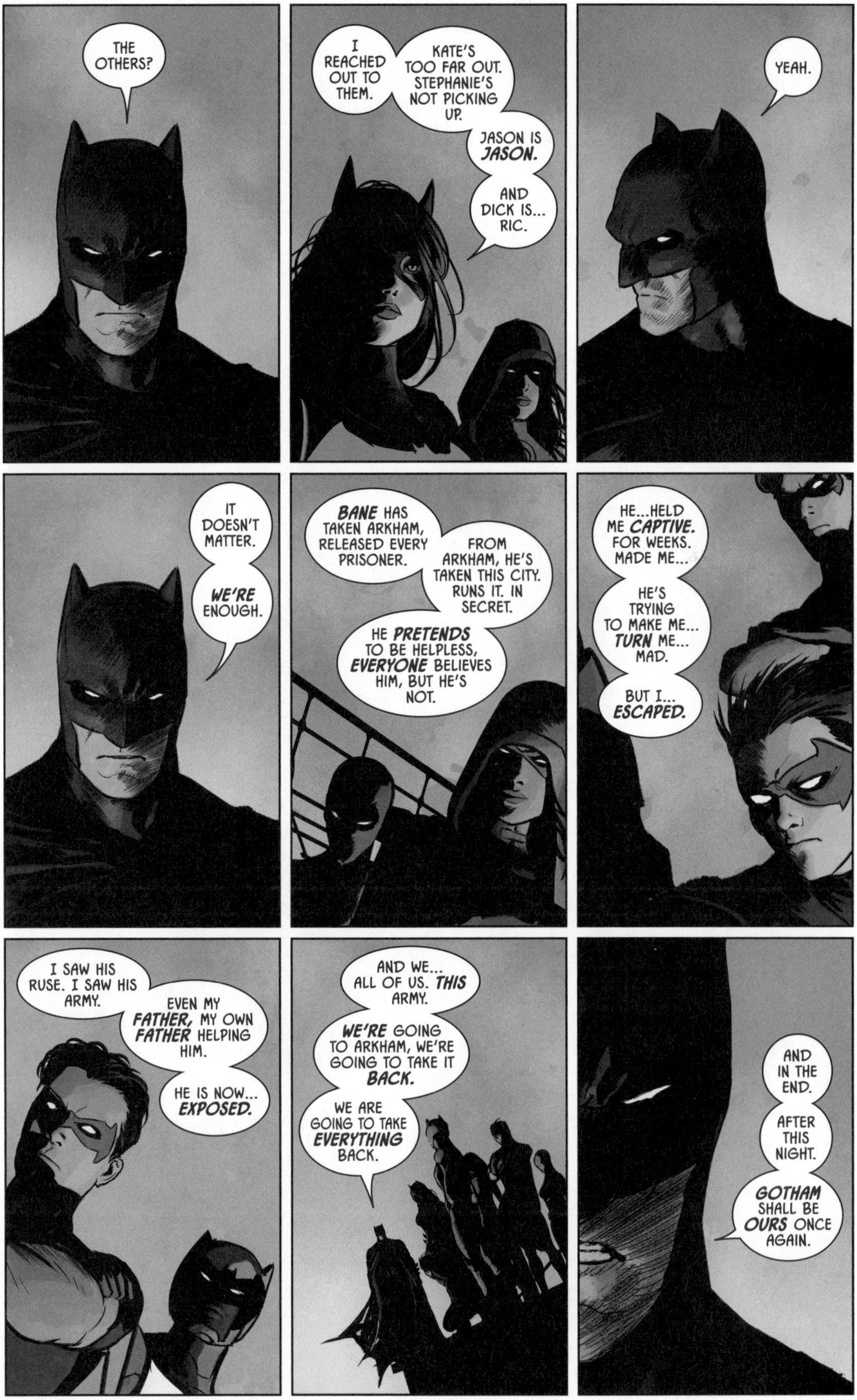
THE OTHERS?
I REACHED OUT TO THEM.
KATE'S TOO FAR OUT. STEPHANIE'S NOT PICKING UP.
JASON IS JASON.
AND DICK IS... RIC.
YEAH.
IT DOESN'T MATTER.
WE'RE ENOUGH.
BANE HAS TAKEN ARKHAM, RELEASED EVERY PRISONER.
FROM ARKHAM, HE'S TAKEN THIS CITY. RUNS IT. IN SECRET.
HE PRETENDS TO BE HELPLESS, EVERYONE BELIEVES HIM, BUT HE'S NOT.
HE...HELD ME CAPTIVE. FOR WEEKS. MADE ME...
HE'S TRYING TO MAKE ME... TURN ME... MAD.
BUT I... ESCAPED.
I SAW HIS RUSE. I SAW HIS ARMY.
EVEN MY FATHER, MY OWN FATHER HELPING HIM.
HE IS NOW... EXPOSED.
AND WE... ALL OF US. THIS ARMY.
WE'RE GOING TO ARKHAM, WE'RE GOING TO TAKE IT BACK.
WE ARE GOING TO TAKE EVERYTHING BACK.
AND IN THE END.
AFTER THIS NIGHT.
GOTHAM SHALL BE OURS ONCE AGAIN.

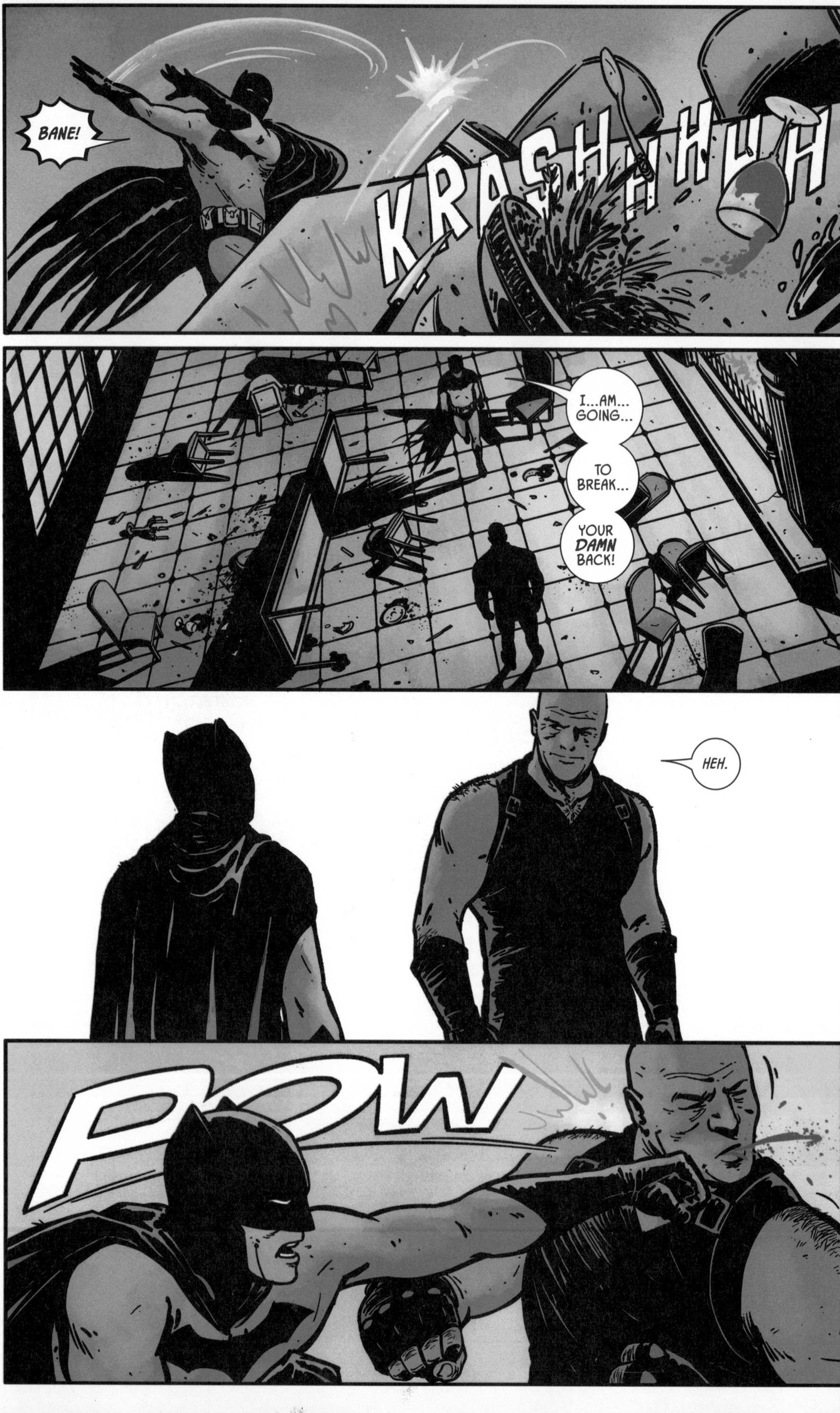
BANE!
KRASHHHHHH
I...AM... GOING...
TO BREAK...
YOUR DAMN BACK!
HEH.
POW

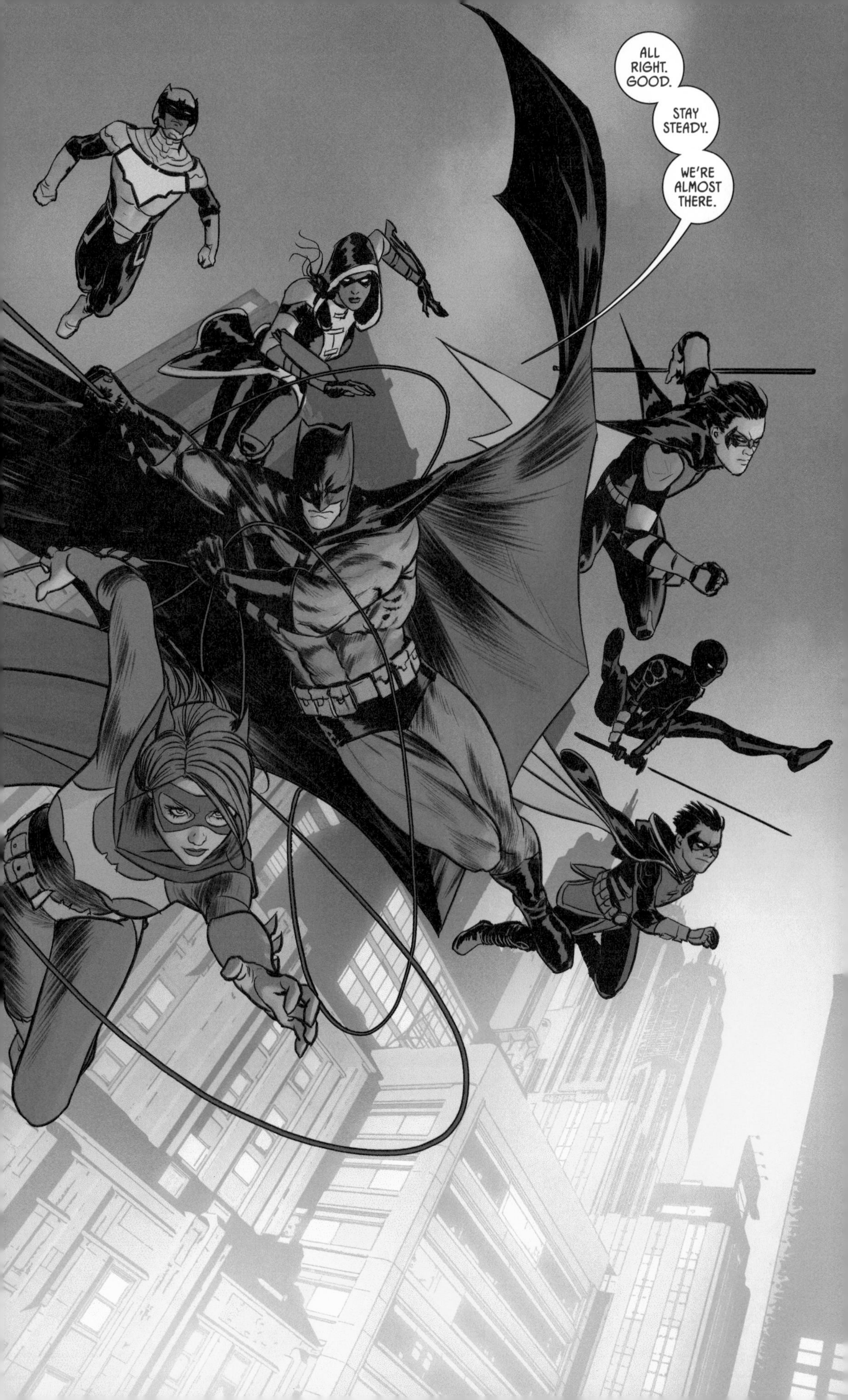
ALL RIGHT. GOOD.
STAY STEADY.
WE'RE ALMOST THERE.

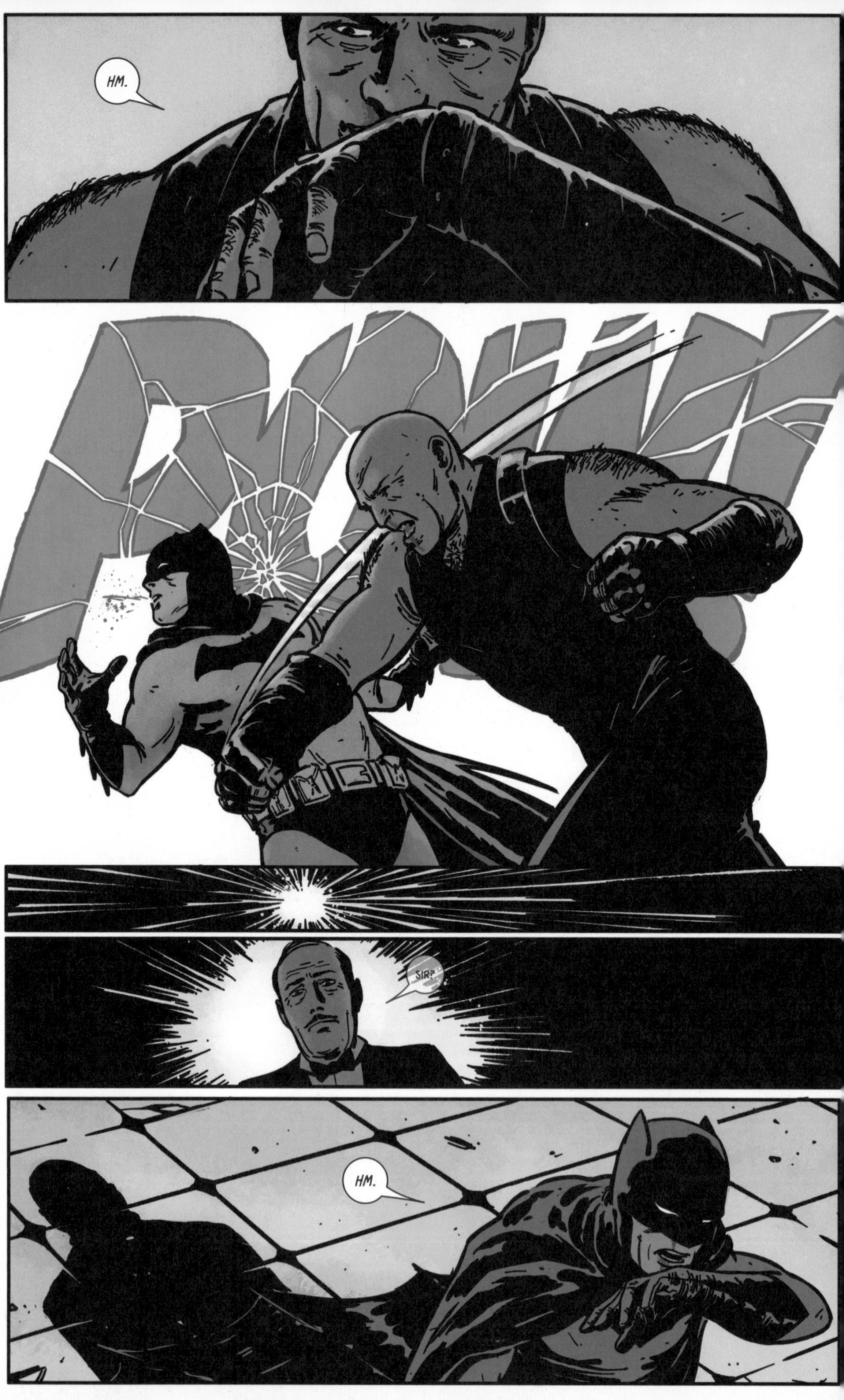
HM.
SIR?
HM.

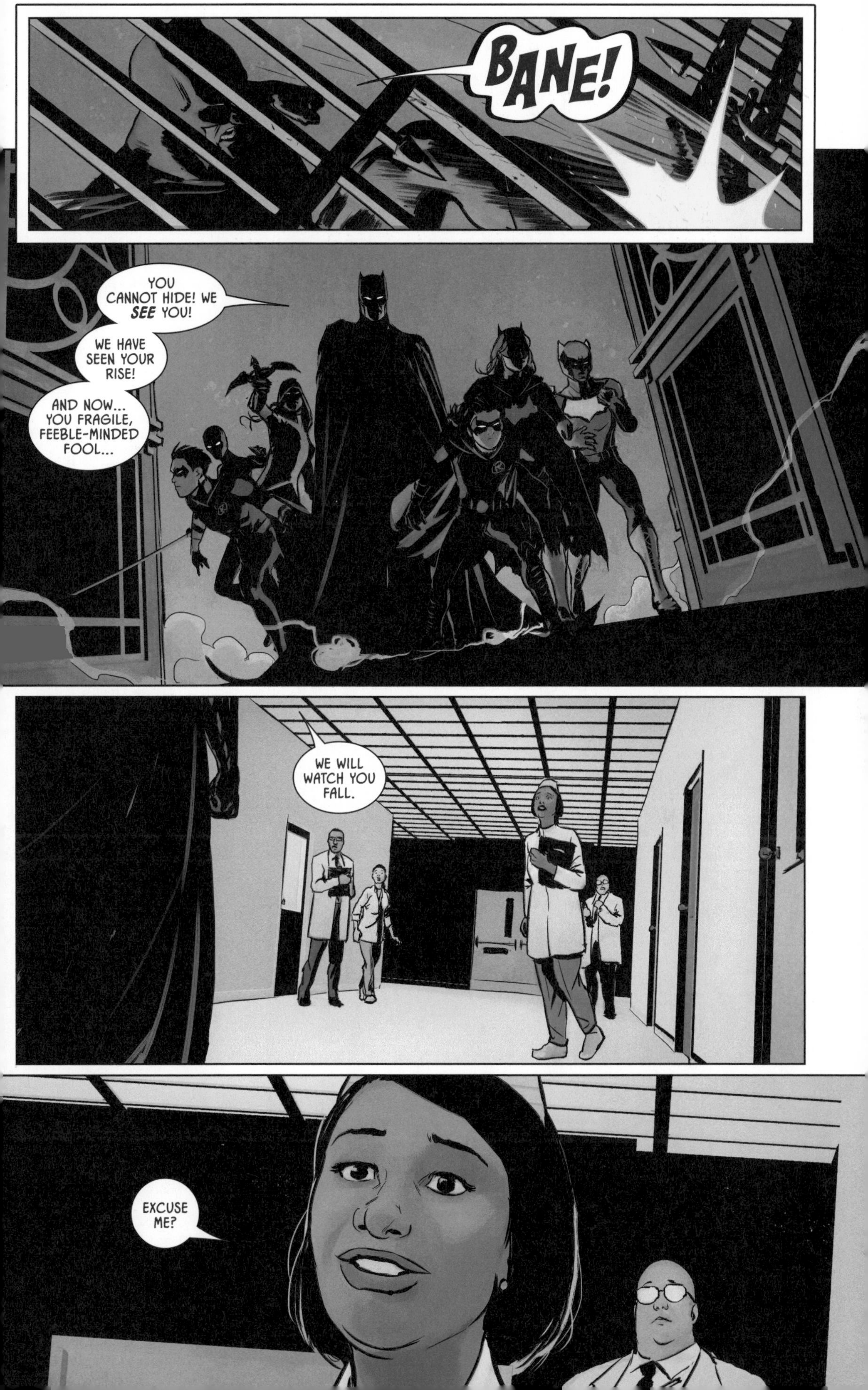
BANE!
YOU CANNOT HIDE! WE SEE YOU!
WE HAVE SEEN YOUR RISE!
AND NOW... YOU FRAGILE, FEEBLE-MINDED FOOL...
WE WILL WATCH YOU FALL.
EXCUSE ME?

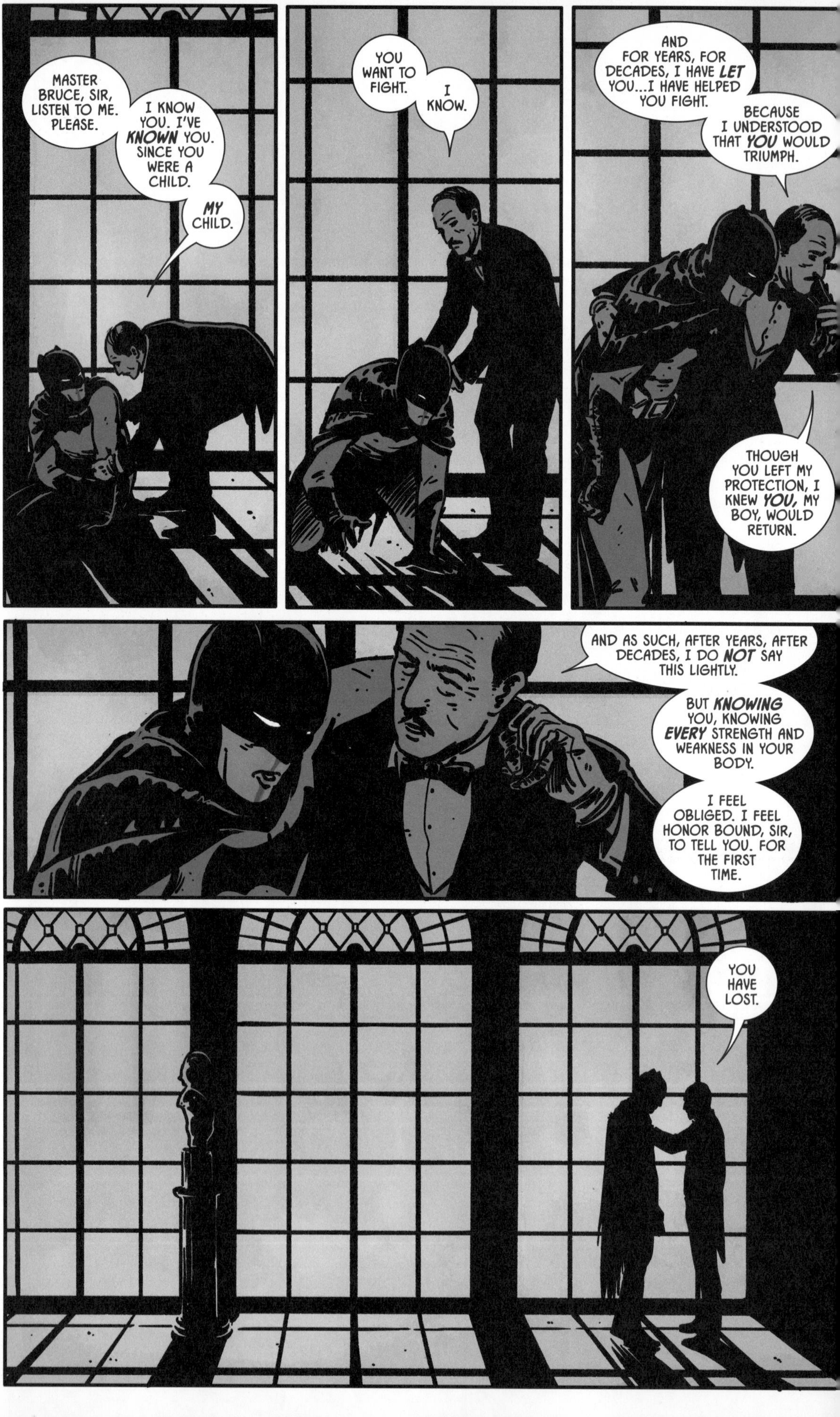
MASTER BRUCE, SIR, LISTEN TO ME. PLEASE.
I KNOW YOU. I'VE KNOWN YOU. SINCE YOU WERE A CHILD.
MY CHILD.
YOU WANT TO FIGHT.
I KNOW.
AND FOR YEARS, FOR DECADES, I HAVE LET YOU...I HAVE HELPED YOU FIGHT.
BECAUSE I UNDERSTOOD THAT YOU WOULD TRIUMPH.
THOUGH YOU LEFT MY PROTECTION, I KNEW YOU, MY BOY, WOULD RETURN.
AND AS SUCH, AFTER YEARS, AFTER DECADES, I DO NOT SAY THIS LIGHTLY.
BUT KNOWING YOU, KNOWING EVERY STRENGTH AND WEAKNESS IN YOUR BODY.
I FEEL OBLIGED. I FEEL HONOR BOUND, SIR, TO TELL YOU. FOR THE FIRST TIME.
YOU HAVE LOST.

IT'S NOT *JUST* THAT WE SAW IT WITH OUR OWN EYES.

I GOT INTO THEIR SYSTEM, THEIR SERVERS, *DEEP* IN.

THERE'S *NO* RECORD OF *ANYONE* GETTING OUT OF THEIR CELLS.

BANE WAS A *WRECK* BEFORE YOU BEAT INTO HIM. NOW HE'S *COMATOSE.*

ALFRED.

HE SAW MY FATHER. MY FATHER *HURT* HIM.

TALK TO HIM. HE'LL TELL YOU.

I...BRUCE, I TALKED TO ALFRED. AT LENGTH.

HE...DOESN'T KNOW WHAT...HE SAYS HE *NEVER* SAW YOUR FATHER. NEVER GOT HURT.

HE SAYS YESTERDAY YOU LEFT THE CAVE IN A STATE OF...HE'S *WORRIED* ABOUT YOU.

HE SAYS... EVER SINCE...SINCE *CATWOMAN*...YOU'VE...

THIS IS *NOT* ABOUT *HER!*

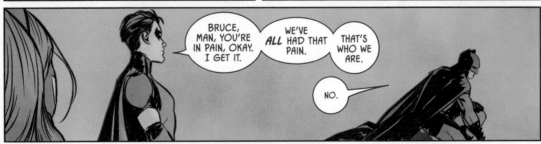

BRUCE, MAN, YOU'RE IN PAIN, OKAY. I GET IT.

WE'VE *ALL* HAD THAT PAIN.

THAT'S WHO WE ARE.

NO.

LET ME...

LET US.

HELP YOU.

I DON'T NEED YOUR HELP, TIM.

BRUCE...I KNOW YOU LOVED HER.

YOU...

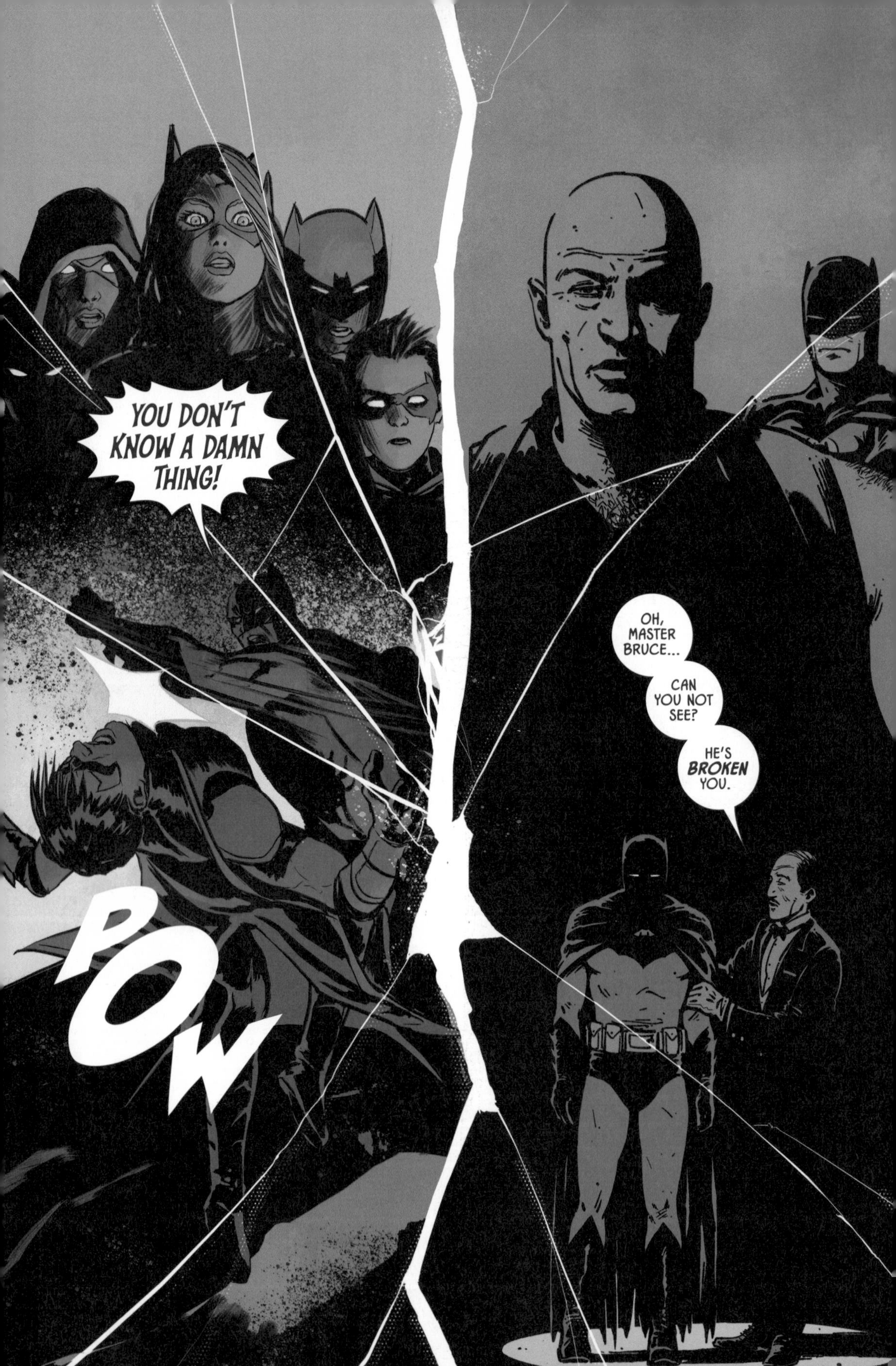
YOU DON'T KNOW A DAMN THING!
POW
OH, MASTER BRUCE...
CAN YOU NOT SEE?
HE'S BROKEN YOU.

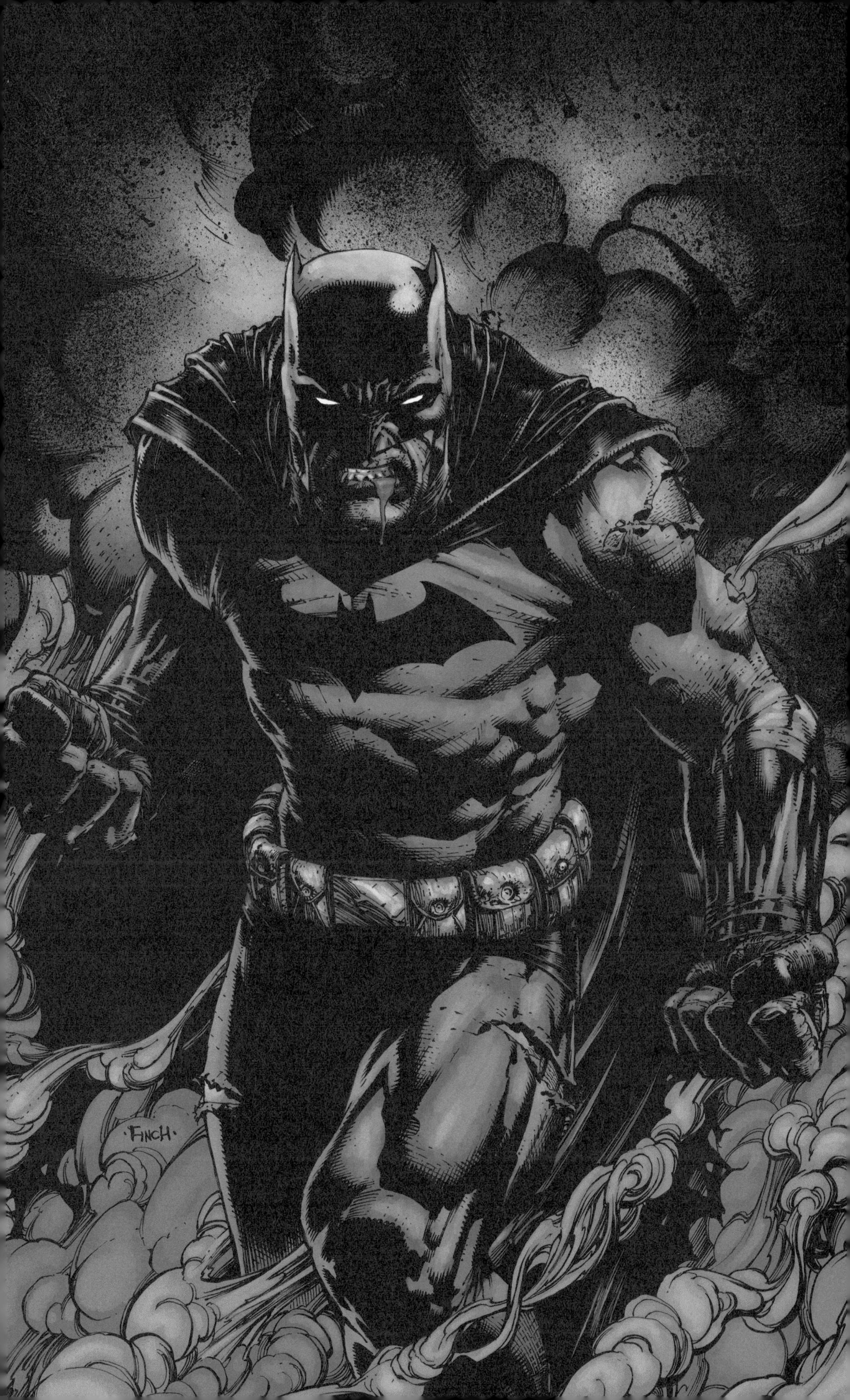
FINCH

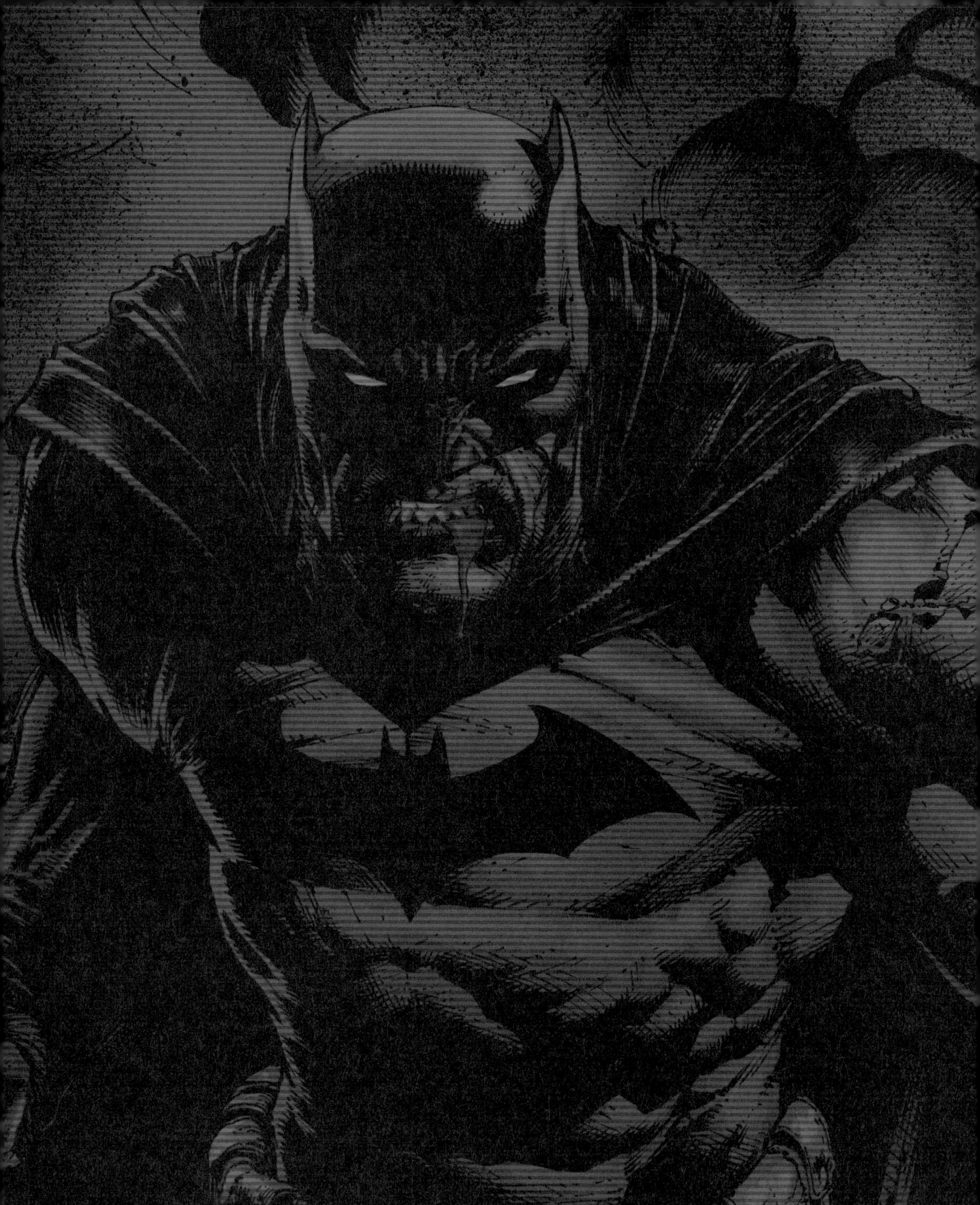

BATMAN

#72

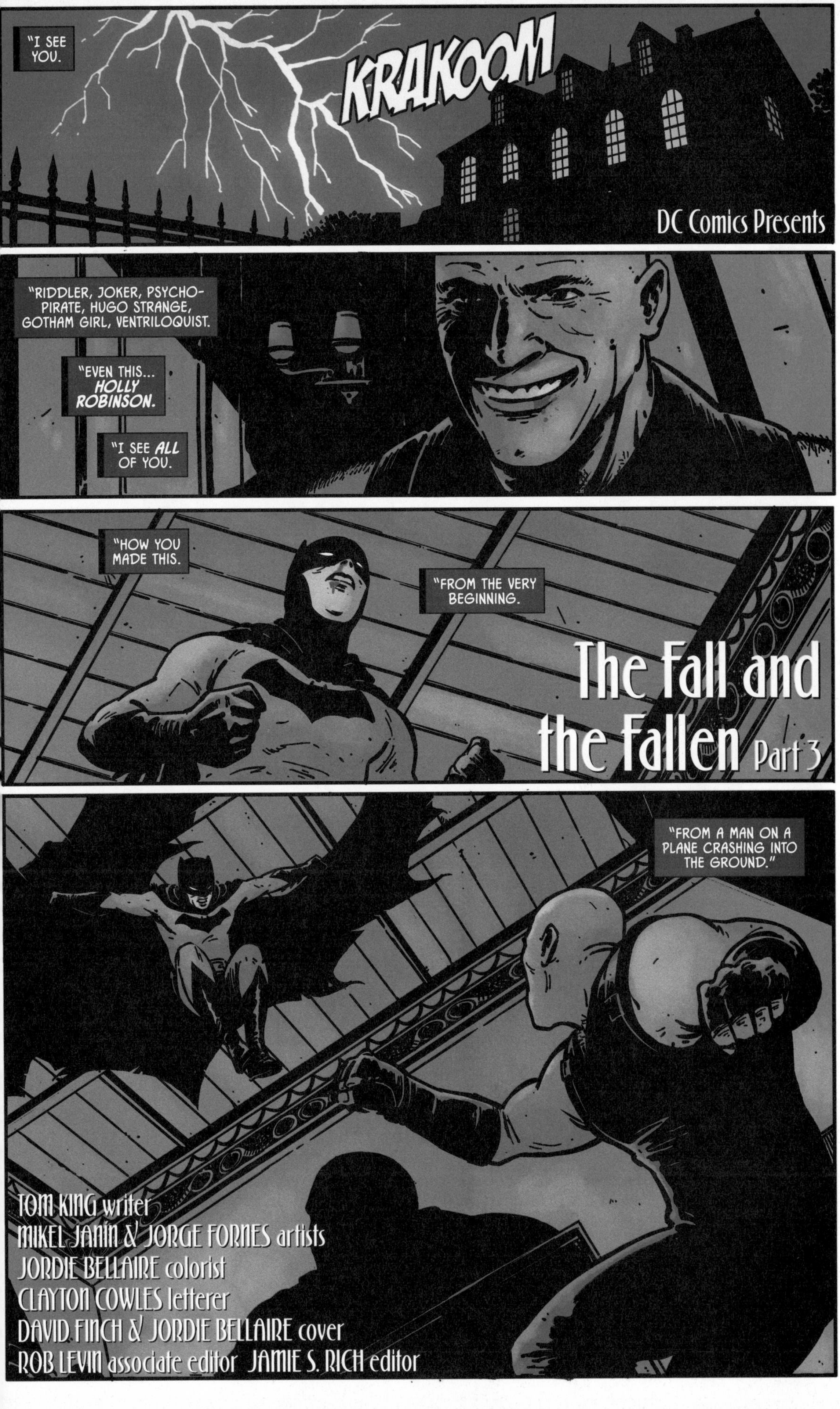
"I SEE YOU.
KRAKOOM
DC Comics Presents
"RIDDLER, JOKER, PSYCHO-PIRATE, HUGO STRANGE, GOTHAM GIRL, VENTRILOQUIST.
"EVEN THIS... HOLLY ROBINSON.
"I SEE ALL OF YOU.
"HOW YOU MADE THIS.
"FROM THE VERY BEGINNING.
The Fall and the Fallen Part 3
"FROM A MAN ON A PLANE CRASHING INTO THE GROUND."
TOM KING writer
MIKEL JANIN & JORGE FORNES artists
JORDIE BELLAIRE colorist
CLAYTON COWLES letterer
DAVID FINCH & JORDIE BELLAIRE cover
ROB LEVIN associate editor JAMIE S. RICH editor

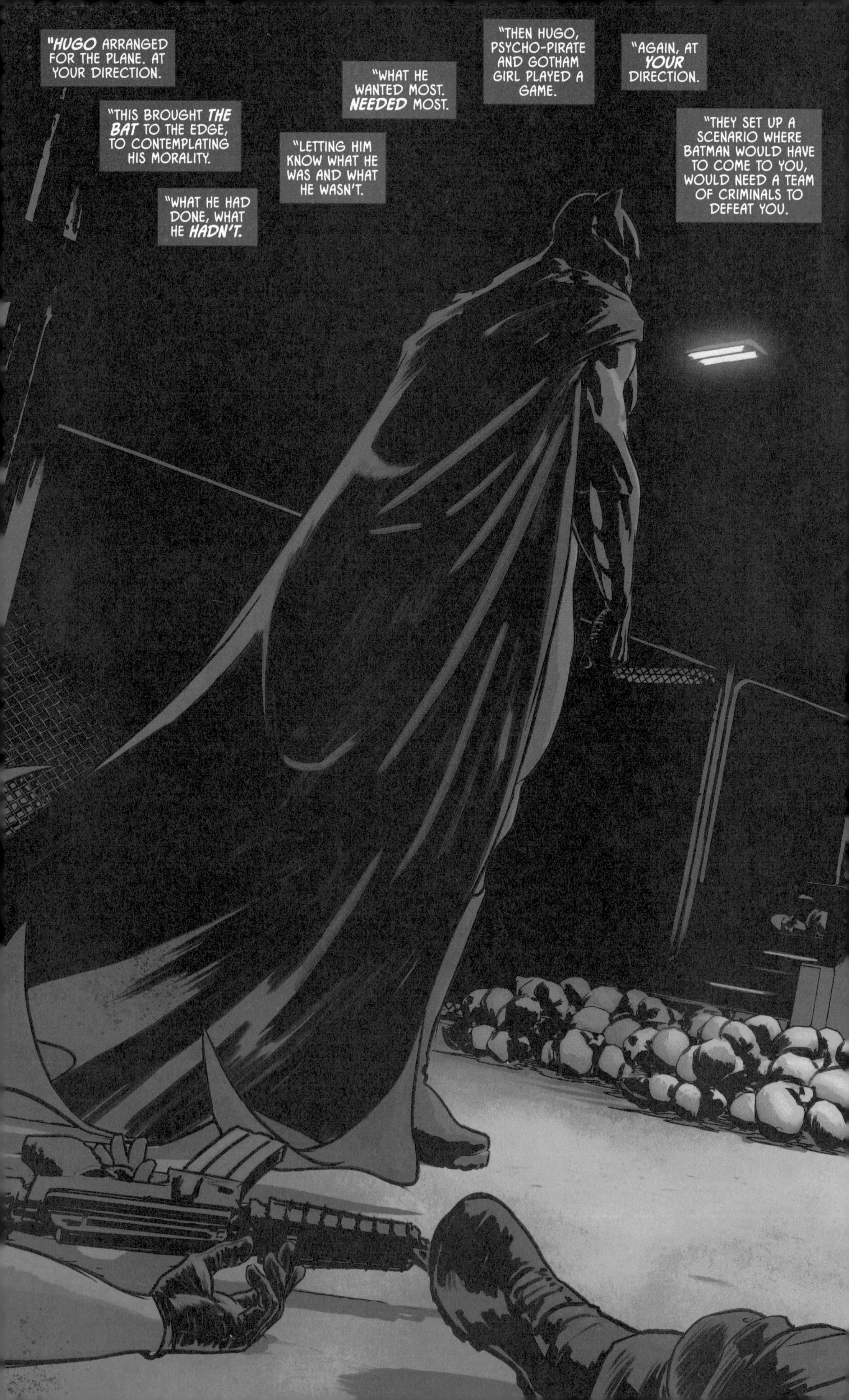
"HUGO ARRANGED FOR THE PLANE. AT YOUR DIRECTION.
"THIS BROUGHT THE BAT TO THE EDGE, TO CONTEMPLATING HIS MORALITY.
"WHAT HE HAD DONE, WHAT HE HADN'T.
"LETTING HIM KNOW WHAT HE WAS AND WHAT HE WASN'T.
"WHAT HE WANTED MOST. NEEDED MOST.
"THEN HUGO, PSYCHO-PIRATE AND GOTHAM GIRL PLAYED A GAME.
"AGAIN, AT YOUR DIRECTION.
"THEY SET UP A SCENARIO WHERE BATMAN WOULD HAVE TO COME TO YOU, WOULD NEED A TEAM OF CRIMINALS TO DEFEAT YOU.

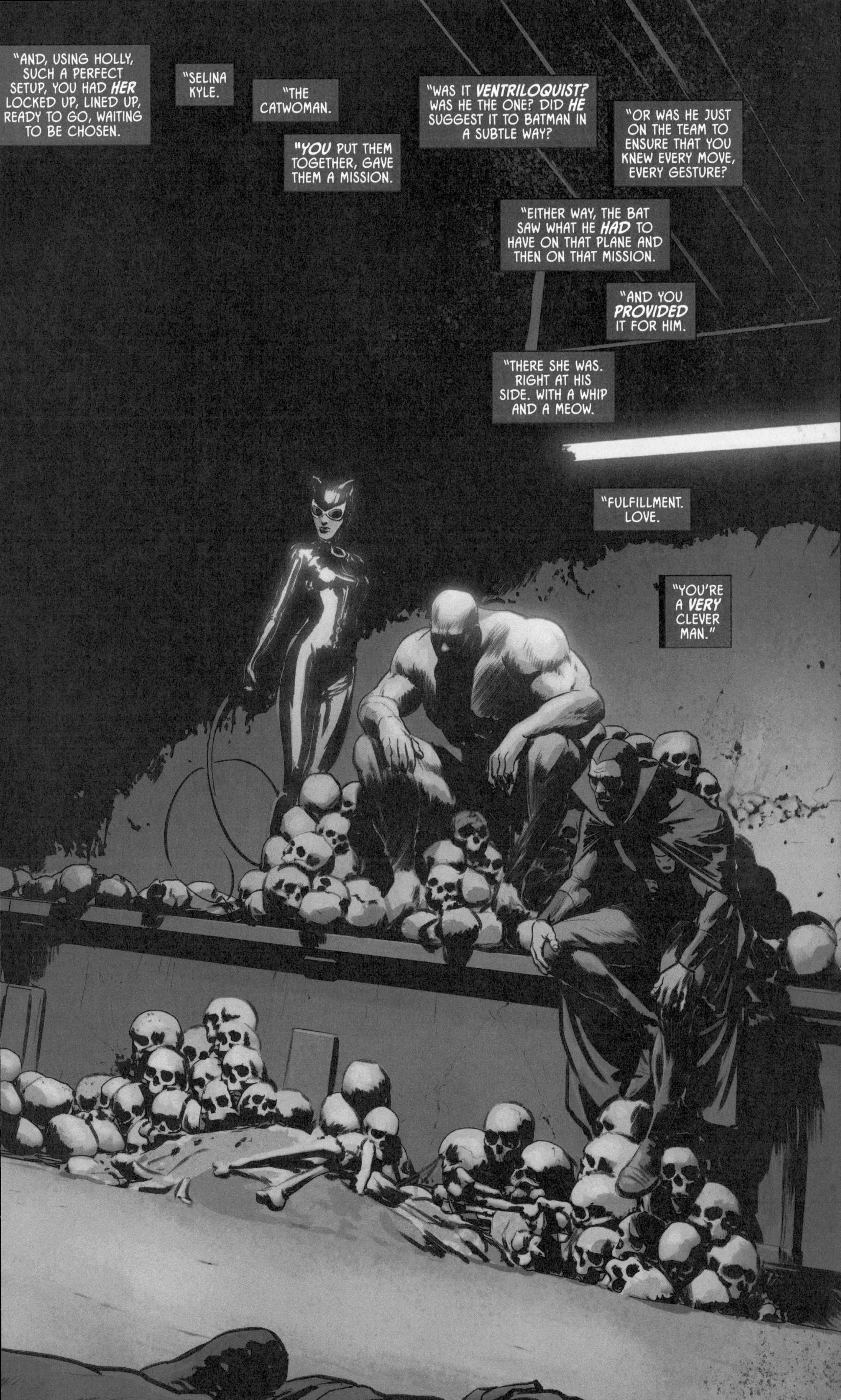
"AND, USING HOLLY, SUCH A PERFECT SETUP, YOU HAD HER LOCKED UP, LINED UP, READY TO GO, WAITING TO BE CHOSEN.
"SELINA KYLE.
"THE CATWOMAN.
"YOU PUT THEM TOGETHER, GAVE THEM A MISSION.
"WAS IT VENTRILOQUIST? WAS HE THE ONE? DID HE SUGGEST IT TO BATMAN IN A SUBTLE WAY?
"OR WAS HE JUST ON THE TEAM TO ENSURE THAT YOU KNEW EVERY MOVE, EVERY GESTURE?
"EITHER WAY, THE BAT SAW WHAT HE HAD TO HAVE ON THAT PLANE AND THEN ON THAT MISSION.
"AND YOU PROVIDED IT FOR HIM.
"THERE SHE WAS. RIGHT AT HIS SIDE. WITH A WHIP AND A MEOW.
"FULFILLMENT. LOVE.
"YOU'RE A VERY CLEVER MAN."

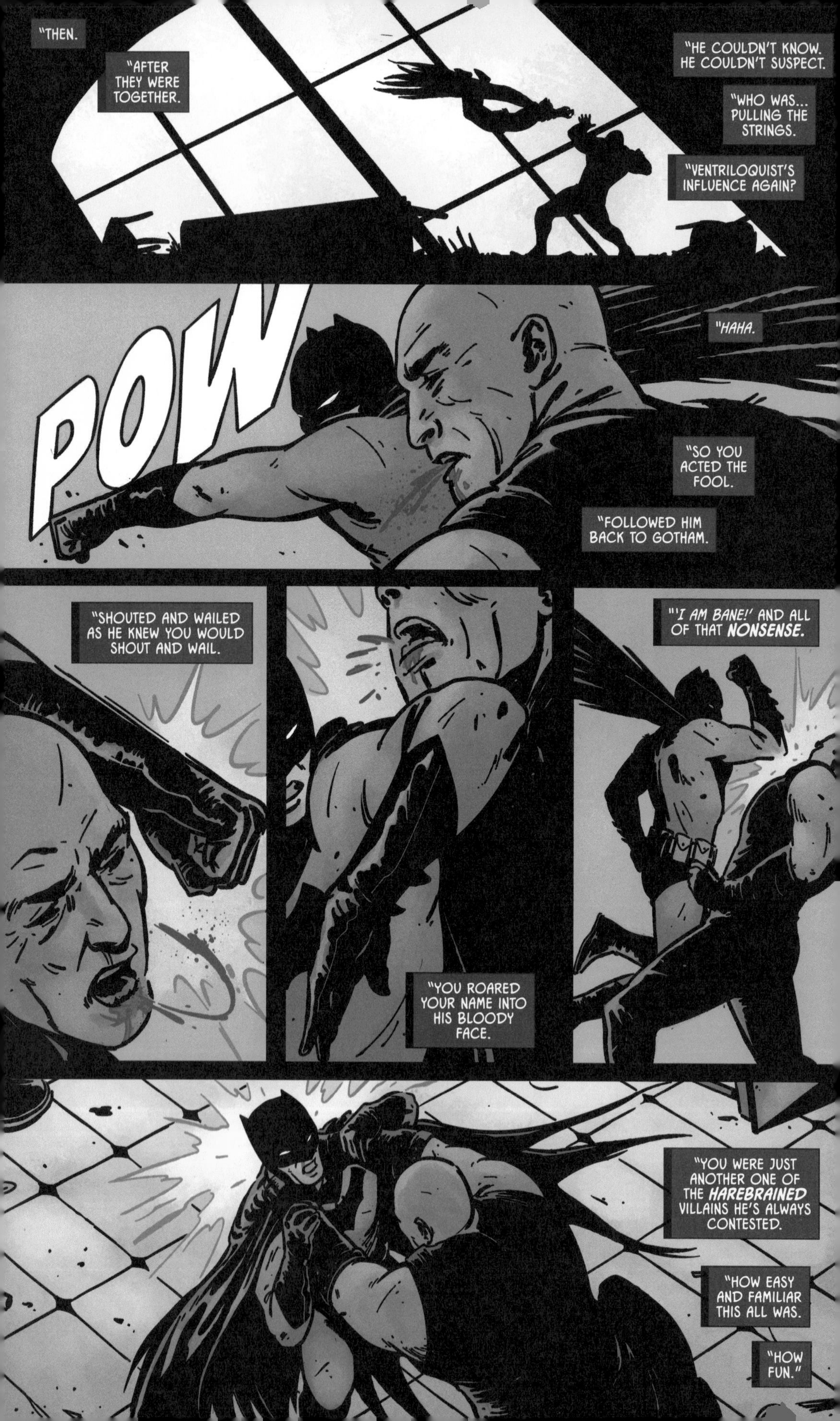
"THEN.
"AFTER THEY WERE TOGETHER.
"HE COULDN'T KNOW. HE COULDN'T SUSPECT.
"WHO WAS... PULLING THE STRINGS.
"VENTRILOQUIST'S INFLUENCE AGAIN?
POW
"HAHA.
"SO YOU ACTED THE FOOL.
"FOLLOWED HIM BACK TO GOTHAM.
"SHOUTED AND WAILED AS HE KNEW YOU WOULD SHOUT AND WAIL.
"YOU ROARED YOUR NAME INTO HIS BLOODY FACE.
"'*I AM BANE!*' AND ALL OF THAT ***NONSENSE.***
"YOU WERE JUST ANOTHER ONE OF THE ***HAREBRAINED*** VILLAINS HE'S ALWAYS CONTESTED.
"HOW EASY AND FAMILIAR THIS ALL WAS.
"HOW FUN."

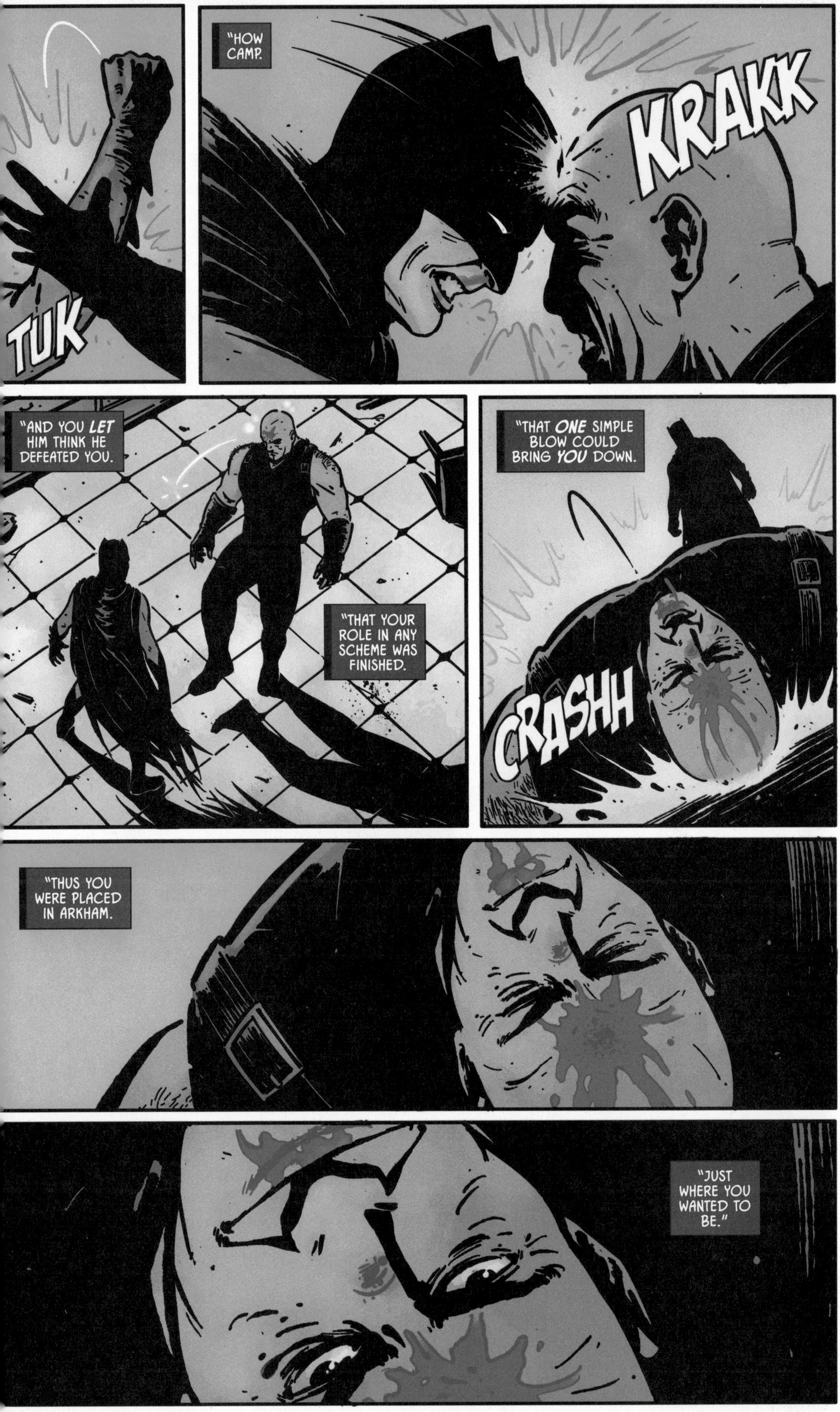
TUK
"HOW CAMP.
KRAKK
"AND YOU LET HIM THINK HE DEFEATED YOU.
"THAT YOUR ROLE IN ANY SCHEME WAS FINISHED.
"THAT ONE SIMPLE BLOW COULD BRING YOU DOWN.
CRASHH
"THUS YOU WERE PLACED IN ARKHAM.
"JUST WHERE YOU WANTED TO BE."

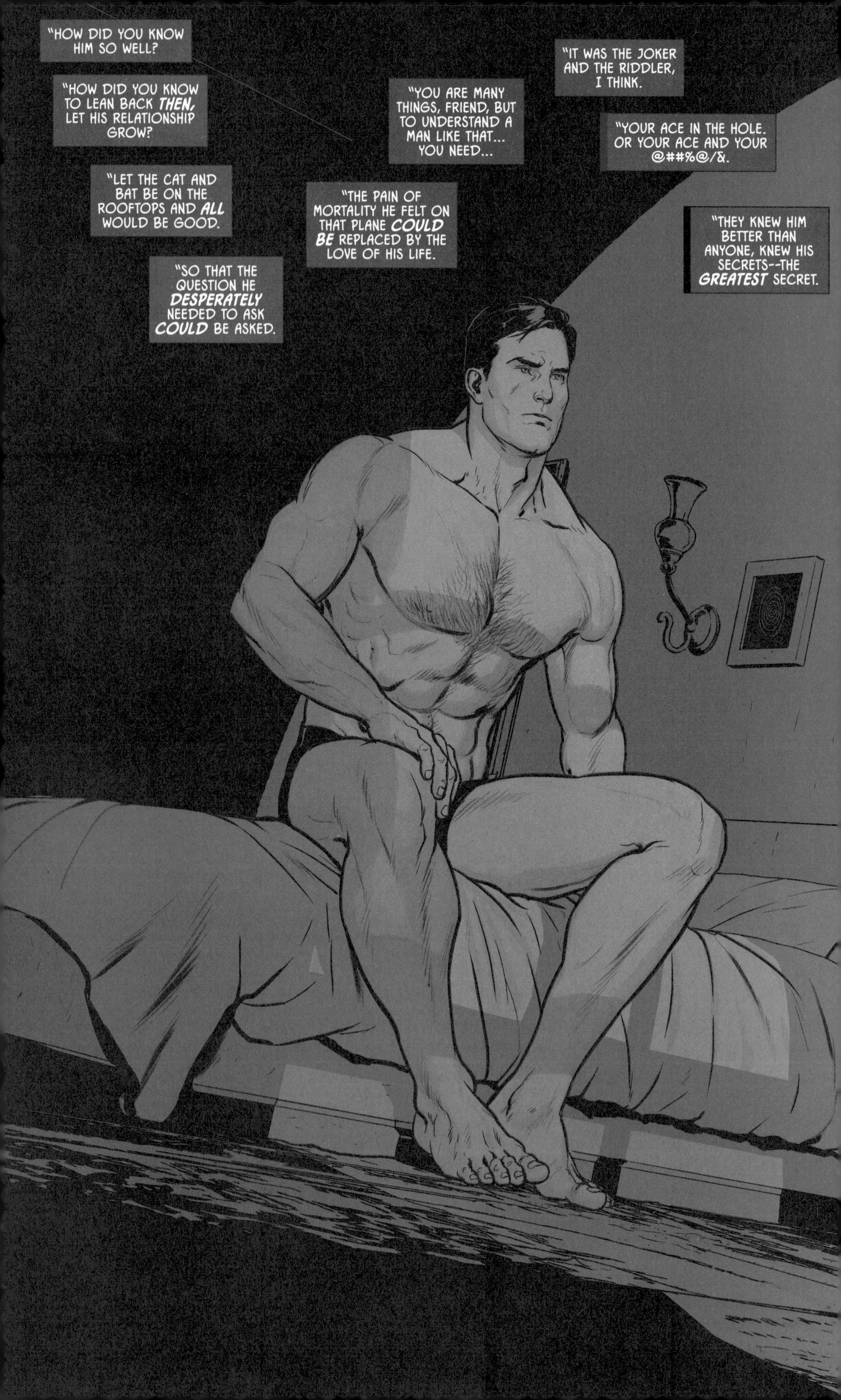
"HOW DID YOU KNOW HIM SO WELL?
"HOW DID YOU KNOW TO LEAN BACK *THEN,* LET HIS RELATIONSHIP GROW?
"LET THE CAT AND BAT BE ON THE ROOFTOPS AND *ALL* WOULD BE GOOD.
"SO THAT THE QUESTION HE *DESPERATELY* NEEDED TO ASK *COULD* BE ASKED.
"THE PAIN OF MORTALITY HE FELT ON THAT PLANE *COULD BE* REPLACED BY THE LOVE OF HIS LIFE.
"YOU ARE MANY THINGS, FRIEND, BUT TO UNDERSTAND A MAN LIKE THAT... YOU NEED...
"IT WAS THE JOKER AND THE RIDDLER, I THINK.
"YOUR ACE IN THE HOLE. OR YOUR ACE AND YOUR @##%@/&.
"THEY KNEW HIM BETTER THAN ANYONE, KNEW HIS SECRETS--THE *GREATEST* SECRET.

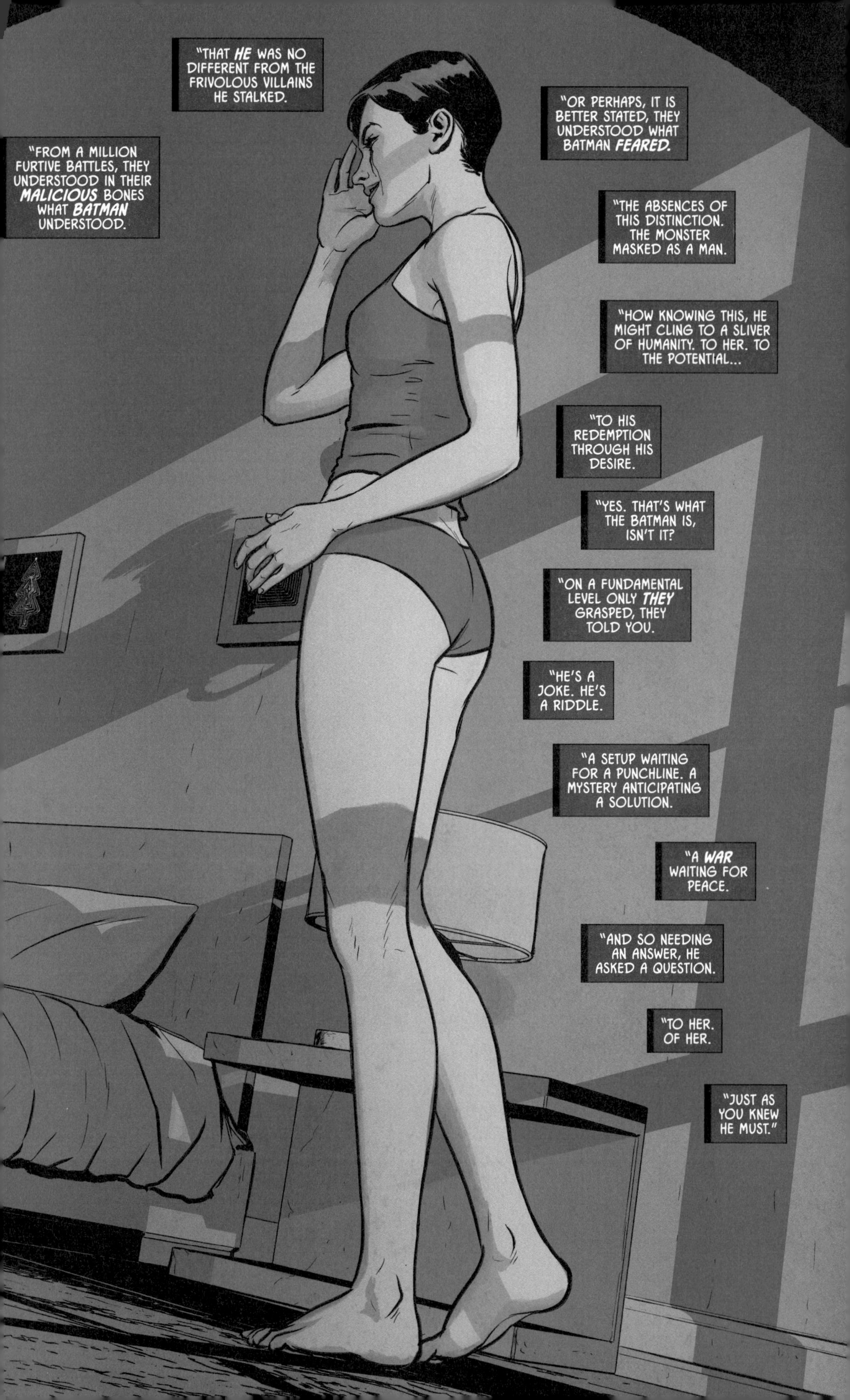
"FROM A MILLION FURTIVE BATTLES, THEY UNDERSTOOD IN THEIR MALICIOUS BONES WHAT BATMAN UNDERSTOOD.
"THAT HE WAS NO DIFFERENT FROM THE FRIVOLOUS VILLAINS HE STALKED.
"OR PERHAPS, IT IS BETTER STATED, THEY UNDERSTOOD WHAT BATMAN FEARED.
"THE ABSENCES OF THIS DISTINCTION. THE MONSTER MASKED AS A MAN.
"HOW KNOWING THIS, HE MIGHT CLING TO A SLIVER OF HUMANITY. TO HER. TO THE POTENTIAL...
"TO HIS REDEMPTION THROUGH HIS DESIRE.
"YES. THAT'S WHAT THE BATMAN IS, ISN'T IT?
"ON A FUNDAMENTAL LEVEL ONLY THEY GRASPED, THEY TOLD YOU.
"HE'S A JOKE. HE'S A RIDDLE.
"A SETUP WAITING FOR A PUNCHLINE. A MYSTERY ANTICIPATING A SOLUTION.
"A WAR WAITING FOR PEACE.
"AND SO NEEDING AN ANSWER, HE ASKED A QUESTION.
"TO HER. OF HER.
"JUST AS YOU KNEW HE MUST."

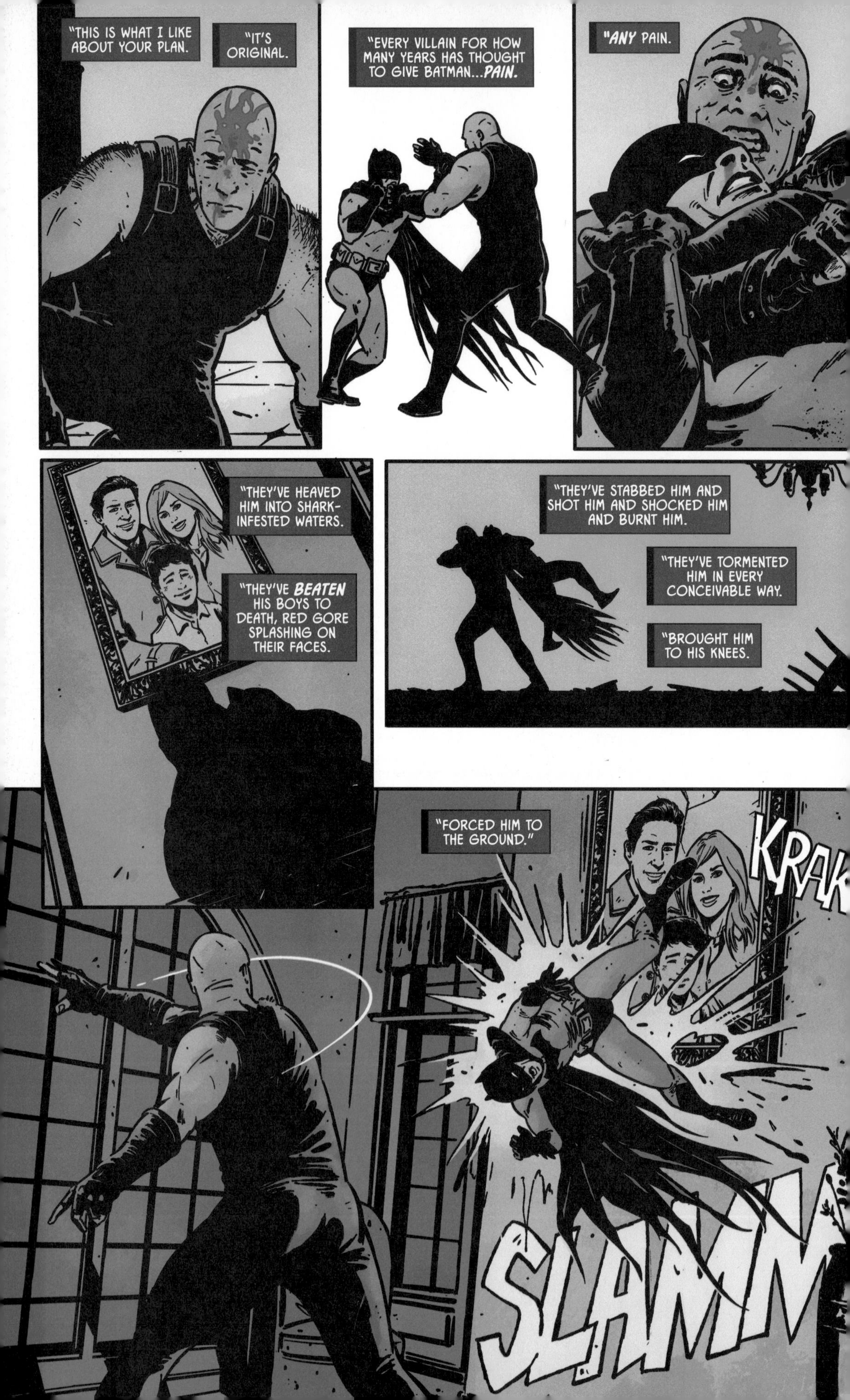
"THIS IS WHAT I LIKE ABOUT YOUR PLAN.
"IT'S ORIGINAL.
"EVERY VILLAIN FOR HOW MANY YEARS HAS THOUGHT TO GIVE BATMAN...PAIN.
"ANY PAIN.
"THEY'VE HEAVED HIM INTO SHARK-INFESTED WATERS.
"THEY'VE BEATEN HIS BOYS TO DEATH, RED GORE SPLASHING ON THEIR FACES.
"THEY'VE STABBED HIM AND SHOT HIM AND SHOCKED HIM AND BURNT HIM.
"THEY'VE TORMENTED HIM IN EVERY CONCEIVABLE WAY.
"BROUGHT HIM TO HIS KNEES.
"FORCED HIM TO THE GROUND."
KRAK
SLAMM

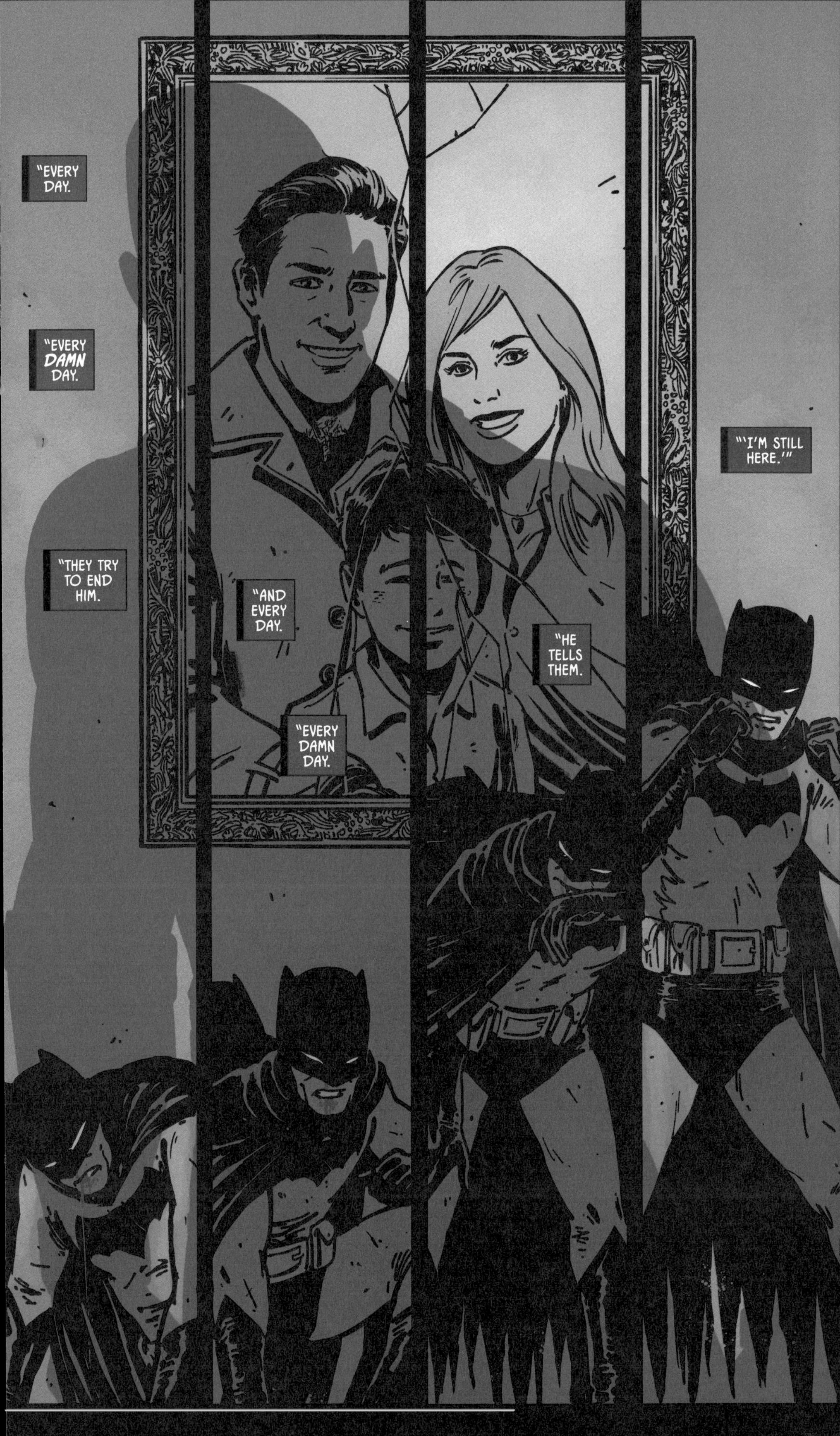
"EVERY DAY.
"EVERY *DAMN* DAY.
"THEY TRY TO END HIM.
"AND EVERY DAY.
"EVERY DAMN DAY.
"HE TELLS THEM.
"'I'M STILL HERE.'"

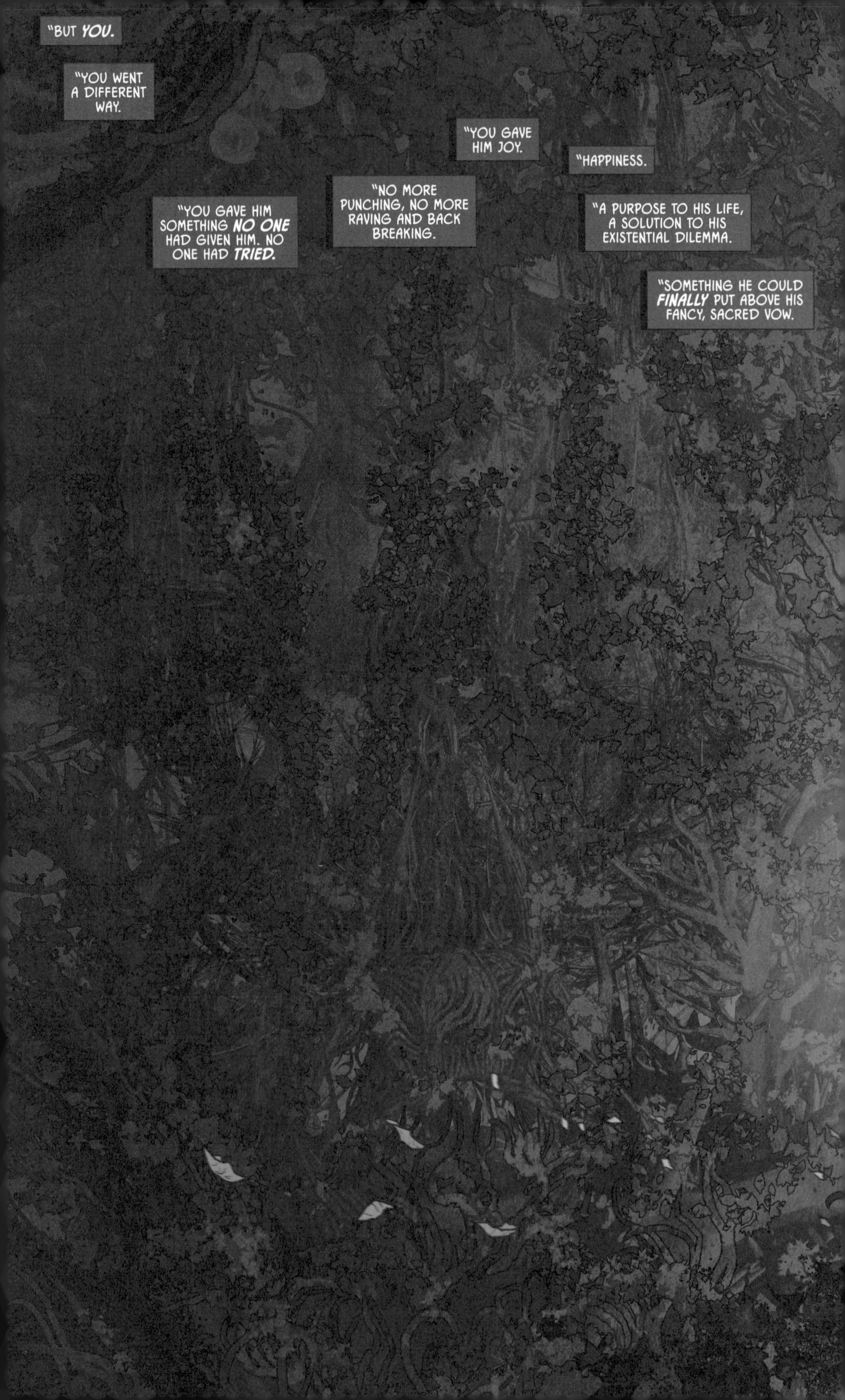
"BUT YOU.
"YOU WENT A DIFFERENT WAY.
"YOU GAVE HIM SOMETHING NO ONE HAD GIVEN HIM. NO ONE HAD TRIED.
"NO MORE PUNCHING, NO MORE RAVING AND BACK BREAKING.
"YOU GAVE HIM JOY.
"HAPPINESS.
"A PURPOSE TO HIS LIFE, A SOLUTION TO HIS EXISTENTIAL DILEMMA.
"SOMETHING HE COULD FINALLY PUT ABOVE HIS FANCY, SACRED VOW.

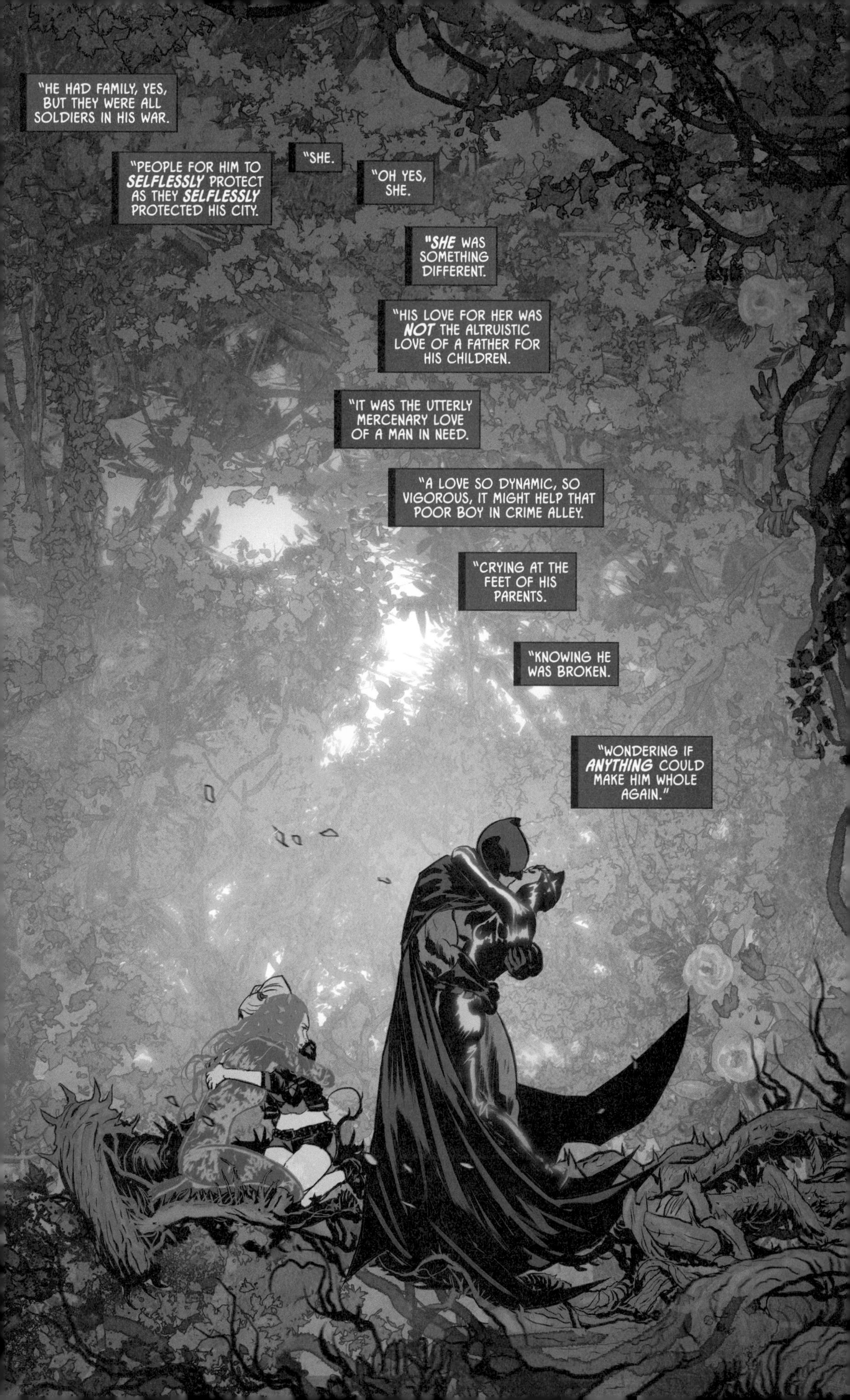
"HE HAD FAMILY, YES, BUT THEY WERE ALL SOLDIERS IN HIS WAR.
"PEOPLE FOR HIM TO ***SELFLESSLY*** PROTECT AS THEY ***SELFLESSLY*** PROTECTED HIS CITY.
"SHE.
"OH YES, SHE.
"***SHE*** WAS SOMETHING DIFFERENT.
"HIS LOVE FOR HER WAS ***NOT*** THE ALTRUISTIC LOVE OF A FATHER FOR HIS CHILDREN.
"IT WAS THE UTTERLY MERCENARY LOVE OF A MAN IN NEED.
"A LOVE SO DYNAMIC, SO VIGOROUS, IT MIGHT HELP THAT POOR BOY IN CRIME ALLEY.
"CRYING AT THE FEET OF HIS PARENTS.
"KNOWING HE WAS BROKEN.
"WONDERING IF ***ANYTHING*** COULD MAKE HIM WHOLE AGAIN."

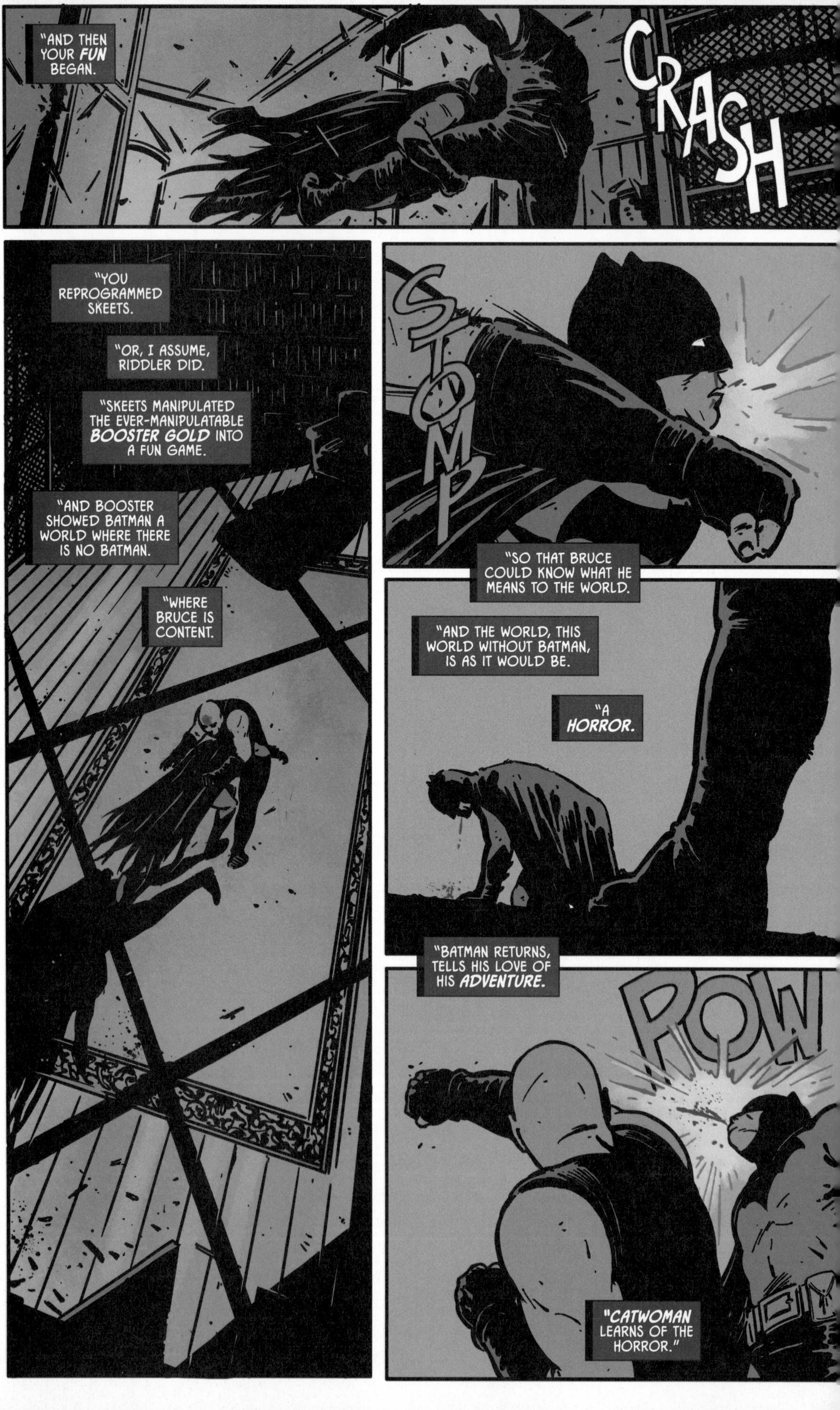
"AND THEN YOUR *FUN* BEGAN.
CRASH
"YOU REPROGRAMMED SKEETS.
"OR, I ASSUME, RIDDLER DID.
"SKEETS MANIPULATED THE EVER-MANIPULATABLE *BOOSTER GOLD* INTO A FUN GAME.
"AND BOOSTER SHOWED BATMAN A WORLD WHERE THERE IS NO BATMAN.
"WHERE BRUCE IS CONTENT.
STOMP
"SO THAT BRUCE COULD KNOW WHAT HE MEANS TO THE WORLD.
"AND THE WORLD, THIS WORLD WITHOUT BATMAN, IS AS IT WOULD BE.
"A *HORROR.*
"BATMAN RETURNS, TELLS HIS LOVE OF HIS *ADVENTURE.*
POW
"*CATWOMAN* LEARNS OF THE HORROR."

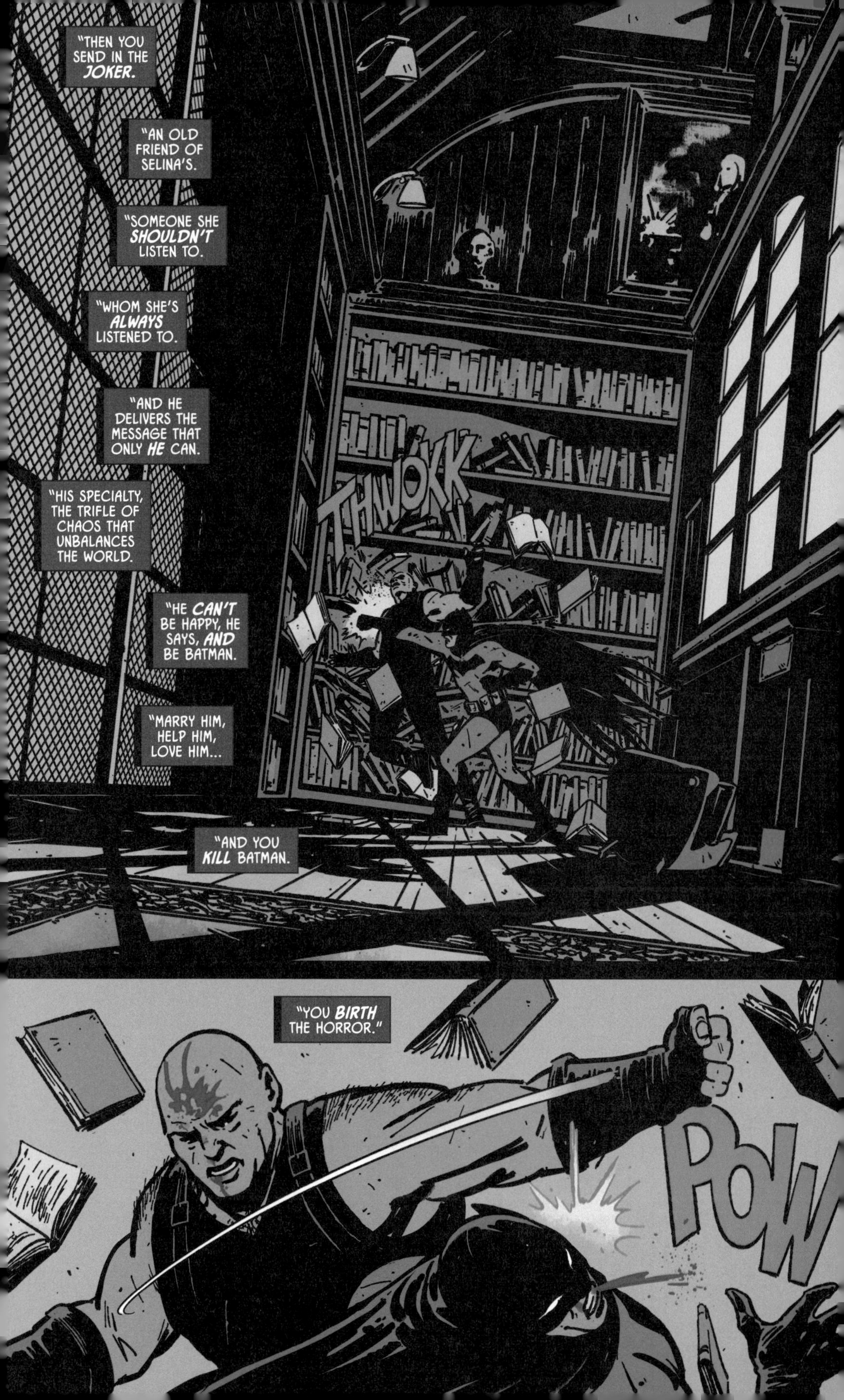
"THEN YOU SEND IN THE JOKER.
"AN OLD FRIEND OF SELINA'S.
"SOMEONE SHE SHOULDN'T LISTEN TO.
"WHOM SHE'S ALWAYS LISTENED TO.
"AND HE DELIVERS THE MESSAGE THAT ONLY HE CAN.
"HIS SPECIALTY, THE TRIFLE OF CHAOS THAT UNBALANCES THE WORLD.
"HE CAN'T BE HAPPY, HE SAYS, AND BE BATMAN.
THWOKK
"MARRY HIM, HELP HIM, LOVE HIM...
"AND YOU KILL BATMAN.
"YOU BIRTH THE HORROR."
POW

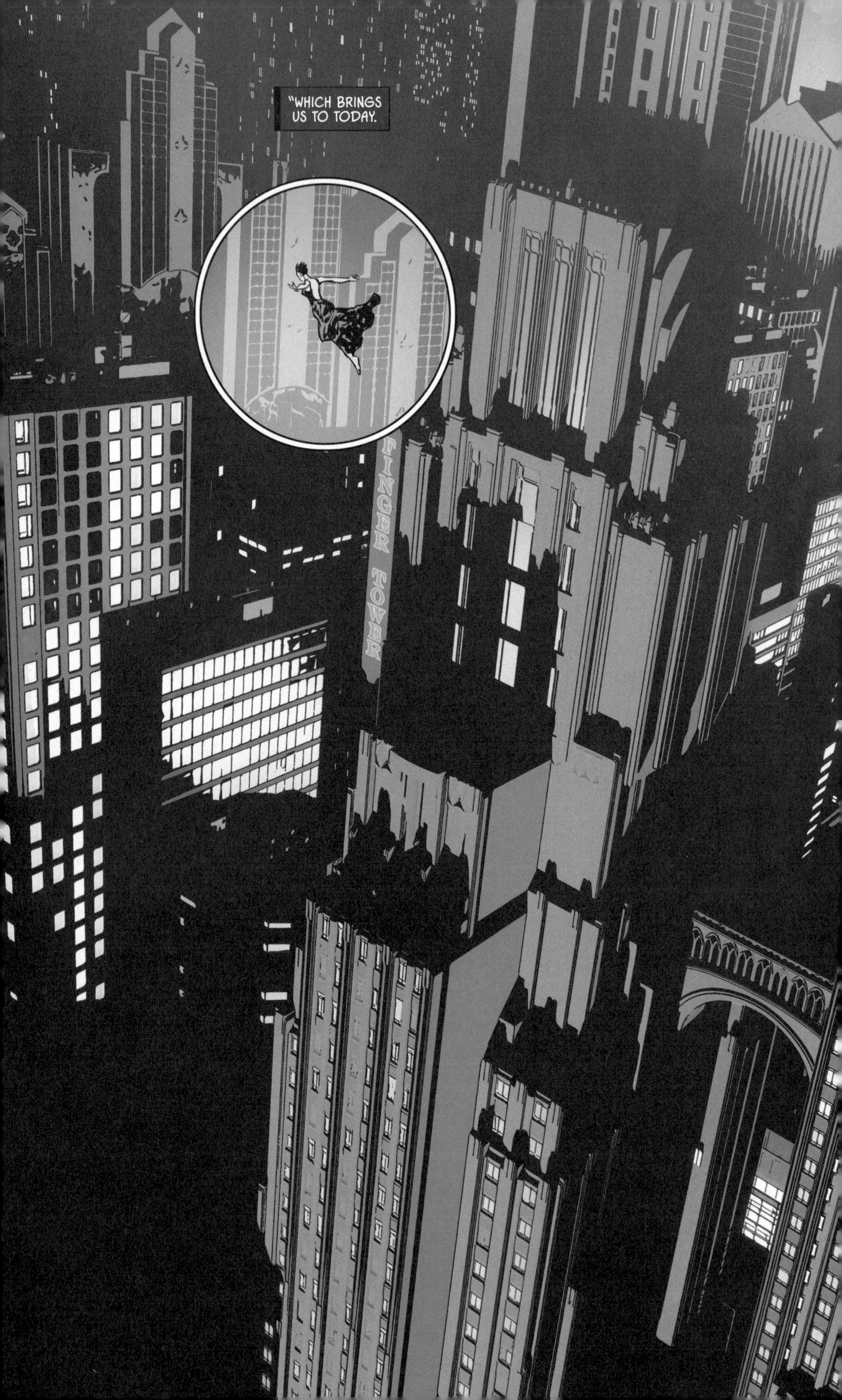
"WHICH BRINGS US TO TODAY.
FINGER TOWER

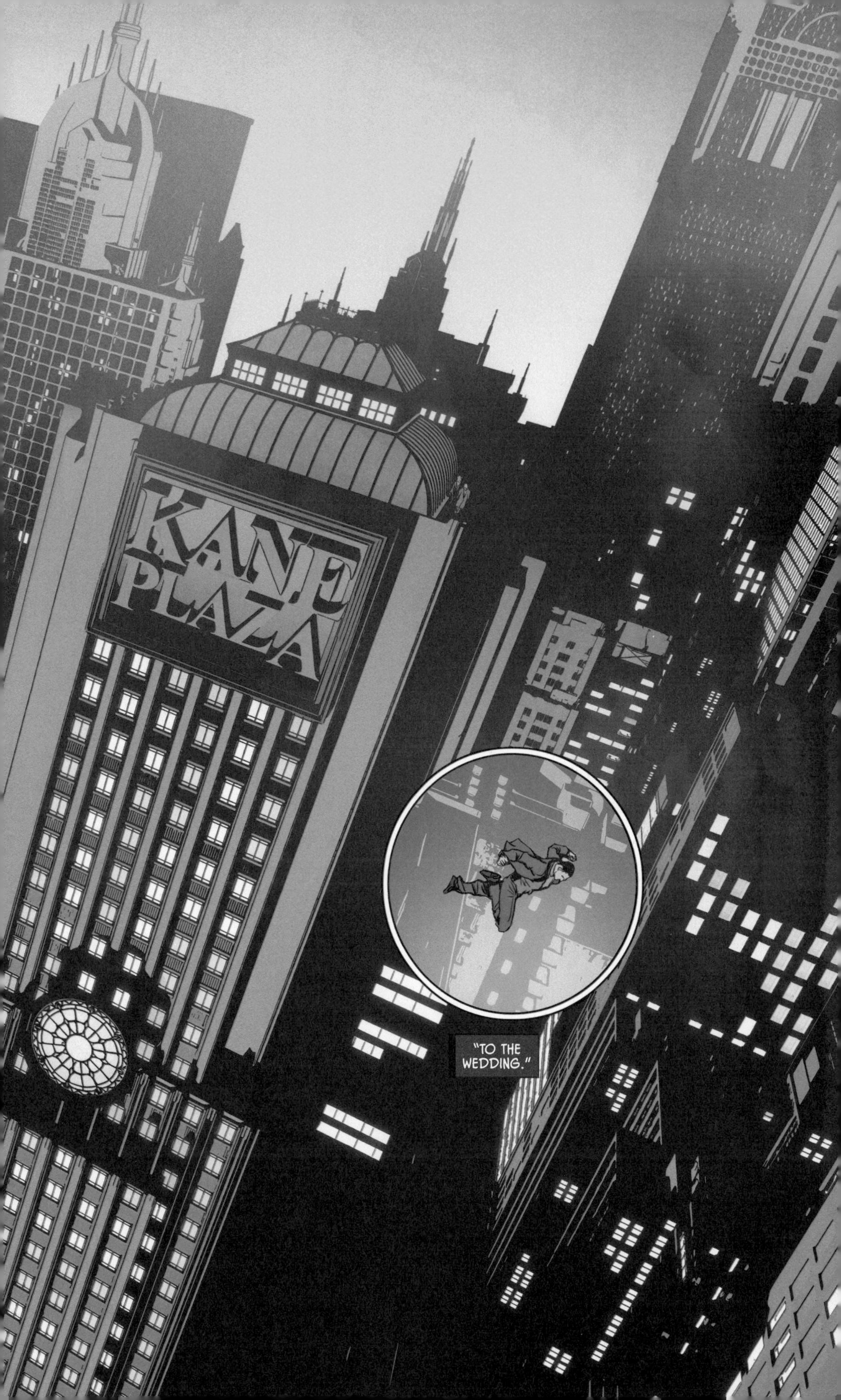
KANE PLAZA
"TO THE WEDDING."

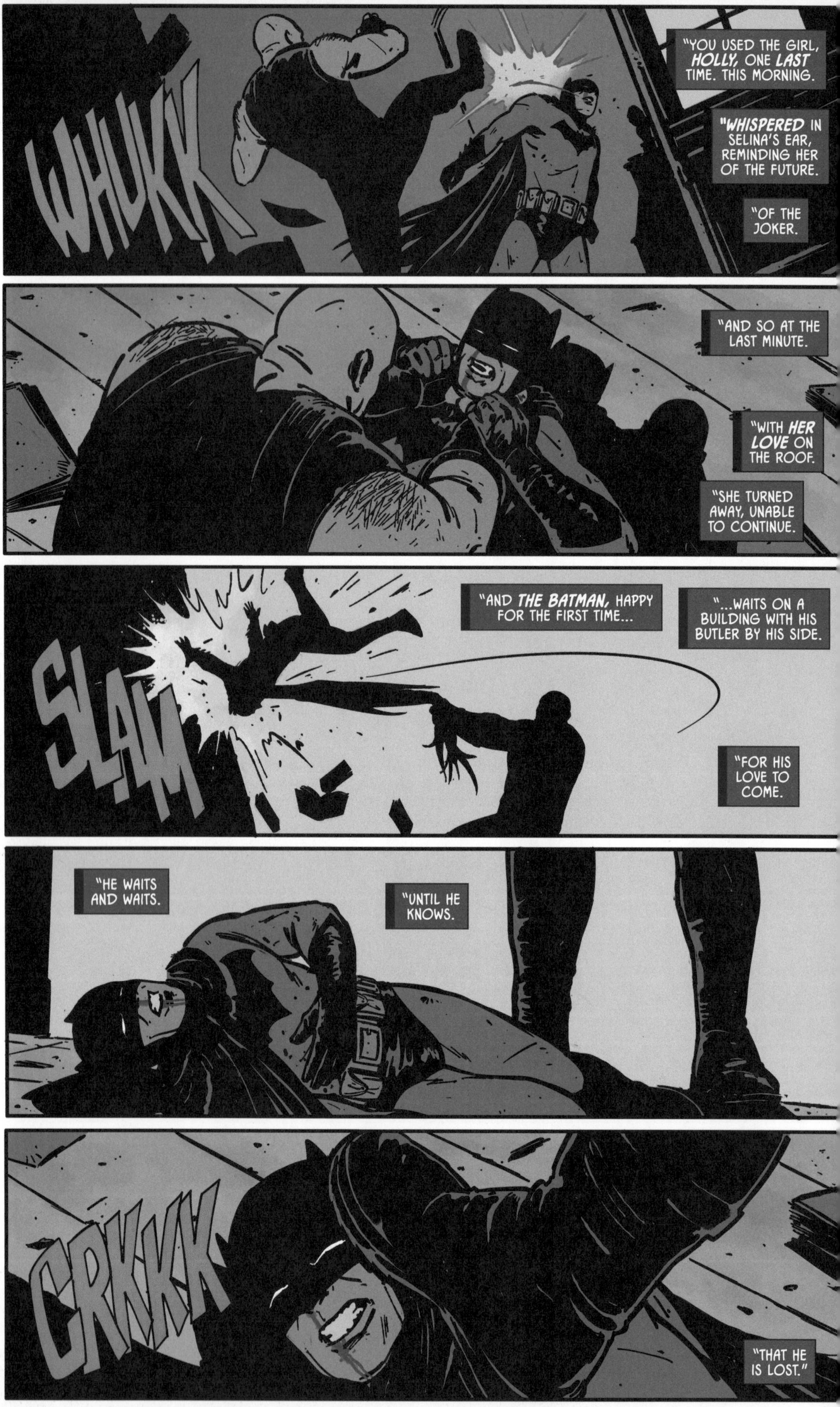
WHUKK
"YOU USED THE GIRL, HOLLY, ONE LAST TIME. THIS MORNING.
"WHISPERED IN SELINA'S EAR, REMINDING HER OF THE FUTURE.
"OF THE JOKER.
"AND SO AT THE LAST MINUTE.
"WITH HER LOVE ON THE ROOF.
"SHE TURNED AWAY, UNABLE TO CONTINUE.
SLAM
"AND THE BATMAN, HAPPY FOR THE FIRST TIME...
"...WAITS ON A BUILDING WITH HIS BUTLER BY HIS SIDE.
"FOR HIS LOVE TO COME.
"HE WAITS AND WAITS.
"UNTIL HE KNOWS.
CRKKK
"THAT HE IS LOST."

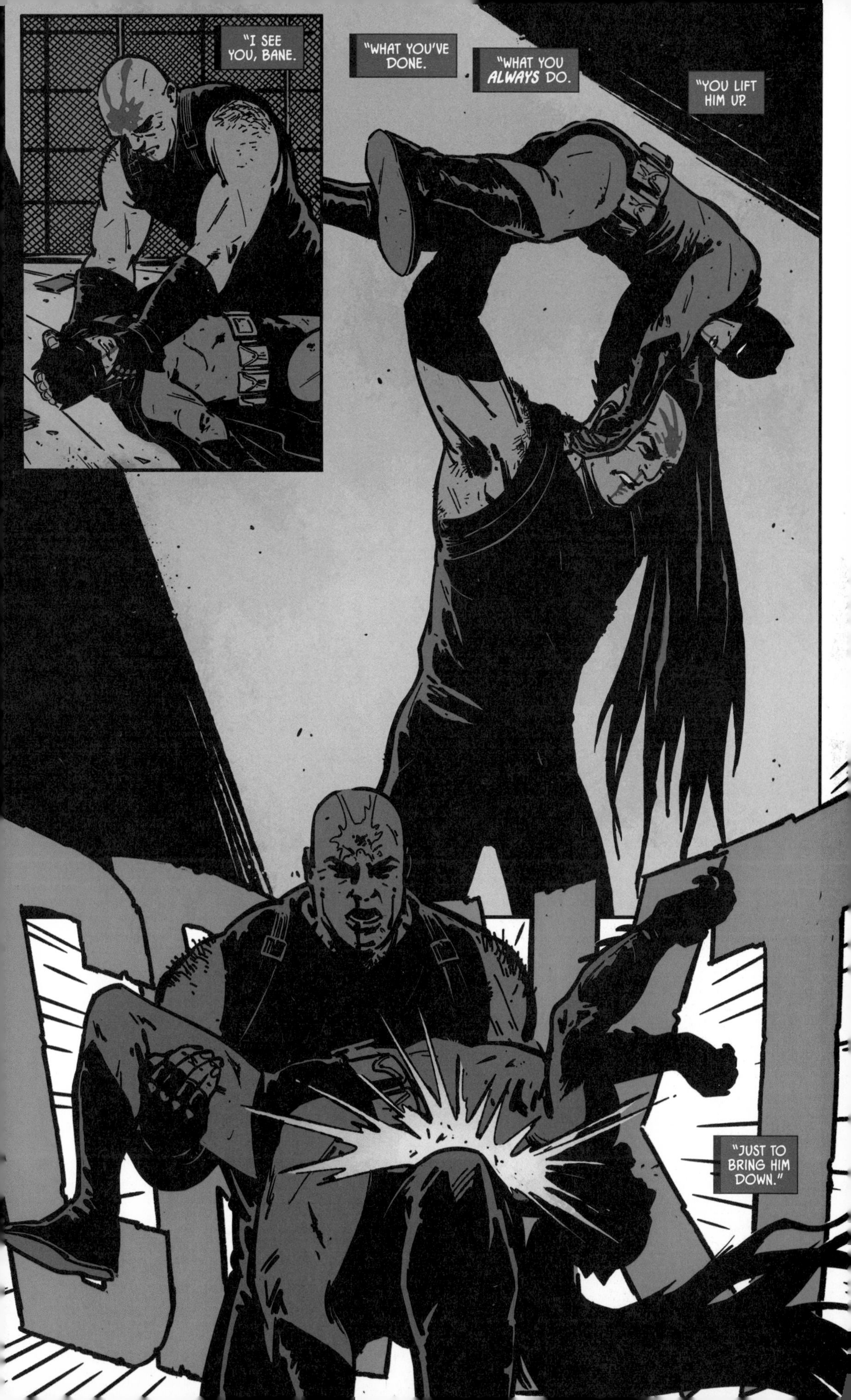
"I SEE YOU, BANE.
"WHAT YOU'VE DONE.
"WHAT YOU *ALWAYS* DO.
"YOU LIFT HIM UP.
"JUST TO BRING HIM DOWN."

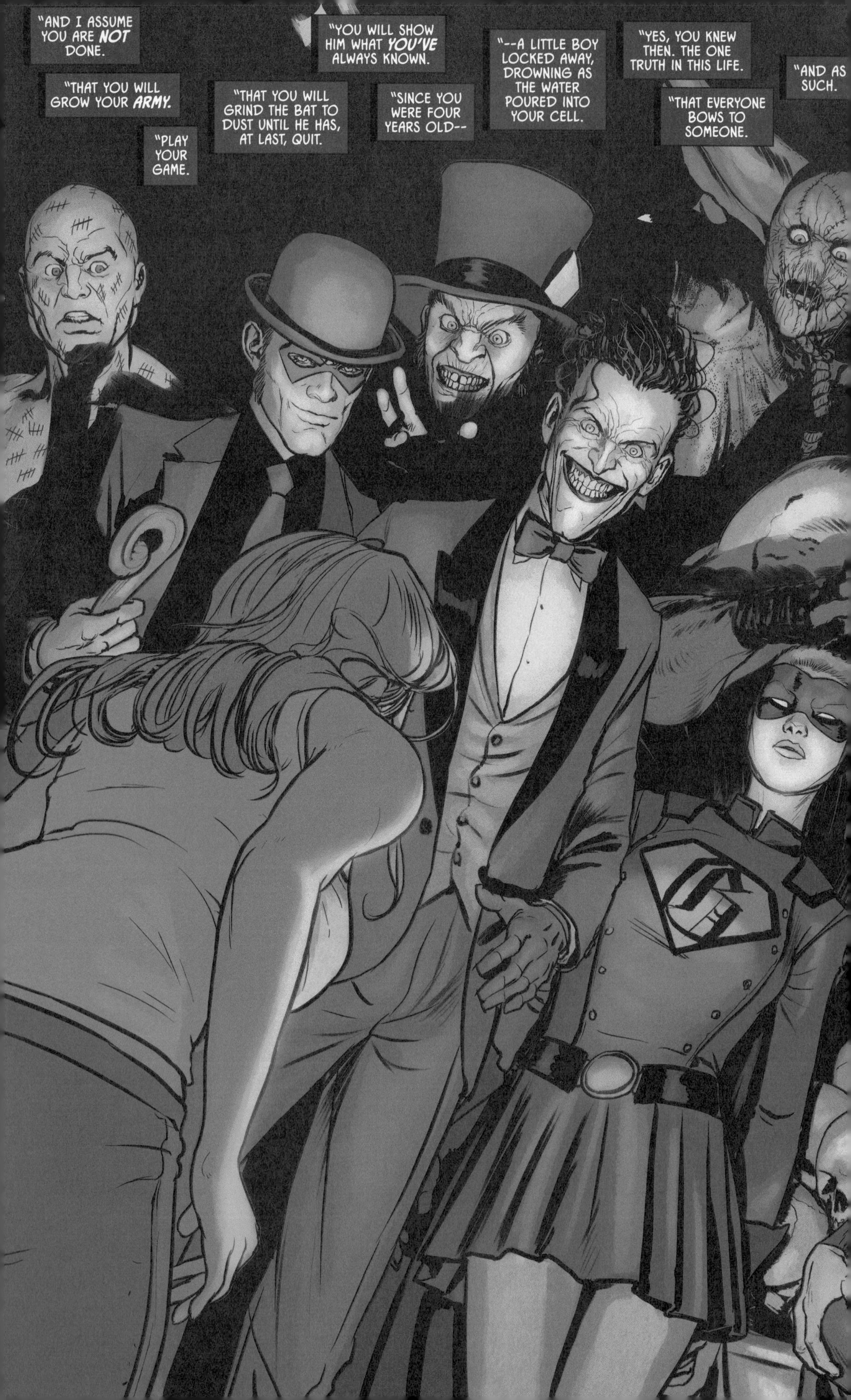
"AND I ASSUME YOU ARE NOT DONE.
"THAT YOU WILL GROW YOUR ARMY.
"PLAY YOUR GAME.
"THAT YOU WILL GRIND THE BAT TO DUST UNTIL HE HAS, AT LAST, QUIT.
"YOU WILL SHOW HIM WHAT YOU'VE ALWAYS KNOWN.
"SINCE YOU WERE FOUR YEARS OLD--
"--A LITTLE BOY LOCKED AWAY, DROWNING AS THE WATER POURED INTO YOUR CELL.
"YES, YOU KNEW THEN. THE ONE TRUTH IN THIS LIFE.
"THAT EVERYONE BOWS TO SOMEONE.
"AND AS SUCH.

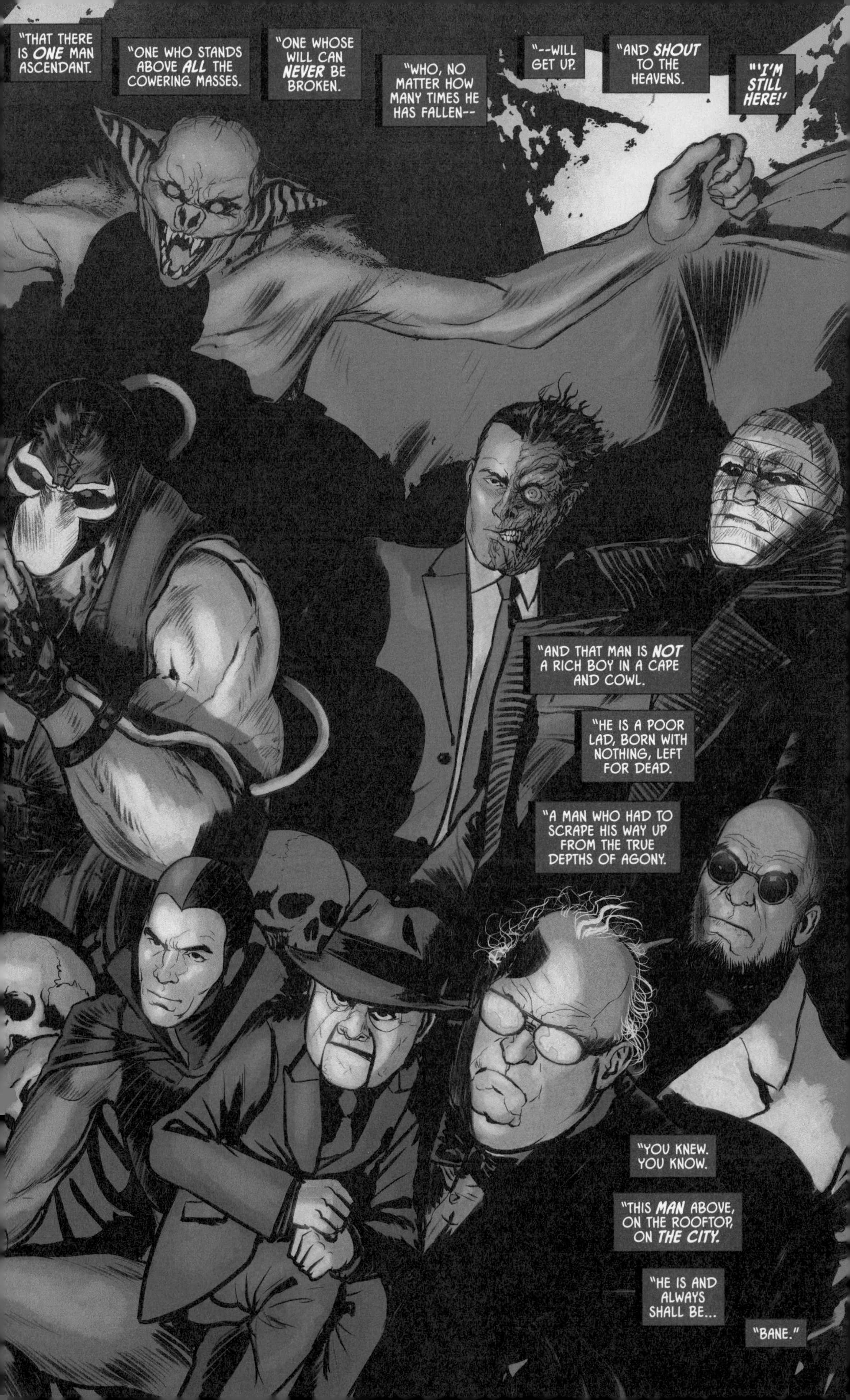
"THAT THERE IS ONE MAN ASCENDANT.
"ONE WHO STANDS ABOVE ALL THE COWERING MASSES.
"ONE WHOSE WILL CAN NEVER BE BROKEN.
"WHO, NO MATTER HOW MANY TIMES HE HAS FALLEN--
"--WILL GET UP.
"AND SHOUT TO THE HEAVENS.
"'I'M STILL HERE!'
"AND THAT MAN IS NOT A RICH BOY IN A CAPE AND COWL.
"HE IS A POOR LAD, BORN WITH NOTHING, LEFT FOR DEAD.
"A MAN WHO HAD TO SCRAPE HIS WAY UP FROM THE TRUE DEPTHS OF AGONY.
"YOU KNEW. YOU KNOW.
"THIS MAN ABOVE, ON THE ROOFTOP, ON THE CITY.
"HE IS AND ALWAYS SHALL BE...
"BANE."

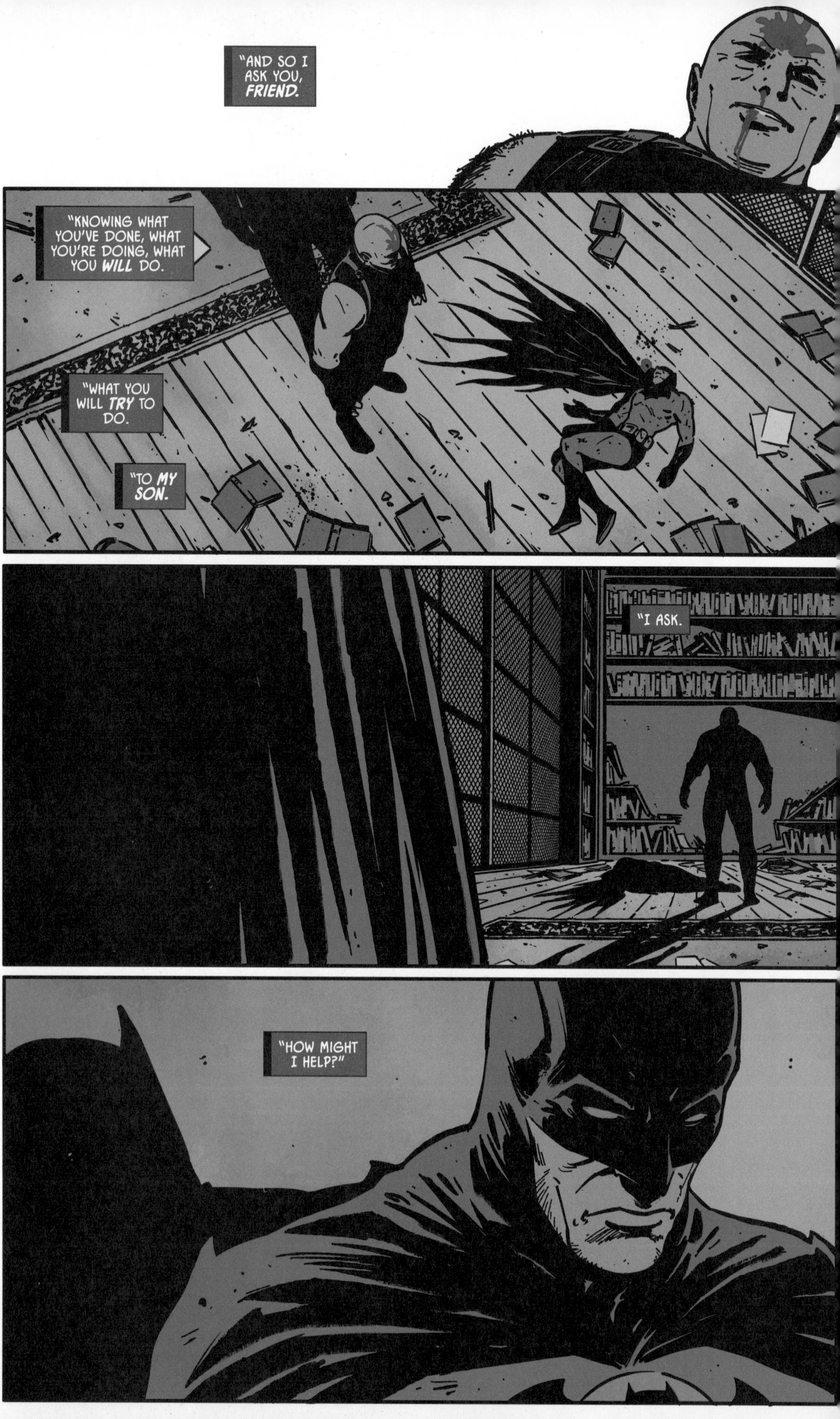
"AND SO I ASK YOU, FRIEND.
"KNOWING WHAT YOU'VE DONE, WHAT YOU'RE DOING, WHAT YOU WILL DO.
"WHAT YOU WILL TRY TO DO.
"TO MY SON.
"I ASK.
"HOW MIGHT I HELP?"

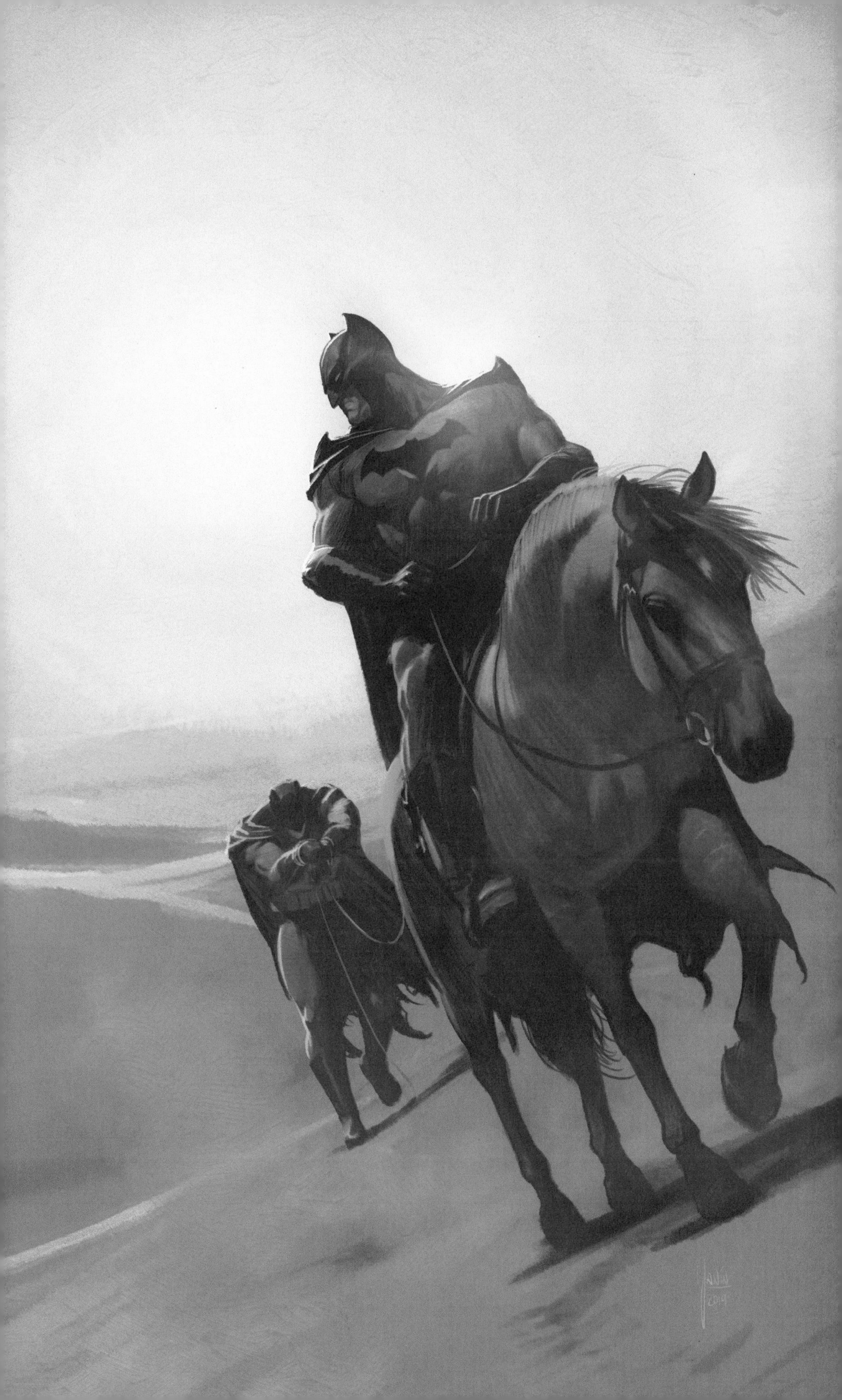

BATMAN
#73

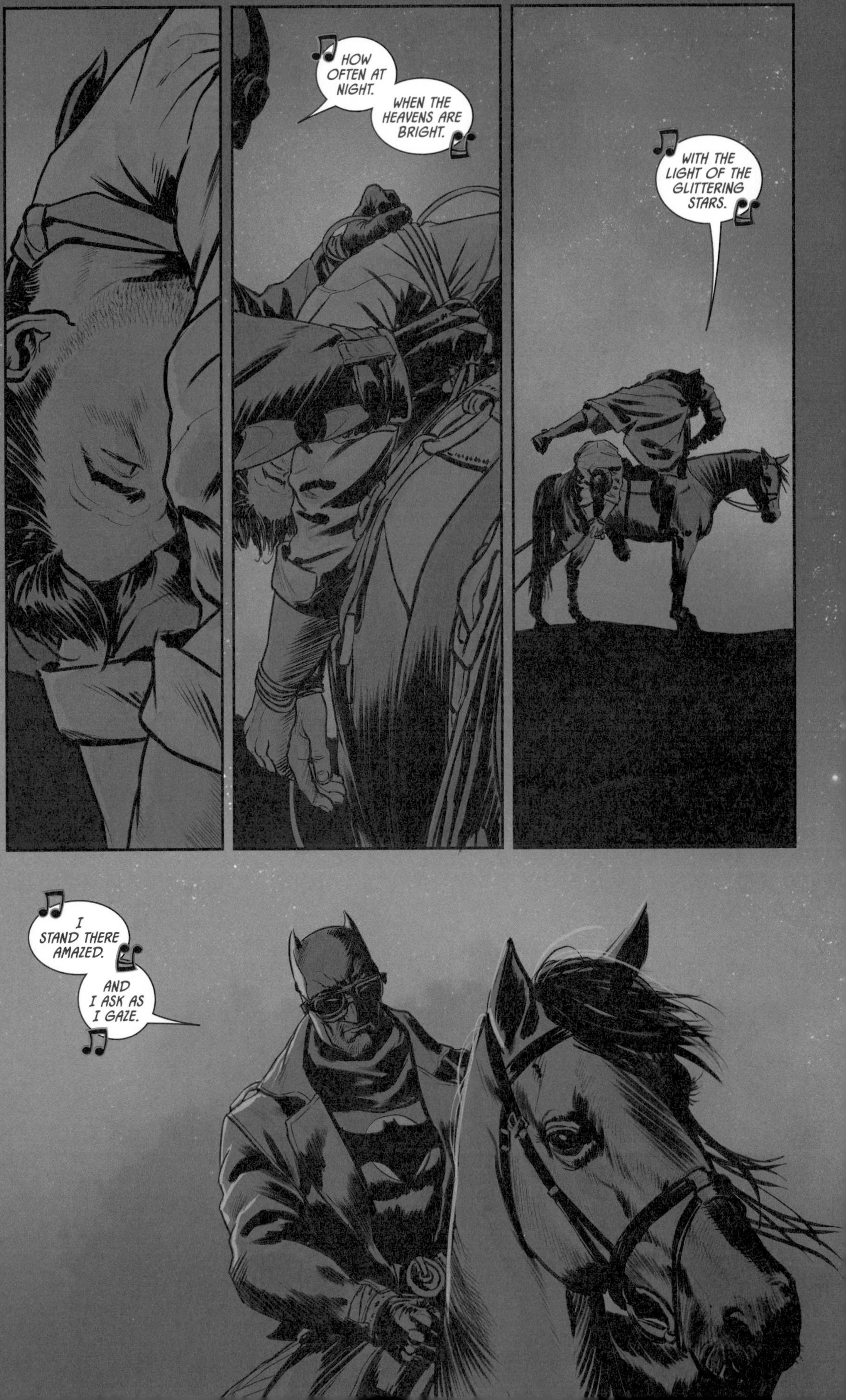
HOW OFTEN AT NIGHT.
WHEN THE HEAVENS ARE BRIGHT.
WITH THE LIGHT OF THE GLITTERING STARS.
I STAND THERE AMAZED.
AND I ASK AS I GAZE.

DC Comics Presents

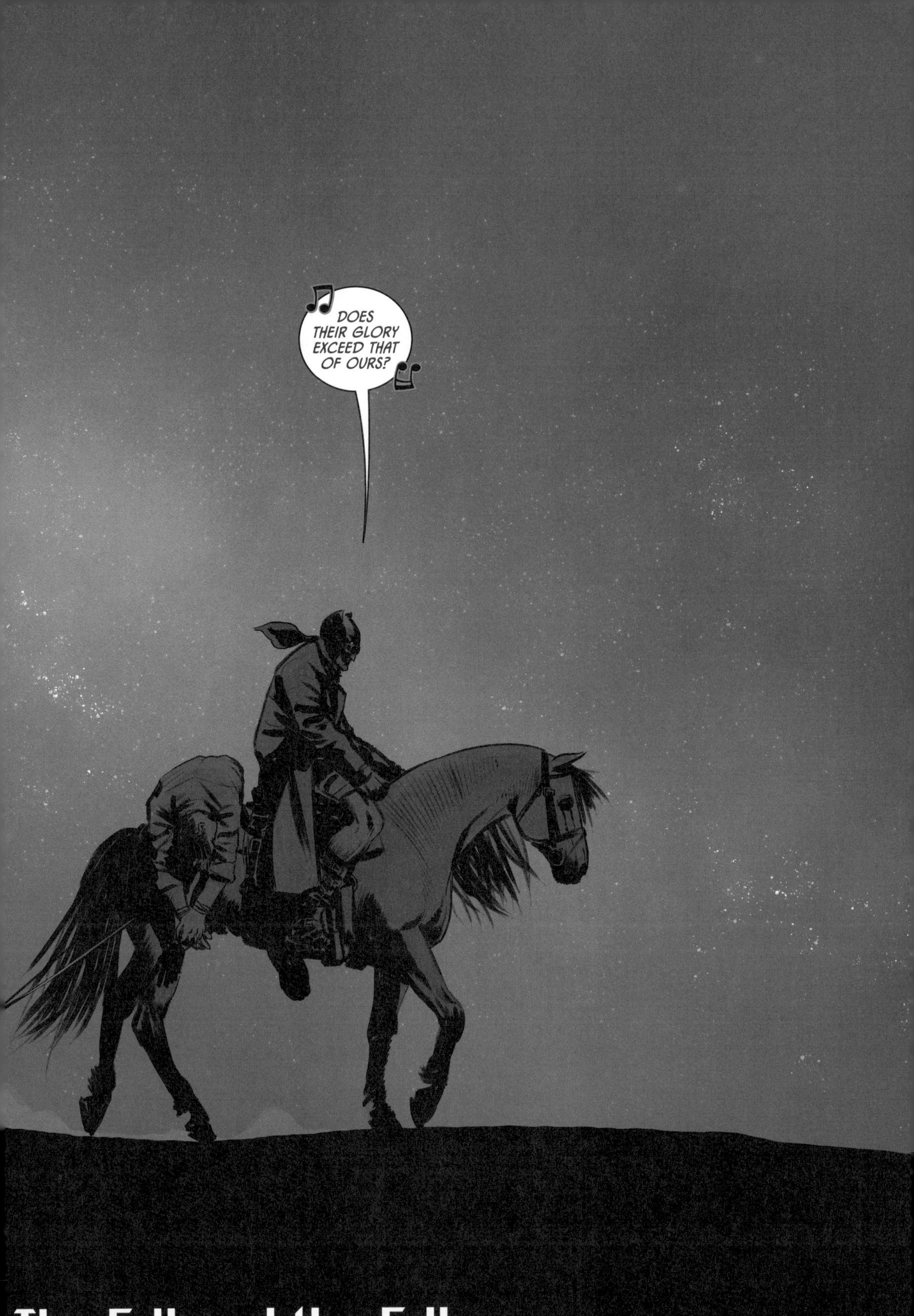
DOES THEIR GLORY EXCEED THAT OF OURS?

The Fall and the Fallen Part 4

TOM KING writer MIKEL JANÍN artist JORDIE BELLAIRE colorist CLAYTON COWLES letterer
MIKEL JANÍN cover ROB LEVIN associate editor JAMIE S. RICH editor

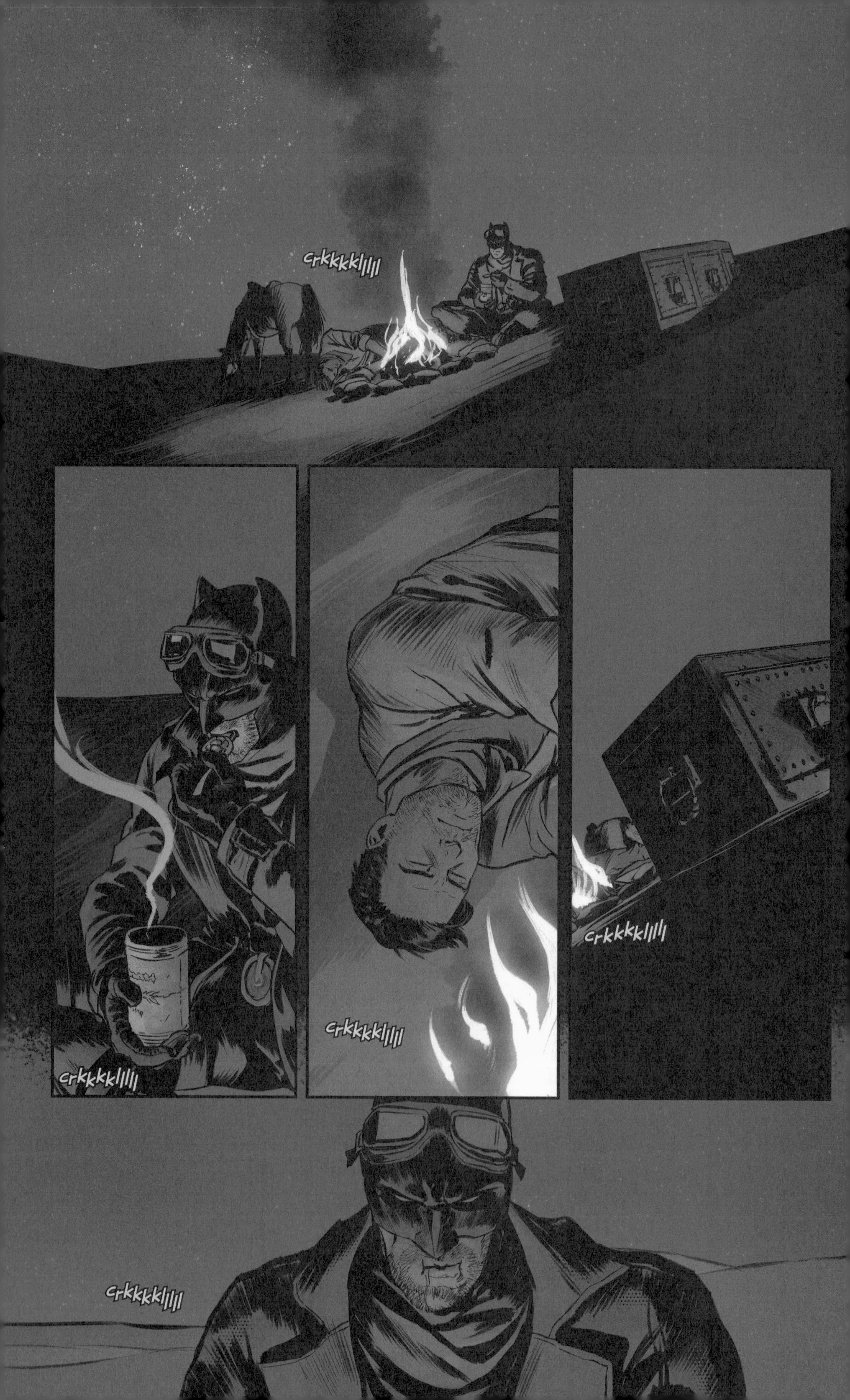
crkkkklllll
crkkkklllll
crkkkklllll
crkkkklllll
crkkkklllll

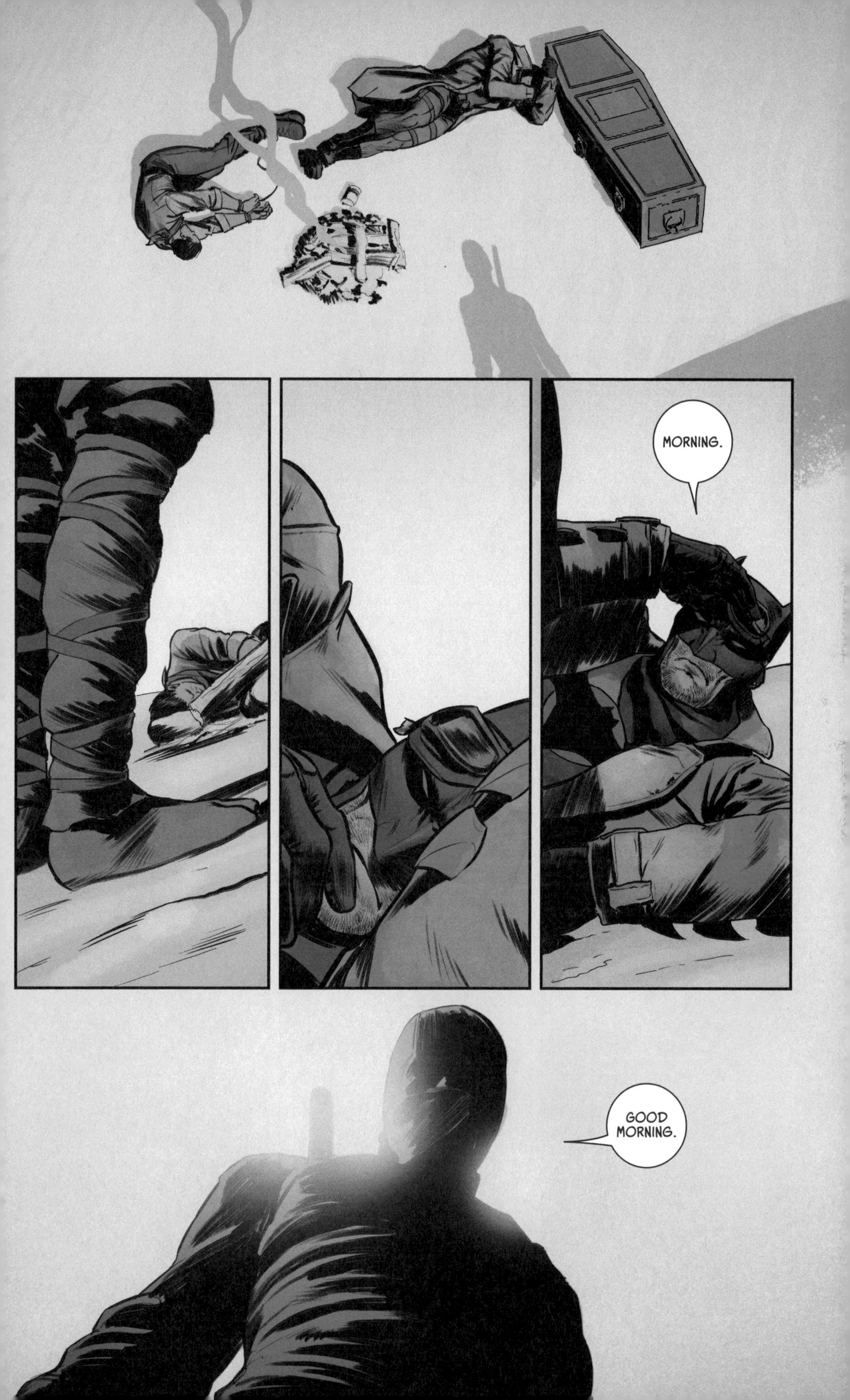
MORNING.
GOOD MORNING.

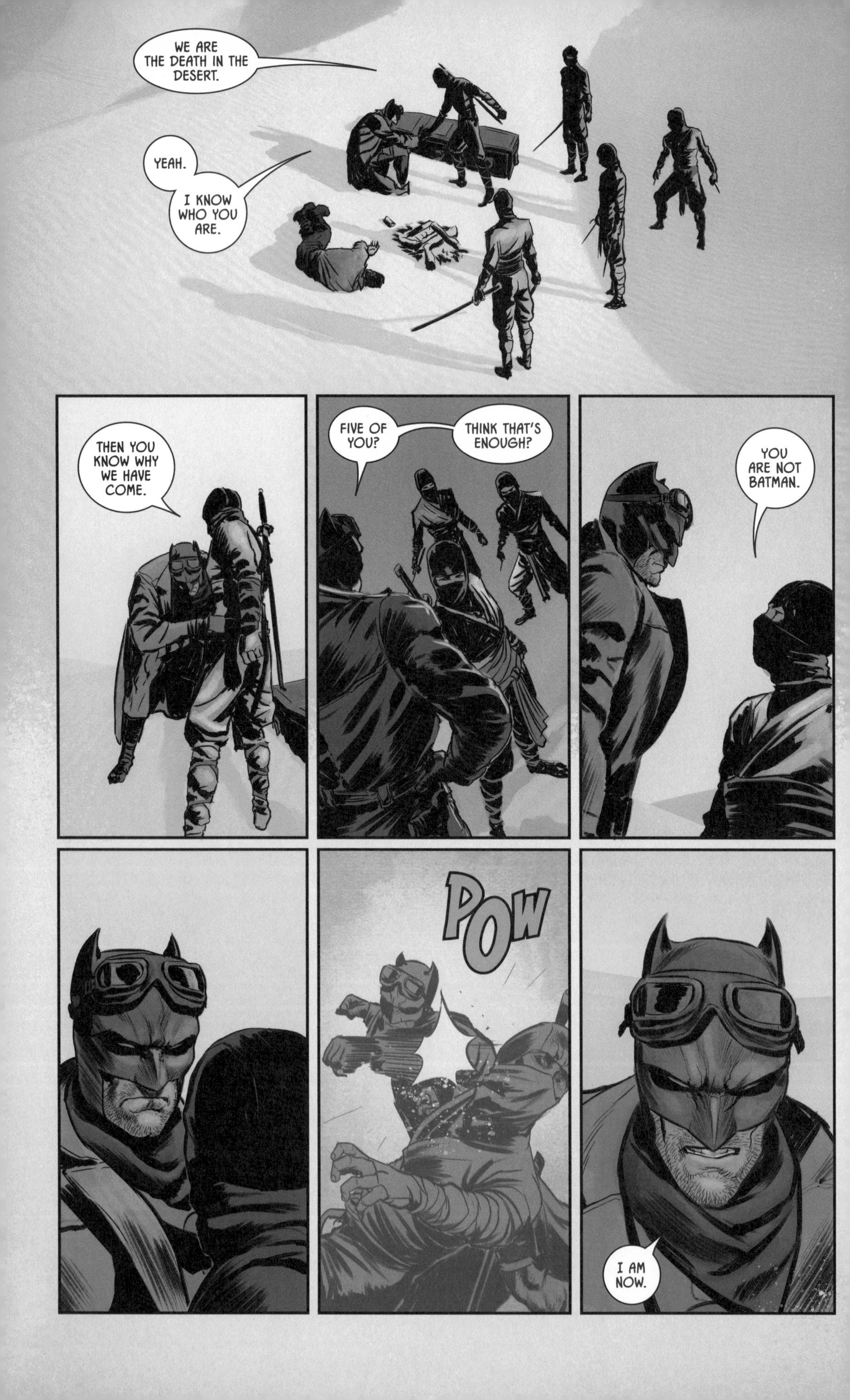
WE ARE THE DEATH IN THE DESERT.
YEAH.
I KNOW WHO YOU ARE.
THEN YOU KNOW WHY WE HAVE COME.
FIVE OF YOU?
THINK THAT'S ENOUGH?
YOU ARE NOT BATMAN.
POW
I AM NOW.

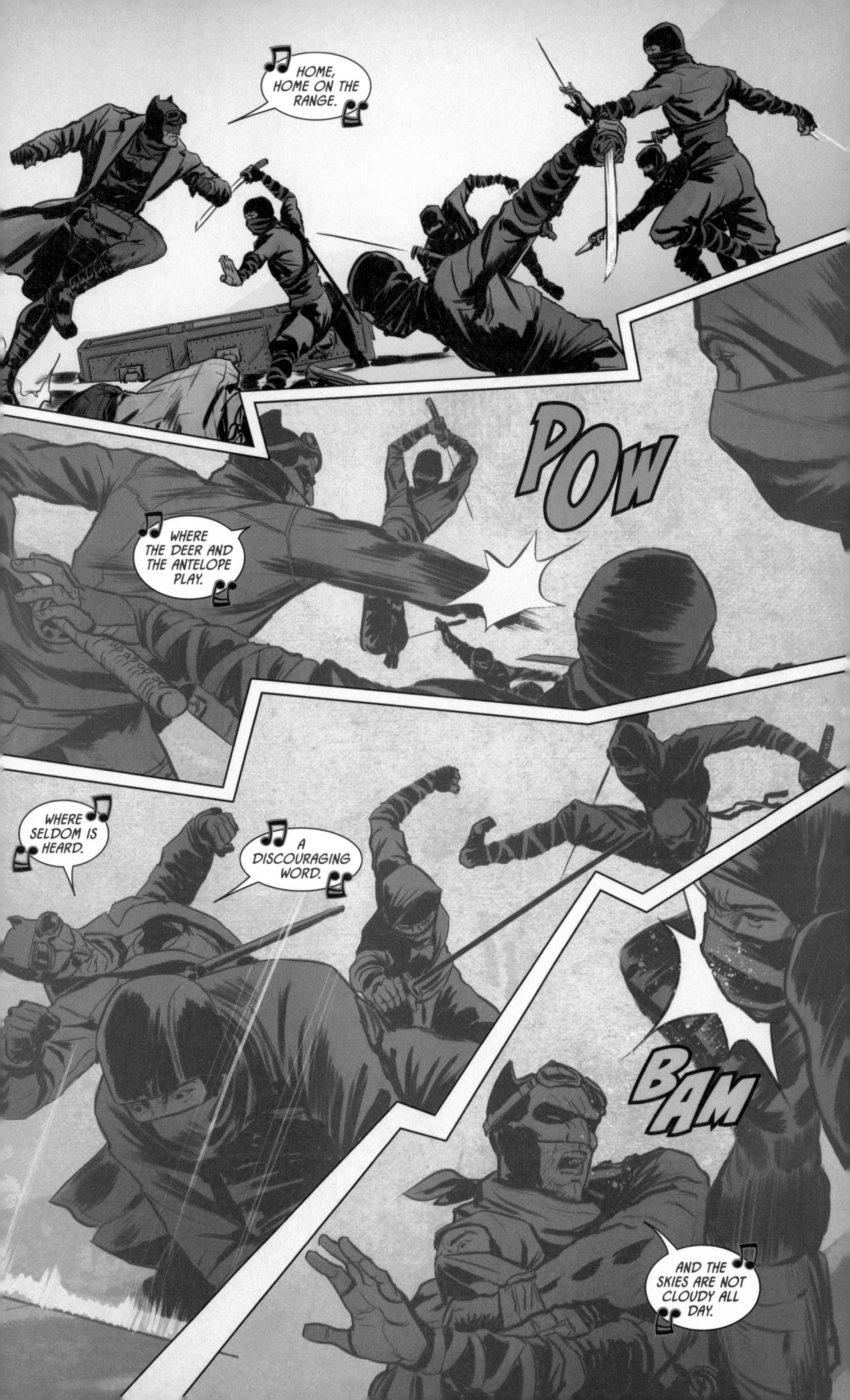
HOME, HOME ON THE RANGE.
POW
WHERE THE DEER AND THE ANTELOPE PLAY.
WHERE SELDOM IS HEARD.
A DISCOURAGING WORD.
BAM
AND THE SKIES ARE NOT CLOUDY ALL DAY.

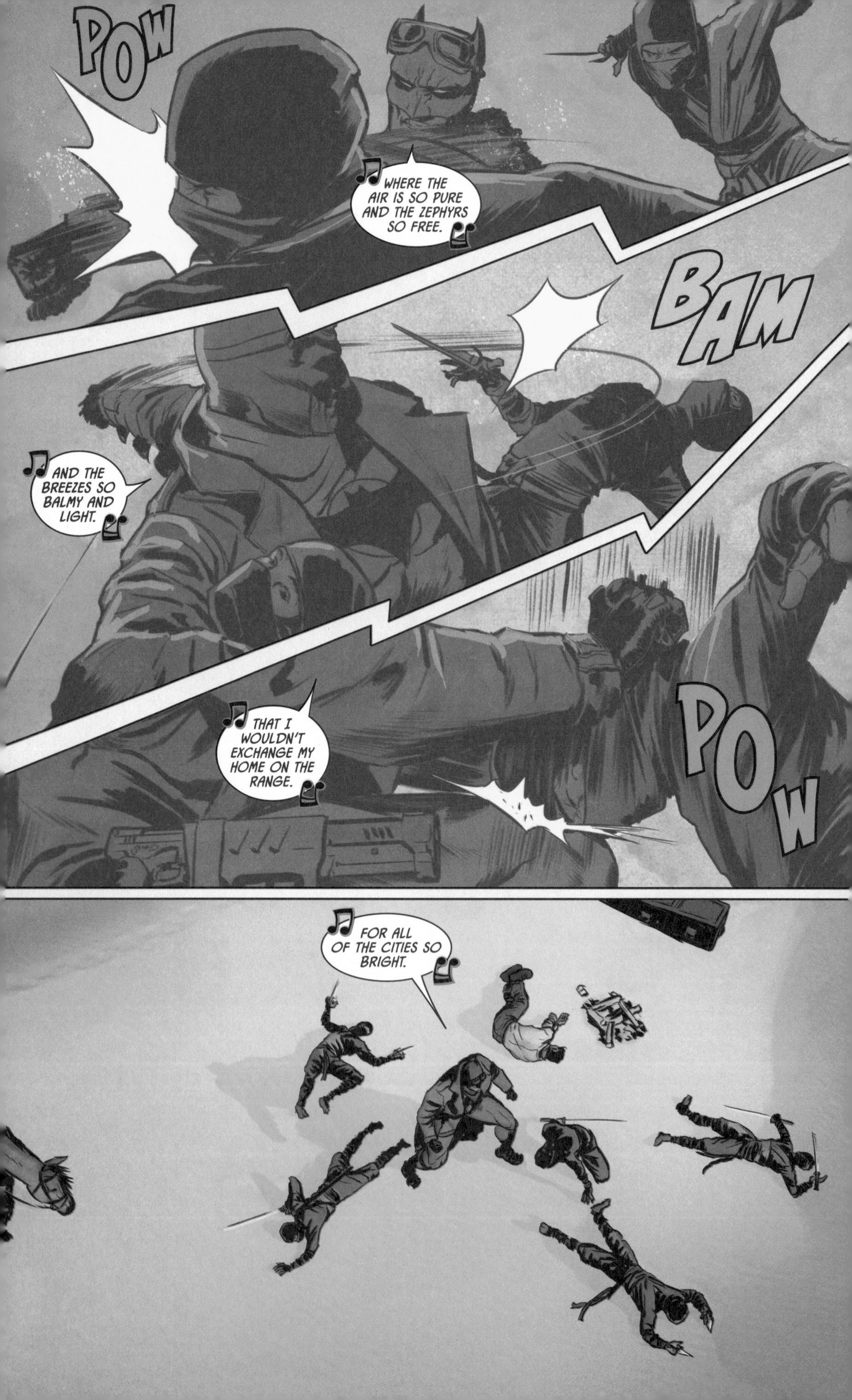
POW
WHERE THE AIR IS SO PURE AND THE ZEPHYRS SO FREE.
BAM
AND THE BREEZES SO BALMY AND LIGHT.
THAT I WOULDN'T EXCHANGE MY HOME ON THE RANGE.
POW
FOR ALL OF THE CITIES SO BRIGHT.

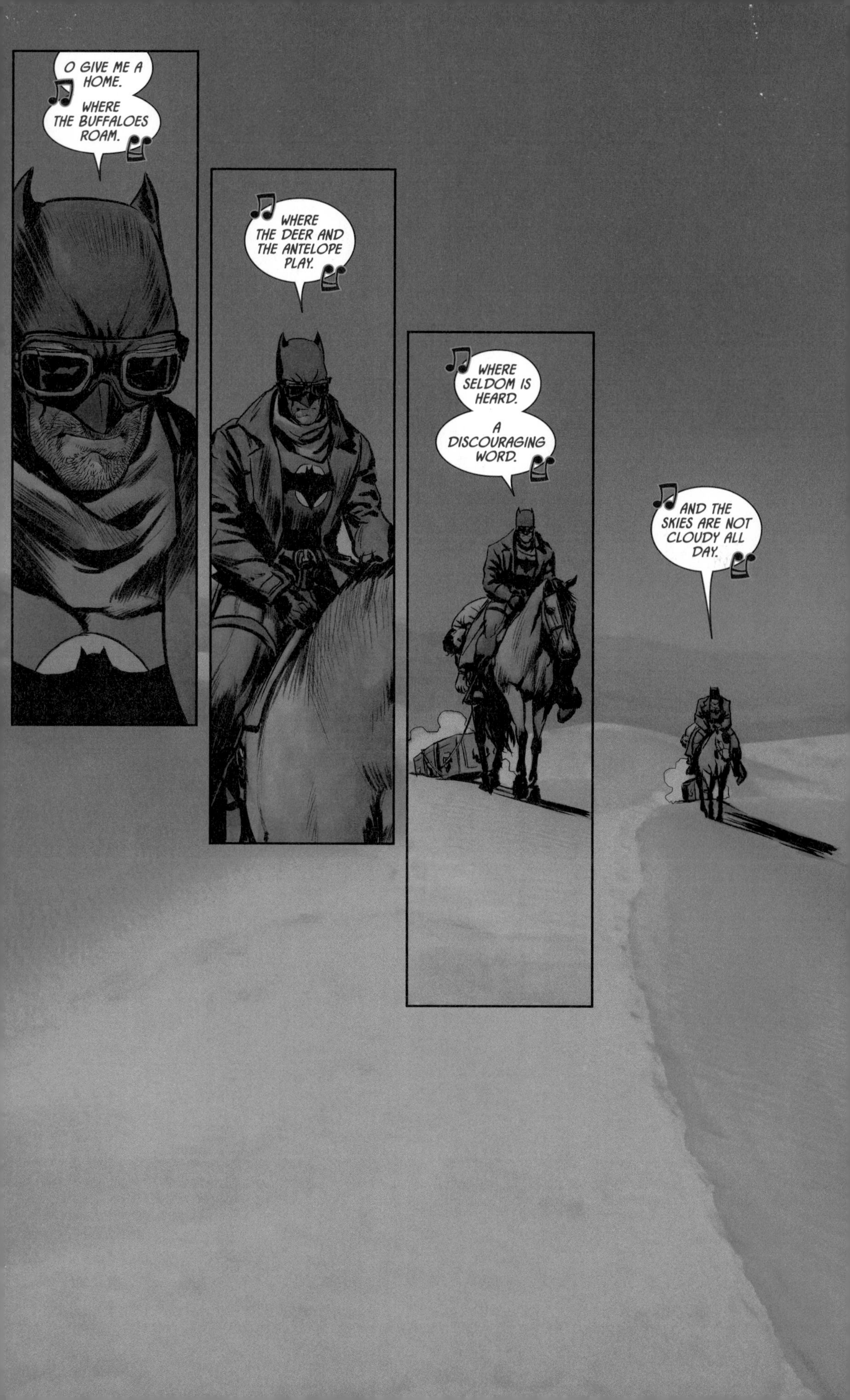
O GIVE ME A HOME.
WHERE THE BUFFALOES ROAM.
WHERE THE DEER AND THE ANTELOPE PLAY.
WHERE SELDOM IS HEARD.
A DISCOURAGING WORD.
AND THE SKIES ARE NOT CLOUDY ALL DAY.

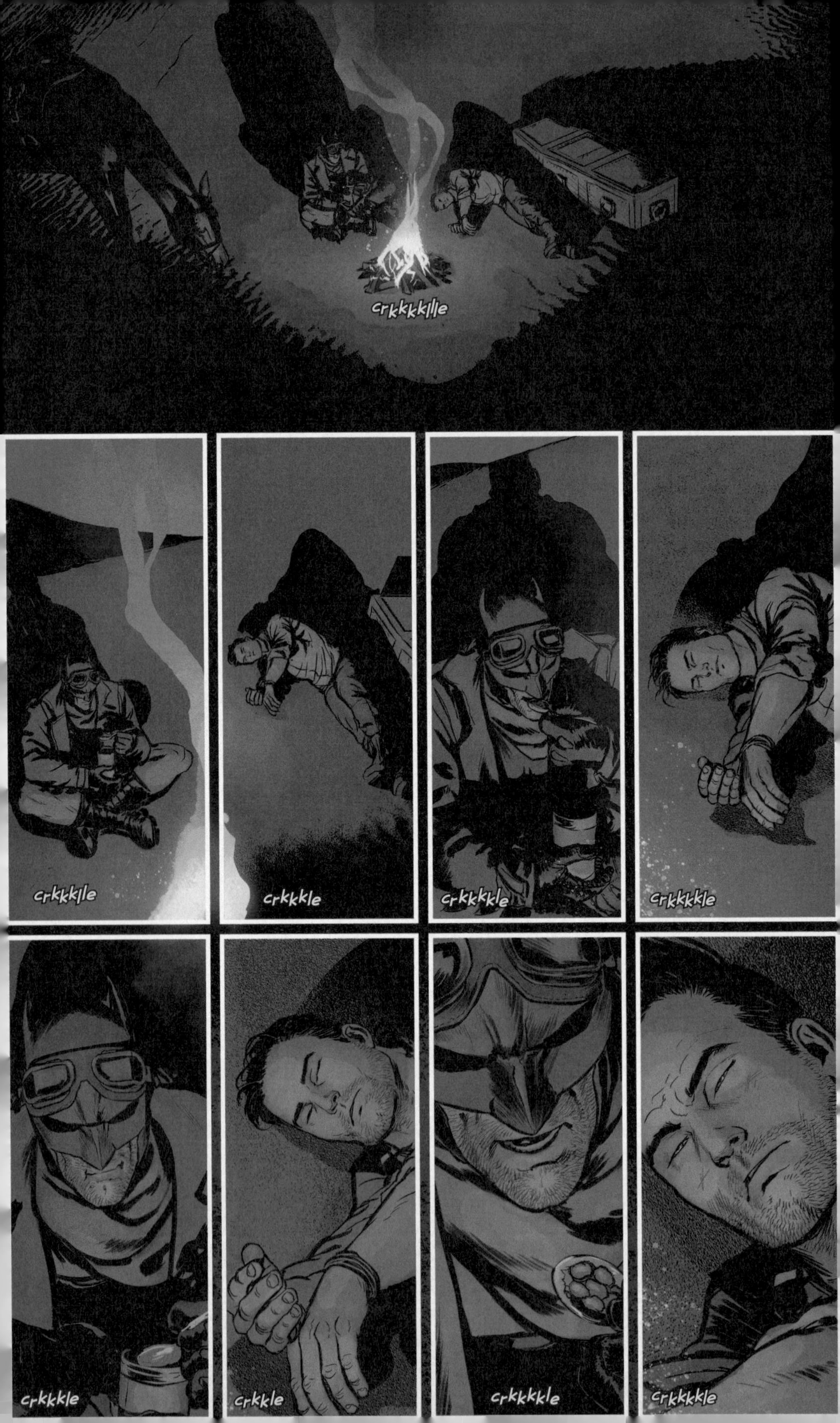

crkkkklle
crkkklle
crkkkle
crkkkkle
crkkkkle
crkkkle
crkkle
crkkkkle
crkkkkle

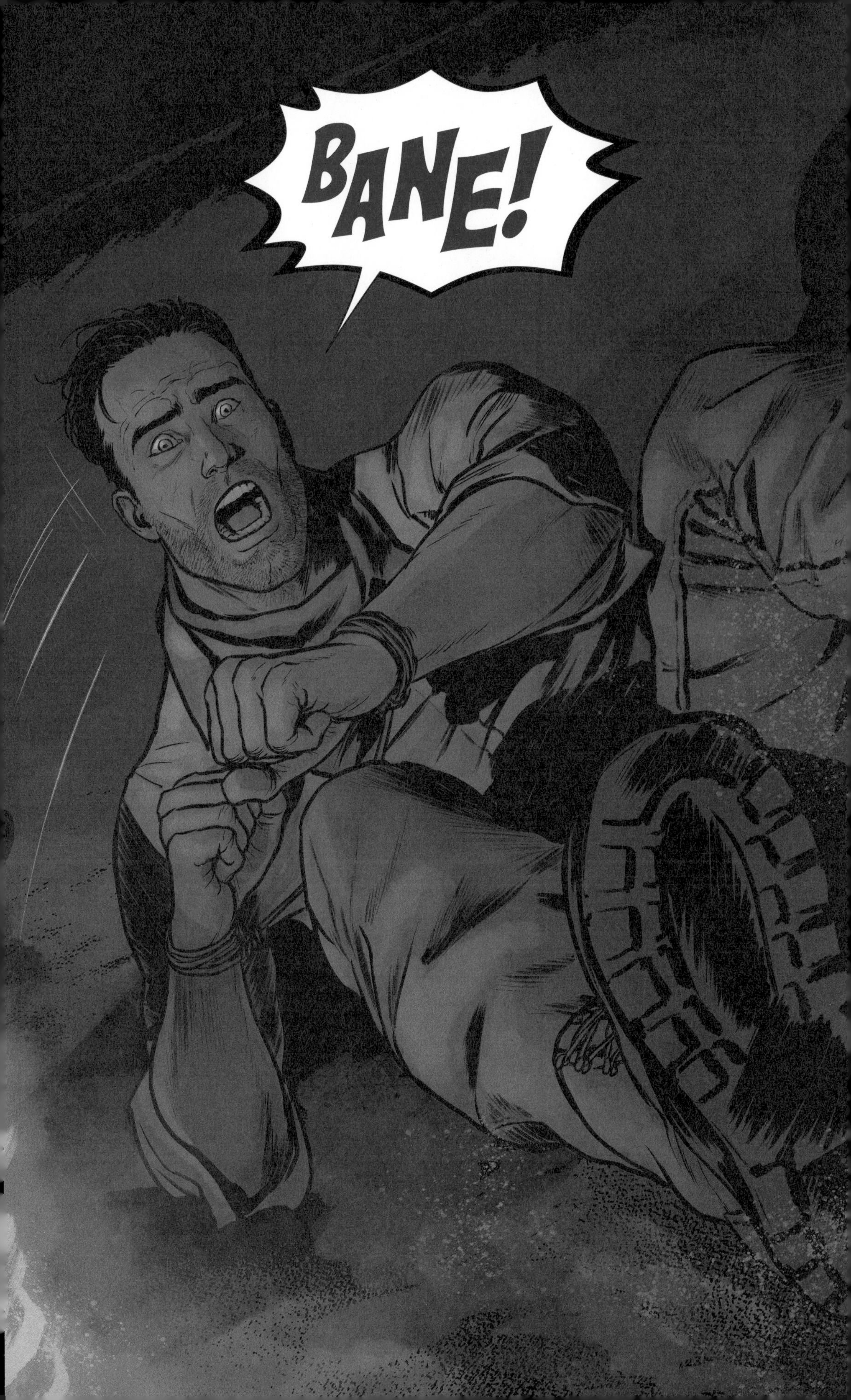
BANE!

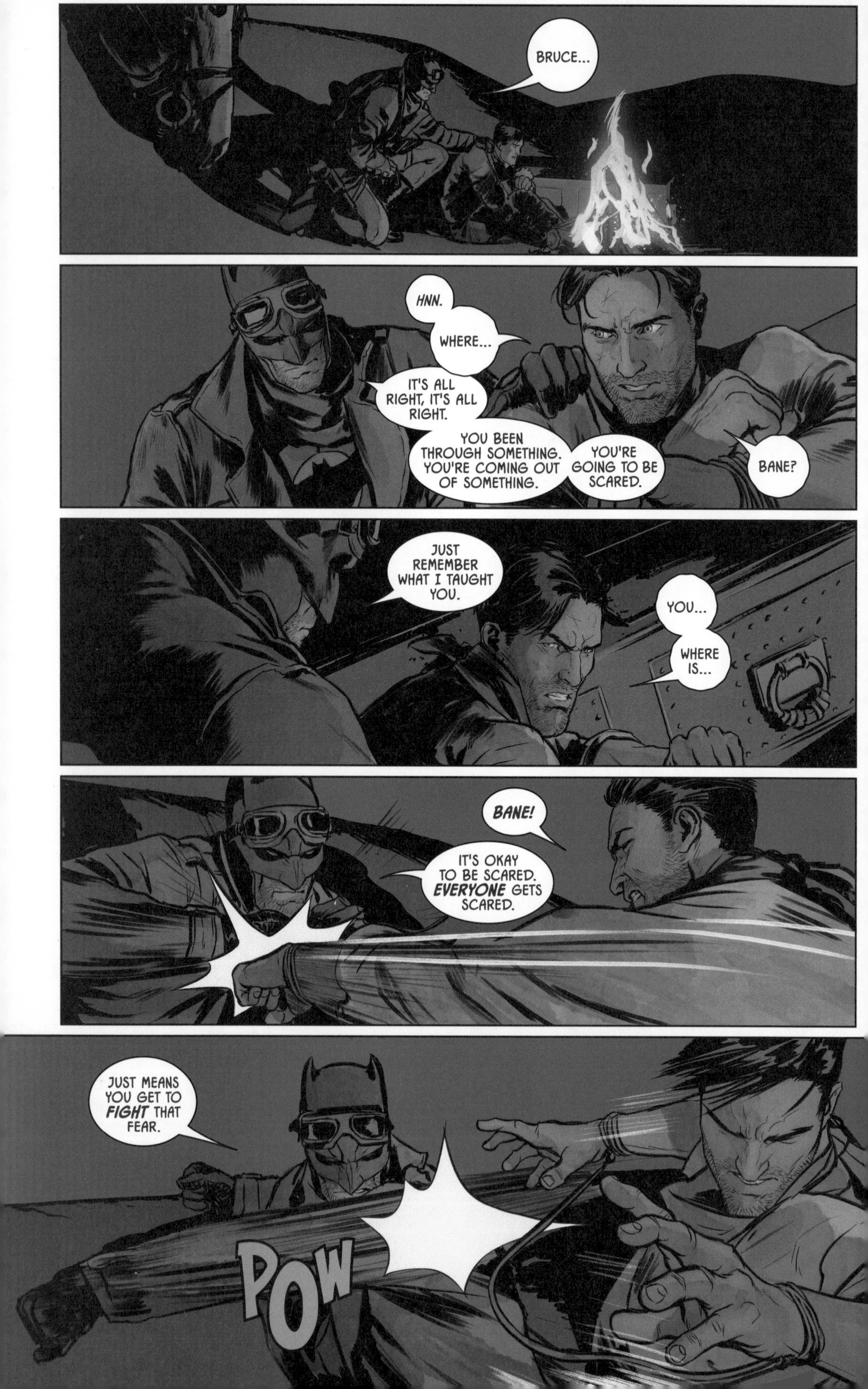
BRUCE...
HNN.
WHERE...
IT'S ALL RIGHT, IT'S ALL RIGHT.
YOU BEEN THROUGH SOMETHING. YOU'RE COMING OUT OF SOMETHING.
YOU'RE GOING TO BE SCARED.
BANE?
JUST REMEMBER WHAT I TAUGHT YOU.
YOU...
WHERE IS...
BANE!
IT'S OKAY TO BE SCARED. EVERYONE GETS SCARED.
JUST MEANS YOU GET TO FIGHT THAT FEAR.
POW

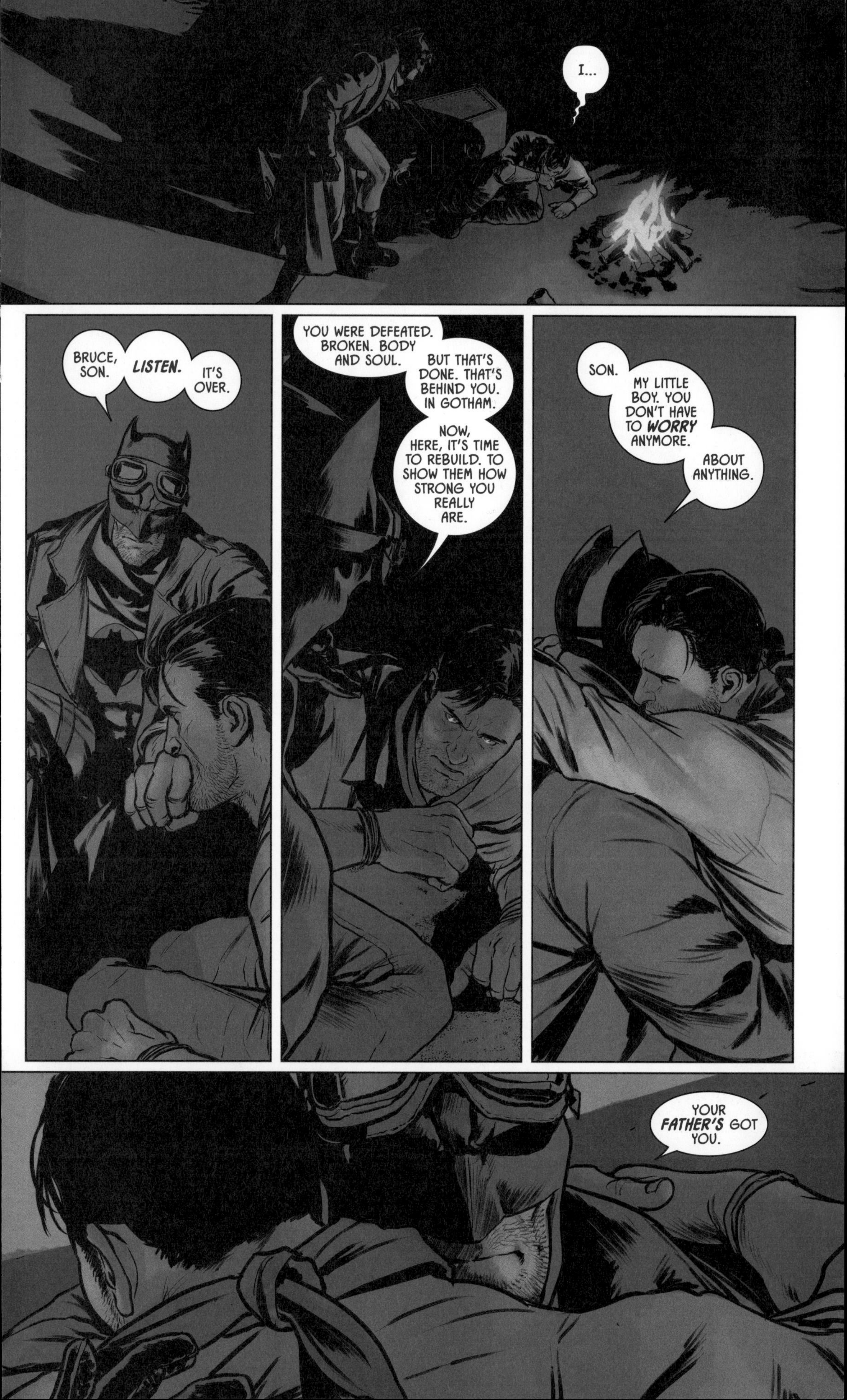
I...
BRUCE, SON.
LISTEN.
IT'S OVER.
YOU WERE DEFEATED. BROKEN. BODY AND SOUL.
BUT THAT'S DONE. THAT'S BEHIND YOU. IN GOTHAM.
NOW, HERE, IT'S TIME TO REBUILD. TO SHOW THEM HOW STRONG YOU REALLY ARE.
SON.
MY LITTLE BOY. YOU DON'T HAVE TO WORRY ANYMORE.
ABOUT ANYTHING.
YOUR FATHER'S GOT YOU.

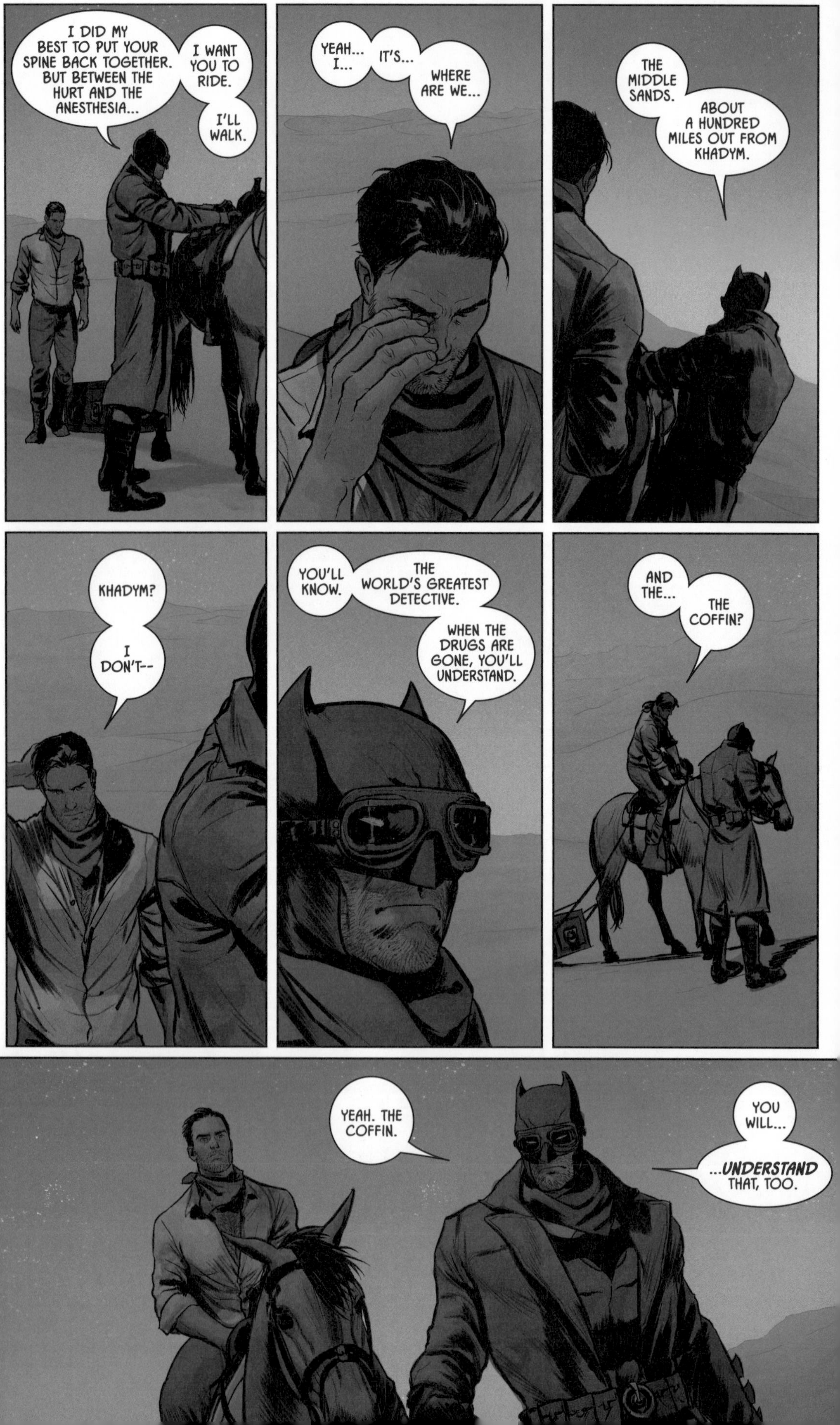
I DID MY BEST TO PUT YOUR SPINE BACK TOGETHER. BUT BETWEEN THE HURT AND THE ANESTHESIA...
I WANT YOU TO RIDE.
I'LL WALK.
YEAH... I...
IT'S...
WHERE ARE WE...
THE MIDDLE SANDS.
ABOUT A HUNDRED MILES OUT FROM KHADYM.
KHADYM?
I DON'T--
YOU'LL KNOW.
THE WORLD'S GREATEST DETECTIVE.
WHEN THE DRUGS ARE GONE, YOU'LL UNDERSTAND.
AND THE...
THE COFFIN?
YEAH. THE COFFIN.
YOU WILL...
...UNDERSTAND THAT, TOO.

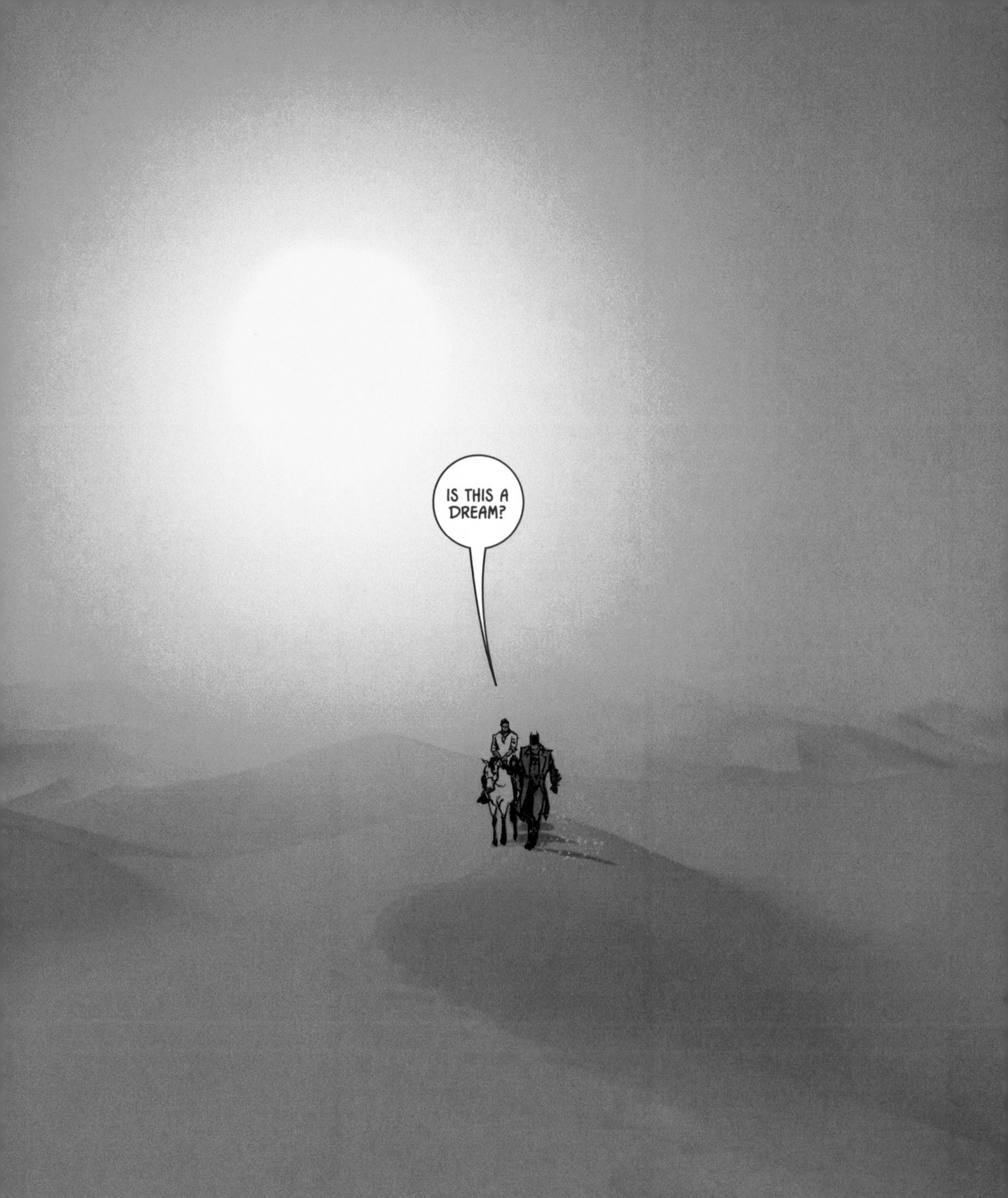
IS THIS A DREAM?

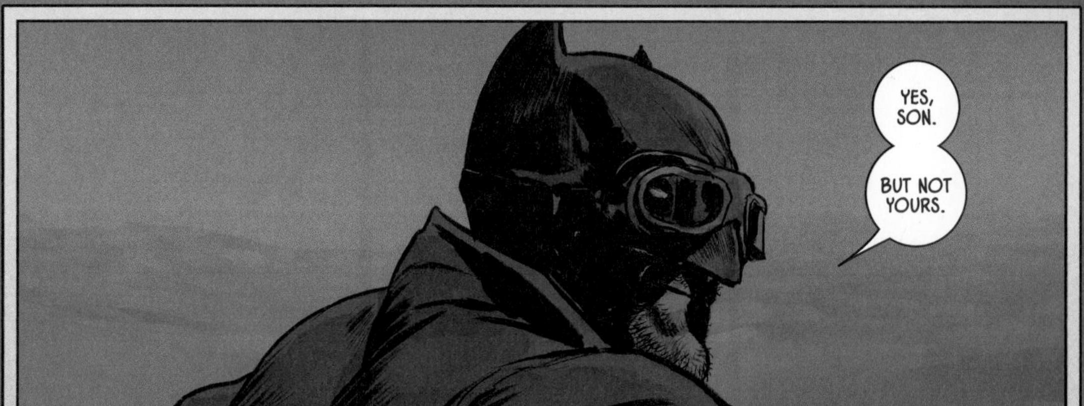
YES, SON.
BUT NOT YOURS.

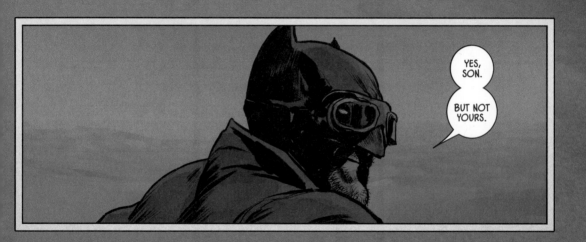

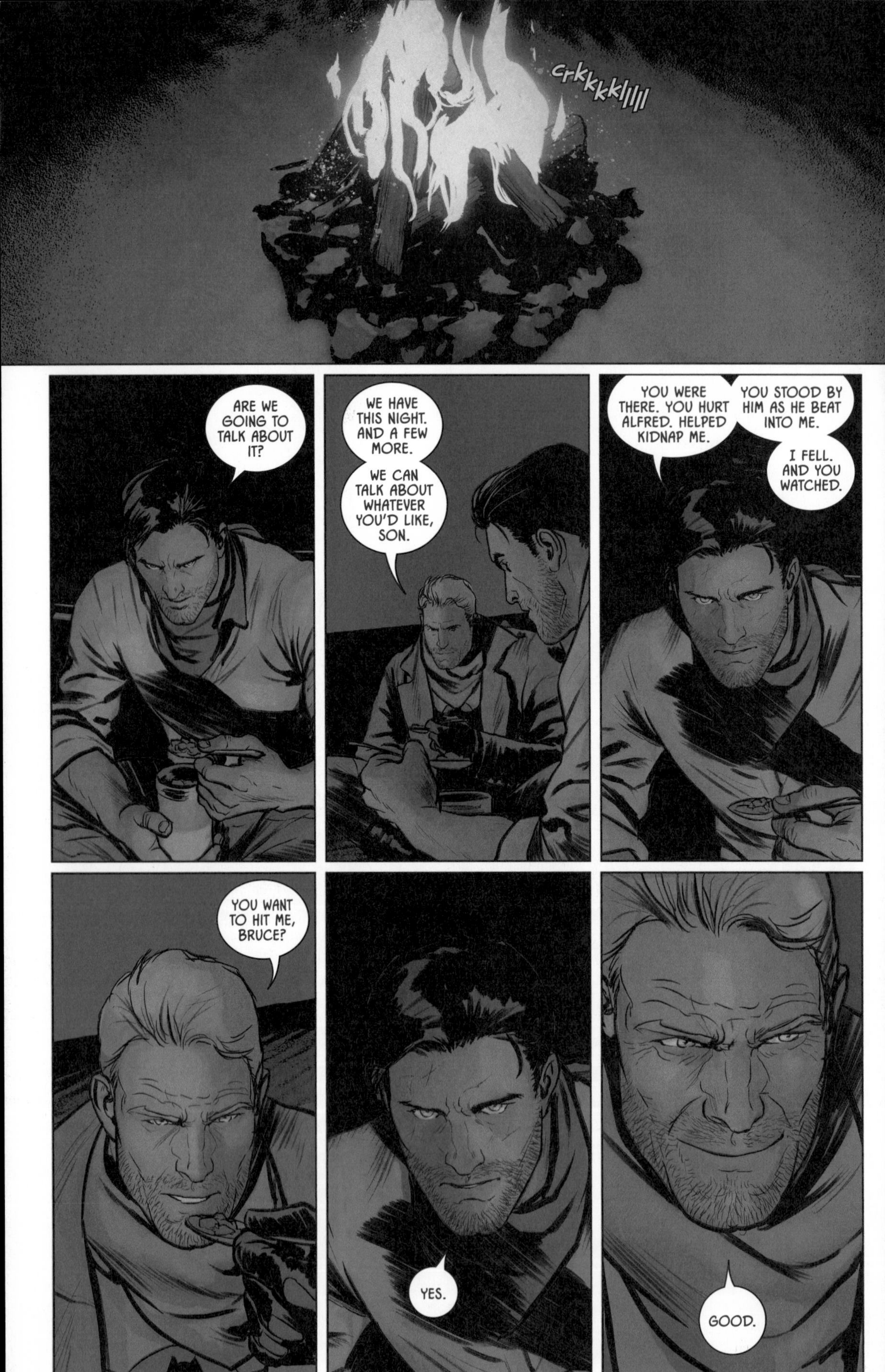
crkkkklllll
ARE WE GOING TO TALK ABOUT IT?
WE HAVE THIS NIGHT. AND A FEW MORE.
WE CAN TALK ABOUT WHATEVER YOU'D LIKE, SON.
YOU WERE THERE. YOU HURT ALFRED. HELPED KIDNAP ME.
YOU STOOD BY HIM AS HE BEAT INTO ME.
I FELL. AND YOU WATCHED.
YOU WANT TO HIT ME, BRUCE?
YES.
GOOD.

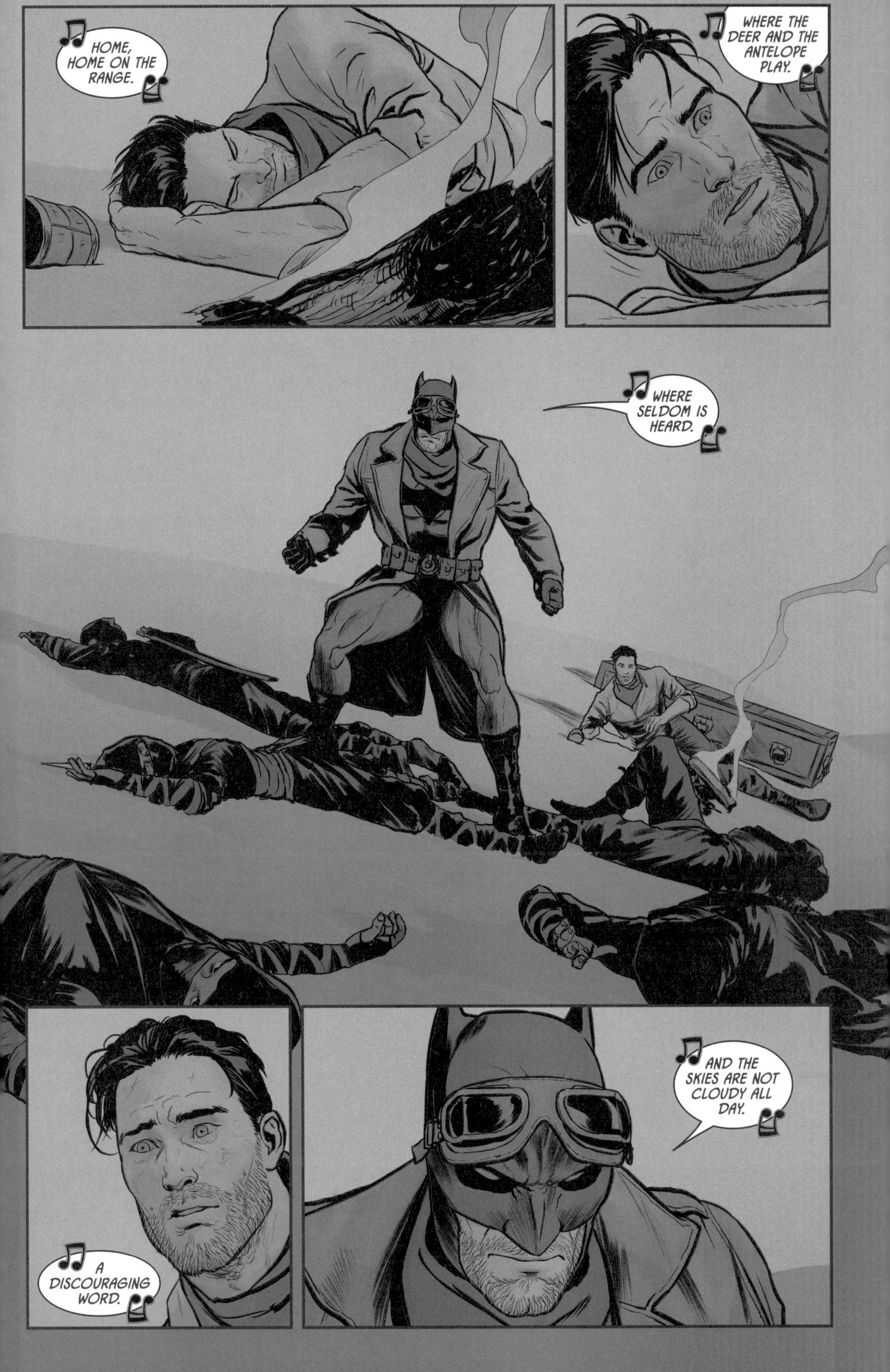
HOME, HOME ON THE RANGE.
WHERE THE DEER AND THE ANTELOPE PLAY.
WHERE SELDOM IS HEARD.
A DISCOURAGING WORD.
AND THE SKIES ARE NOT CLOUDY ALL DAY.

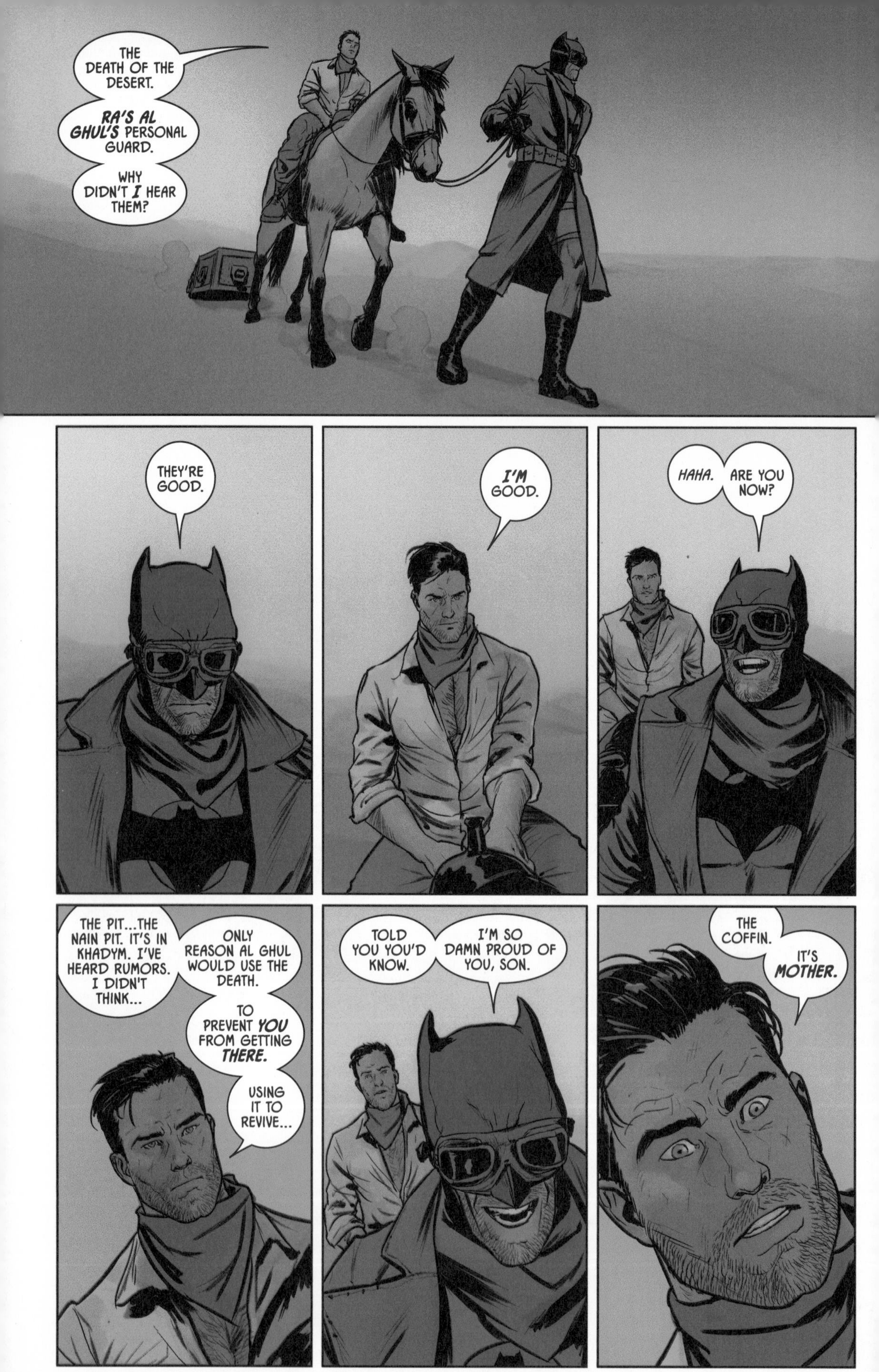
THE DEATH OF THE DESERT.
RA'S AL GHUL'S PERSONAL GUARD.
WHY DIDN'T I HEAR THEM?
THEY'RE GOOD.
I'M GOOD.
HAHA.
ARE YOU NOW?
THE PIT...THE NAIN PIT. IT'S IN KHADYM. I'VE HEARD RUMORS. I DIDN'T THINK...
ONLY REASON AL GHUL WOULD USE THE DEATH.
TO PREVENT YOU FROM GETTING THERE.
USING IT TO REVIVE...
TOLD YOU YOU'D KNOW.
I'M SO DAMN PROUD OF YOU, SON.
THE COFFIN.
IT'S MOTHER.

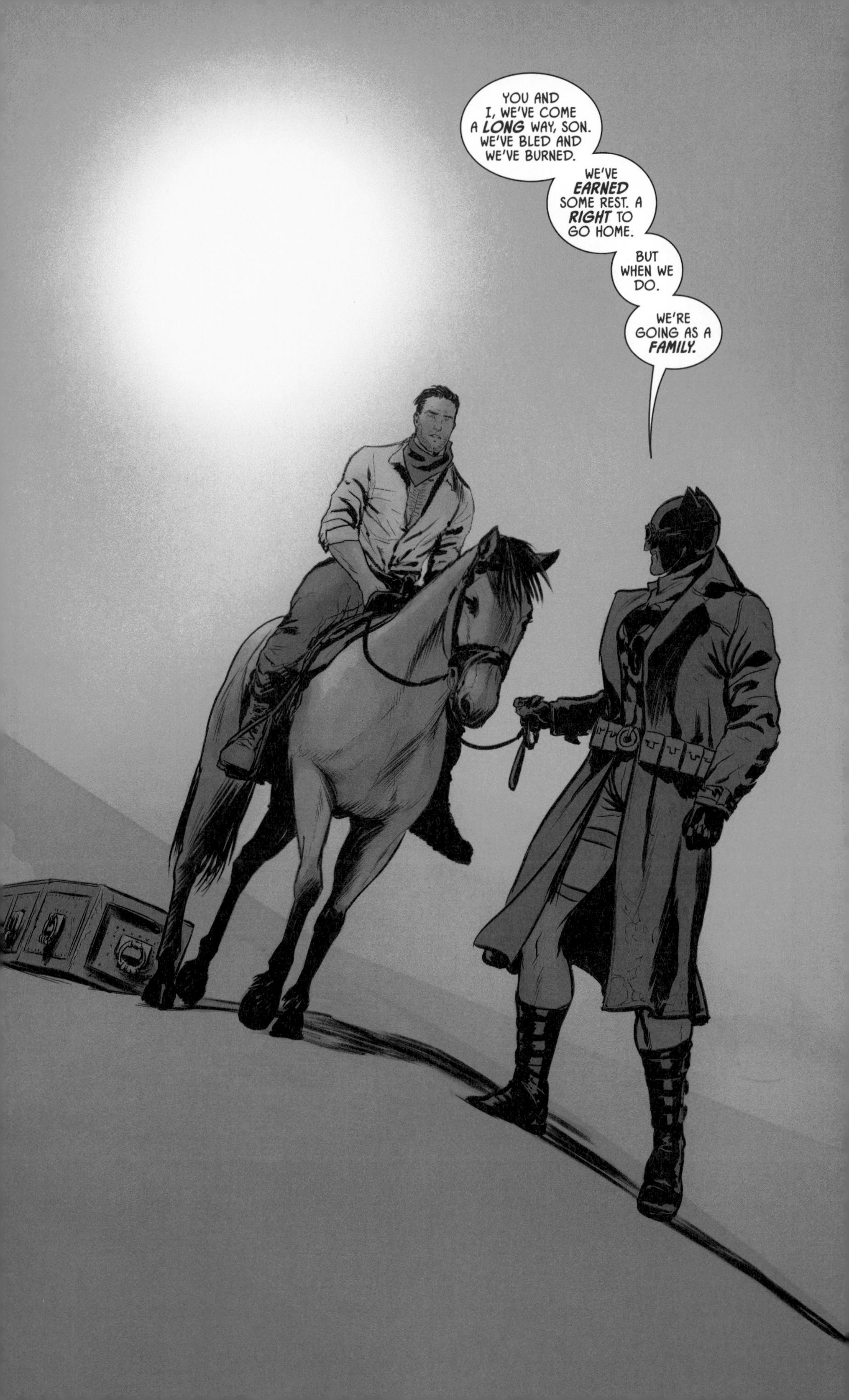
YOU AND I, WE'VE COME A LONG WAY, SON. WE'VE BLED AND WE'VE BURNED.
WE'VE EARNED SOME REST. A RIGHT TO GO HOME.
BUT WHEN WE DO.
WE'RE GOING AS A FAMILY.

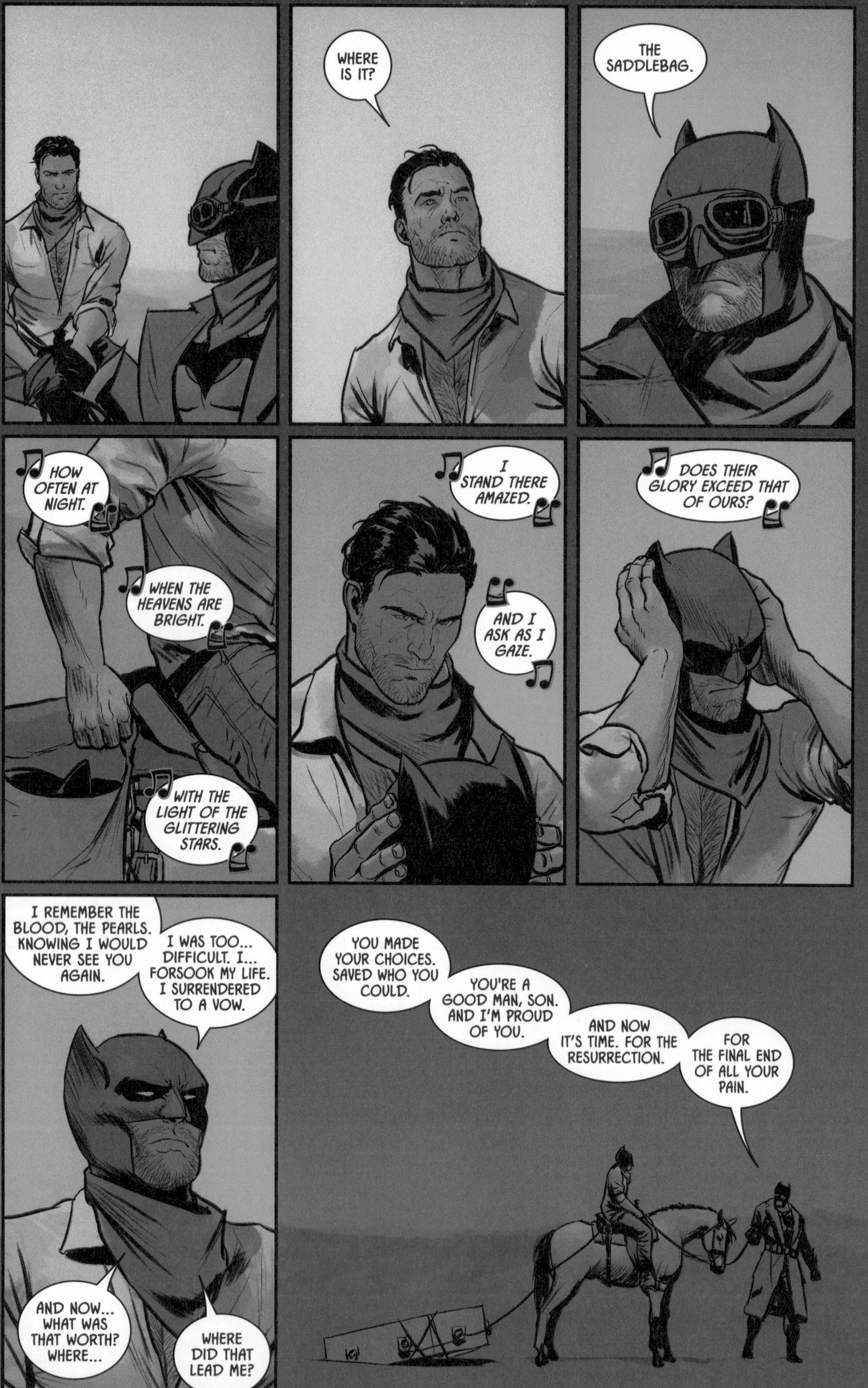
WHERE IS IT?
THE SADDLEBAG.
HOW OFTEN AT NIGHT.
WHEN THE HEAVENS ARE BRIGHT.
WITH THE LIGHT OF THE GLITTERING STARS.
I STAND THERE AMAZED.
AND I ASK AS I GAZE.
DOES THEIR GLORY EXCEED THAT OF OURS?
I REMEMBER THE BLOOD, THE PEARLS. KNOWING I WOULD NEVER SEE YOU AGAIN.
I WAS TOO... DIFFICULT. I... FORSOOK MY LIFE. I SURRENDERED TO A VOW.
AND NOW... WHAT WAS THAT WORTH? WHERE...
WHERE DID THAT LEAD ME?
YOU MADE YOUR CHOICES. SAVED WHO YOU COULD.
YOU'RE A GOOD MAN, SON. AND I'M PROUD OF YOU.
AND NOW IT'S TIME. FOR THE RESURRECTION.
FOR THE FINAL END OF ALL YOUR PAIN.

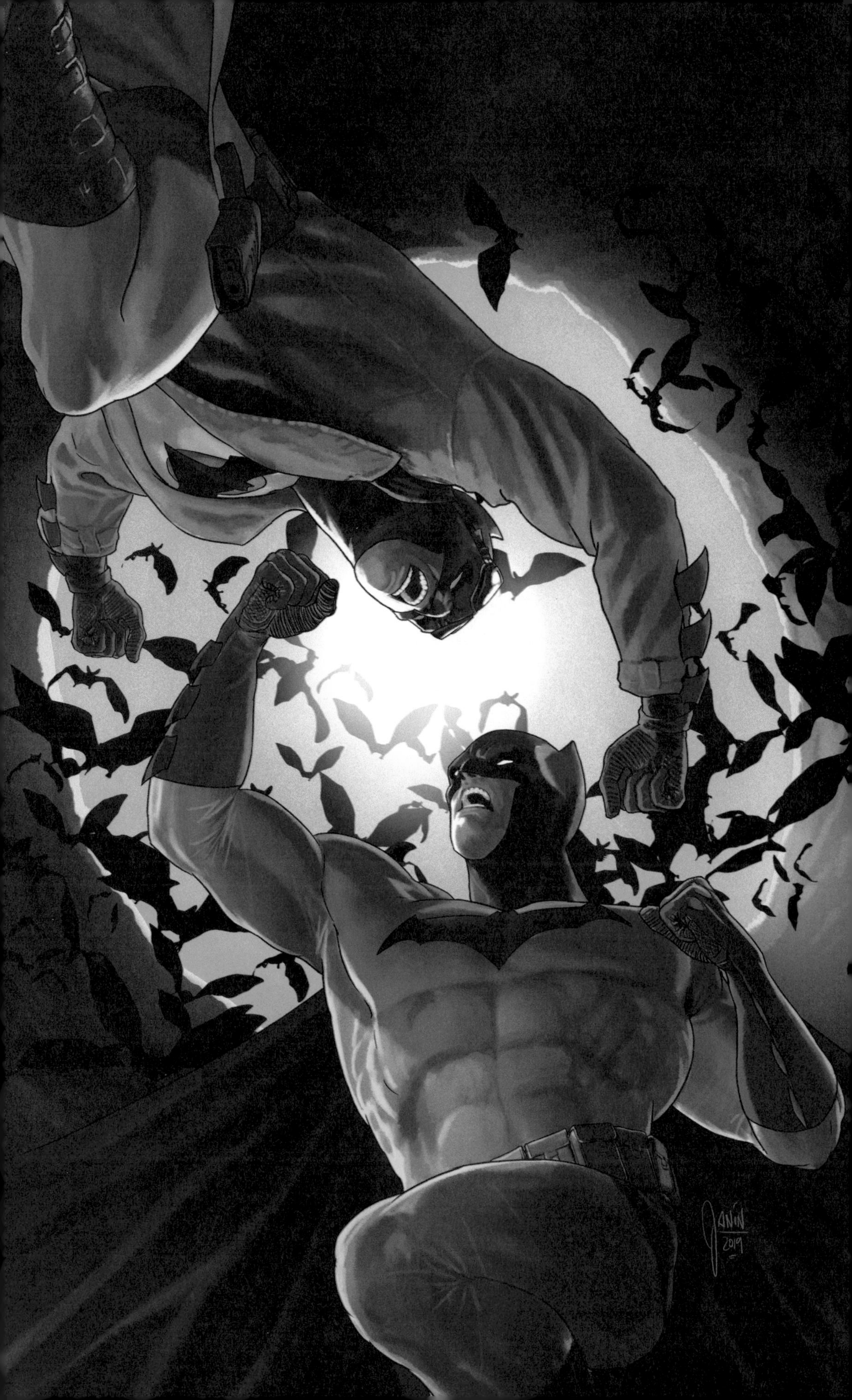

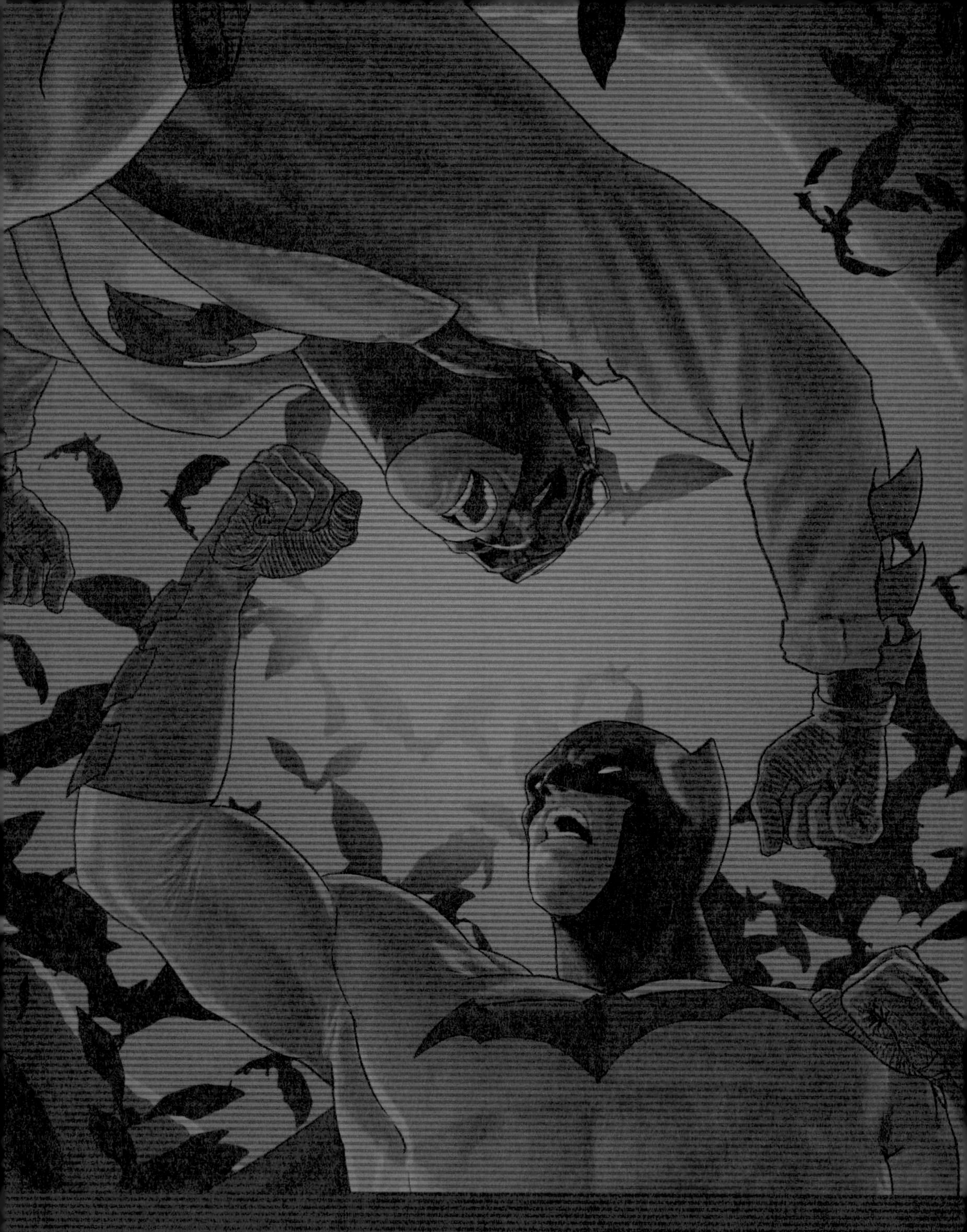

BATMAN
#74

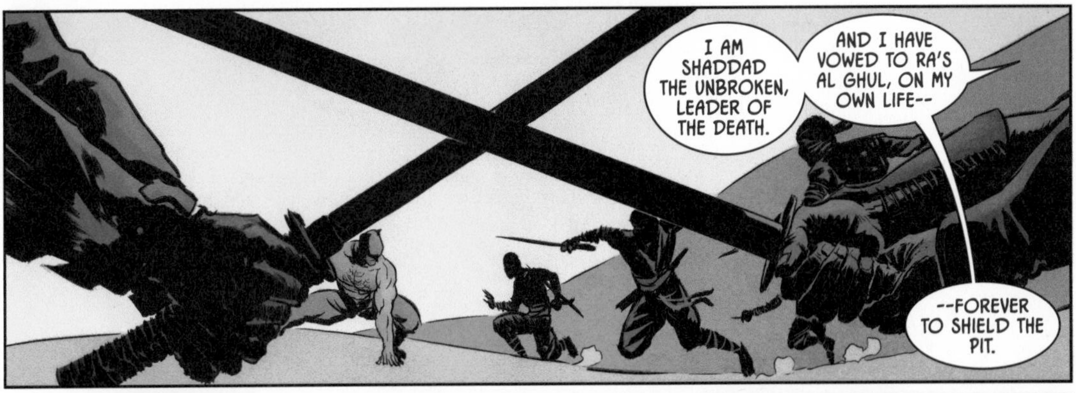
I AM SHADDAD THE UNBROKEN, LEADER OF THE DEATH.
AND I HAVE VOWED TO RA'S AL GHUL, ON MY OWN LIFE--
--FOREVER TO SHIELD THE PIT.

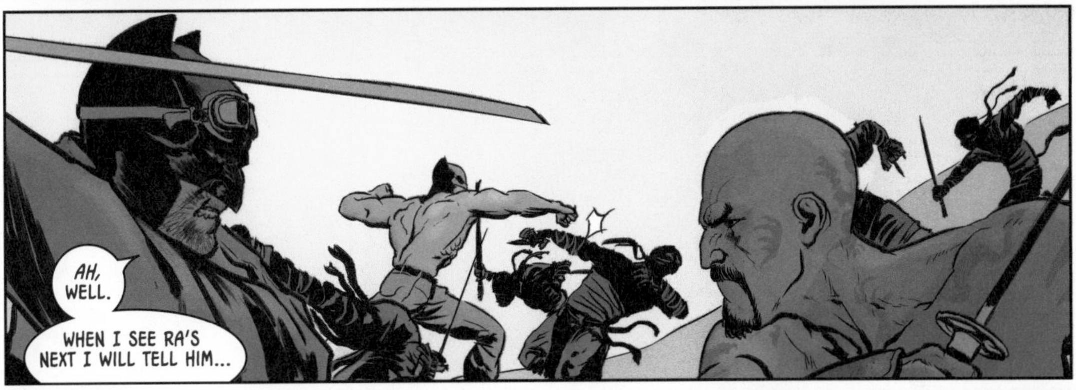
AH, WELL.
WHEN I SEE RA'S NEXT I WILL TELL HIM...

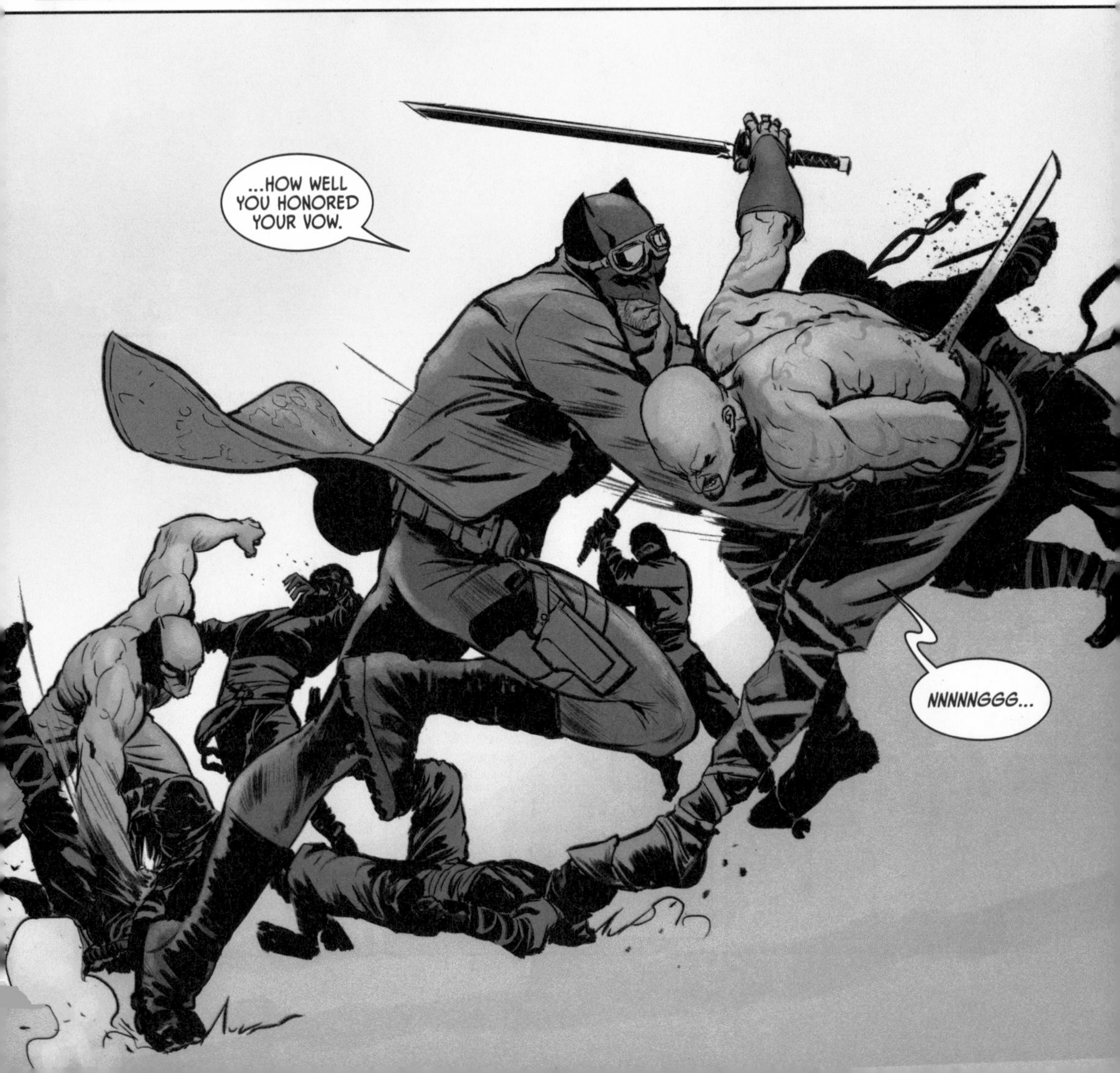
...HOW WELL YOU HONORED YOUR VOW.
NNNNNGGG...

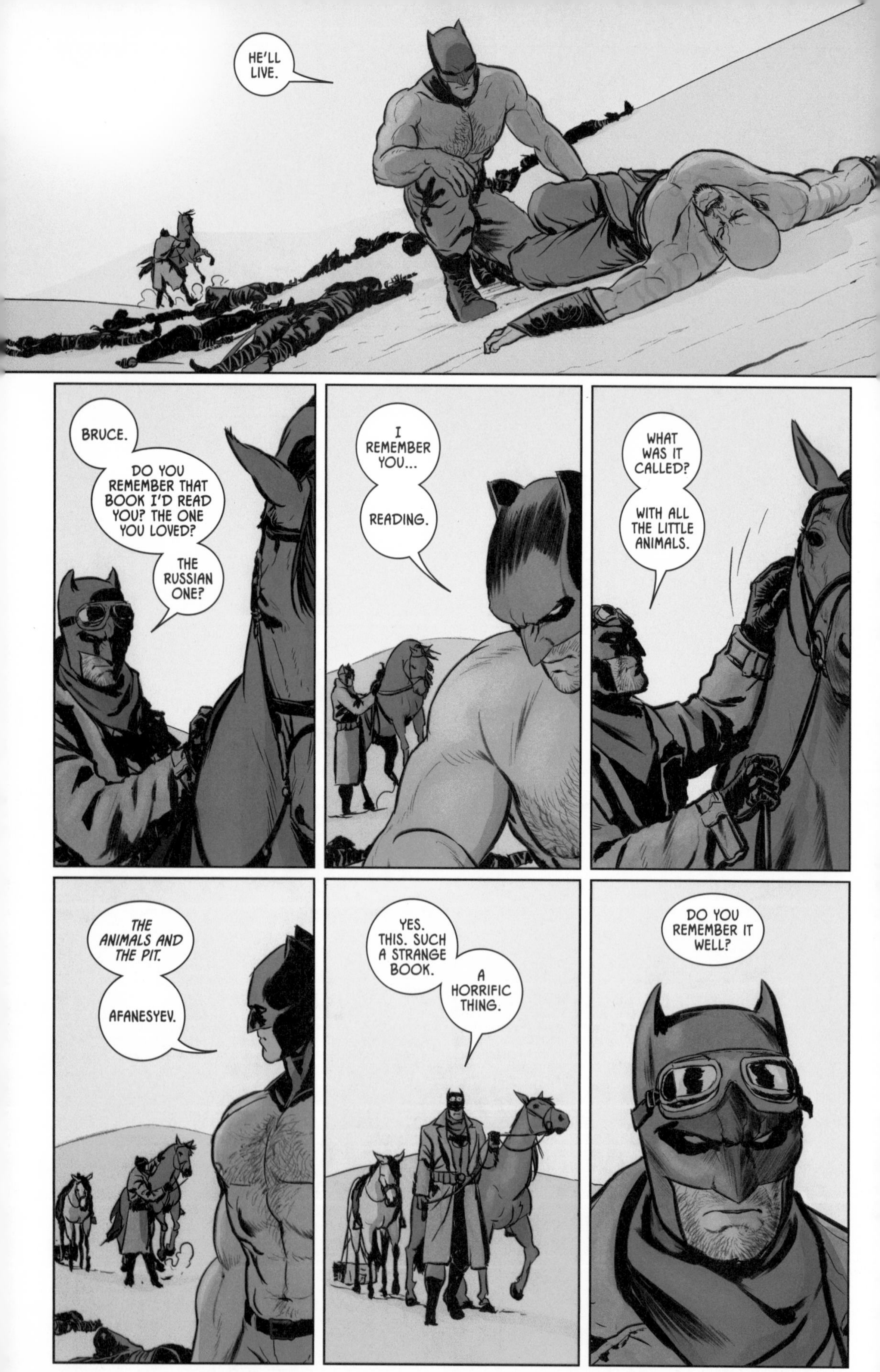

HE'LL LIVE.
BRUCE.
DO YOU REMEMBER THAT BOOK I'D READ YOU? THE ONE YOU LOVED?
THE RUSSIAN ONE?
I REMEMBER YOU...
READING.
WHAT WAS IT CALLED?
WITH ALL THE LITTLE ANIMALS.
THE ANIMALS AND THE PIT.
AFANESYEV.
YES. THIS. SUCH A STRANGE BOOK.
A HORRIFIC THING.
DO YOU REMEMBER IT WELL?

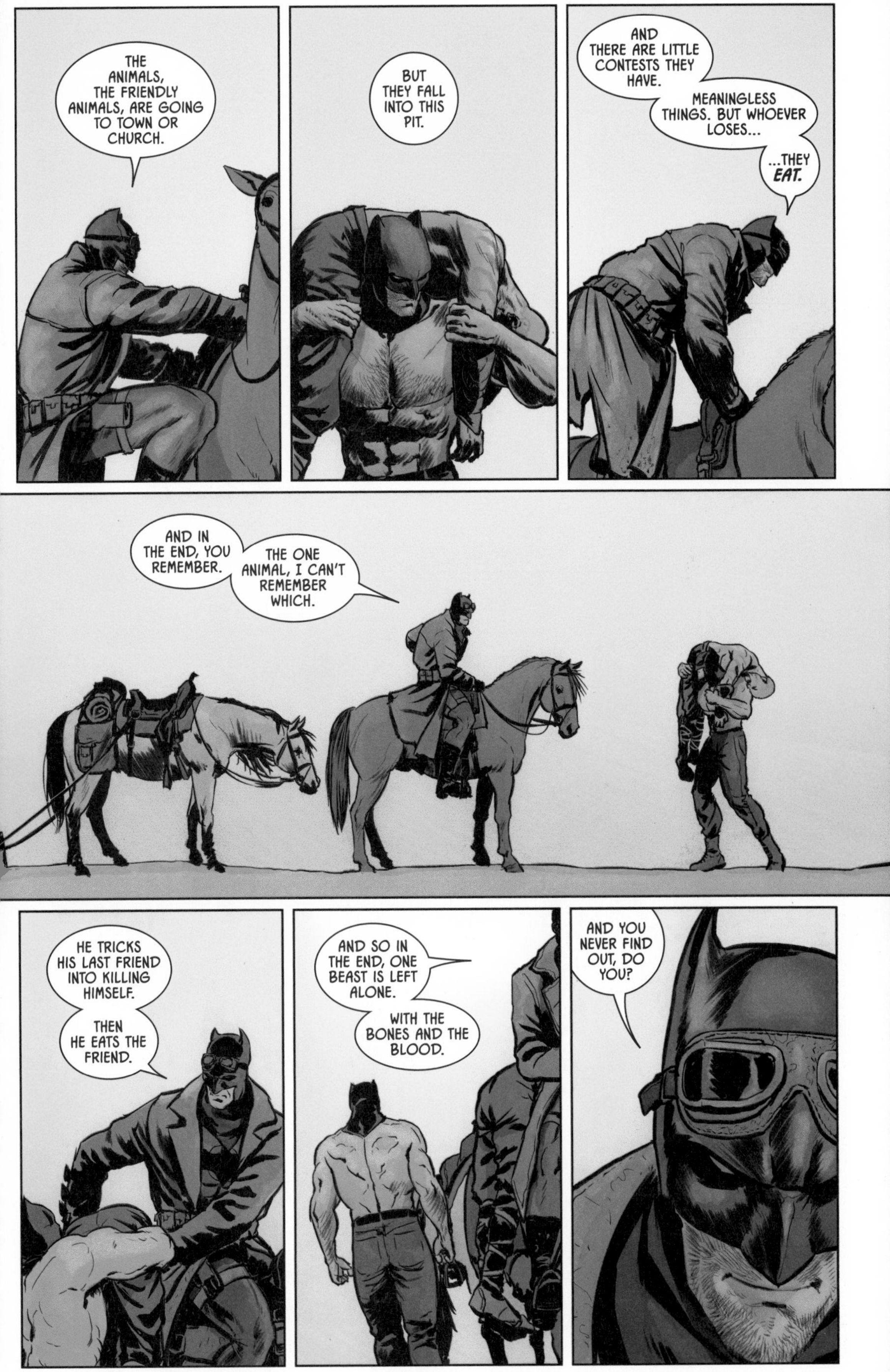
THE ANIMALS, THE FRIENDLY ANIMALS, ARE GOING TO TOWN OR CHURCH.
BUT THEY FALL INTO THIS PIT.
AND THERE ARE LITTLE CONTESTS THEY HAVE.
MEANINGLESS THINGS. BUT WHOEVER LOSES...
...THEY *EAT.*
AND IN THE END, YOU REMEMBER.
THE ONE ANIMAL, I CAN'T REMEMBER WHICH.
HE TRICKS HIS LAST FRIEND INTO KILLING HIMSELF.
THEN HE EATS THE FRIEND.
AND SO IN THE END, ONE BEAST IS LEFT ALONE.
WITH THE BONES AND THE BLOOD.
AND YOU NEVER FIND OUT, DO YOU?

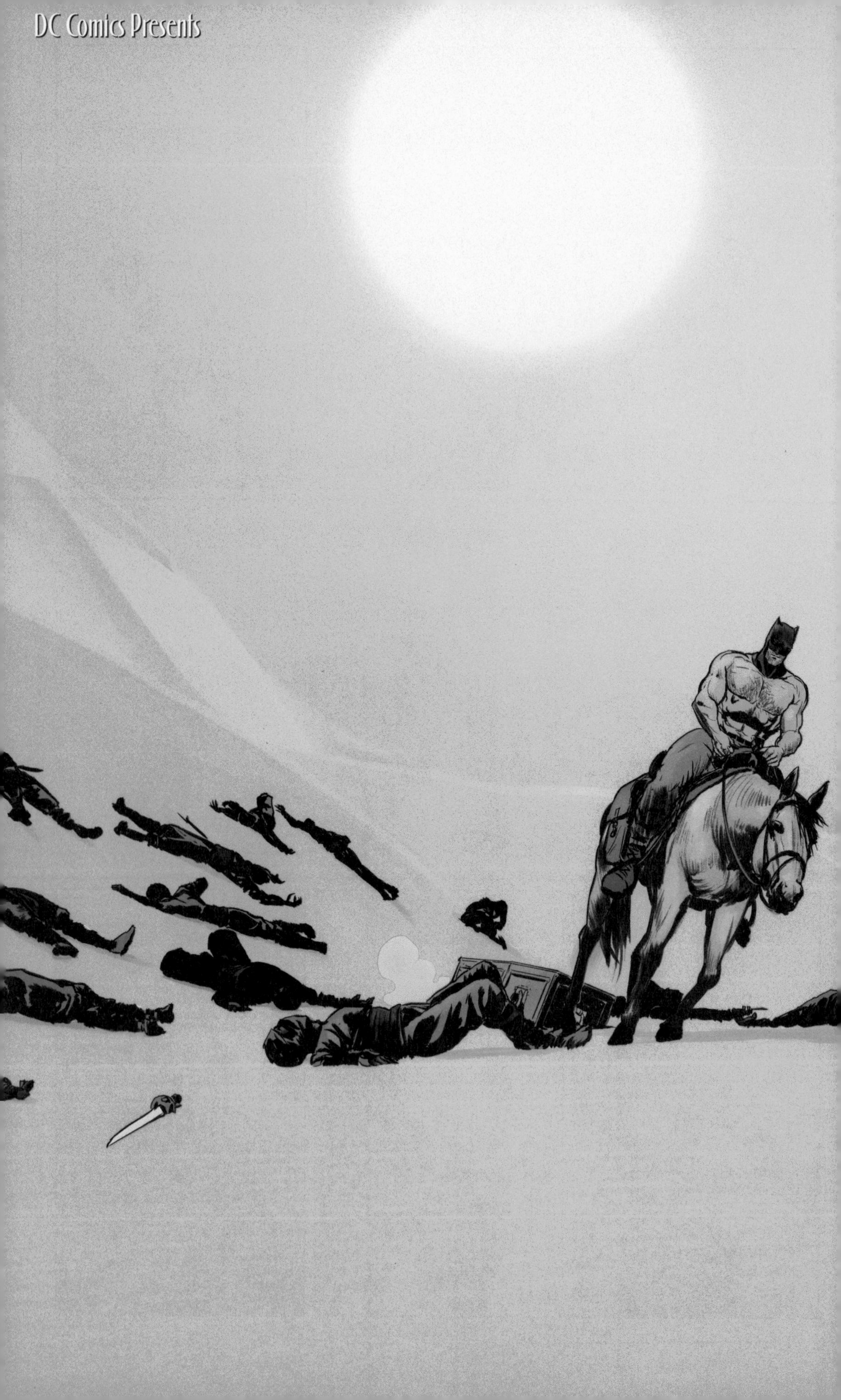

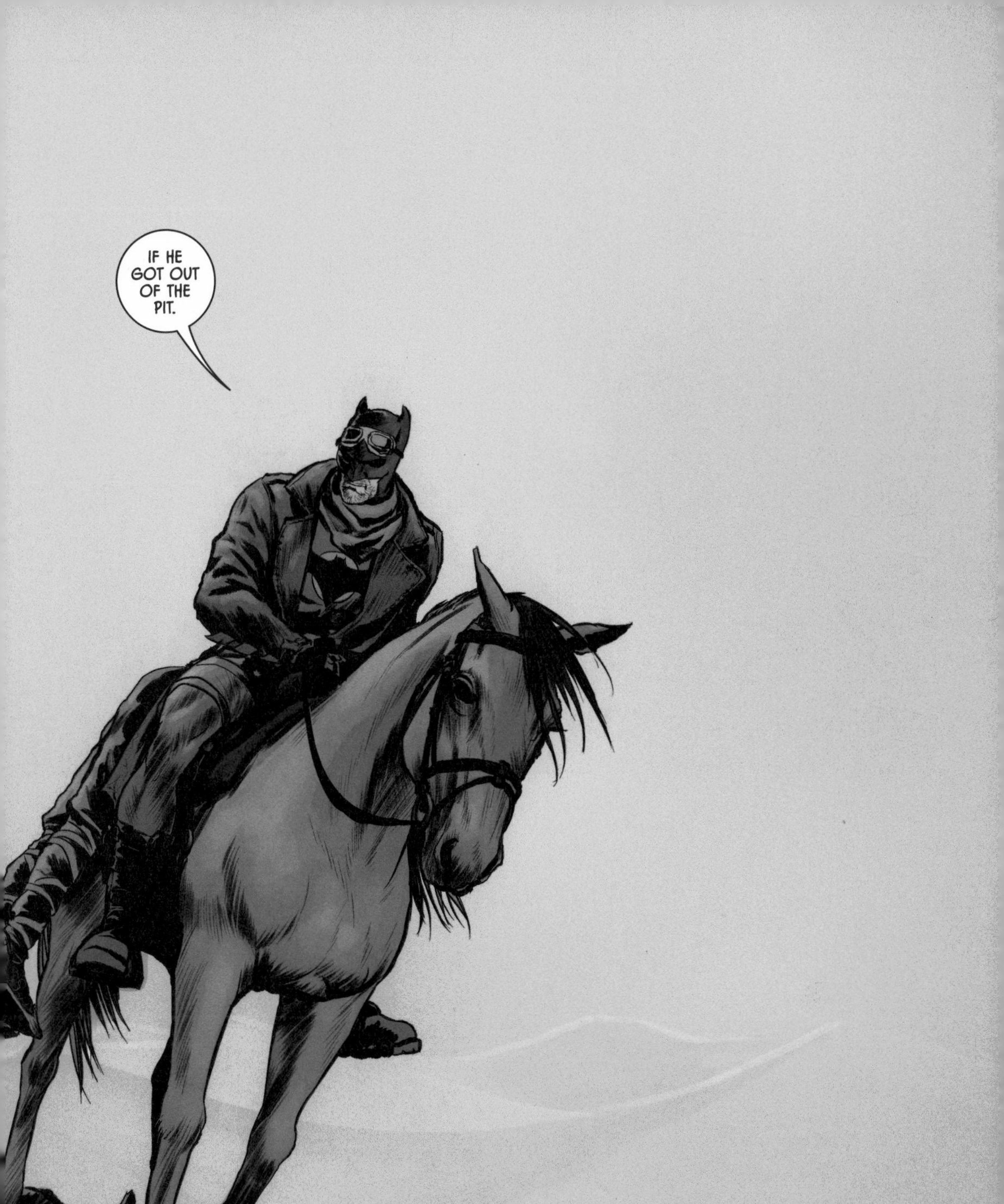
IF HE GOT OUT OF THE PIT.

The Fall and the Fallen Conclusion

TOM KING writer MIKEL JANÍN artist JORDIE BELLAIRE colorist CLAYTON COWLES letterer
MIKEL JANÍN cover ROB LEVIN associate editor JAMIE S. RICH editor

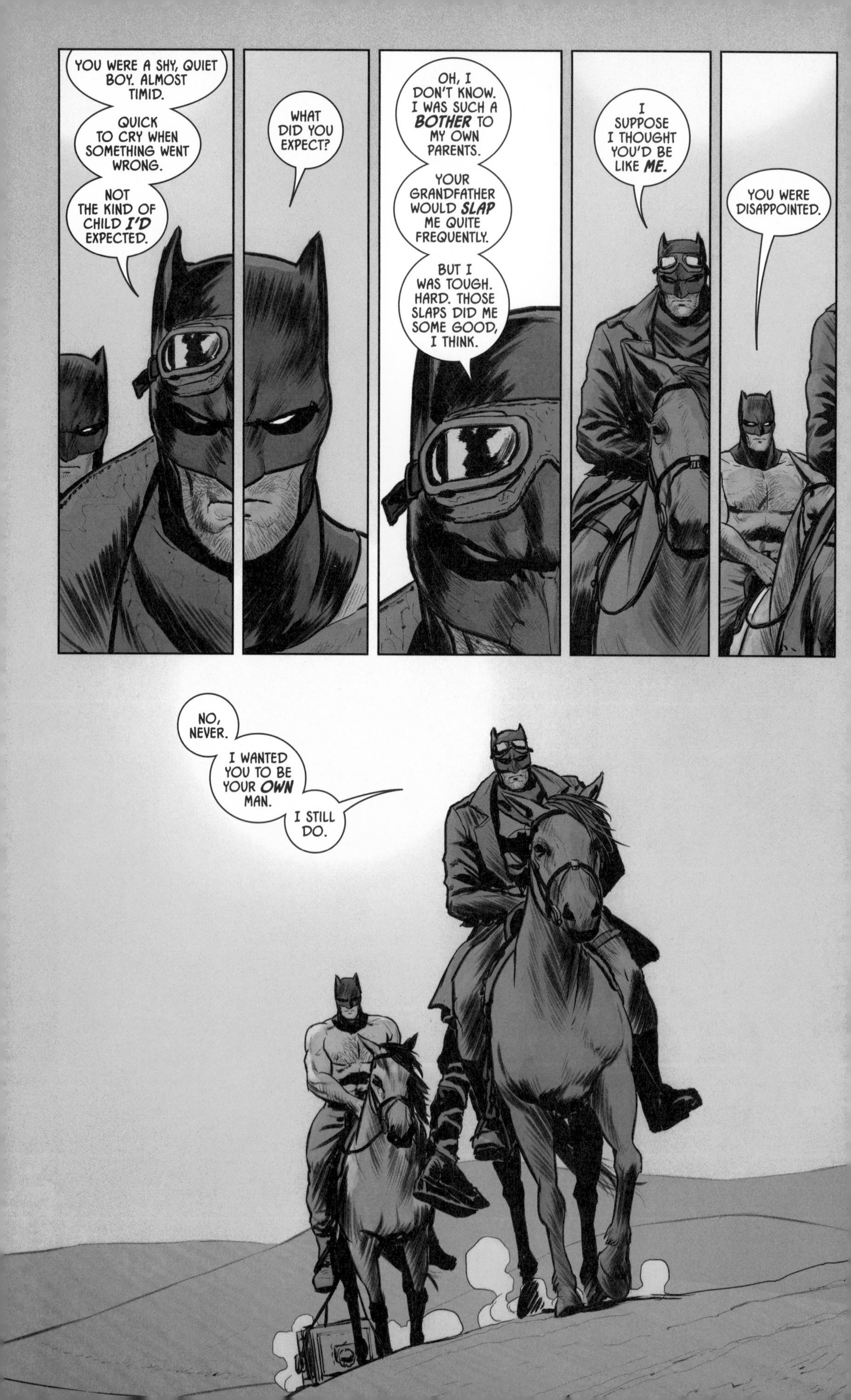
YOU WERE A SHY, QUIET BOY. ALMOST TIMID.
QUICK TO CRY WHEN SOMETHING WENT WRONG.
NOT THE KIND OF CHILD I'D EXPECTED.
WHAT DID YOU EXPECT?
OH, I DON'T KNOW. I WAS SUCH A BOTHER TO MY OWN PARENTS.
YOUR GRANDFATHER WOULD SLAP ME QUITE FREQUENTLY.
BUT I WAS TOUGH. HARD. THOSE SLAPS DID ME SOME GOOD, I THINK.
I SUPPOSE I THOUGHT YOU'D BE LIKE ME.
YOU WERE DISAPPOINTED.
NO, NEVER.
I WANTED YOU TO BE YOUR OWN MAN.
I STILL DO.

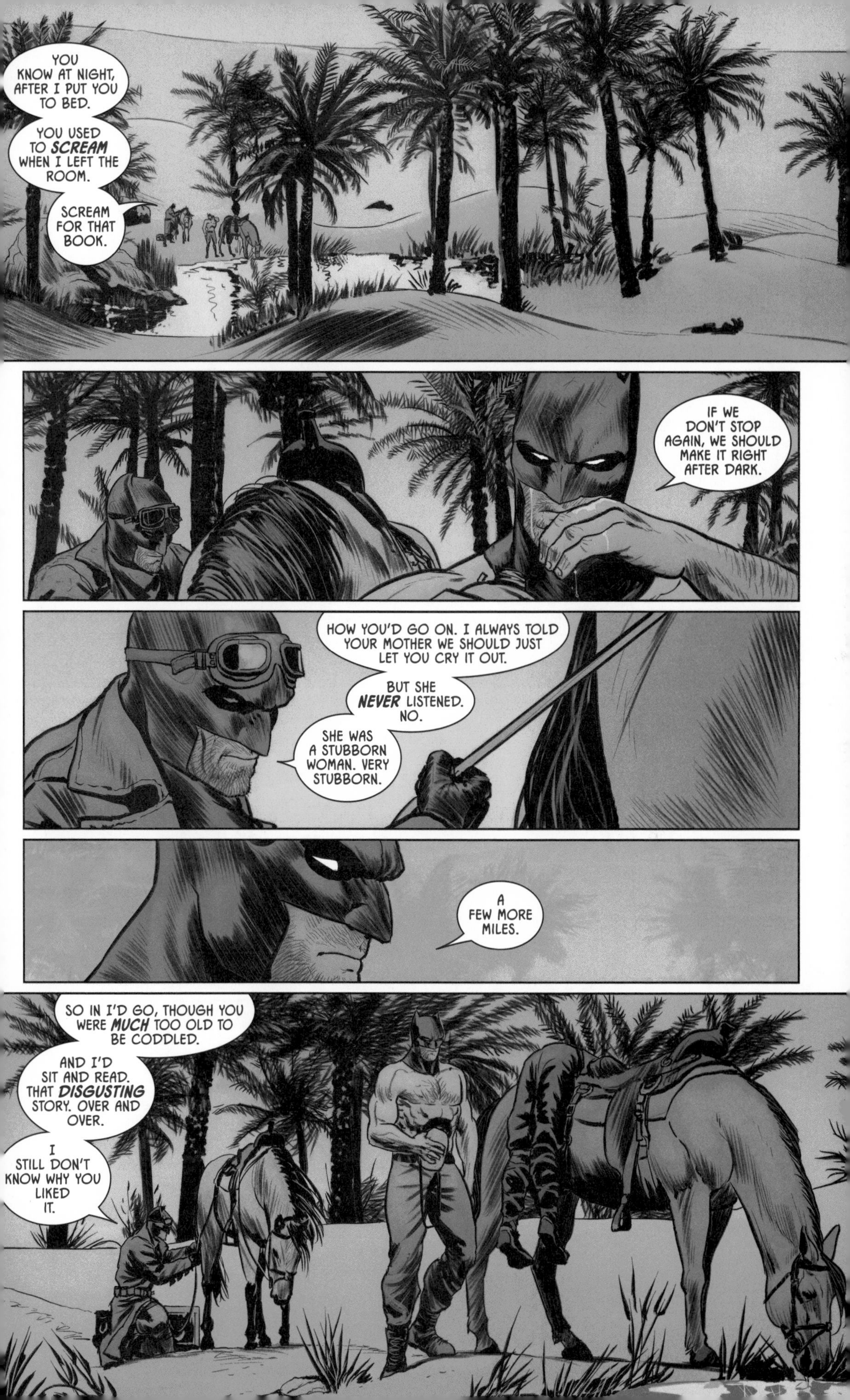
YOU KNOW AT NIGHT, AFTER I PUT YOU TO BED.
YOU USED TO *SCREAM* WHEN I LEFT THE ROOM.
SCREAM FOR THAT BOOK.
IF WE DON'T STOP AGAIN, WE SHOULD MAKE IT RIGHT AFTER DARK.
HOW YOU'D GO ON. I ALWAYS TOLD YOUR MOTHER WE SHOULD JUST LET YOU CRY IT OUT.
BUT SHE *NEVER* LISTENED. NO.
SHE WAS A STUBBORN WOMAN. VERY STUBBORN.
A FEW MORE MILES.
SO IN I'D GO, THOUGH YOU WERE *MUCH* TOO OLD TO BE CODDLED.
AND I'D SIT AND READ. THAT *DISGUSTING* STORY. OVER AND OVER.
I STILL DON'T KNOW WHY YOU LIKED IT.

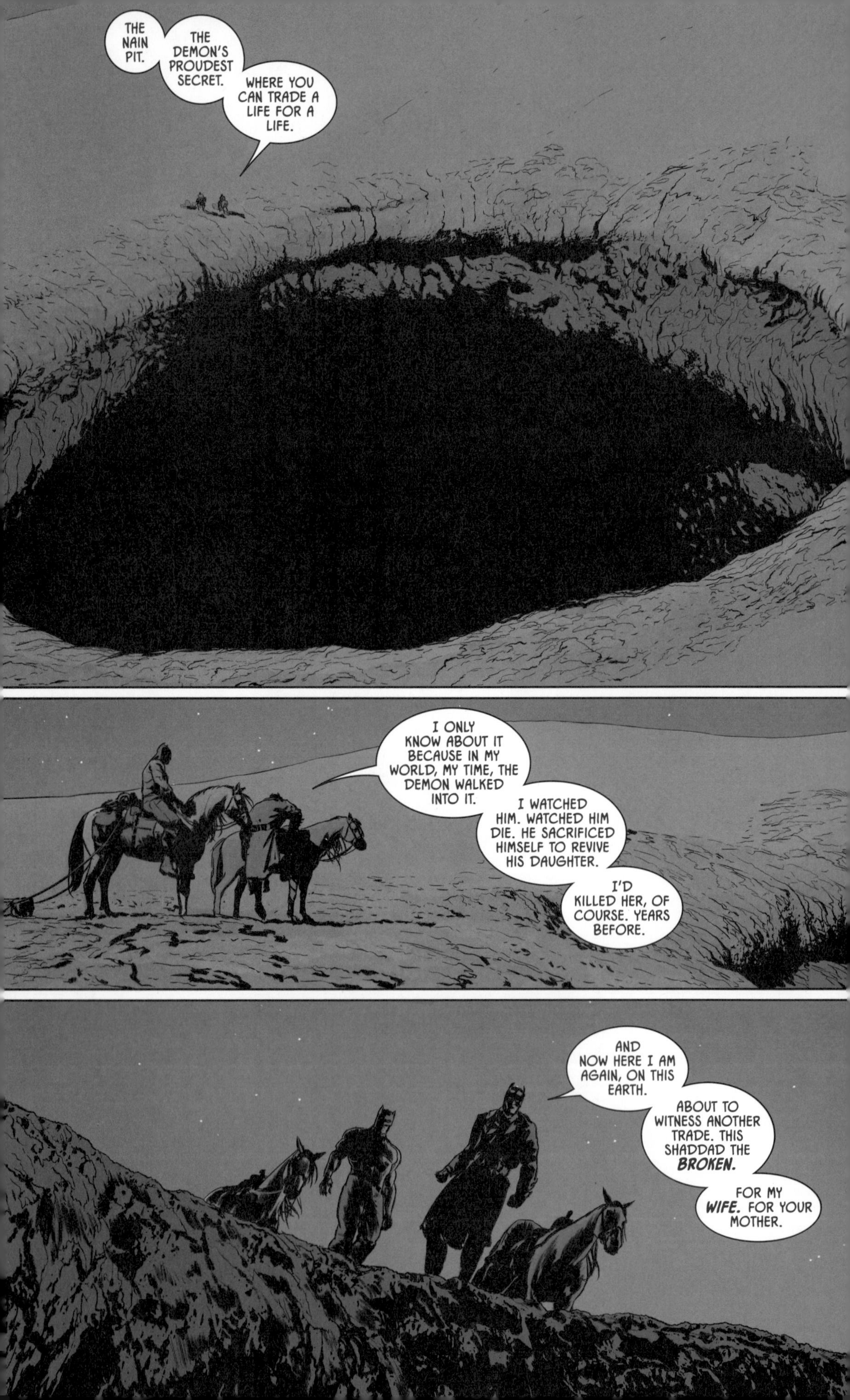
THE NAIN PIT.
THE DEMON'S PROUDEST SECRET.
WHERE YOU CAN TRADE A LIFE FOR A LIFE.
I ONLY KNOW ABOUT IT BECAUSE IN MY WORLD, MY TIME, THE DEMON WALKED INTO IT.
I WATCHED HIM. WATCHED HIM DIE. HE SACRIFICED HIMSELF TO REVIVE HIS DAUGHTER.
I'D KILLED HER, OF COURSE. YEARS BEFORE.
AND NOW HERE I AM AGAIN, ON THIS EARTH.
ABOUT TO WITNESS ANOTHER TRADE. THIS SHADDAD THE ***BROKEN.***
FOR MY ***WIFE.*** FOR YOUR MOTHER.

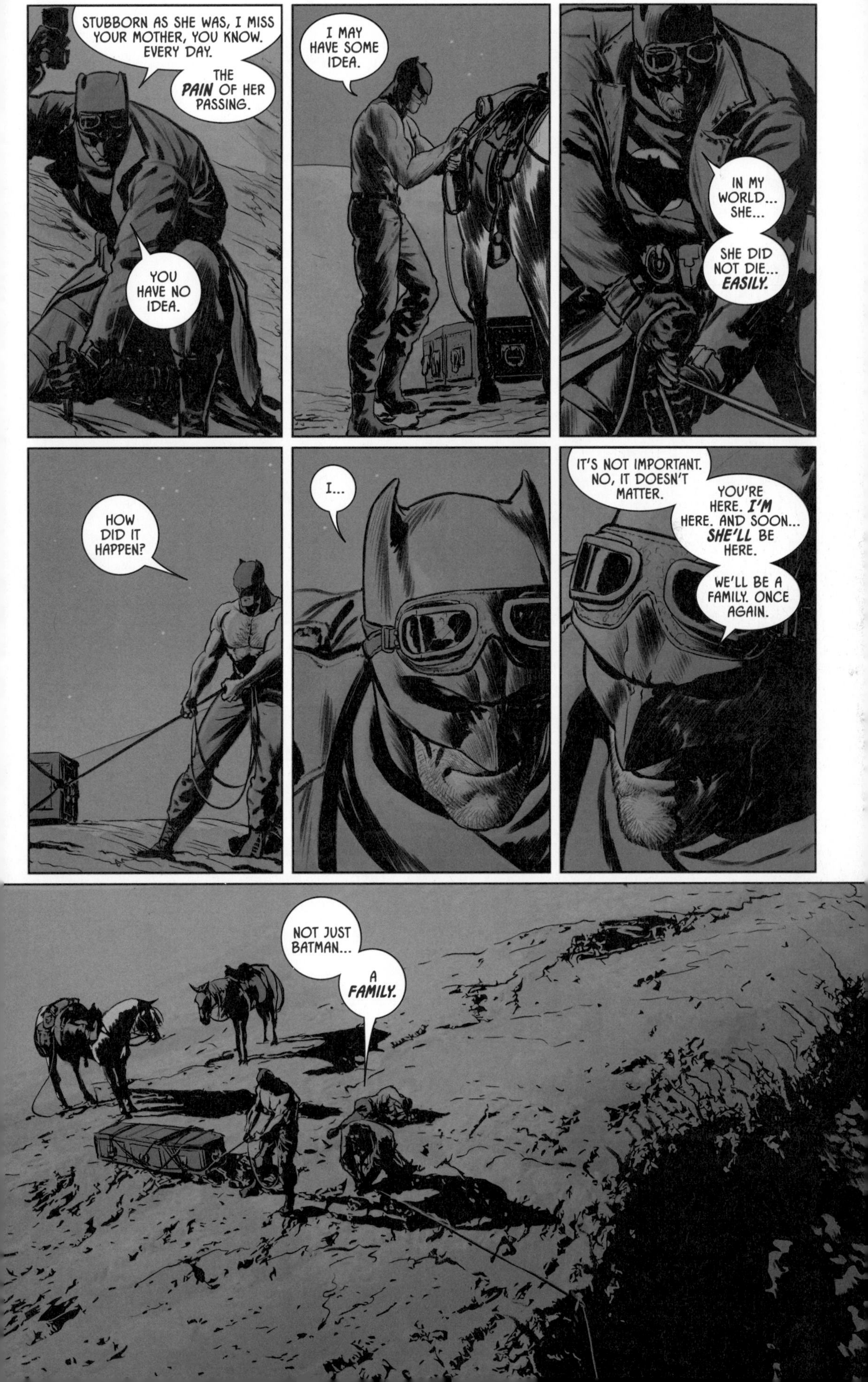
STUBBORN AS SHE WAS, I MISS YOUR MOTHER, YOU KNOW. EVERY DAY.
THE PAIN OF HER PASSING.
YOU HAVE NO IDEA.
I MAY HAVE SOME IDEA.
IN MY WORLD... SHE...
SHE DID NOT DIE... EASILY.
HOW DID IT HAPPEN?
I...
IT'S NOT IMPORTANT. NO, IT DOESN'T MATTER.
YOU'RE HERE. I'M HERE. AND SOON... SHE'LL BE HERE.
WE'LL BE A FAMILY. ONCE AGAIN.
NOT JUST BATMAN...
A FAMILY.

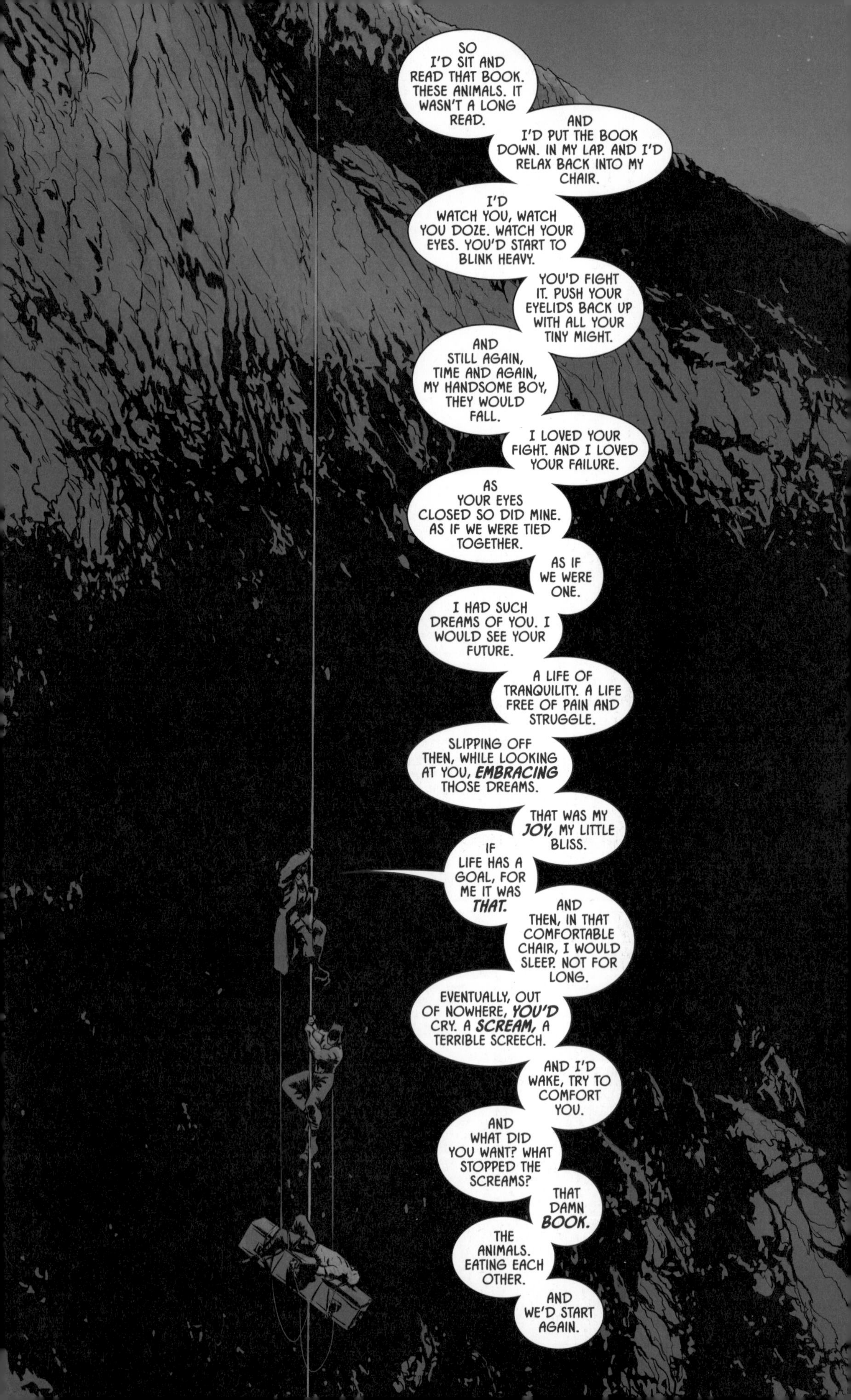
SO I'D SIT AND READ THAT BOOK. THESE ANIMALS. IT WASN'T A LONG READ.
AND I'D PUT THE BOOK DOWN. IN MY LAP. AND I'D RELAX BACK INTO MY CHAIR.
I'D WATCH YOU, WATCH YOU DOZE. WATCH YOUR EYES. YOU'D START TO BLINK HEAVY.
YOU'D FIGHT IT. PUSH YOUR EYELIDS BACK UP WITH ALL YOUR TINY MIGHT.
AND STILL AGAIN, TIME AND AGAIN, MY HANDSOME BOY, THEY WOULD FALL.
I LOVED YOUR FIGHT. AND I LOVED YOUR FAILURE.
AS YOUR EYES CLOSED SO DID MINE. AS IF WE WERE TIED TOGETHER.
AS IF WE WERE ONE.
I HAD SUCH DREAMS OF YOU. I WOULD SEE YOUR FUTURE.
A LIFE OF TRANQUILITY. A LIFE FREE OF PAIN AND STRUGGLE.
SLIPPING OFF THEN, WHILE LOOKING AT YOU, ***EMBRACING*** THOSE DREAMS.
THAT WAS MY ***JOY,*** MY LITTLE BLISS.
IF LIFE HAS A GOAL, FOR ME IT WAS ***THAT.***
AND THEN, IN THAT COMFORTABLE CHAIR, I WOULD SLEEP. NOT FOR LONG.
EVENTUALLY, OUT OF NOWHERE, ***YOU'D*** CRY. A ***SCREAM,*** A TERRIBLE SCREECH.
AND I'D WAKE, TRY TO COMFORT YOU.
AND WHAT DID YOU WANT? WHAT STOPPED THE SCREAMS?
THAT DAMN ***BOOK.***
THE ANIMALS. EATING EACH OTHER.
AND WE'D START AGAIN.

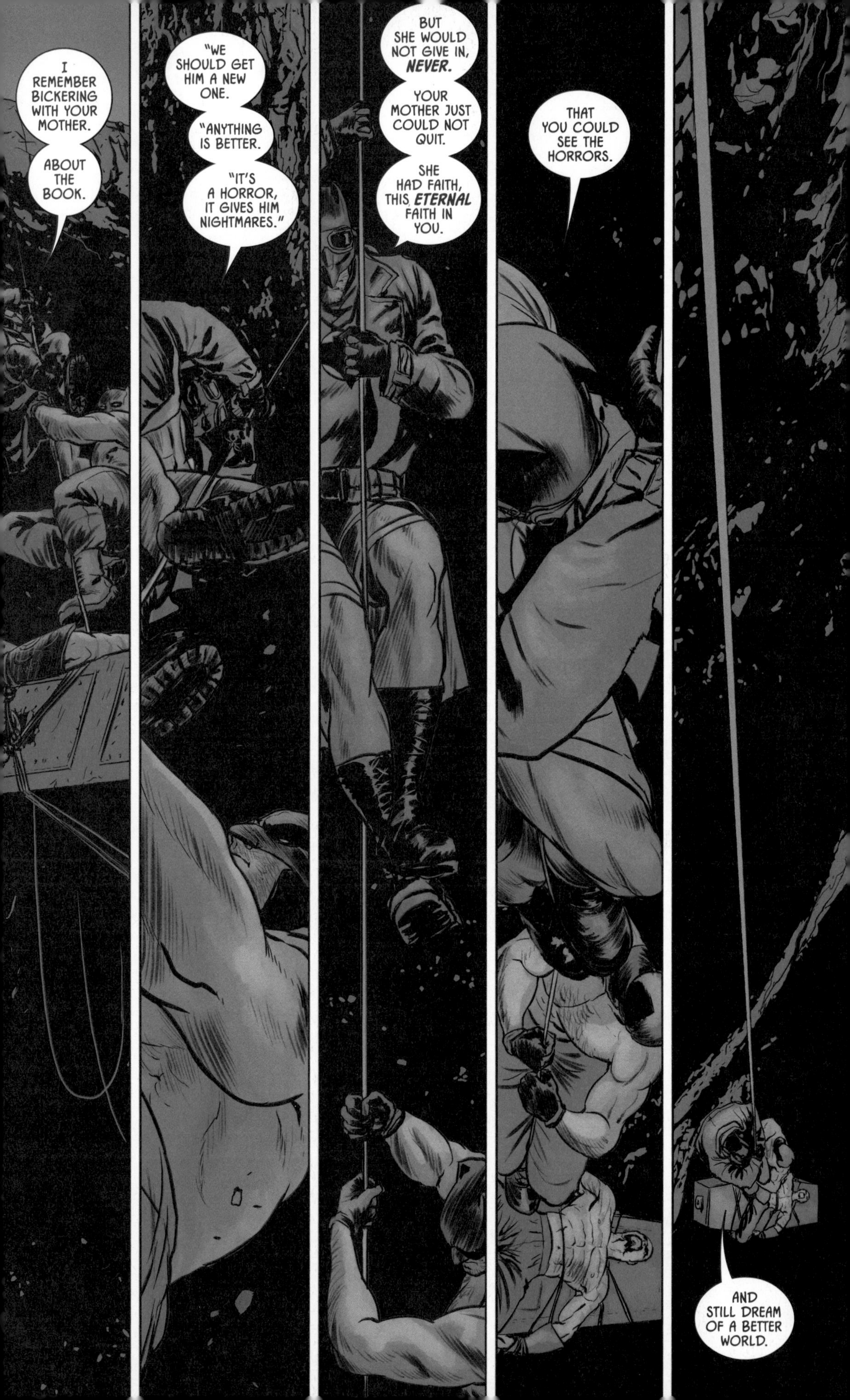
I REMEMBER BICKERING WITH YOUR MOTHER.
ABOUT THE BOOK.
"WE SHOULD GET HIM A NEW ONE.
"ANYTHING IS BETTER.
"IT'S A HORROR, IT GIVES HIM NIGHTMARES."
BUT SHE WOULD NOT GIVE IN, NEVER.
YOUR MOTHER JUST COULD NOT QUIT.
SHE HAD FAITH, THIS ETERNAL FAITH IN YOU.
THAT YOU COULD SEE THE HORRORS.
AND STILL DREAM OF A BETTER WORLD.

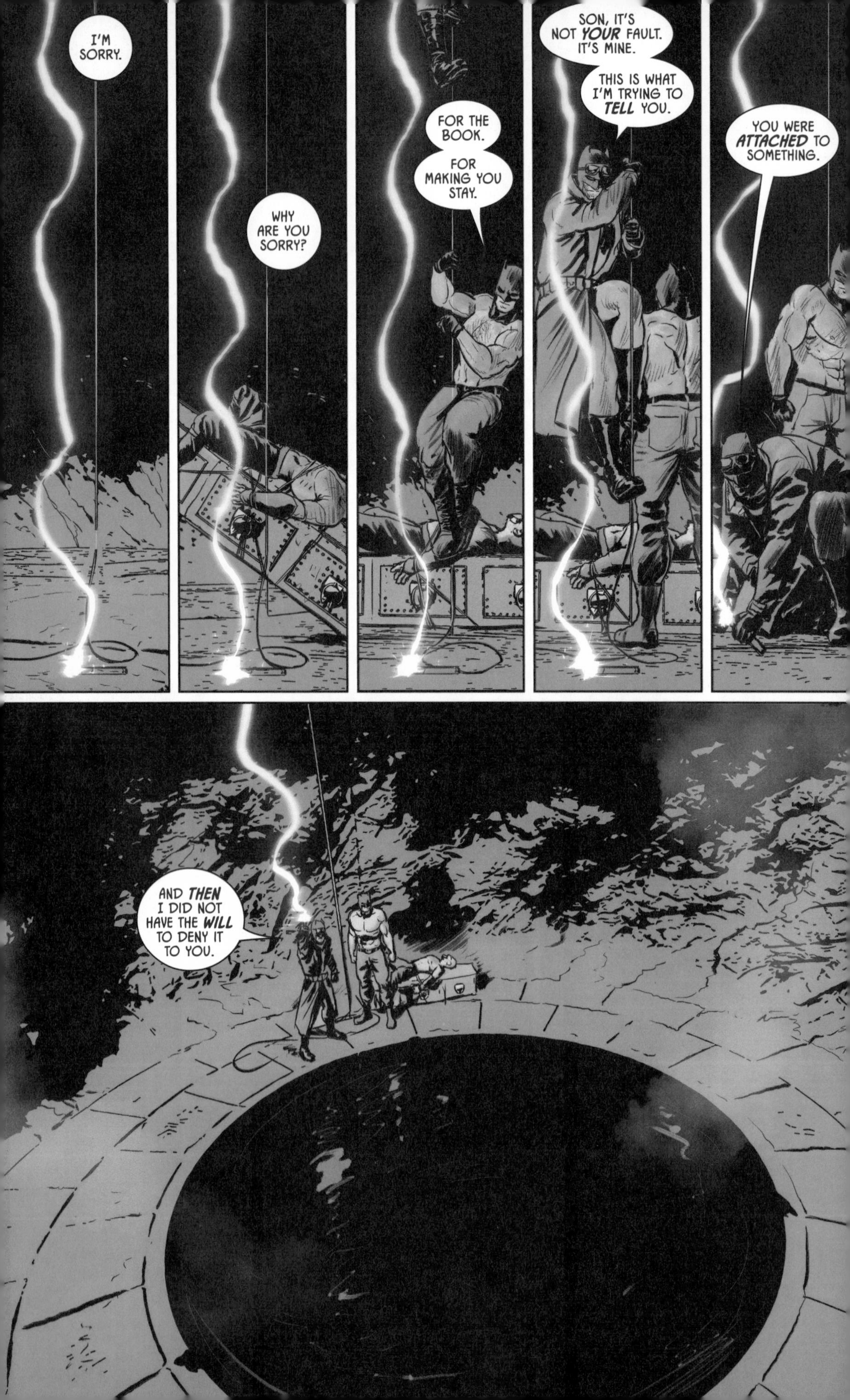
I'M SORRY.
WHY ARE YOU SORRY?
FOR THE BOOK.
FOR MAKING YOU STAY.
SON, IT'S NOT *YOUR* FAULT. IT'S MINE.
THIS IS WHAT I'M TRYING TO *TELL* YOU.
YOU WERE *ATTACHED* TO SOMETHING.
AND *THEN* I DID NOT HAVE THE *WILL* TO DENY IT TO YOU.

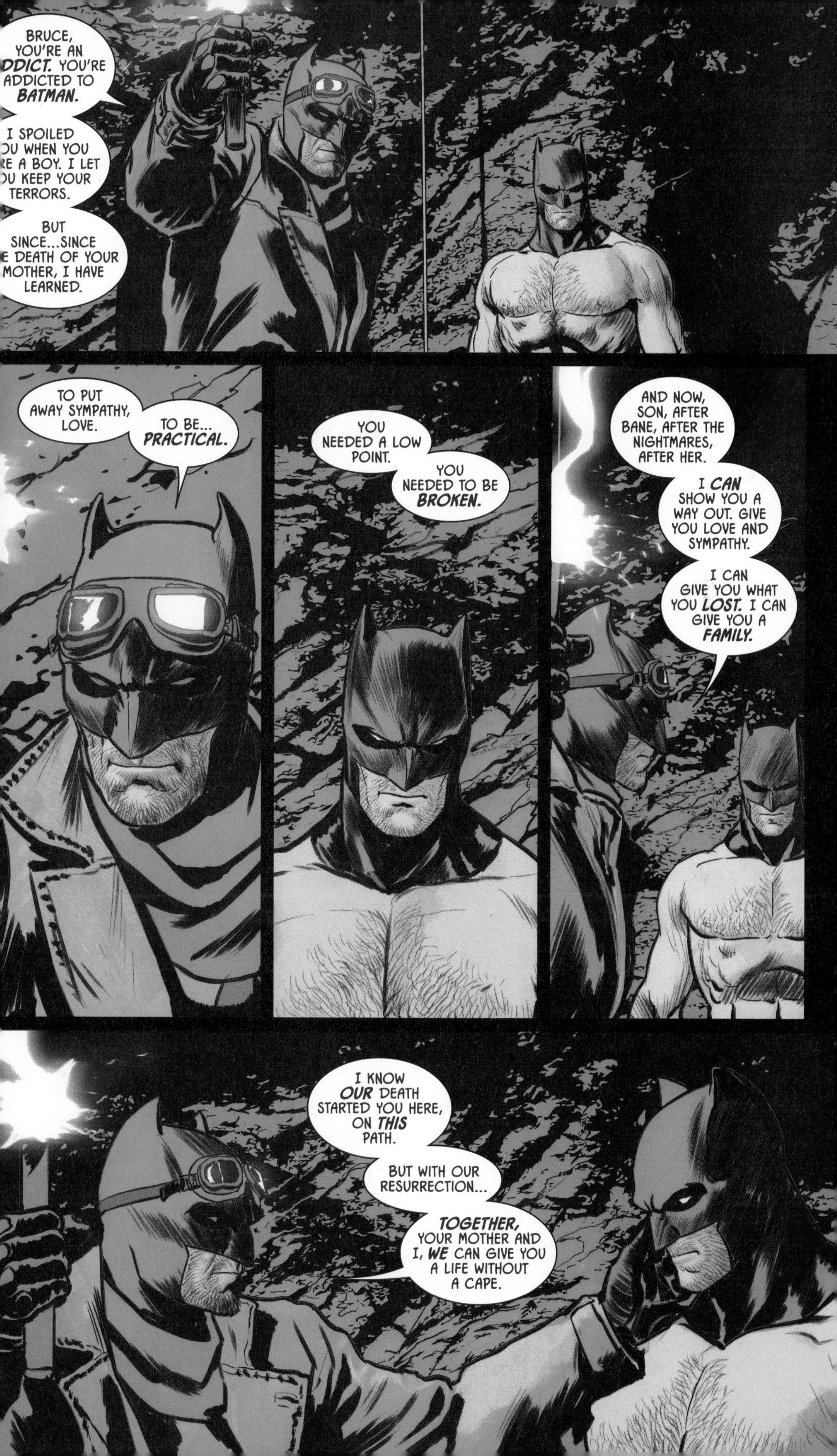
BRUCE, YOU'RE AN DDICT. YOU'RE ADDICTED TO BATMAN.
I SPOILED OU WHEN YOU RE A BOY. I LET OU KEEP YOUR TERRORS.
BUT SINCE...SINCE E DEATH OF YOUR MOTHER, I HAVE LEARNED.
TO PUT AWAY SYMPATHY, LOVE.
TO BE... PRACTICAL.
YOU NEEDED A LOW POINT.
YOU NEEDED TO BE BROKEN.
AND NOW, SON, AFTER BANE, AFTER THE NIGHTMARES, AFTER HER.
I CAN SHOW YOU A WAY OUT. GIVE YOU LOVE AND SYMPATHY.
I CAN GIVE YOU WHAT YOU LOST. I CAN GIVE YOU A FAMILY.
I KNOW OUR DEATH STARTED YOU HERE, ON THIS PATH.
BUT WITH OUR RESURRECTION...
TOGETHER, YOUR MOTHER AND I, WE CAN GIVE YOU A LIFE WITHOUT A CAPE.

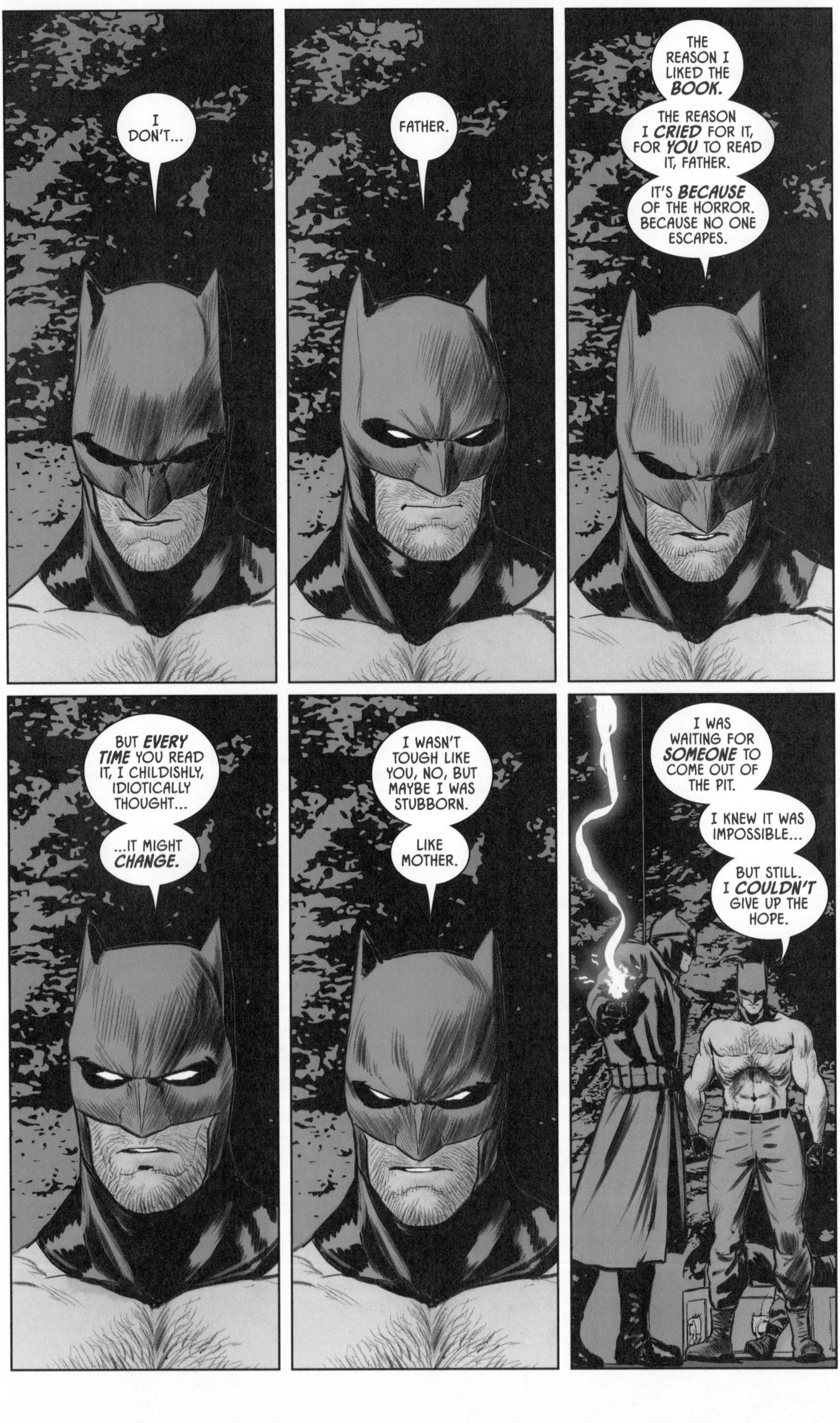
I DON'T...
FATHER.
THE REASON I LIKED THE BOOK.
THE REASON I CRIED FOR IT, FOR YOU TO READ IT, FATHER.
IT'S BECAUSE OF THE HORROR. BECAUSE NO ONE ESCAPES.
BUT EVERY TIME YOU READ IT, I CHILDISHLY, IDIOTICALLY THOUGHT...
...IT MIGHT CHANGE.
I WASN'T TOUGH LIKE YOU, NO, BUT MAYBE I WAS STUBBORN.
LIKE MOTHER.
I WAS WAITING FOR SOMEONE TO COME OUT OF THE PIT.
I KNEW IT WAS IMPOSSIBLE...
BUT STILL. I COULDN'T GIVE UP THE HOPE.

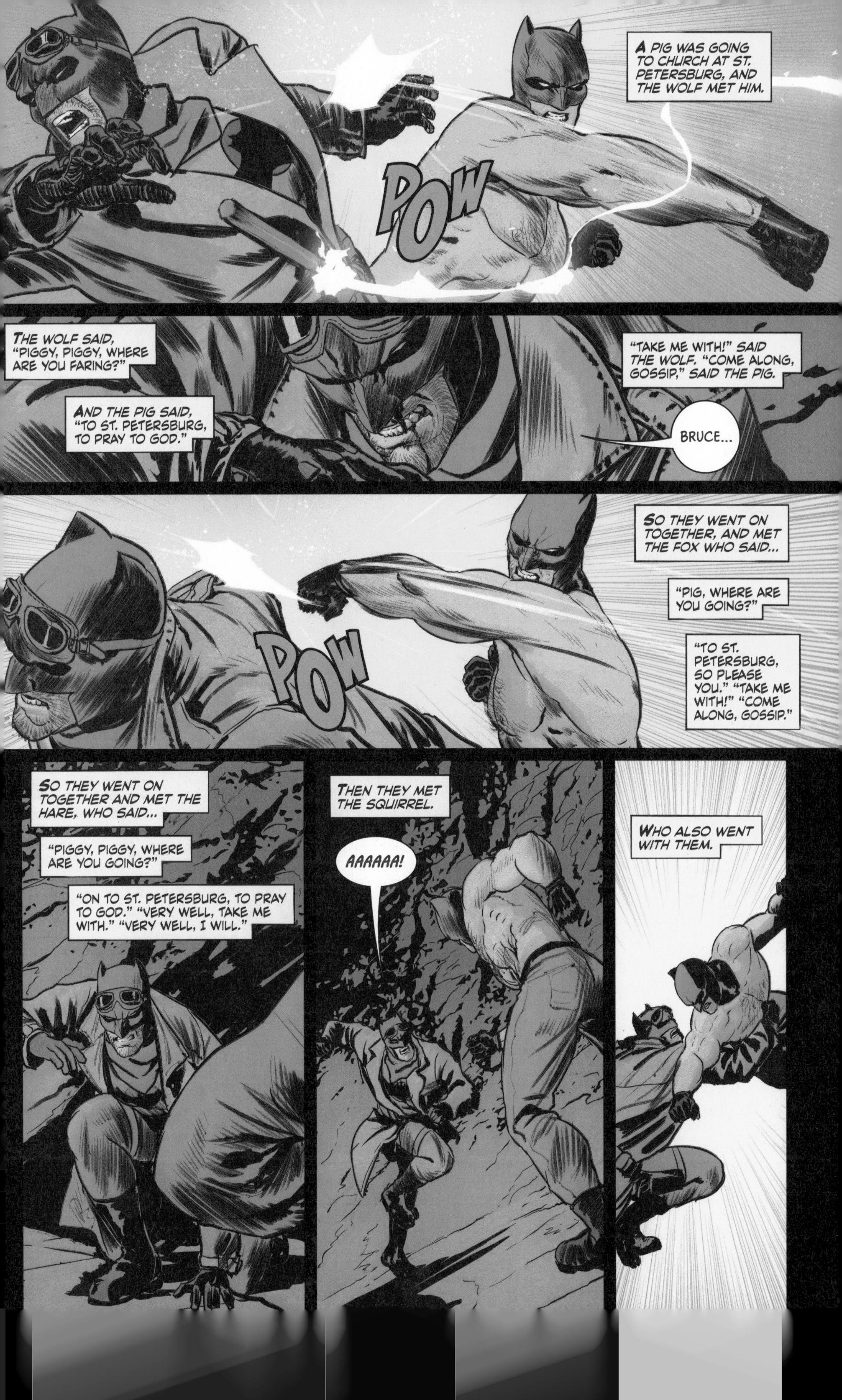
A PIG WAS GOING TO CHURCH AT ST. PETERSBURG, AND THE WOLF MET HIM.
POW
THE WOLF SAID, "PIGGY, PIGGY, WHERE ARE YOU FARING?"
AND THE PIG SAID, "TO ST. PETERSBURG, TO PRAY TO GOD."
"TAKE ME WITH!" SAID THE WOLF. "COME ALONG, GOSSIP," SAID THE PIG.
BRUCE...
SO THEY WENT ON TOGETHER, AND MET THE FOX WHO SAID...
"PIG, WHERE ARE YOU GOING?"
"TO ST. PETERSBURG, SO PLEASE YOU." "TAKE ME WITH!" "COME ALONG, GOSSIP."
POW
SO THEY WENT ON TOGETHER AND MET THE HARE, WHO SAID...
"PIGGY, PIGGY, WHERE ARE YOU GOING?"
"ON TO ST. PETERSBURG, TO PRAY TO GOD." "VERY WELL, TAKE ME WITH." "VERY WELL, I WILL."
THEN THEY MET THE SQUIRREL.
AAAAAA!
WHO ALSO WENT WITH THEM.

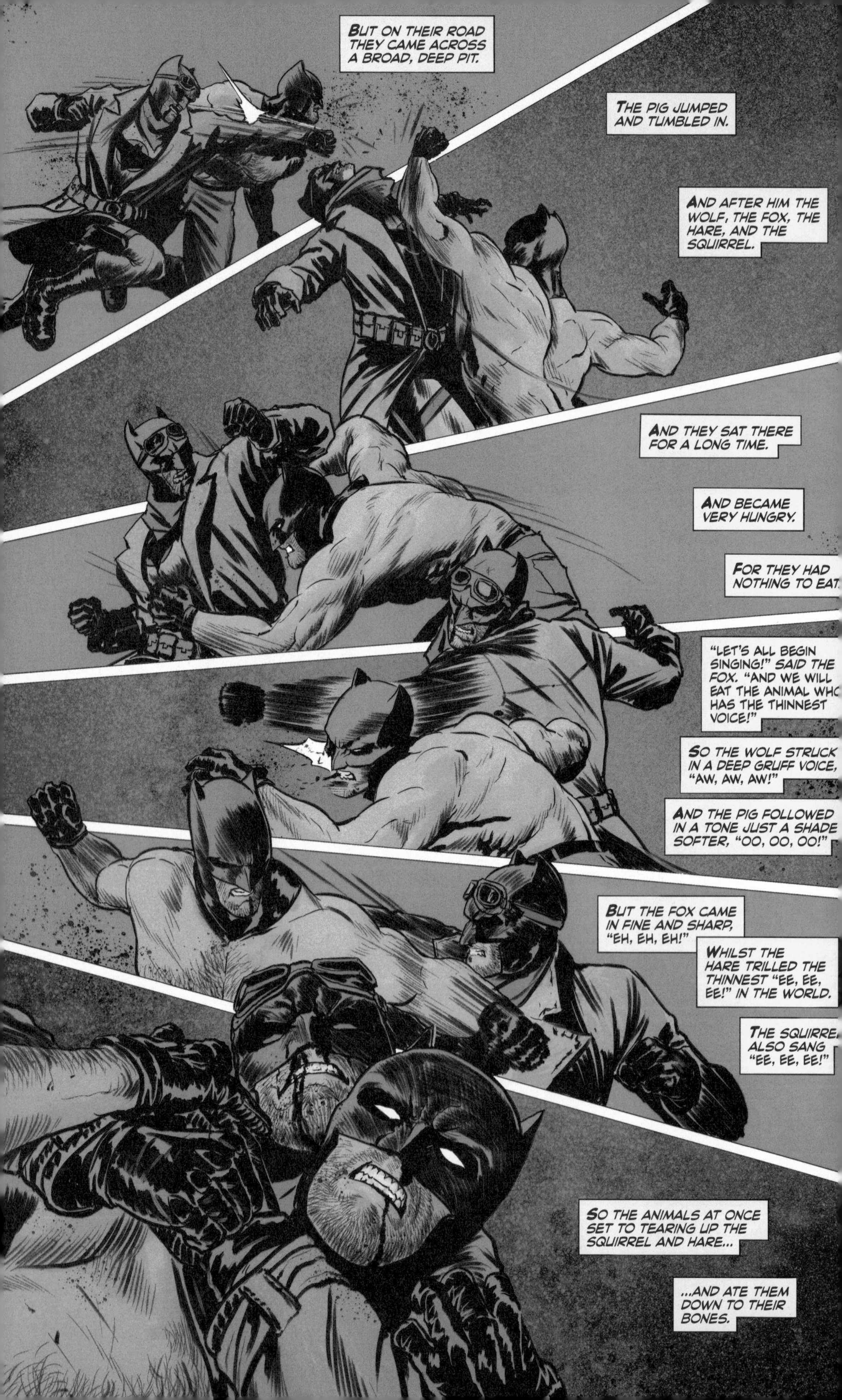
BUT ON THEIR ROAD THEY CAME ACROSS A BROAD, DEEP PIT.
THE PIG JUMPED AND TUMBLED IN.
AND AFTER HIM THE WOLF, THE FOX, THE HARE, AND THE SQUIRREL.
AND THEY SAT THERE FOR A LONG TIME.
AND BECAME VERY HUNGRY.
FOR THEY HAD NOTHING TO EAT.
"LET'S ALL BEGIN SINGING!" SAID THE FOX. "AND WE WILL EAT THE ANIMAL WHO HAS THE THINNEST VOICE!"
SO THE WOLF STRUCK IN A DEEP GRUFF VOICE, "AW, AW, AW!"
AND THE PIG FOLLOWED IN A TONE JUST A SHADE SOFTER, "OO, OO, OO!"
BUT THE FOX CAME IN FINE AND SHARP, "EH, EH, EH!"
WHILST THE HARE TRILLED THE THINNEST "EE, EE, EE!" IN THE WORLD.
THE SQUIRREL ALSO SANG "EE, EE, EE!"
SO THE ANIMALS AT ONCE SET TO TEARING UP THE SQUIRREL AND HARE...
...AND ATE THEM DOWN TO THEIR BONES.

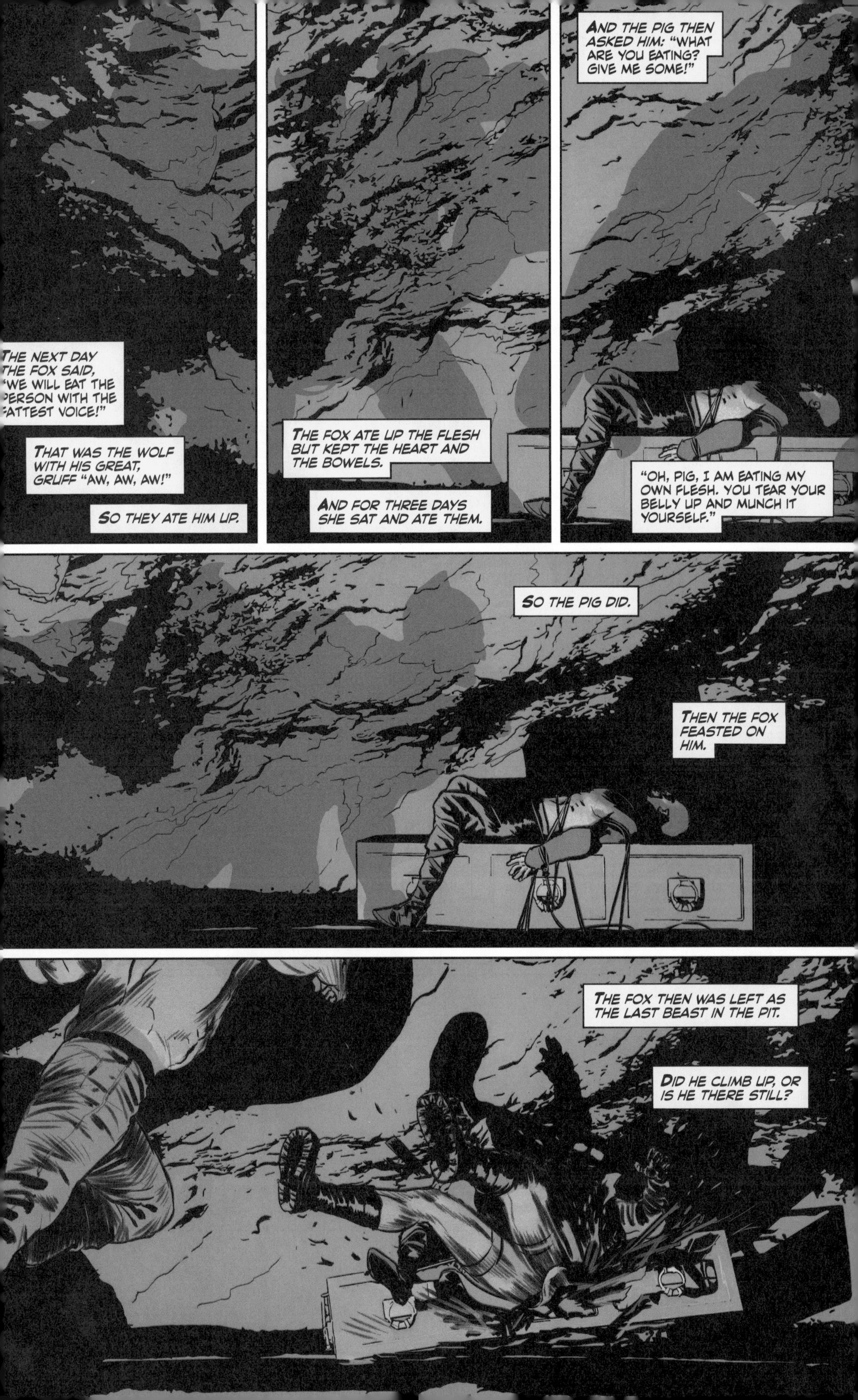
THE NEXT DAY THE FOX SAID, "WE WILL EAT THE PERSON WITH THE FATTEST VOICE!"
THAT WAS THE WOLF WITH HIS GREAT, GRUFF "AW, AW, AW!"
SO THEY ATE HIM UP.
THE FOX ATE UP THE FLESH BUT KEPT THE HEART AND THE BOWELS.
AND FOR THREE DAYS SHE SAT AND ATE THEM.
AND THE PIG THEN ASKED HIM: "WHAT ARE YOU EATING? GIVE ME SOME!"
"OH, PIG, I AM EATING MY OWN FLESH. YOU TEAR YOUR BELLY UP AND MUNCH IT YOURSELF."
SO THE PIG DID.
THEN THE FOX FEASTED ON HIM.
THE FOX THEN WAS LEFT AS THE LAST BEAST IN THE PIT.
DID HE CLIMB UP, OR IS HE THERE STILL?

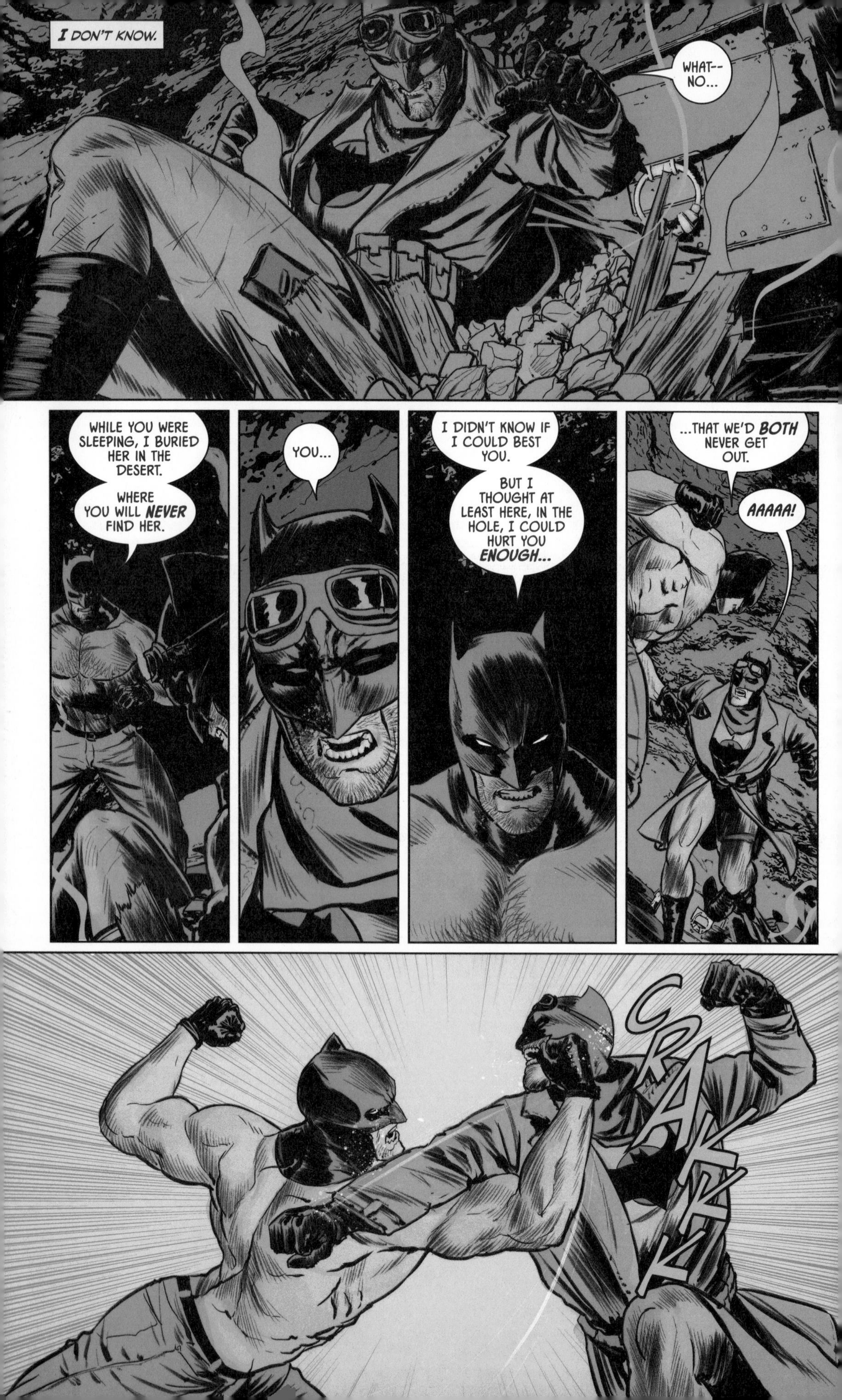
I DON'T KNOW.
WHAT-- NO...
WHILE YOU WERE SLEEPING, I BURIED HER IN THE DESERT.
WHERE YOU WILL NEVER FIND HER.
YOU...
I DIDN'T KNOW IF I COULD BEST YOU.
BUT I THOUGHT AT LEAST HERE, IN THE HOLE, I COULD HURT YOU ENOUGH...
...THAT WE'D BOTH NEVER GET OUT.
AAAAA!
CRAKKK

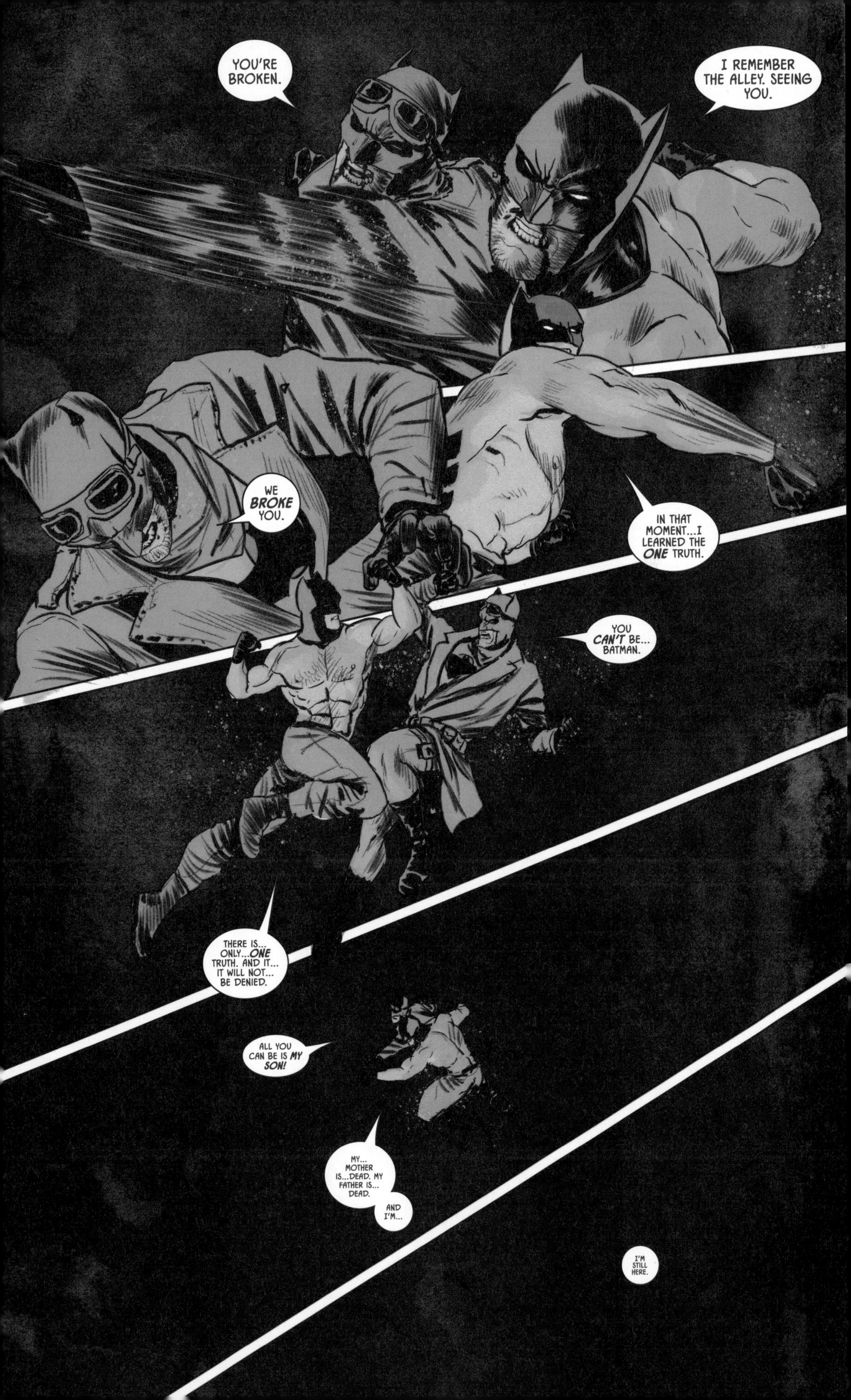
YOU'RE BROKEN.
I REMEMBER THE ALLEY. SEEING YOU.
WE BROKE YOU.
IN THAT MOMENT...I LEARNED THE ONE TRUTH.
YOU CAN'T BE... BATMAN.
THERE IS... ONLY...ONE TRUTH. AND IT... IT WILL NOT... BE DENIED.
ALL YOU CAN BE IS MY SON!
MY... MOTHER IS...DEAD. MY FATHER IS... DEAD.
AND I'M...
I'M STILL HERE.

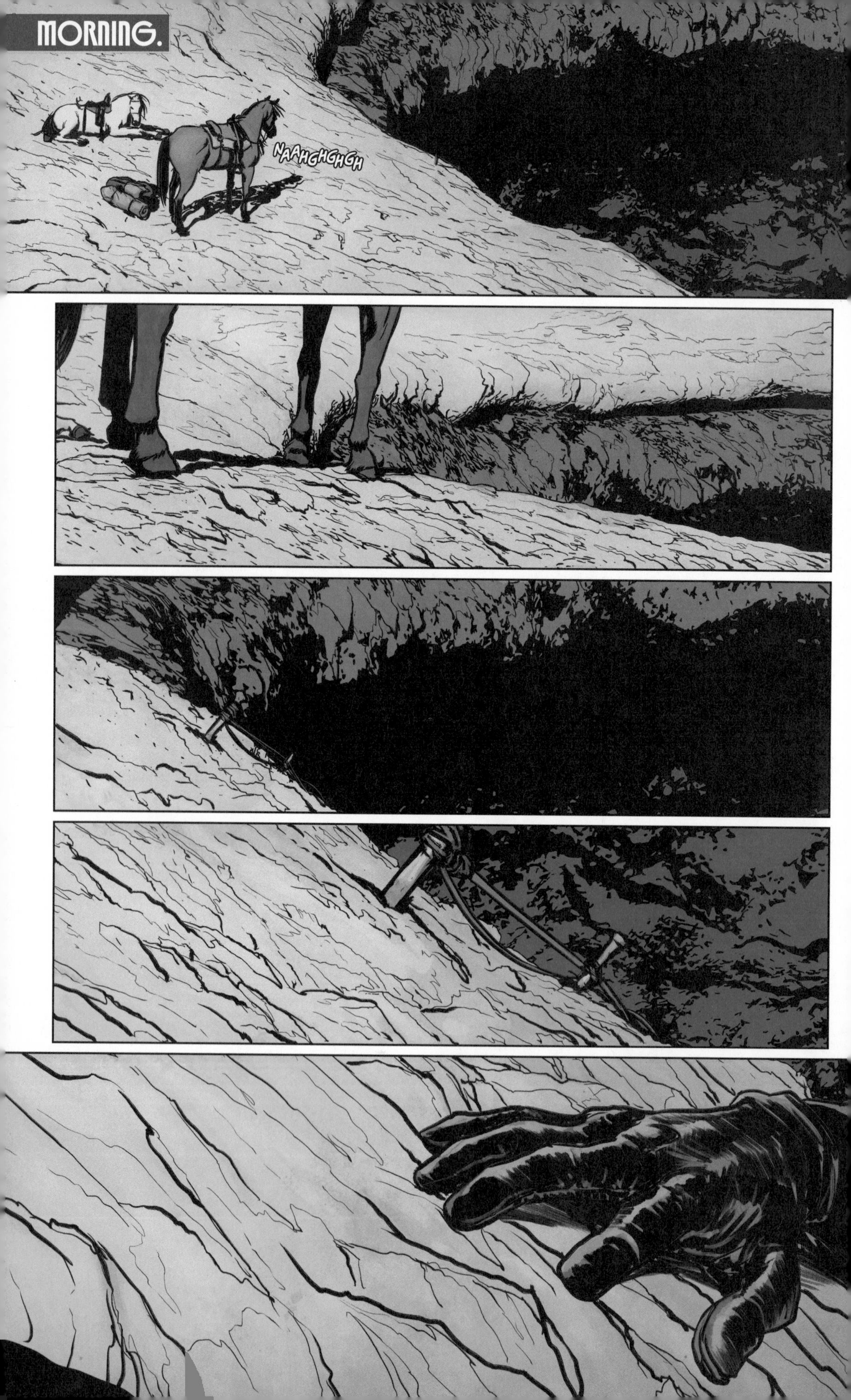
MORNING.
NAAHGHGHGH

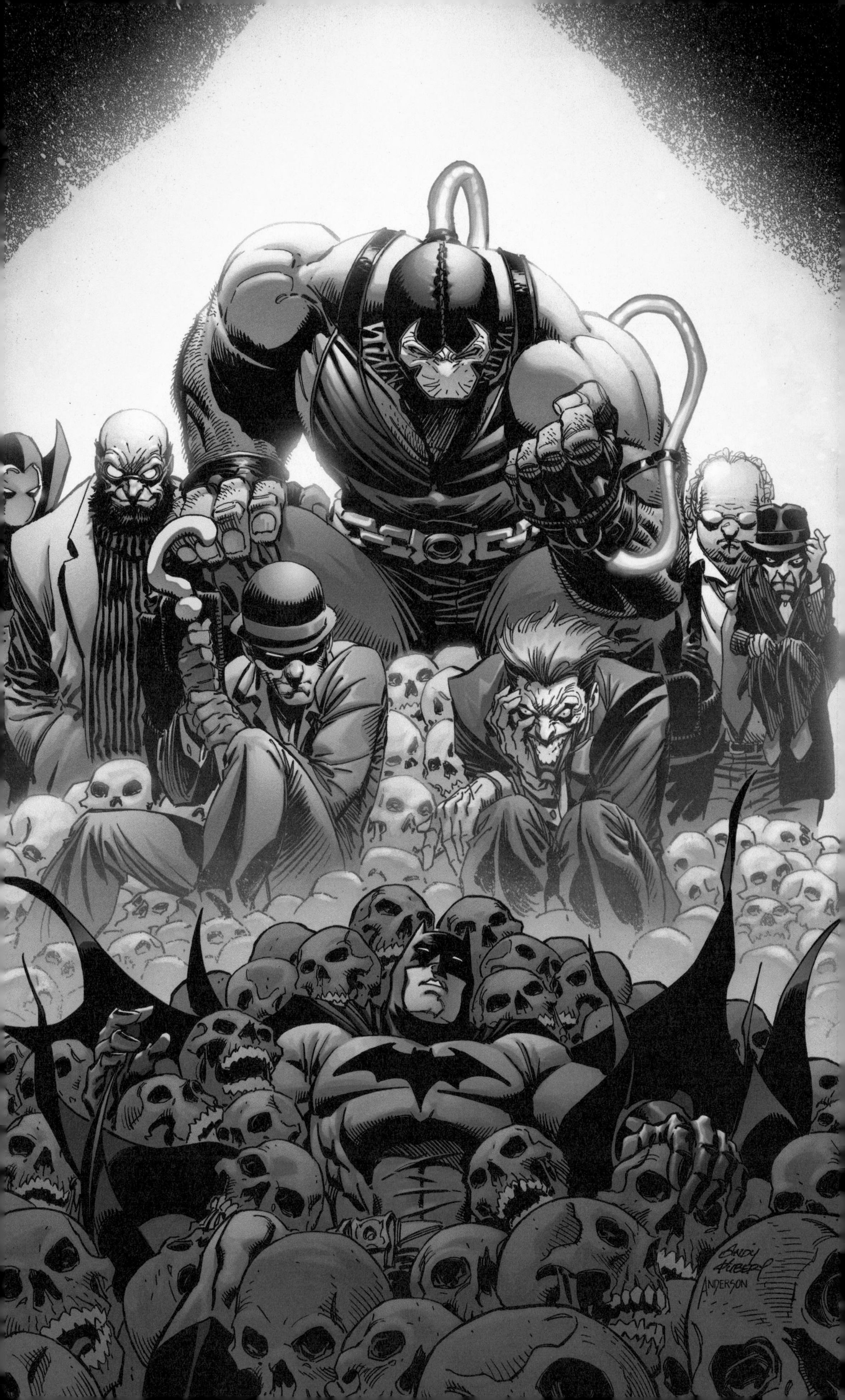
ANDY KUBERT
ANDERSON

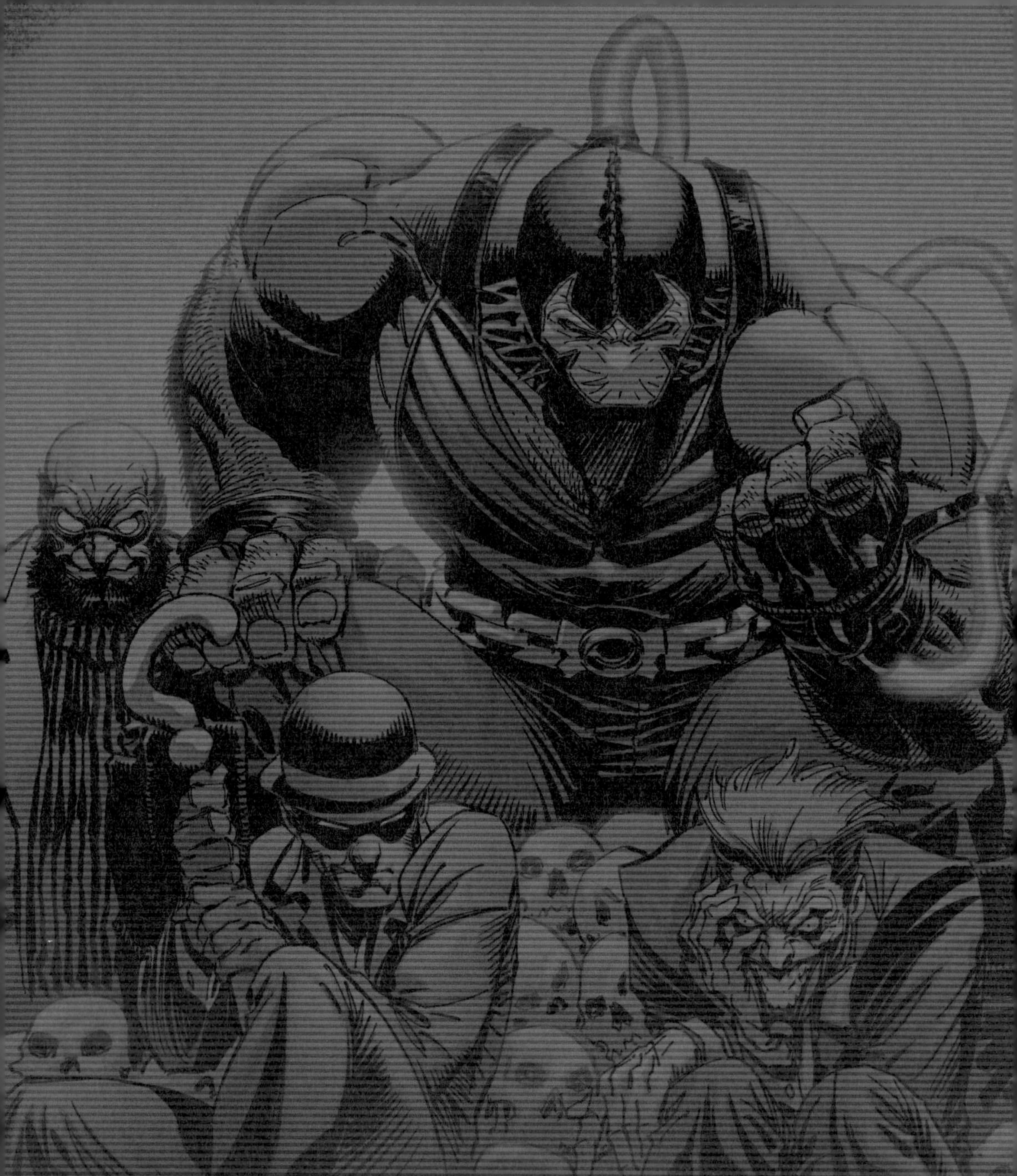

BATMAN
SECRET FILES #2

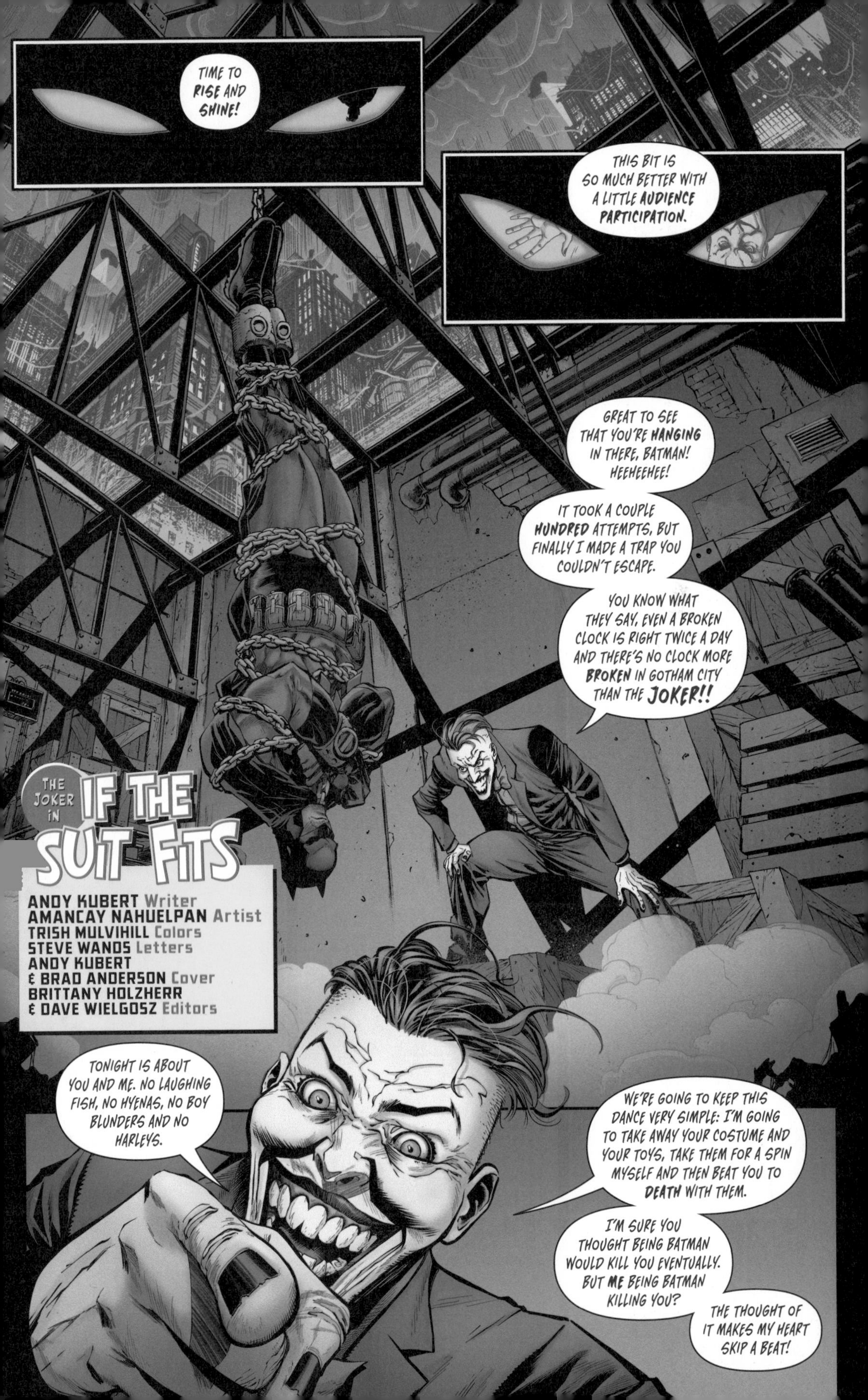

TIME TO RISE AND SHINE!
THIS BIT IS SO MUCH BETTER WITH A LITTLE AUDIENCE PARTICIPATION.
GREAT TO SEE THAT YOU'RE HANGING IN THERE, BATMAN! HEEHEEHEE!
IT TOOK A COUPLE HUNDRED ATTEMPTS, BUT FINALLY I MADE A TRAP YOU COULDN'T ESCAPE.
YOU KNOW WHAT THEY SAY, EVEN A BROKEN CLOCK IS RIGHT TWICE A DAY AND THERE'S NO CLOCK MORE BROKEN IN GOTHAM CITY THAN THE JOKER!!
THE JOKER in IF THE SUIT FITS
ANDY KUBERT Writer
AMANCAY NAHUELPAN Artist
TRISH MULVIHILL Colors
STEVE WANDS Letters
ANDY KUBERT & BRAD ANDERSON Cover
BRITTANY HOLZHERR & DAVE WIELGOSZ Editors
TONIGHT IS ABOUT YOU AND ME. NO LAUGHING FISH, NO HYENAS, NO BOY BLUNDERS AND NO HARLEYS.
WE'RE GOING TO KEEP THIS DANCE VERY SIMPLE: I'M GOING TO TAKE AWAY YOUR COSTUME AND YOUR TOYS, TAKE THEM FOR A SPIN MYSELF AND THEN BEAT YOU TO DEATH WITH THEM.
I'M SURE YOU THOUGHT BEING BATMAN WOULD KILL YOU EVENTUALLY. BUT ME BEING BATMAN KILLING YOU?
THE THOUGHT OF IT MAKES MY HEART SKIP A BEAT!

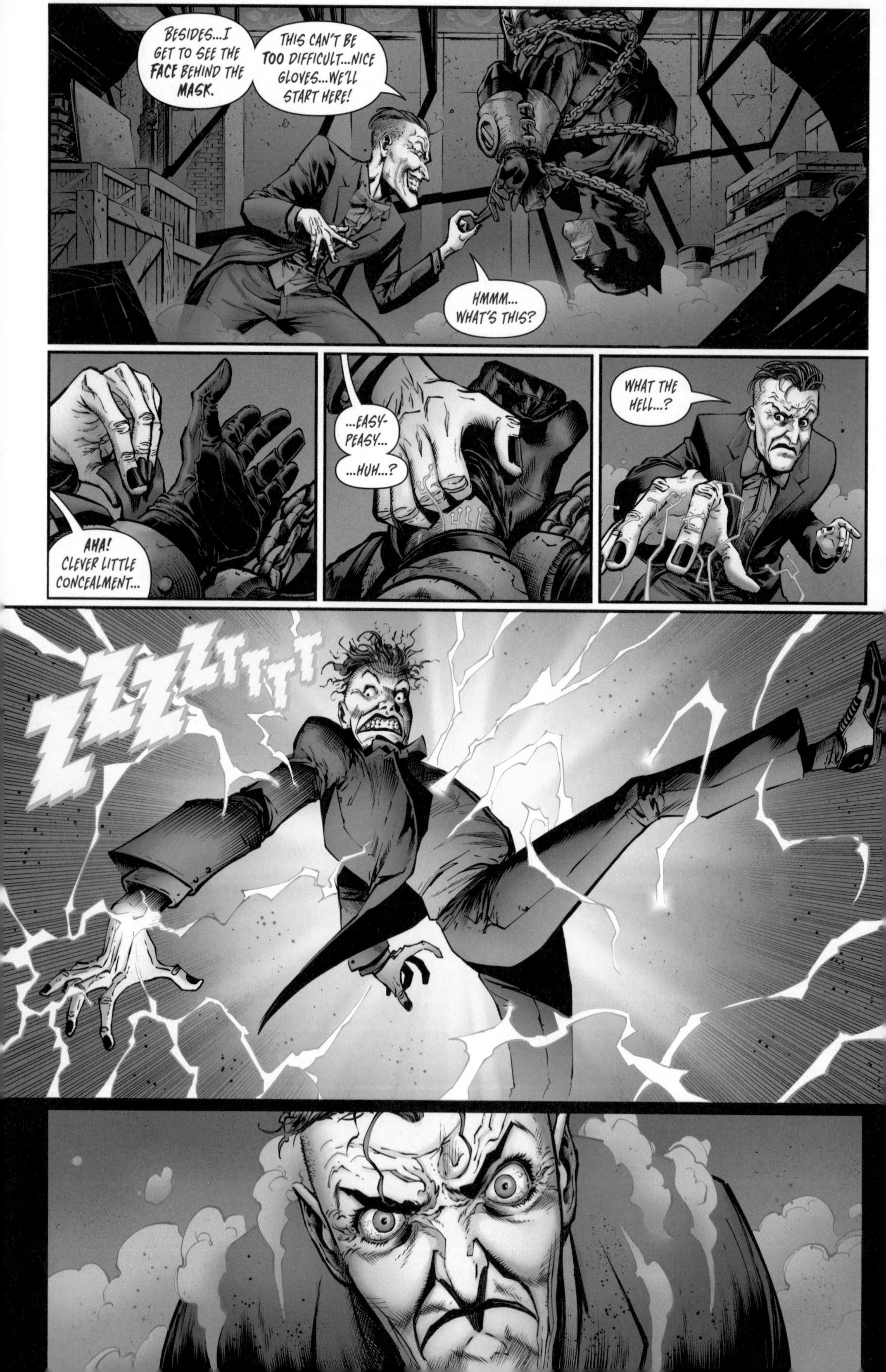
BESIDES...I GET TO SEE THE FACE BEHIND THE MASK.
THIS CAN'T BE TOO DIFFICULT...NICE GLOVES...WE'LL START HERE!
HMMM... WHAT'S THIS?
AHA! CLEVER LITTLE CONCEALMENT...
...EASY-PEASY...
...HUH...?
WHAT THE HELL...?
ZZZZTTTTT

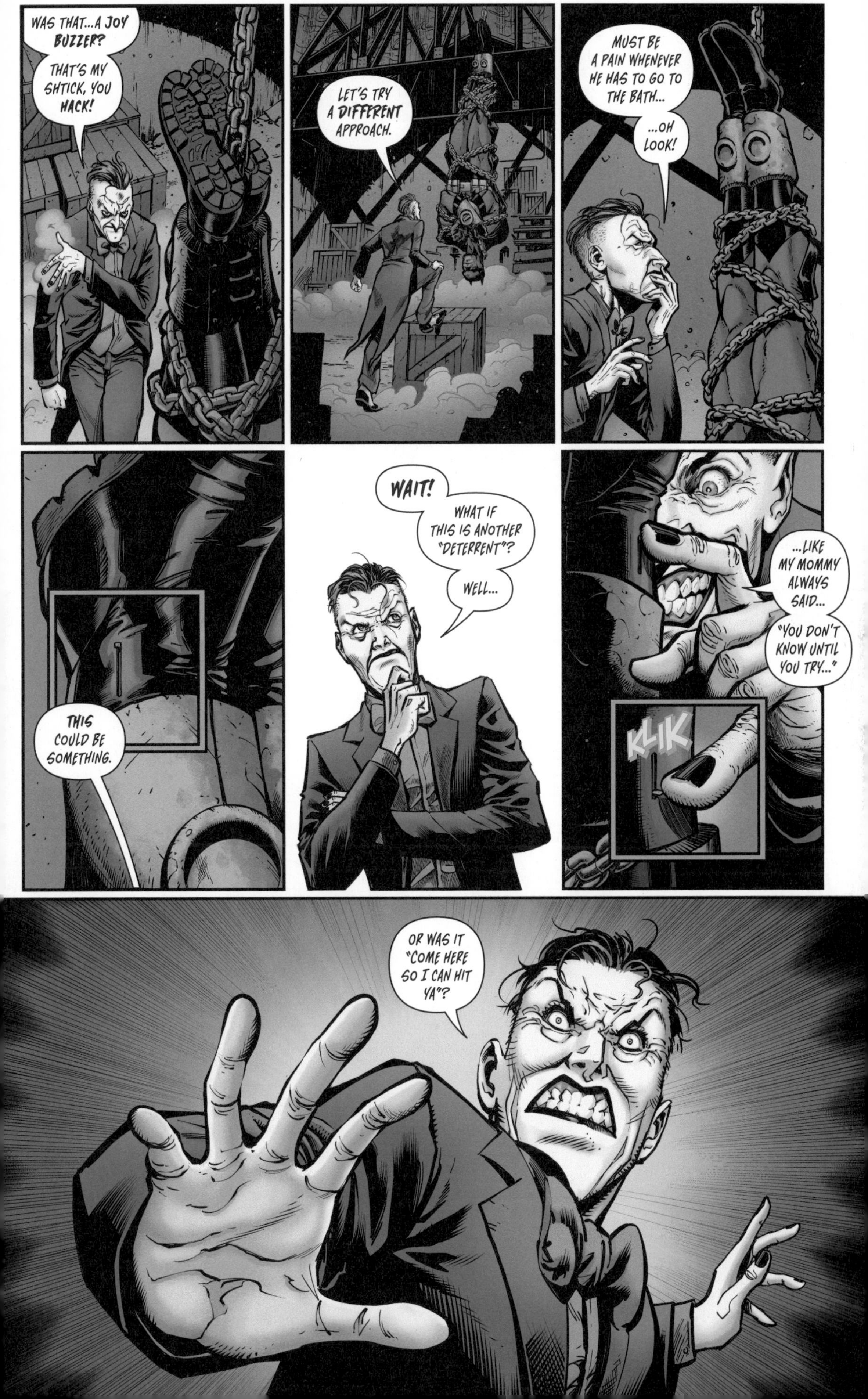
WAS THAT...A JOY BUZZER?
THAT'S MY SHTICK, YOU HACK!
LET'S TRY A DIFFERENT APPROACH.
MUST BE A PAIN WHENEVER HE HAS TO GO TO THE BATH...
...OH LOOK!
THIS COULD BE SOMETHING.
WAIT!
WHAT IF THIS IS ANOTHER "DETERRENT"?
WELL...
...LIKE MY MOMMY ALWAYS SAID...
"YOU DON'T KNOW UNTIL YOU TRY..."
KLIK
OR WAS IT "COME HERE SO I CAN HIT YA"?

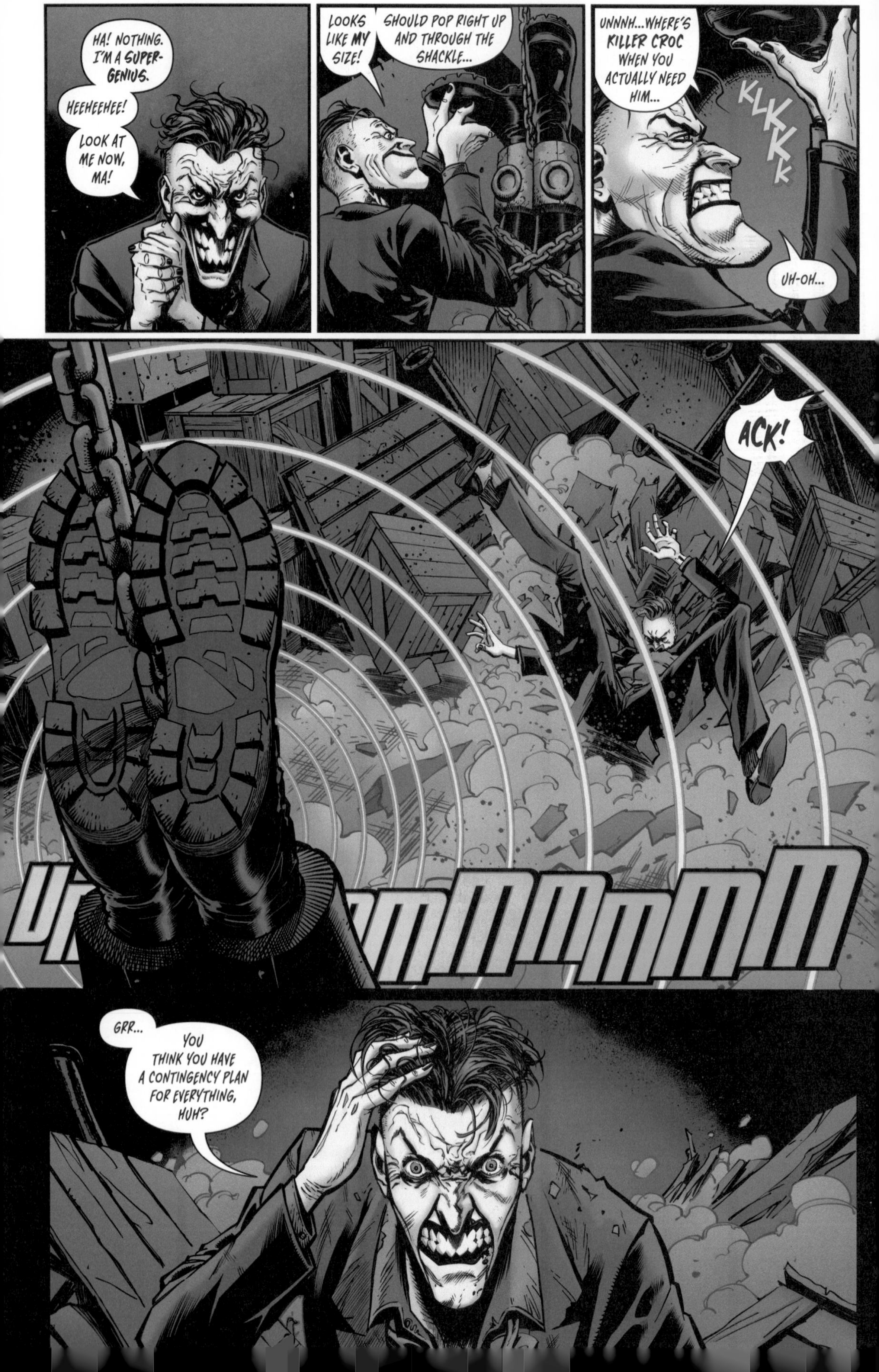
HA! NOTHING. I'M A SUPER-GENIUS.
HEEHEEHEE!
LOOK AT ME NOW, MA!
LOOKS LIKE MY SIZE!
SHOULD POP RIGHT UP AND THROUGH THE SHACKLE...
UNNNH...WHERE'S KILLER CROC WHEN YOU ACTUALLY NEED HIM...
UH-OH...
ACK!
GRR...
YOU THINK YOU HAVE A CONTINGENCY PLAN FOR EVERYTHING, HUH?

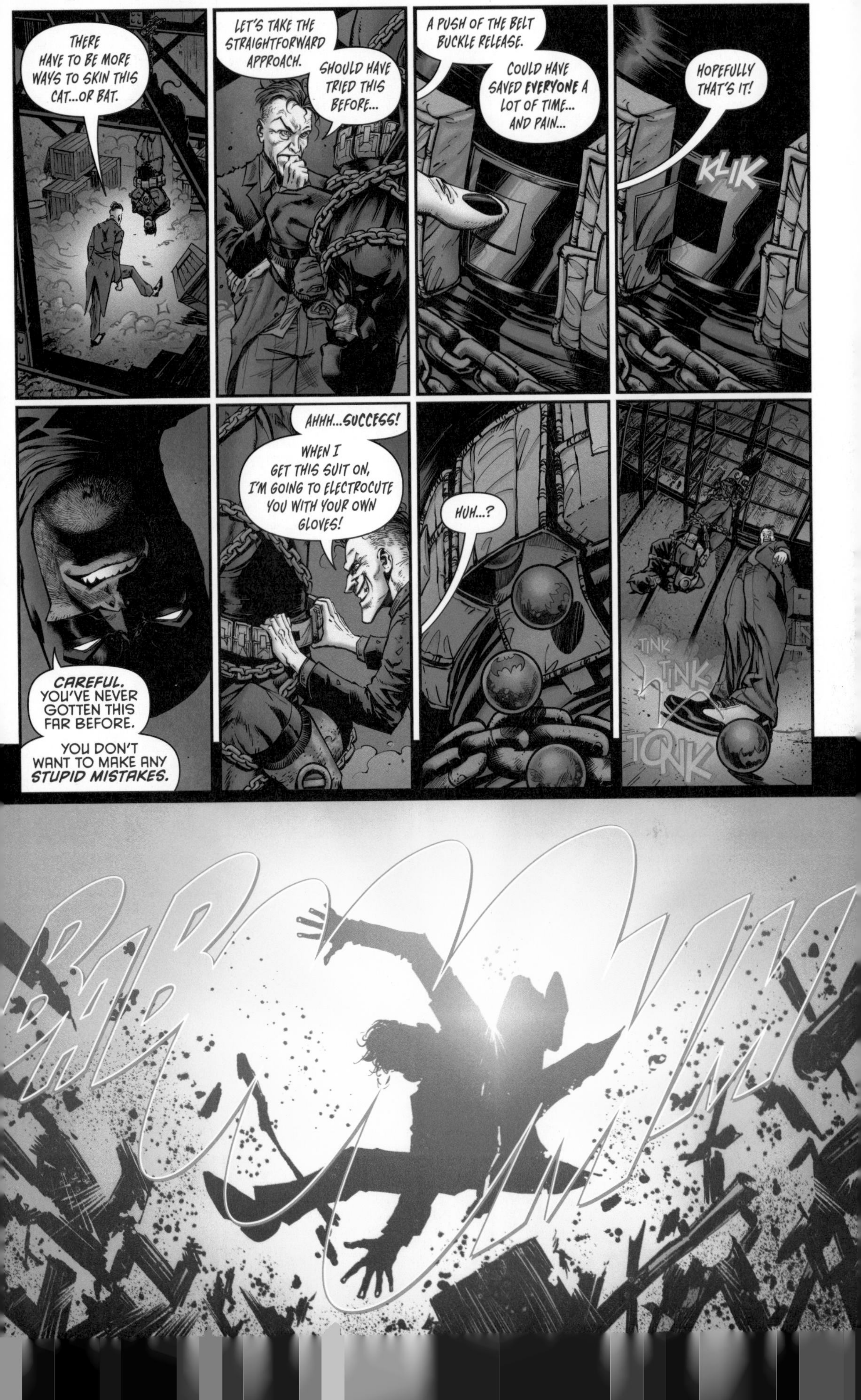
THERE HAVE TO BE MORE WAYS TO SKIN THIS CAT...OR BAT.
LET'S TAKE THE STRAIGHTFORWARD APPROACH.
SHOULD HAVE TRIED THIS BEFORE...
A PUSH OF THE BELT BUCKLE RELEASE.
COULD HAVE SAVED EVERYONE A LOT OF TIME... AND PAIN...
HOPEFULLY THAT'S IT!
KLIK
CAREFUL. YOU'VE NEVER GOTTEN THIS FAR BEFORE.
YOU DON'T WANT TO MAKE ANY STUPID MISTAKES.
AHHH...SUCCESS!
WHEN I GET THIS SUIT ON, I'M GOING TO ELECTROCUTE YOU WITH YOUR OWN GLOVES!
HUH...?
TINK
TINK
TONK
BBOOOM

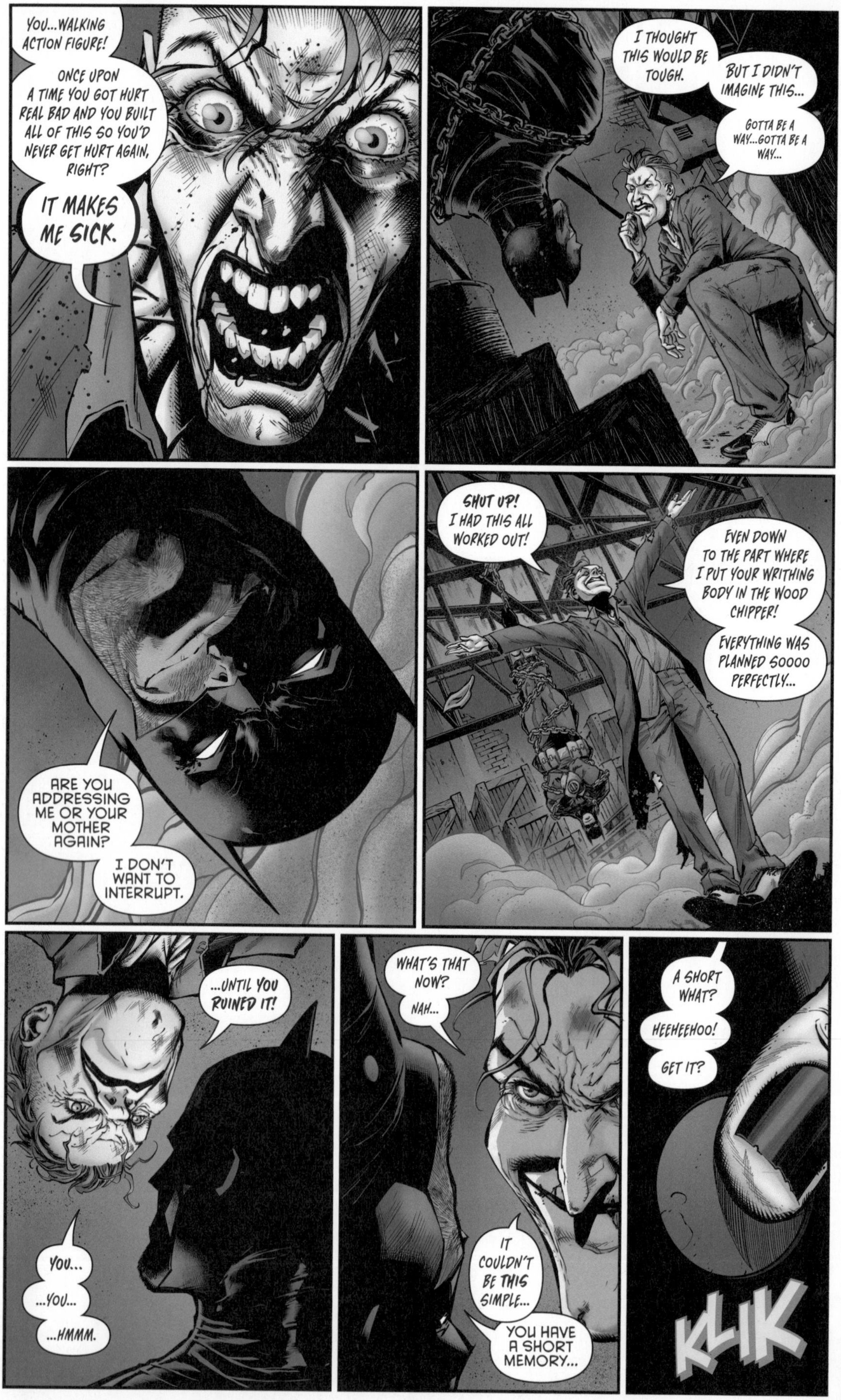

YOU...WALKING ACTION FIGURE!
ONCE UPON A TIME YOU GOT HURT REAL BAD AND YOU BUILT ALL OF THIS SO YOU'D NEVER GET HURT AGAIN, RIGHT?
IT MAKES ME SICK.
I THOUGHT THIS WOULD BE TOUGH.
BUT I DIDN'T IMAGINE THIS...
GOTTA BE A WAY...GOTTA BE A WAY...
ARE YOU ADDRESSING ME OR YOUR MOTHER AGAIN?
I DON'T WANT TO INTERRUPT.
SHUT UP! I HAD THIS ALL WORKED OUT!
EVEN DOWN TO THE PART WHERE I PUT YOUR WRITHING BODY IN THE WOOD CHIPPER!
EVERYTHING WAS PLANNED SOOOO PERFECTLY...
...UNTIL YOU RUINED IT!
YOU...
...YOU...
...HMMM.
WHAT'S THAT NOW?
NAH...
IT COULDN'T BE THIS SIMPLE...
YOU HAVE A SHORT MEMORY...
A SHORT WHAT?
HEEHEEHOO!
GET IT?
KLIK

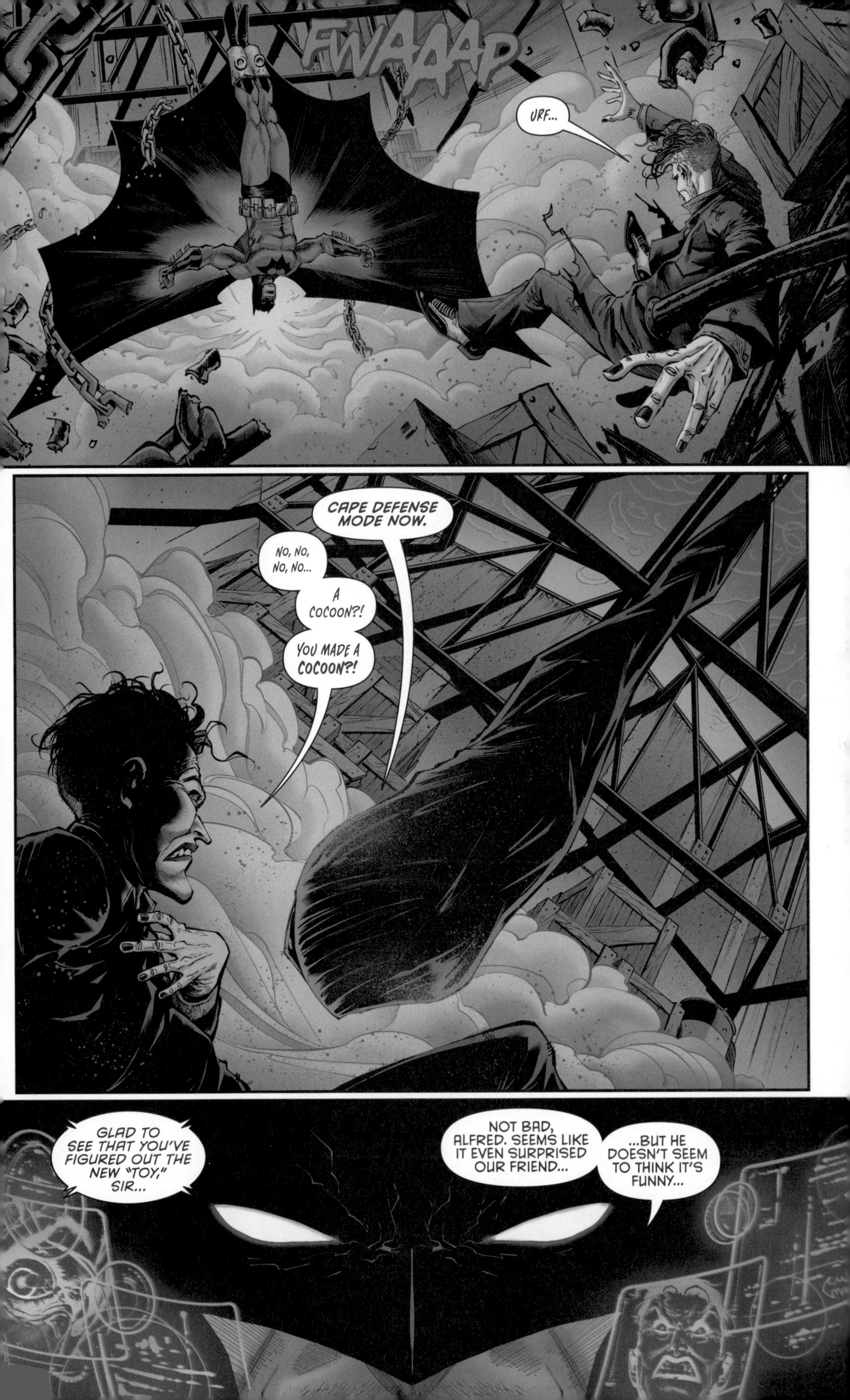
FWAAAP
URF...
CAPE DEFENSE MODE NOW.
NO, NO, NO, NO...
A COCOON?!
YOU MADE A COCOON?!
GLAD TO SEE THAT YOU'VE FIGURED OUT THE NEW "TOY," SIR...
NOT BAD, ALFRED. SEEMS LIKE IT EVEN SURPRISED OUR FRIEND...
...BUT HE DOESN'T SEEM TO THINK IT'S FUNNY...

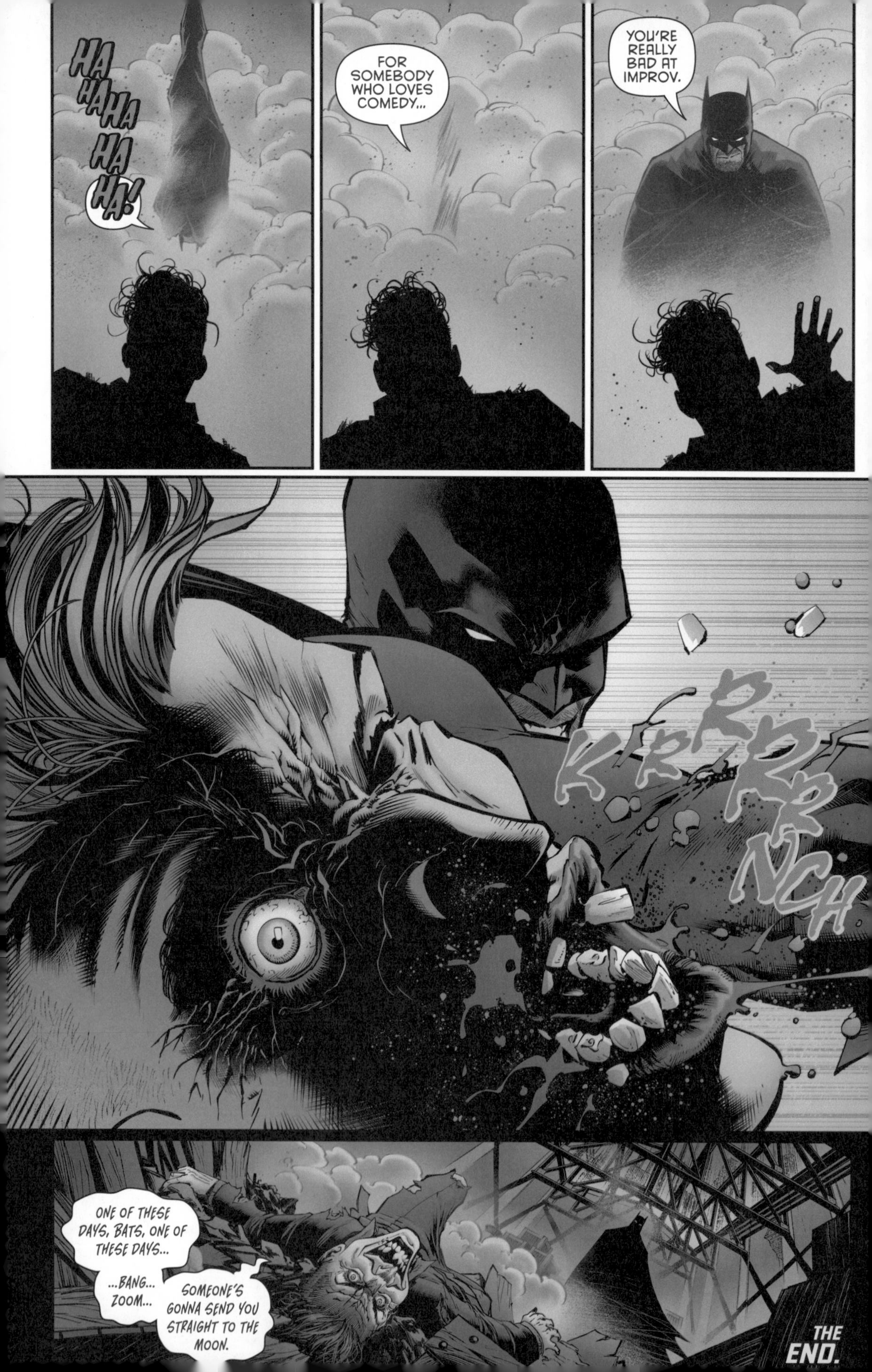

HA HAHA HAHA HA HA!
FOR SOMEBODY WHO LOVES COMEDY...
YOU'RE REALLY BAD AT IMPROV.
KRRRRNCH
ONE OF THESE DAYS, BATS, ONE OF THESE DAYS...
...BANG... ZOOM...
SOMEONE'S GONNA SEND YOU STRAIGHT TO THE MOON.
THE END.

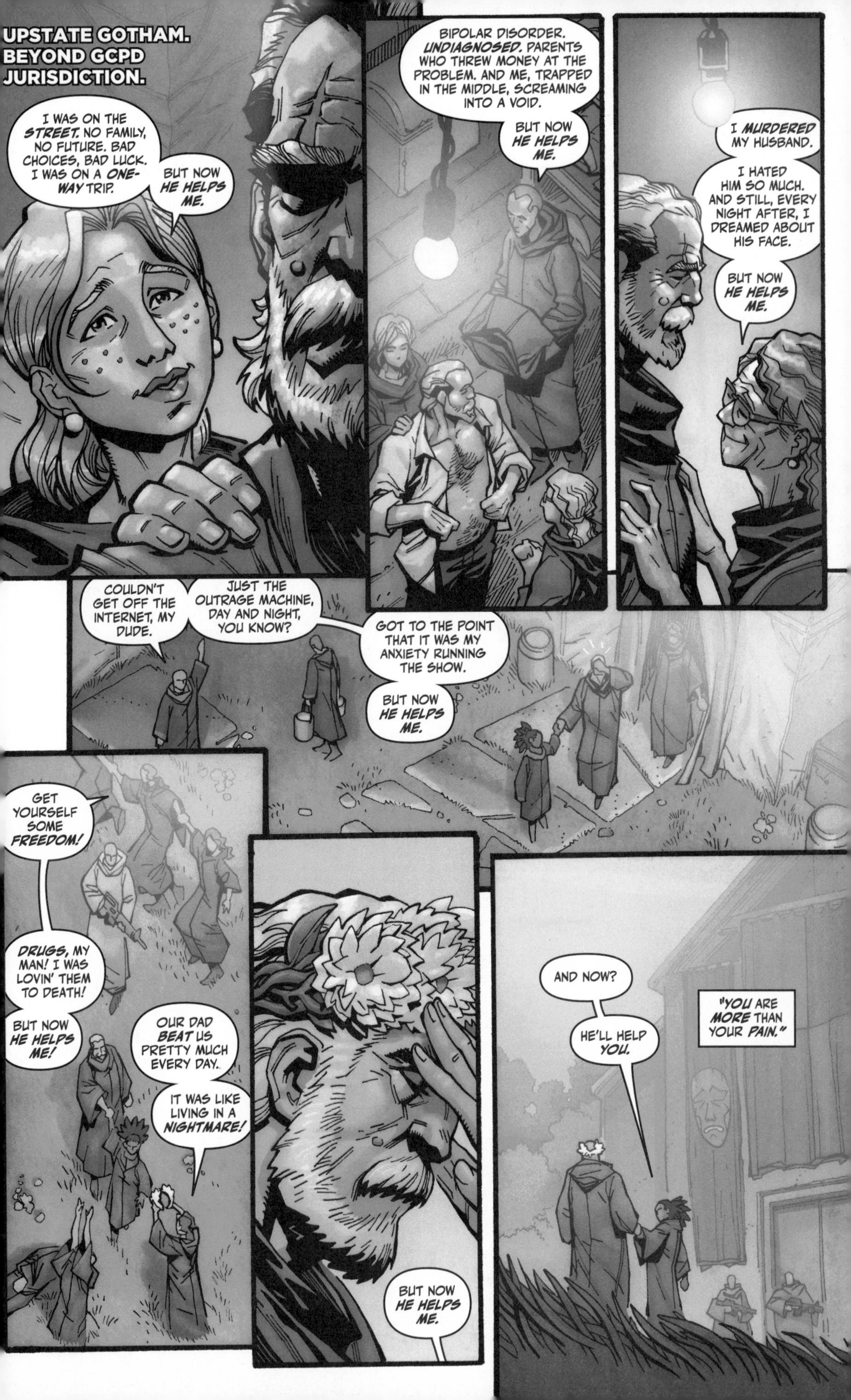
UPSTATE GOTHAM. BEYOND GCPD JURISDICTION.
I WAS ON THE STREET. NO FAMILY, NO FUTURE. BAD CHOICES, BAD LUCK. I WAS ON A ONE-WAY TRIP.
BUT NOW HE HELPS ME.
BIPOLAR DISORDER. UNDIAGNOSED. PARENTS WHO THREW MONEY AT THE PROBLEM. AND ME, TRAPPED IN THE MIDDLE, SCREAMING INTO A VOID.
BUT NOW HE HELPS ME.
I MURDERED MY HUSBAND.
I HATED HIM SO MUCH. AND STILL, EVERY NIGHT AFTER, I DREAMED ABOUT HIS FACE.
BUT NOW HE HELPS ME.
COULDN'T GET OFF THE INTERNET, MY DUDE.
JUST THE OUTRAGE MACHINE, DAY AND NIGHT, YOU KNOW?
GOT TO THE POINT THAT IT WAS MY ANXIETY RUNNING THE SHOW.
BUT NOW HE HELPS ME.
GET YOURSELF SOME FREEDOM!
DRUGS, MY MAN! I WAS LOVIN' THEM TO DEATH!
BUT NOW HE HELPS ME!
OUR DAD BEAT US PRETTY MUCH EVERY DAY.
IT WAS LIKE LIVING IN A NIGHTMARE!
BUT NOW HE HELPS ME.
AND NOW?
HE'LL HELP YOU.
"YOU ARE MORE THAN YOUR PAIN."

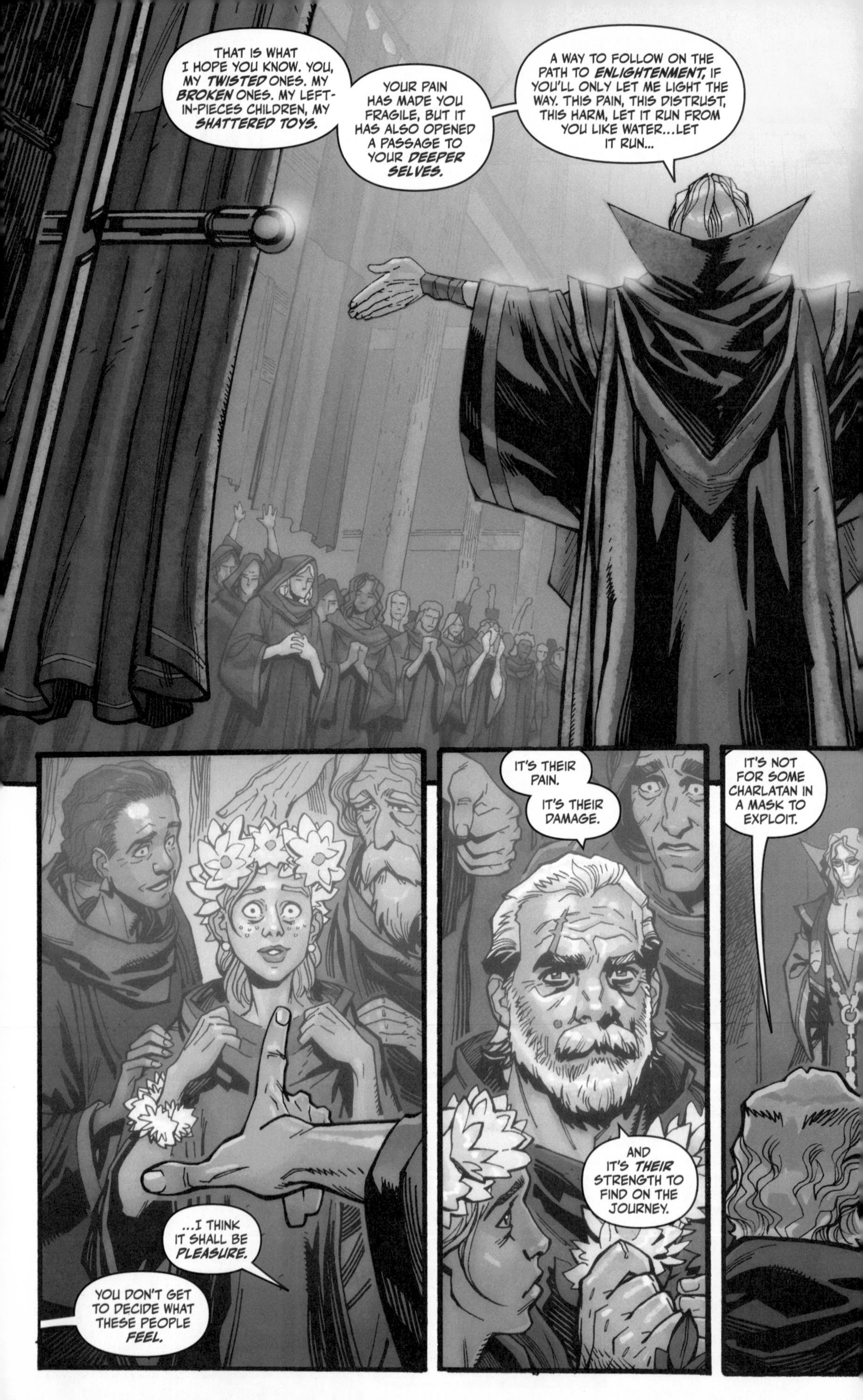
THAT IS WHAT I HOPE YOU KNOW. YOU, MY TWISTED ONES. MY BROKEN ONES. MY LEFT-IN-PIECES CHILDREN, MY SHATTERED TOYS.
YOUR PAIN HAS MADE YOU FRAGILE, BUT IT HAS ALSO OPENED A PASSAGE TO YOUR DEEPER SELVES.
A WAY TO FOLLOW ON THE PATH TO ENLIGHTENMENT, IF YOU'LL ONLY LET ME LIGHT THE WAY. THIS PAIN, THIS DISTRUST, THIS HARM, LET IT RUN FROM YOU LIKE WATER...LET IT RUN...
...I THINK IT SHALL BE PLEASURE.
YOU DON'T GET TO DECIDE WHAT THESE PEOPLE FEEL.
IT'S THEIR PAIN.
IT'S THEIR DAMAGE.
AND IT'S THEIR STRENGTH TO FIND ON THE JOURNEY.
IT'S NOT FOR SOME CHARLATAN IN A MASK TO EXPLOIT.

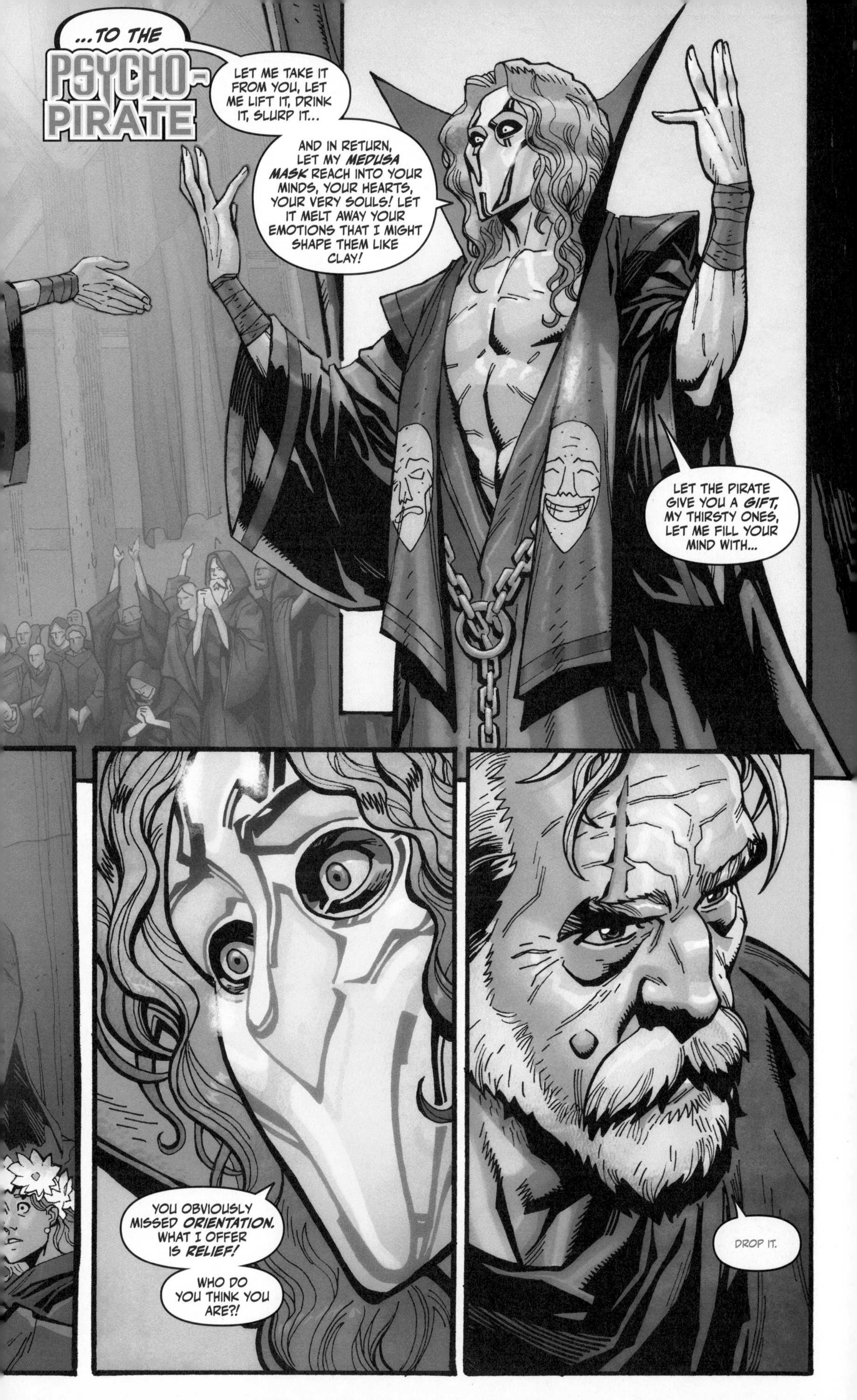
...TO THE PSYCHO-PIRATE
LET ME TAKE IT FROM YOU, LET ME LIFT IT, DRINK IT, SLURP IT...
AND IN RETURN, LET MY MEDUSA MASK REACH INTO YOUR MINDS, YOUR HEARTS, YOUR VERY SOULS! LET IT MELT AWAY YOUR EMOTIONS THAT I MIGHT SHAPE THEM LIKE CLAY!
LET THE PIRATE GIVE YOU A GIFT, MY THIRSTY ONES, LET ME FILL YOUR MIND WITH...
YOU OBVIOUSLY MISSED ORIENTATION. WHAT I OFFER IS RELIEF!
WHO DO YOU THINK YOU ARE?!
DROP IT.

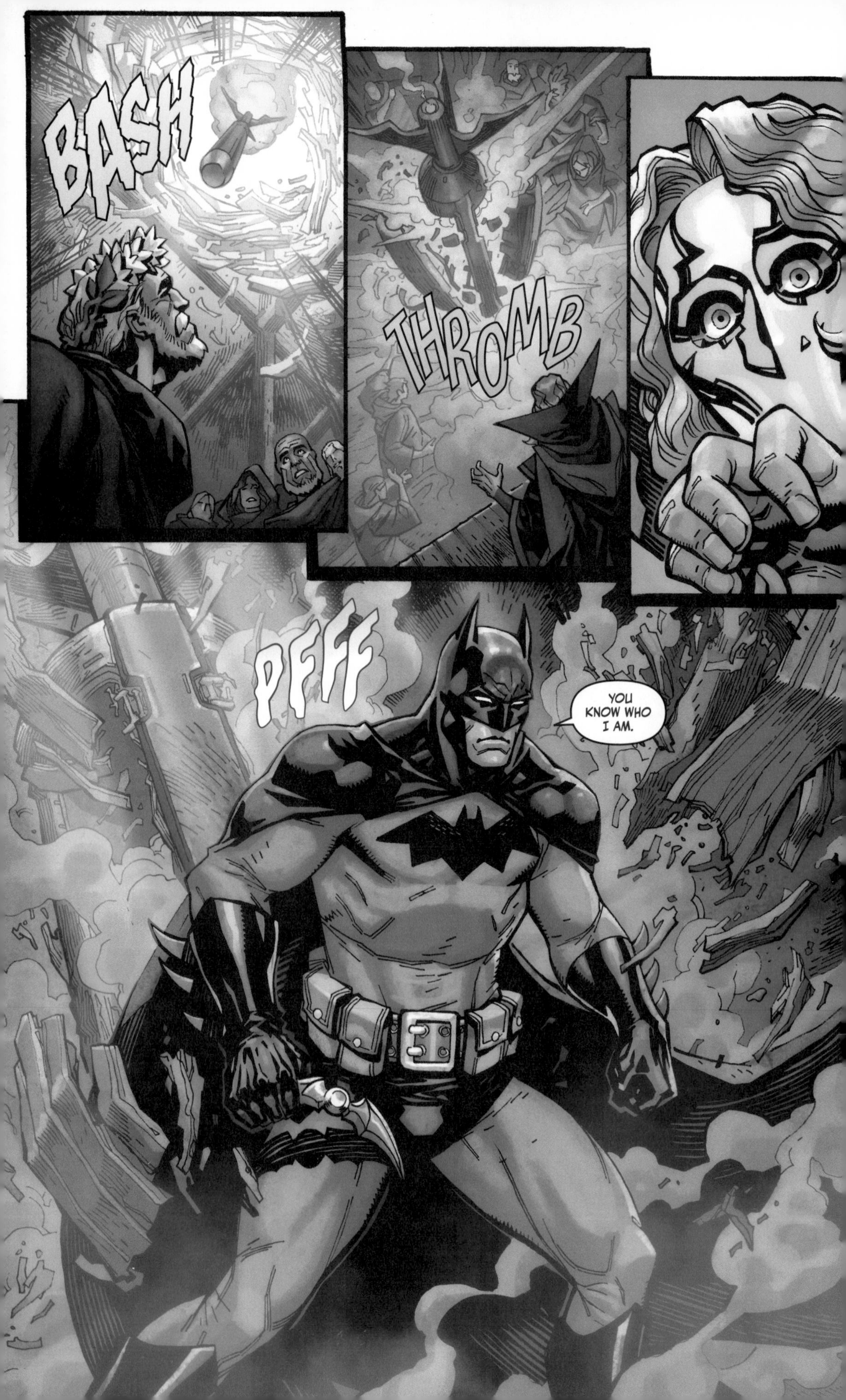
BASH
THROMB
PFFF
YOU KNOW WHO I AM.

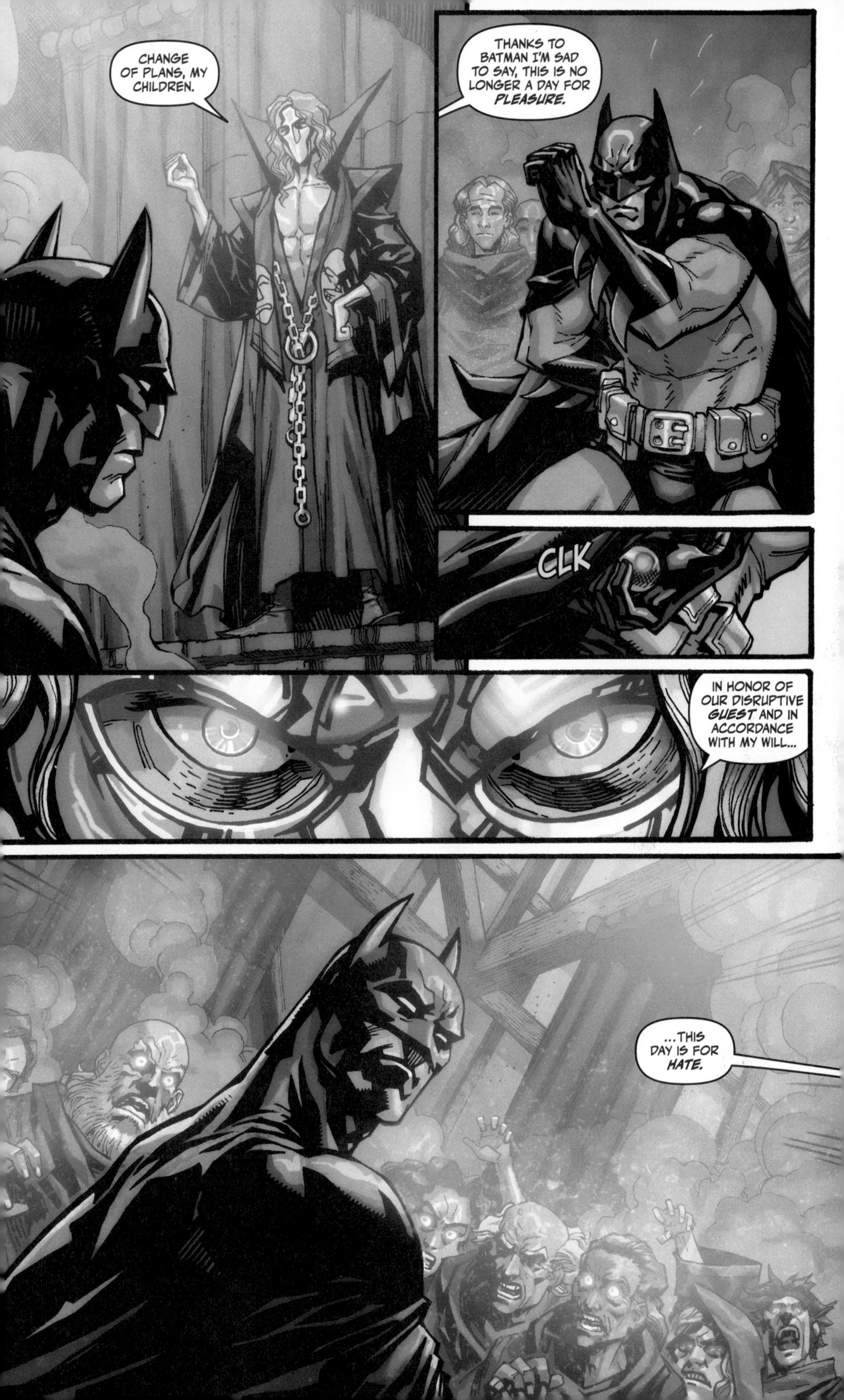
CHANGE OF PLANS, MY CHILDREN.
THANKS TO BATMAN I'M SAD TO SAY, THIS IS NO LONGER A DAY FOR PLEASURE.
CLK
IN HONOR OF OUR DISRUPTIVE GUEST AND IN ACCORDANCE WITH MY WILL...
...THIS DAY IS FOR HATE.

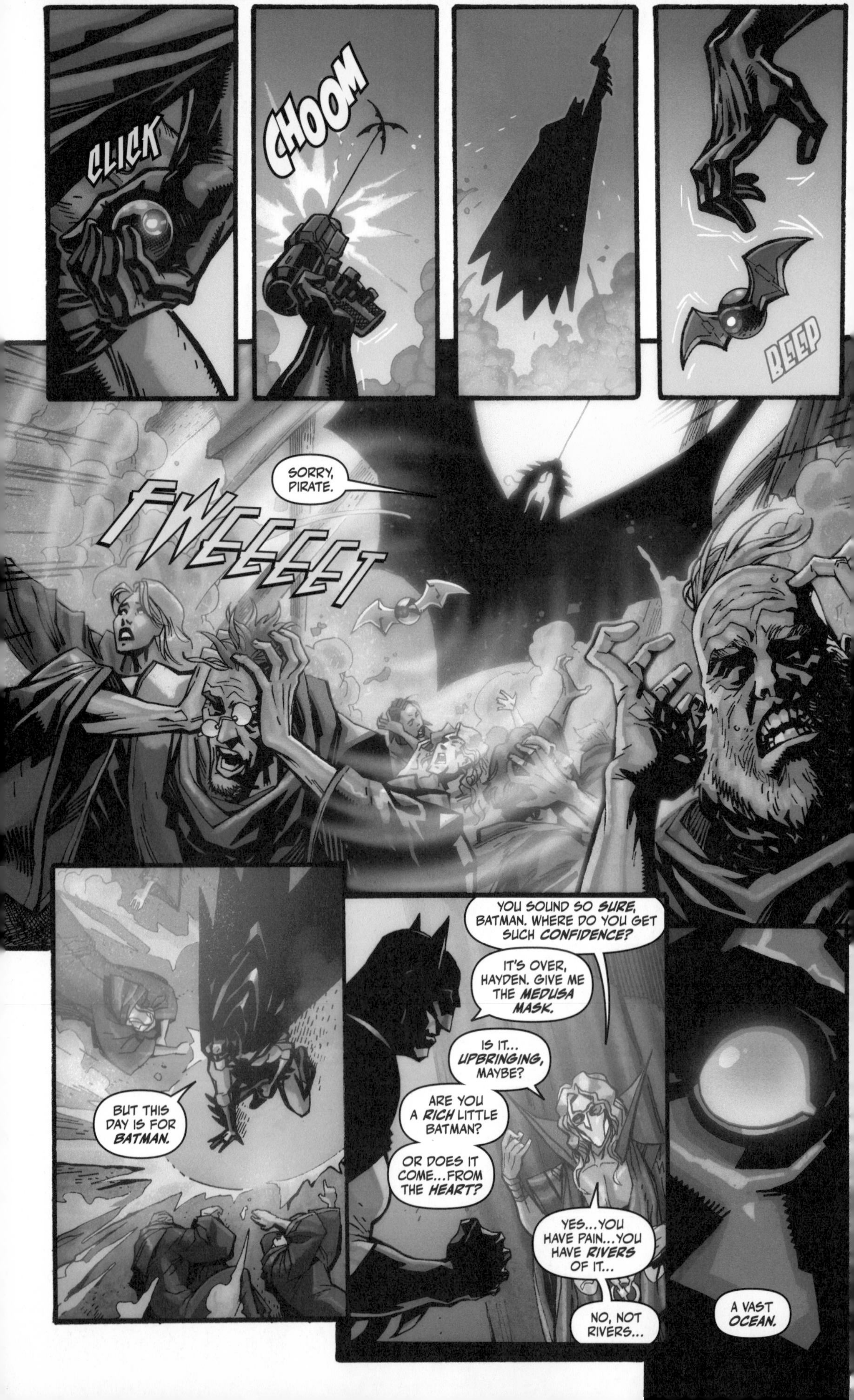
CLICK
CHOOM
BEEP
SORRY, PIRATE.
FWEEEEET
BUT THIS DAY IS FOR BATMAN.
YOU SOUND SO SURE, BATMAN. WHERE DO YOU GET SUCH CONFIDENCE?
IT'S OVER, HAYDEN. GIVE ME THE MEDUSA MASK.
IS IT... UPBRINGING, MAYBE?
ARE YOU A RICH LITTLE BATMAN?
OR DOES IT COME...FROM THE HEART?
YES...YOU HAVE PAIN...YOU HAVE RIVERS OF IT...
NO, NOT RIVERS...
A VAST OCEAN.

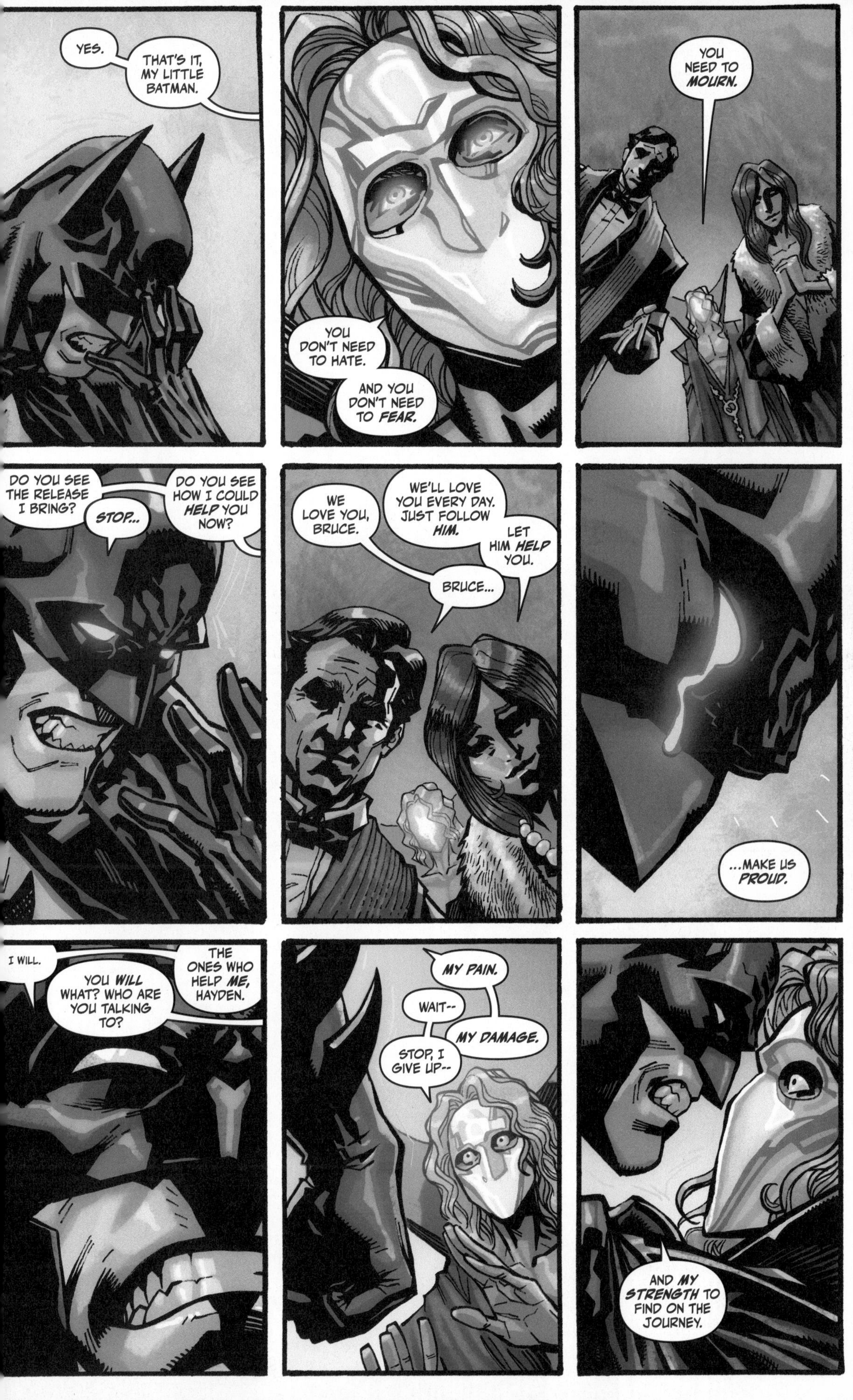
YES.
THAT'S IT, MY LITTLE BATMAN.
YOU DON'T NEED TO HATE.
AND YOU DON'T NEED TO FEAR.
YOU NEED TO MOURN.
DO YOU SEE THE RELEASE I BRING?
STOP...
DO YOU SEE HOW I COULD HELP YOU NOW?
WE LOVE YOU, BRUCE.
WE'LL LOVE YOU EVERY DAY. JUST FOLLOW HIM.
LET HIM HELP YOU.
BRUCE...
...MAKE US PROUD.
I WILL.
YOU WILL WHAT? WHO ARE YOU TALKING TO?
THE ONES WHO HELP ME, HAYDEN.
MY PAIN.
WAIT--
MY DAMAGE.
STOP, I GIVE UP--
AND MY STRENGTH TO FIND ON THE JOURNEY.

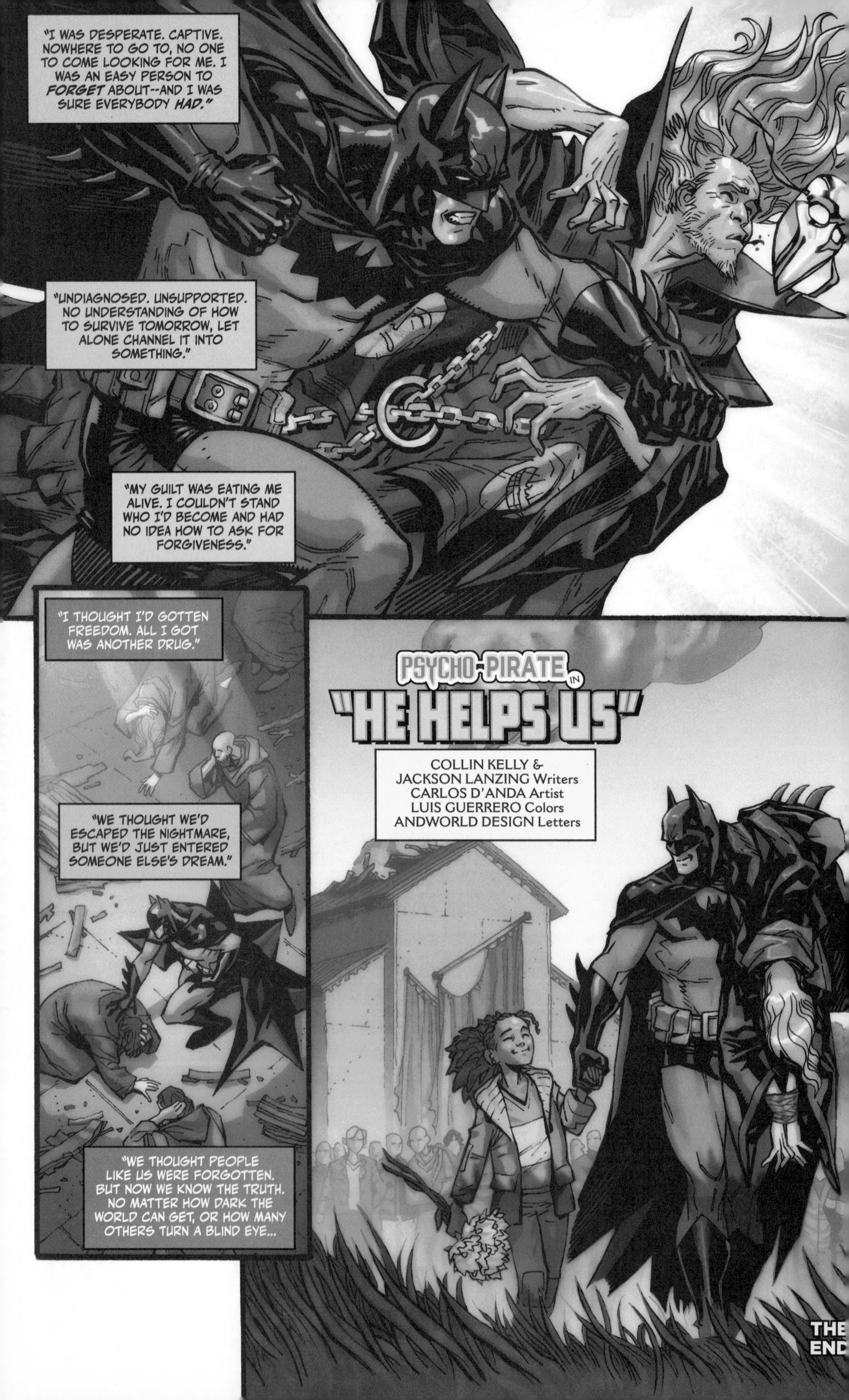
"I WAS DESPERATE. CAPTIVE. NOWHERE TO GO TO, NO ONE TO COME LOOKING FOR ME. I WAS AN EASY PERSON TO *FORGET* ABOUT--AND I WAS SURE EVERYBODY *HAD.*"
"UNDIAGNOSED. UNSUPPORTED. NO UNDERSTANDING OF HOW TO SURVIVE TOMORROW, LET ALONE CHANNEL IT INTO SOMETHING."
"MY GUILT WAS EATING ME ALIVE. I COULDN'T STAND WHO I'D BECOME AND HAD NO IDEA HOW TO ASK FOR FORGIVENESS."
"I THOUGHT I'D GOTTEN FREEDOM. ALL I GOT WAS ANOTHER DRUG."
"WE THOUGHT WE'D ESCAPED THE NIGHTMARE, BUT WE'D JUST ENTERED SOMEONE ELSE'S DREAM."
"WE THOUGHT PEOPLE LIKE US WERE FORGOTTEN. BUT NOW WE KNOW THE TRUTH. NO MATTER HOW DARK THE WORLD CAN GET, OR HOW MANY OTHERS TURN A BLIND EYE...
PSYCHO-PIRATE IN
"HE HELPS US"
COLLIN KELLY & JACKSON LANZING Writers
CARLOS D'ANDA Artist
LUIS GUERRERO Colors
ANDWORLD DESIGN Letters
THE END

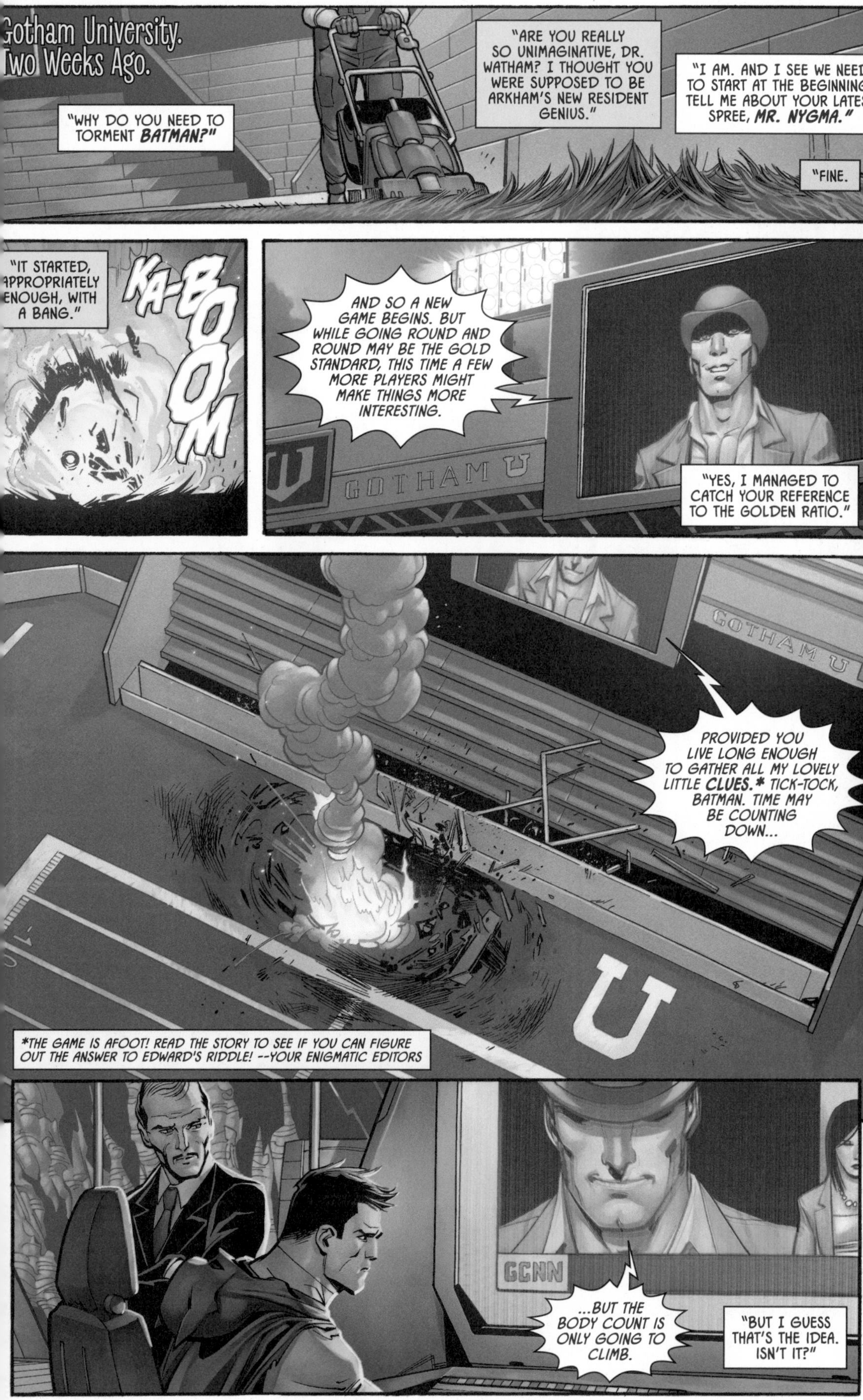
Gotham University. Two Weeks Ago.
"WHY DO YOU NEED TO TORMENT BATMAN?"
"ARE YOU REALLY SO UNIMAGINATIVE, DR. WATHAM? I THOUGHT YOU WERE SUPPOSED TO BE ARKHAM'S NEW RESIDENT GENIUS."
"I AM. AND I SEE WE NEED TO START AT THE BEGINNING. TELL ME ABOUT YOUR LATEST SPREE, MR. NYGMA."
"FINE.
"IT STARTED, APPROPRIATELY ENOUGH, WITH A BANG."
KA-BOOM
AND SO A NEW GAME BEGINS. BUT WHILE GOING ROUND AND ROUND MAY BE THE GOLD STANDARD, THIS TIME A FEW MORE PLAYERS MIGHT MAKE THINGS MORE INTERESTING.
GOTHAM U
"YES, I MANAGED TO CATCH YOUR REFERENCE TO THE GOLDEN RATIO."
GOTHAM U
PROVIDED YOU LIVE LONG ENOUGH TO GATHER ALL MY LOVELY LITTLE CLUES.* TICK-TOCK, BATMAN. TIME MAY BE COUNTING DOWN...
U
*THE GAME IS AFOOT! READ THE STORY TO SEE IF YOU CAN FIGURE OUT THE ANSWER TO EDWARD'S RIDDLE! --YOUR ENIGMATIC EDITORS
GCNN
...BUT THE BODY COUNT IS ONLY GOING TO CLIMB.
"BUT I GUESS THAT'S THE IDEA. ISN'T IT?"

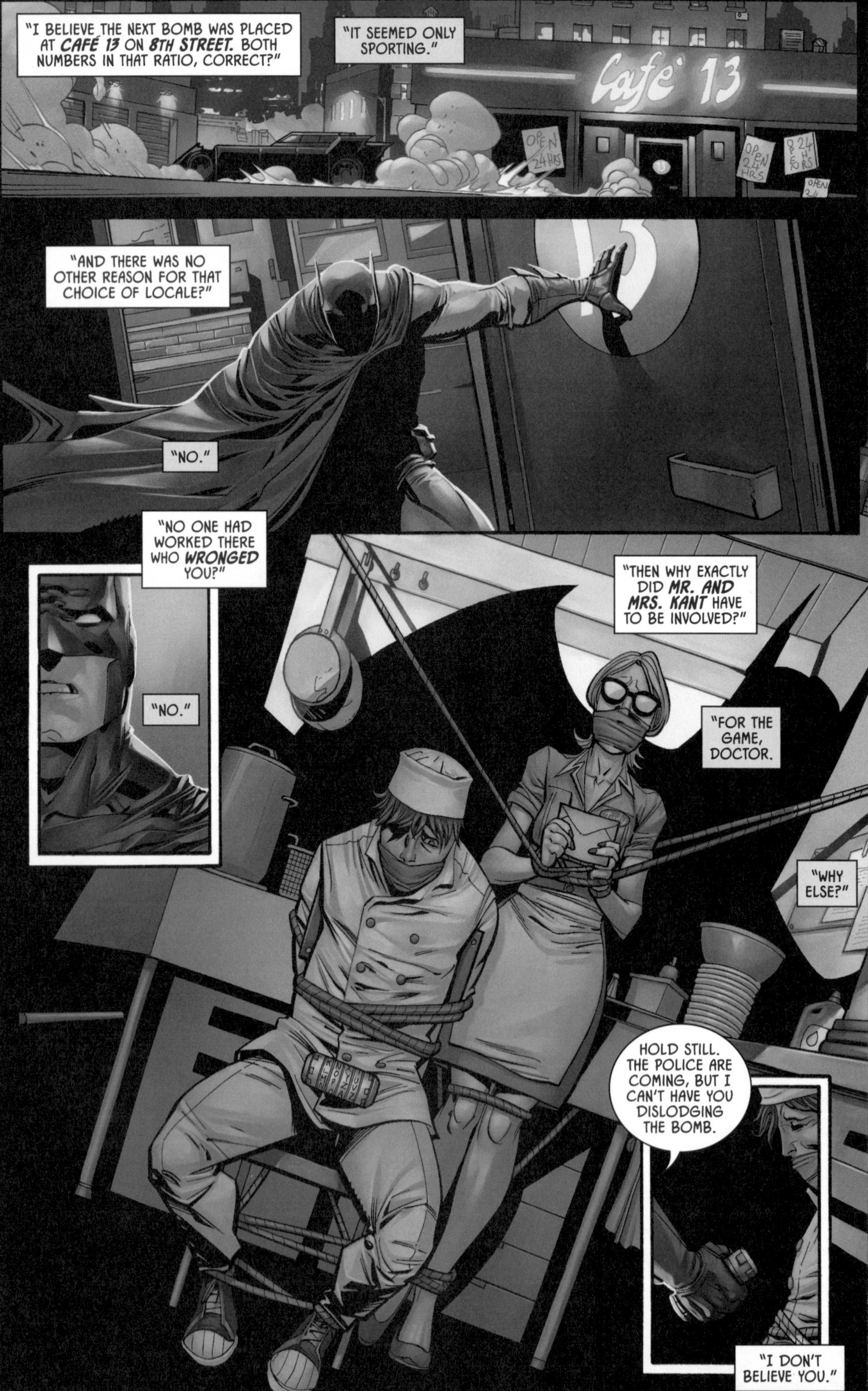
"I BELIEVE THE NEXT BOMB WAS PLACED AT CAFÉ 13 ON 8TH STREET. BOTH NUMBERS IN THAT RATIO, CORRECT?"
"IT SEEMED ONLY SPORTING."
Café 13
OPEN 24 HRS
"AND THERE WAS NO OTHER REASON FOR THAT CHOICE OF LOCALE?"
"NO."
"NO ONE HAD WORKED THERE WHO WRONGED YOU?"
"NO."
"THEN WHY EXACTLY DID MR. AND MRS. KANT HAVE TO BE INVOLVED?"
"FOR THE GAME, DOCTOR.
"WHY ELSE?"
HOLD STILL. THE POLICE ARE COMING, BUT I CAN'T HAVE YOU DISLODGING THE BOMB.
"I DON'T BELIEVE YOU."

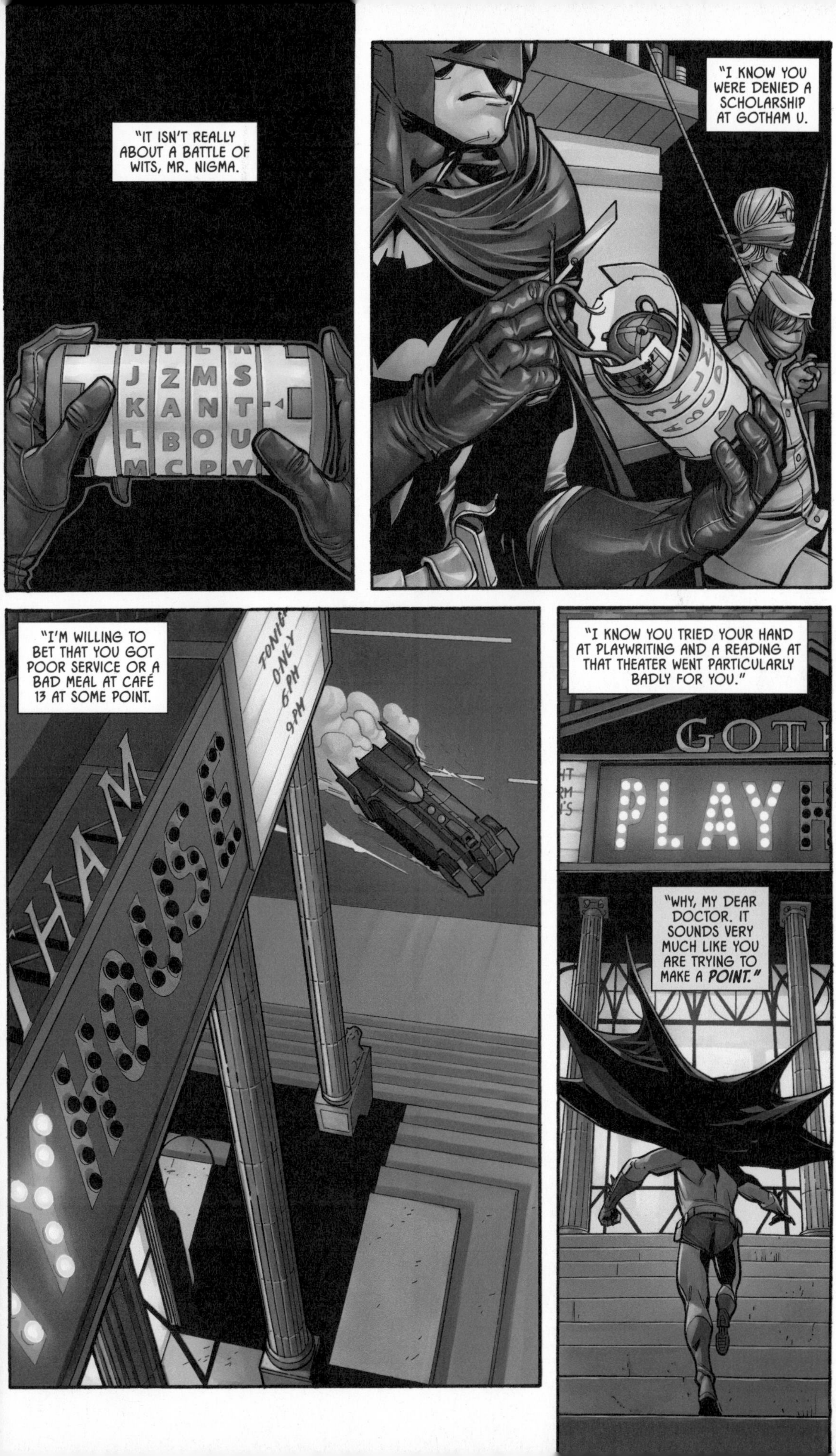

"IT ISN'T REALLY ABOUT A BATTLE OF WITS, MR. NIGMA.
J Z M S
K A N T
L B O U
"I KNOW YOU WERE DENIED A SCHOLARSHIP AT GOTHAM U.
"I'M WILLING TO BET THAT YOU GOT POOR SERVICE OR A BAD MEAL AT CAFÉ 13 AT SOME POINT.
ONLY
6PM
9PM
HAM
HOUSE
"I KNOW YOU TRIED YOUR HAND AT PLAYWRITING AND A READING AT THAT THEATER WENT PARTICULARLY BADLY FOR YOU."
GOT
PLAY
"WHY, MY DEAR DOCTOR. IT SOUNDS VERY MUCH LIKE YOU ARE TRYING TO MAKE A *POINT.*"

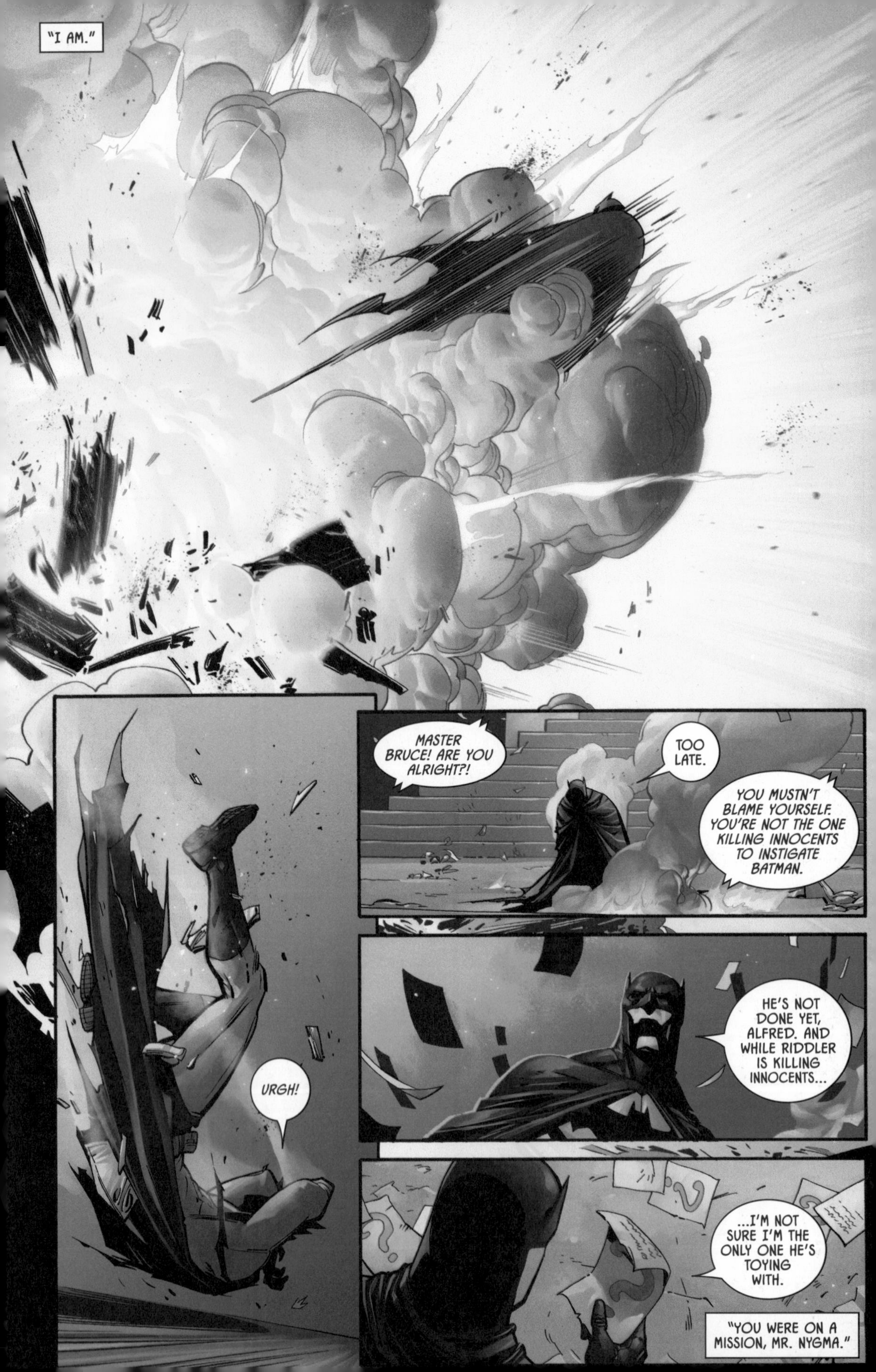
"I AM."
URGH!
MASTER BRUCE! ARE YOU ALRIGHT?!
TOO LATE.
YOU MUSTN'T BLAME YOURSELF. YOU'RE NOT THE ONE KILLING INNOCENTS TO INSTIGATE BATMAN.
HE'S NOT DONE YET, ALFRED. AND WHILE RIDDLER IS KILLING INNOCENTS...
...I'M NOT SURE I'M THE ONLY ONE HE'S TOYING WITH.
"YOU WERE ON A MISSION, MR. NYGMA."

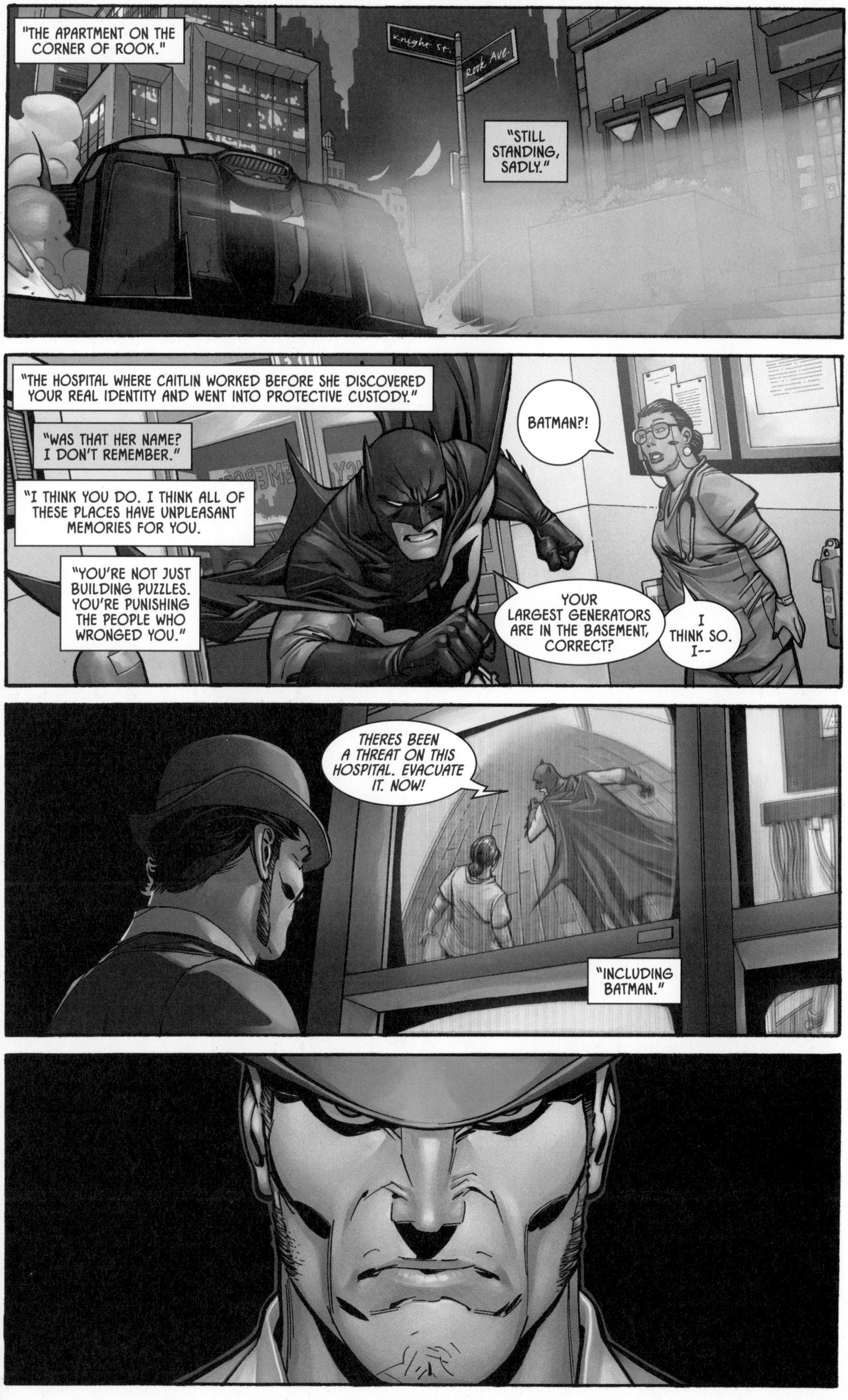
Knight St.
Rook Ave.
"THE APARTMENT ON THE CORNER OF ROOK."
"STILL STANDING, SADLY."
"THE HOSPITAL WHERE CAITLIN WORKED BEFORE SHE DISCOVERED YOUR REAL IDENTITY AND WENT INTO PROTECTIVE CUSTODY."
"WAS THAT HER NAME? I DON'T REMEMBER."
"I THINK YOU DO. I THINK ALL OF THESE PLACES HAVE UNPLEASANT MEMORIES FOR YOU.
"YOU'RE NOT JUST BUILDING PUZZLES. YOU'RE PUNISHING THE PEOPLE WHO WRONGED YOU."
BATMAN?!
YOUR LARGEST GENERATORS ARE IN THE BASEMENT, CORRECT?
I THINK SO. I--
THERES BEEN A THREAT ON THIS HOSPITAL. EVACUATE IT. NOW!
"INCLUDING BATMAN."

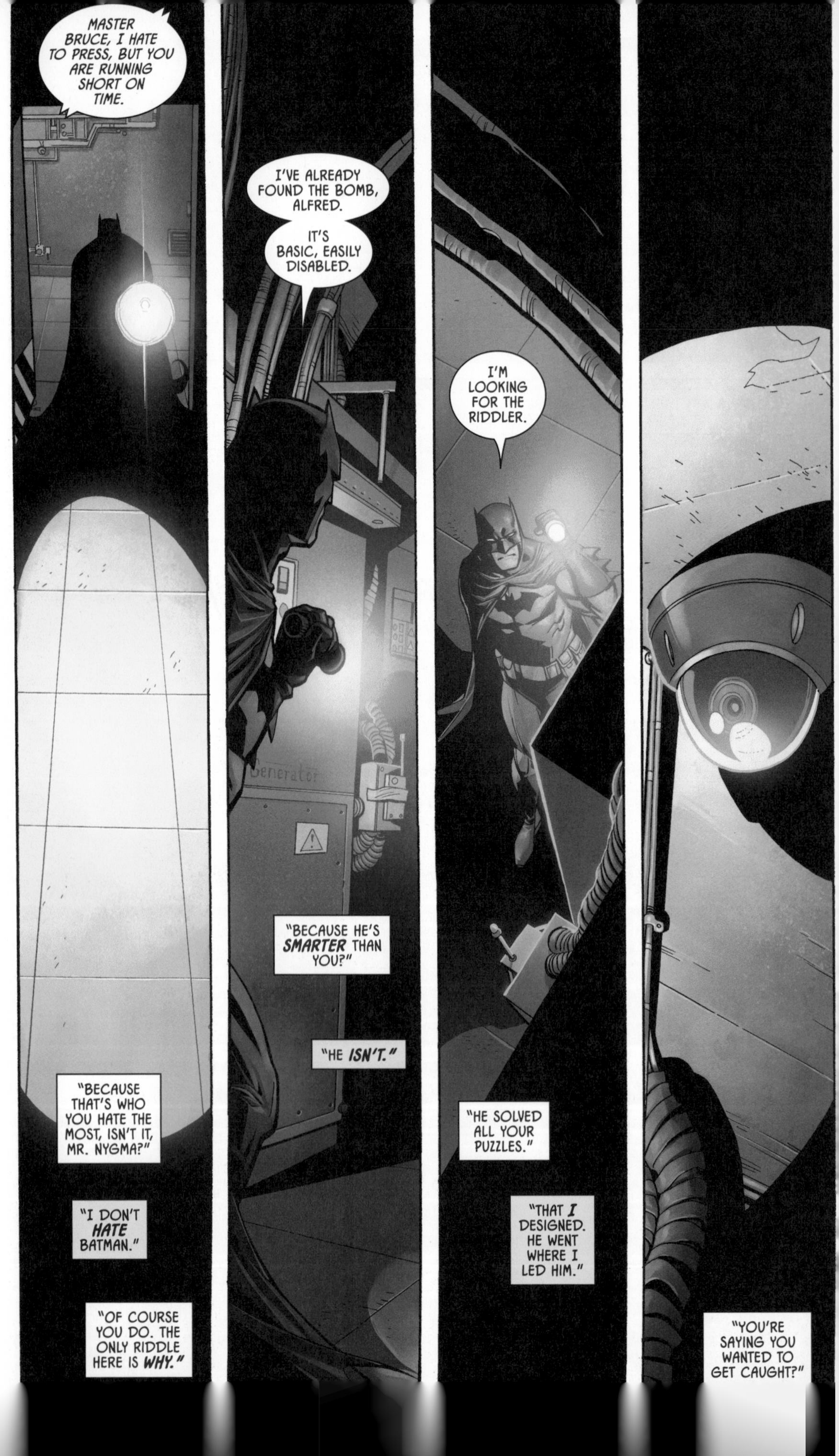
MASTER BRUCE, I HATE TO PRESS, BUT YOU ARE RUNNING SHORT ON TIME.
"BECAUSE THAT'S WHO YOU HATE THE MOST, ISN'T IT, MR. NYGMA?"
"I DON'T *HATE* BATMAN."
"OF COURSE YOU DO. THE ONLY RIDDLE HERE IS *WHY.*"
I'VE ALREADY FOUND THE BOMB, ALFRED.
IT'S BASIC, EASILY DISABLED.
Generator
"BECAUSE HE'S *SMARTER* THAN YOU?"
"HE *ISN'T.*"
I'M LOOKING FOR THE RIDDLER.
"HE SOLVED ALL YOUR PUZZLES."
"THAT *I* DESIGNED. HE WENT WHERE I LED HIM."
"YOU'RE SAYING YOU WANTED TO GET CAUGHT?"

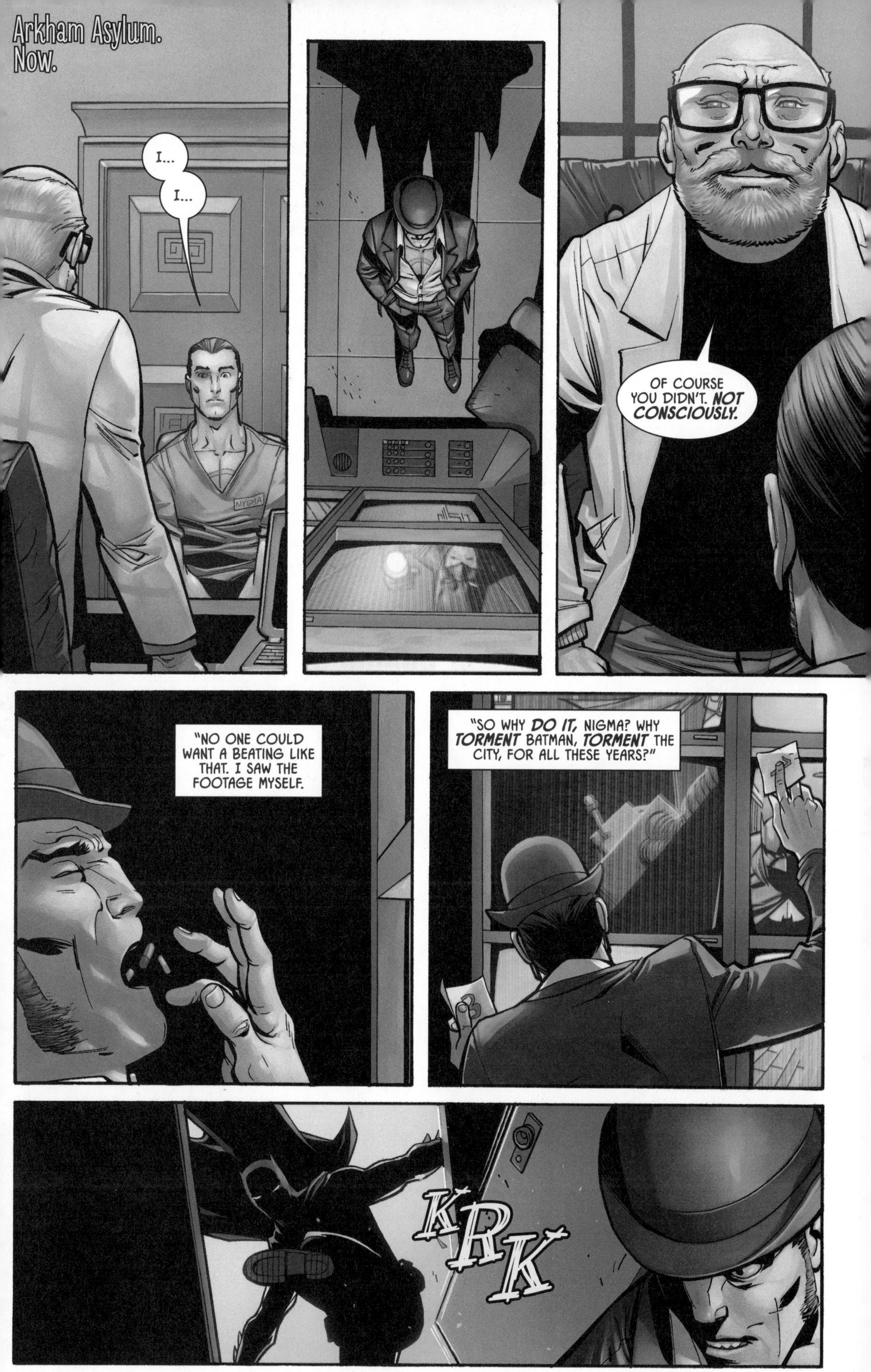
Arkham Asylum.
Now.
I...
I...
OF COURSE YOU DIDN'T. NOT CONSCIOUSLY.
NYGMA
"NO ONE COULD WANT A BEATING LIKE THAT. I SAW THE FOOTAGE MYSELF.
"SO WHY DO IT, NIGMA? WHY TORMENT BATMAN, TORMENT THE CITY, FOR ALL THESE YEARS?"
KRK

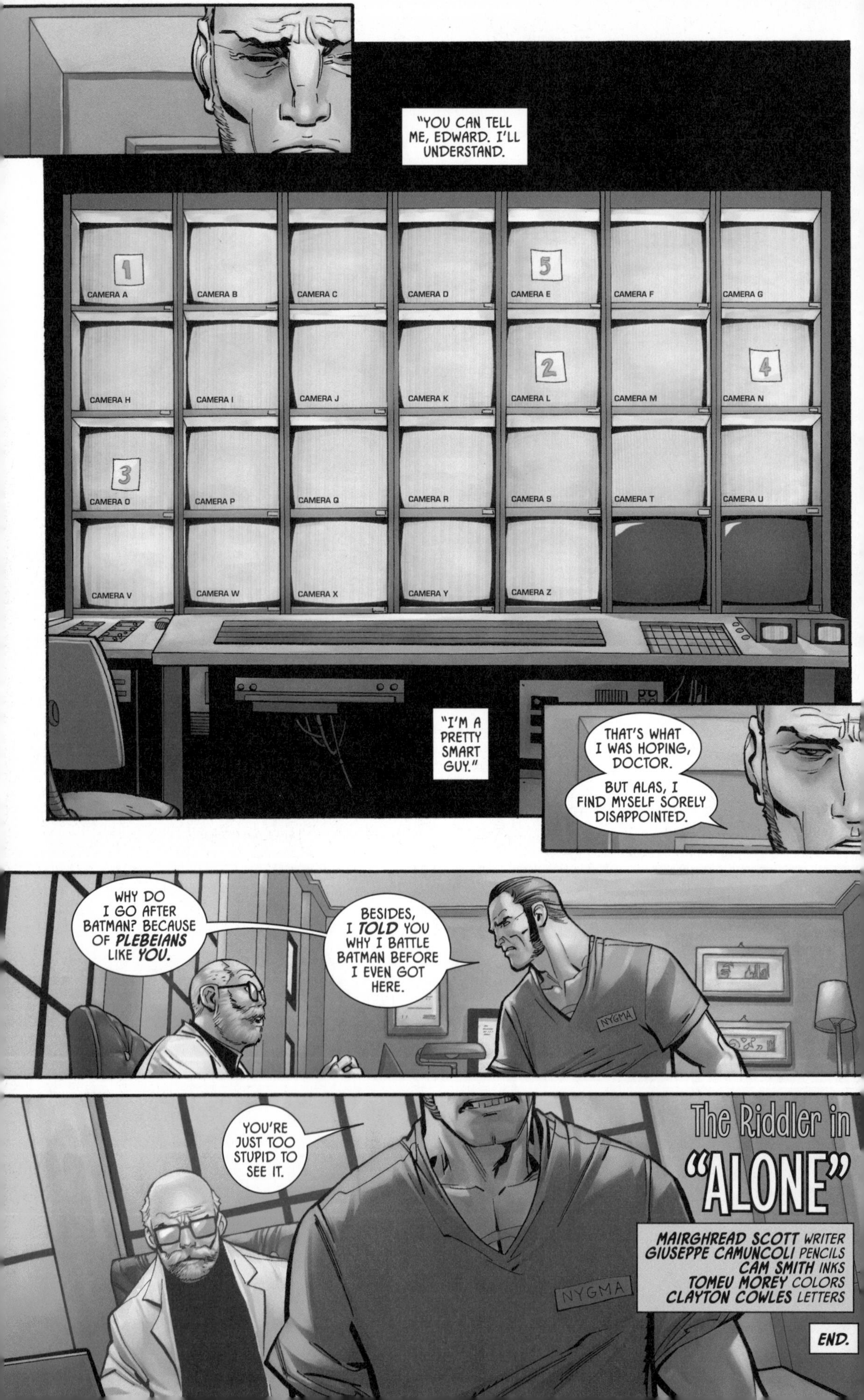
"YOU CAN TELL ME, EDWARD. I'LL UNDERSTAND.
1
CAMERA A
CAMERA B
CAMERA C
CAMERA D
5
CAMERA E
CAMERA F
CAMERA G
CAMERA H
CAMERA I
CAMERA J
CAMERA K
2
CAMERA L
CAMERA M
4
CAMERA N
3
CAMERA O
CAMERA P
CAMERA Q
CAMERA R
CAMERA S
CAMERA T
CAMERA U
CAMERA V
CAMERA W
CAMERA X
CAMERA Y
CAMERA Z
"I'M A PRETTY SMART GUY."
THAT'S WHAT I WAS HOPING, DOCTOR.
BUT ALAS, I FIND MYSELF SORELY DISAPPOINTED.
WHY DO I GO AFTER BATMAN? BECAUSE OF **PLEBEIANS** LIKE **YOU.**
BESIDES, I **TOLD** YOU WHY I BATTLE BATMAN BEFORE I EVEN GOT HERE.
NYGMA
YOU'RE JUST TOO STUPID TO SEE IT.
NYGMA
The Riddler in
"ALONE"
MAIRGHREAD SCOTT WRITER
GIUSEPPE CAMUNCOLI PENCILS
CAM SMITH INKS
TOMEU MOREY COLORS
CLAYTON COWLES LETTERS
END.

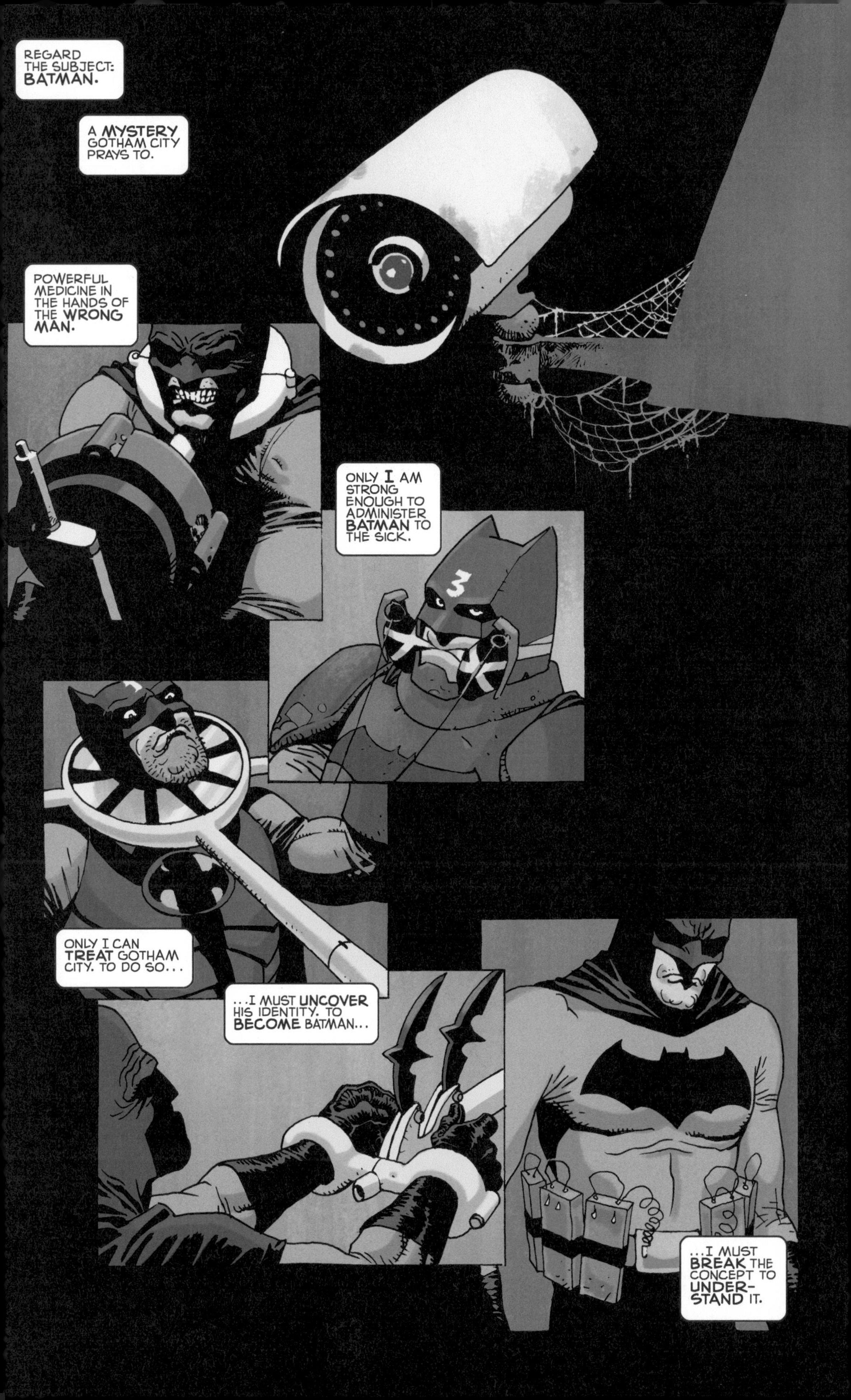
REGARD THE SUBJECT: BATMAN.
A MYSTERY GOTHAM CITY PRAYS TO.
POWERFUL MEDICINE IN THE HANDS OF THE WRONG MAN.
ONLY I AM STRONG ENOUGH TO ADMINISTER BATMAN TO THE SICK.
3
ONLY I CAN TREAT GOTHAM CITY. TO DO SO...
...I MUST UNCOVER HIS IDENTITY. TO BECOME BATMAN...
...I MUST BREAK THE CONCEPT TO UNDER-STAND IT.

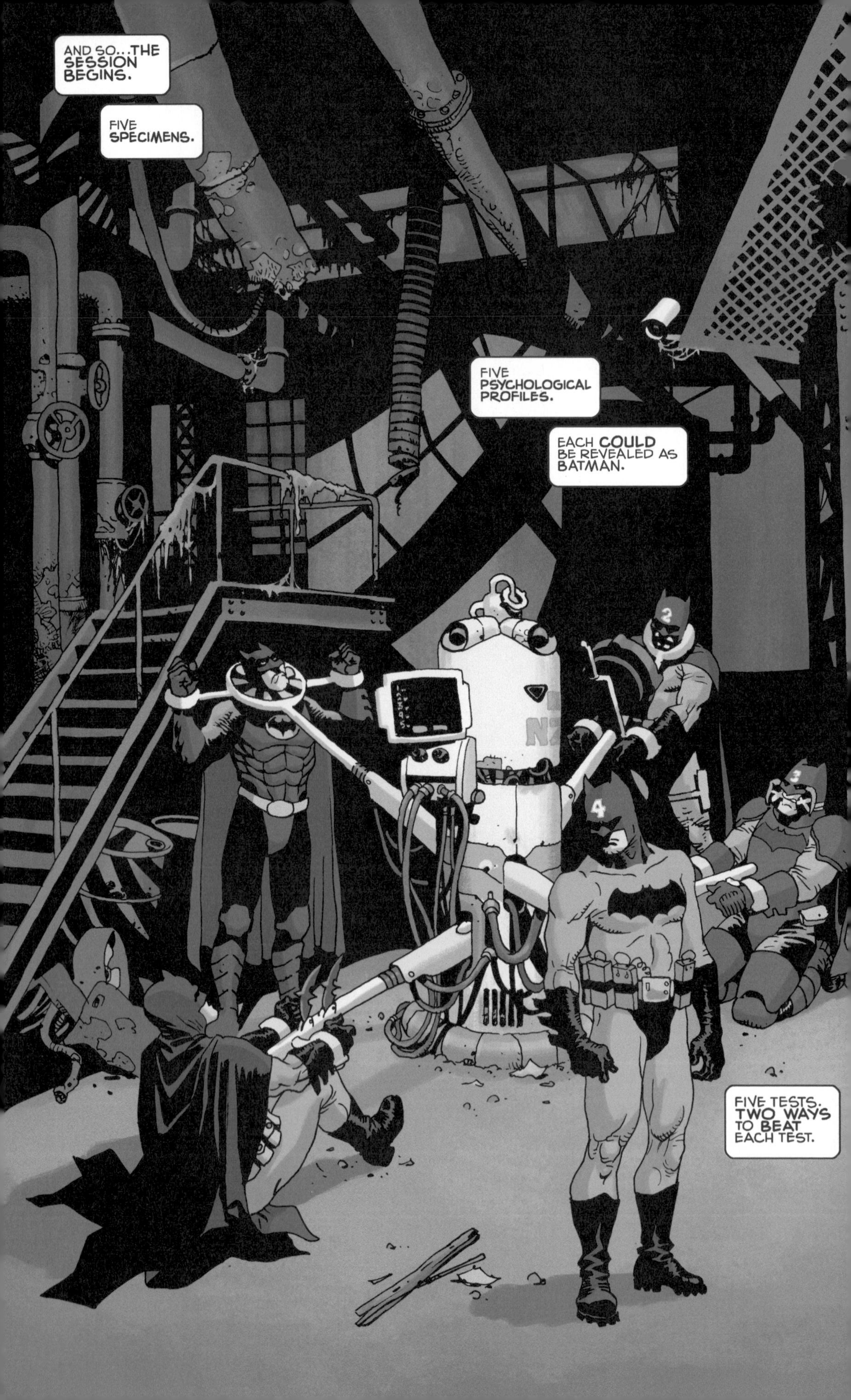

AND SO... THE SESSION BEGINS.
FIVE SPECIMENS.
FIVE PSYCHOLOGICAL PROFILES.
EACH COULD BE REVEALED AS BATMAN.
FIVE TESTS. TWO WAYS TO BEAT EACH TEST.

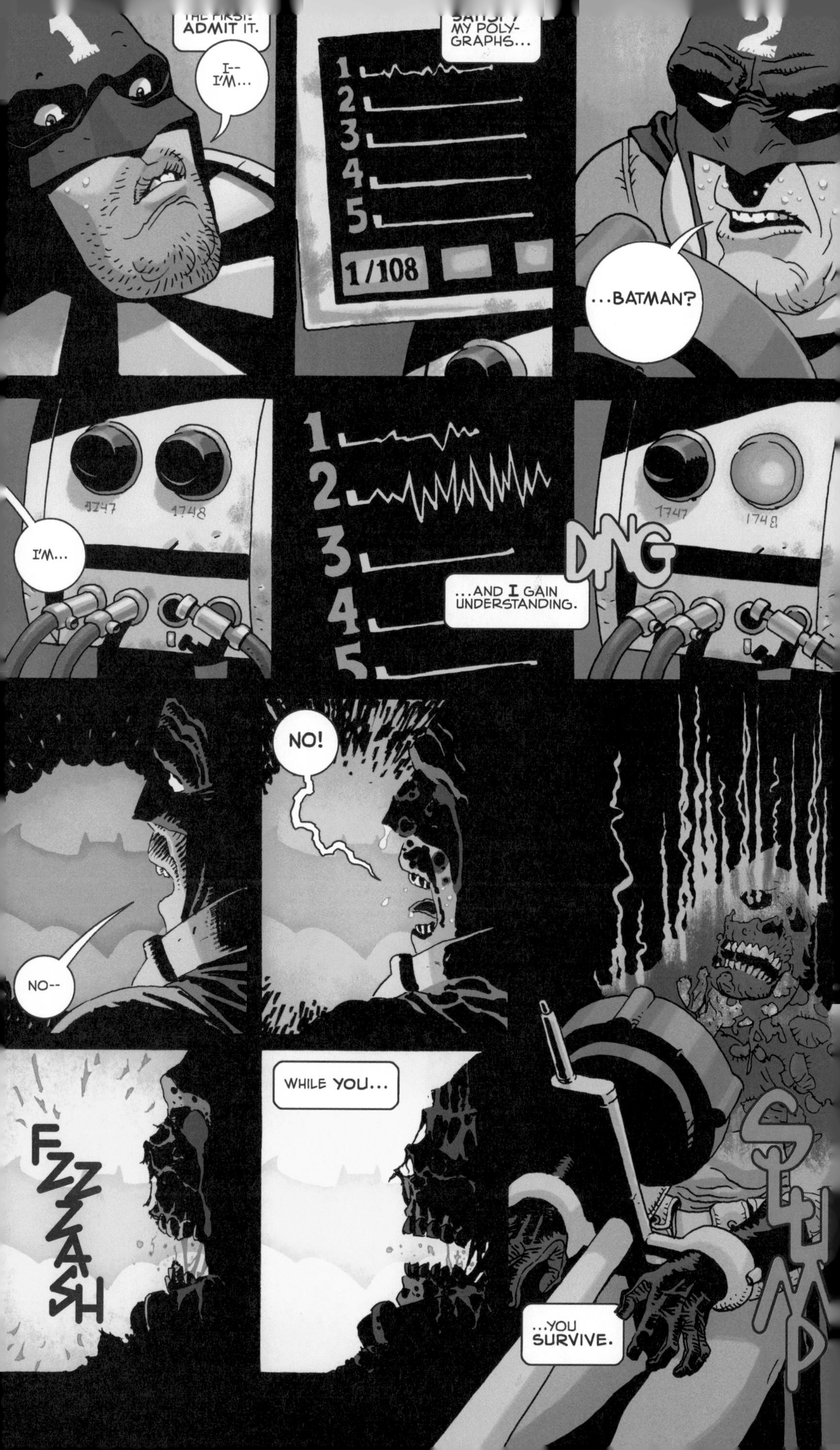

ADMIT IT.
I-- I'M...
MY POLY-GRAPHS...
1
2
3
4
5
1/108
...BATMAN?
1747
1748
I'M...
1
2
3
4
5
...AND I GAIN UNDERSTANDING.
DING
1747
1748
NO--
NO!
FZZZASH
WHILE YOU...
...YOU SURVIVE.
SLUMP

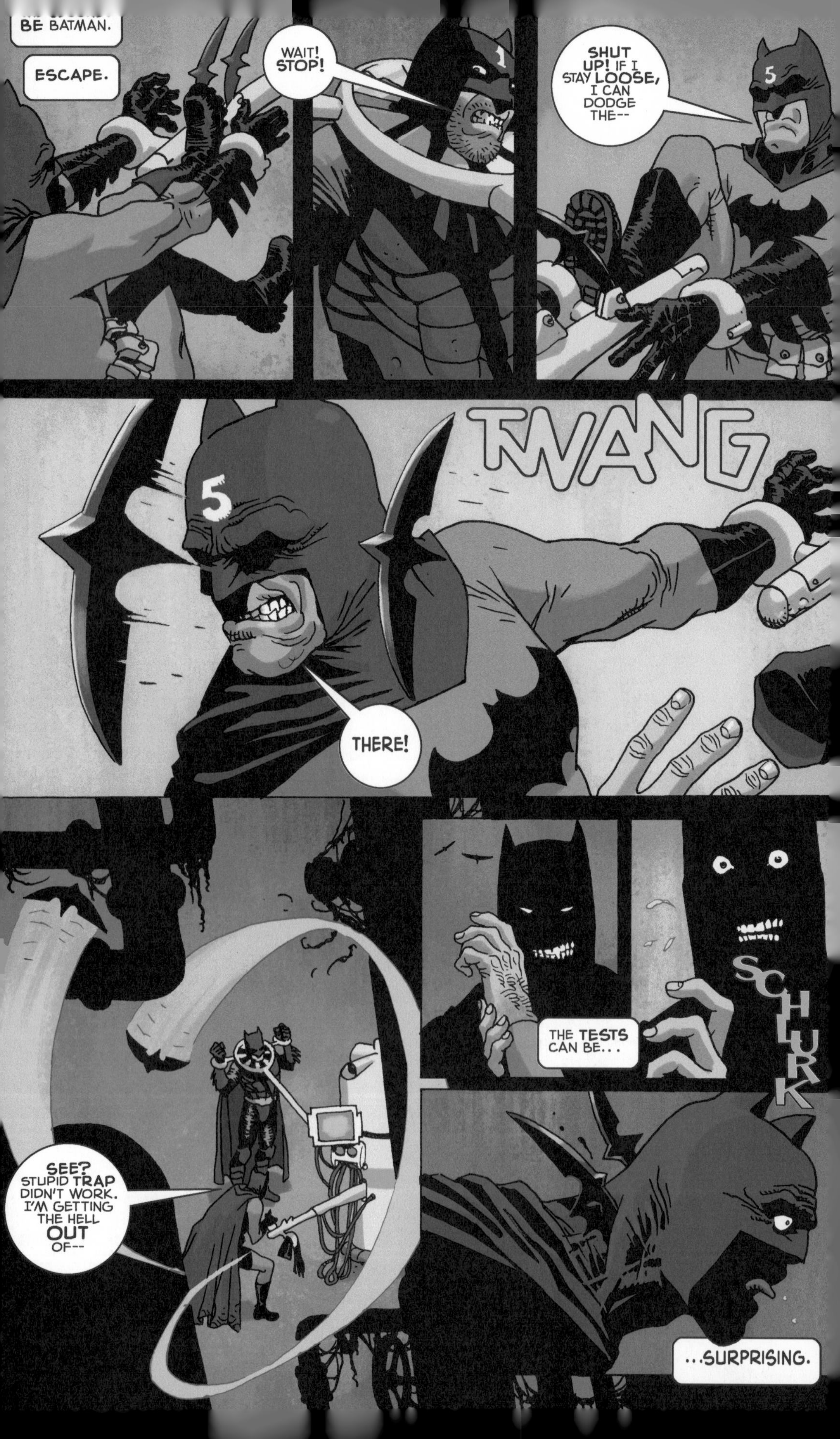

BE BATMAN.
ESCAPE.
WAIT! STOP!
SHUT UP! IF I STAY LOOSE, I CAN DODGE THE--
TWANG
THERE!
SEE? STUPID TRAP DIDN'T WORK. I'M GETTING THE HELL OUT OF--
THE TESTS CAN BE...
SCHURK
...SURPRISING.

I'VE ISOLATED THE LIFE-AND-DEATH **STRESSES** BATMAN FACES NIGHTLY.

STUMP

EACH SPECIMEN...

...ALIVE...

...OR...

3

...DEAD...

4

FINE! FINE! I'M BATMAN!

I'M BATMAN!

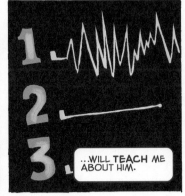

1.

2.

3.

...WILL **TEACH** ME ABOUT HIM.

DING

HERK!

SNAP

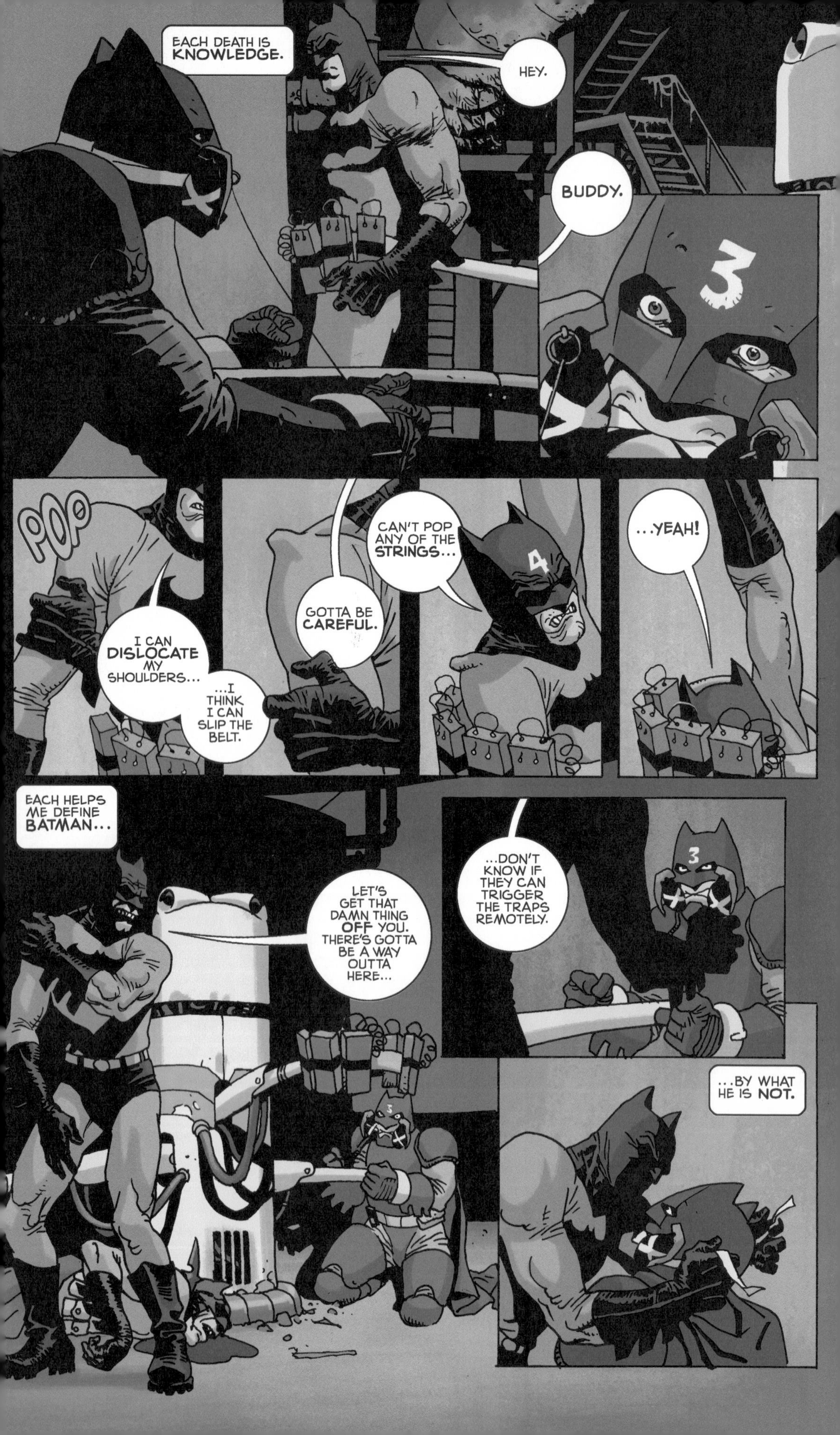
EACH DEATH IS KNOWLEDGE.
HEY.
BUDDY.
POP
I CAN DISLOCATE MY SHOULDERS...
...I THINK I CAN SLIP THE BELT.
GOTTA BE CAREFUL.
CAN'T POP ANY OF THE STRINGS...
...YEAH!
EACH HELPS ME DEFINE BATMAN...
LET'S GET THAT DAMN THING OFF YOU. THERE'S GOTTA BE A WAY OUTTA HERE...
...DON'T KNOW IF THEY CAN TRIGGER THE TRAPS REMOTELY.
...BY WHAT HE IS NOT.

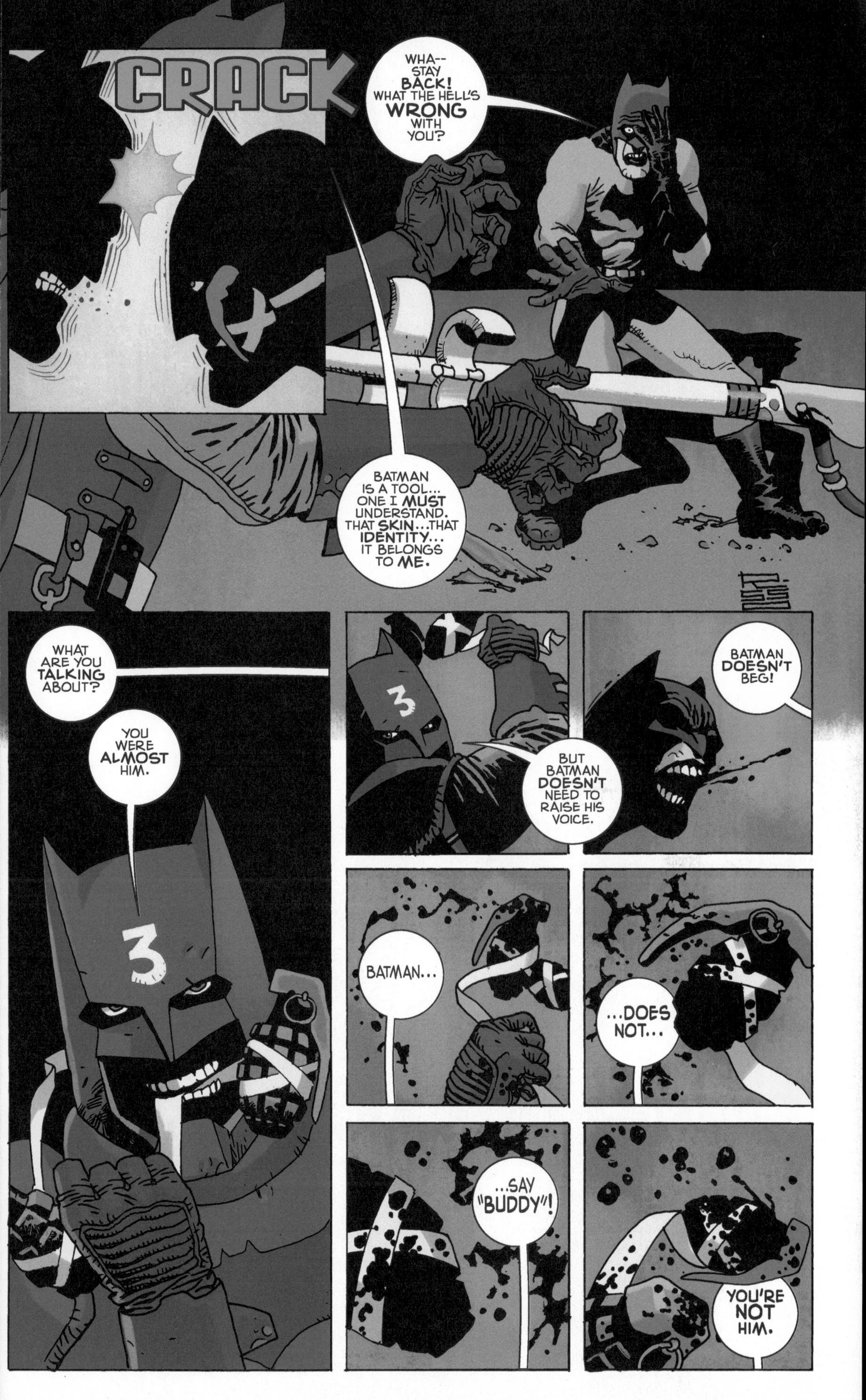
CRACK
WHA-- STAY BACK! WHAT THE HELL'S WRONG WITH YOU?
BATMAN IS A TOOL... ONE I MUST UNDERSTAND. THAT SKIN...THAT IDENTITY... IT BELONGS TO ME.
WHAT ARE YOU TALKING ABOUT?
YOU WERE ALMOST HIM.
BATMAN DOESN'T BEG!
BUT BATMAN DOESN'T NEED TO RAISE HIS VOICE.
BATMAN...
...DOES NOT...
...SAY "BUDDY"!
YOU'RE NOT HIM.

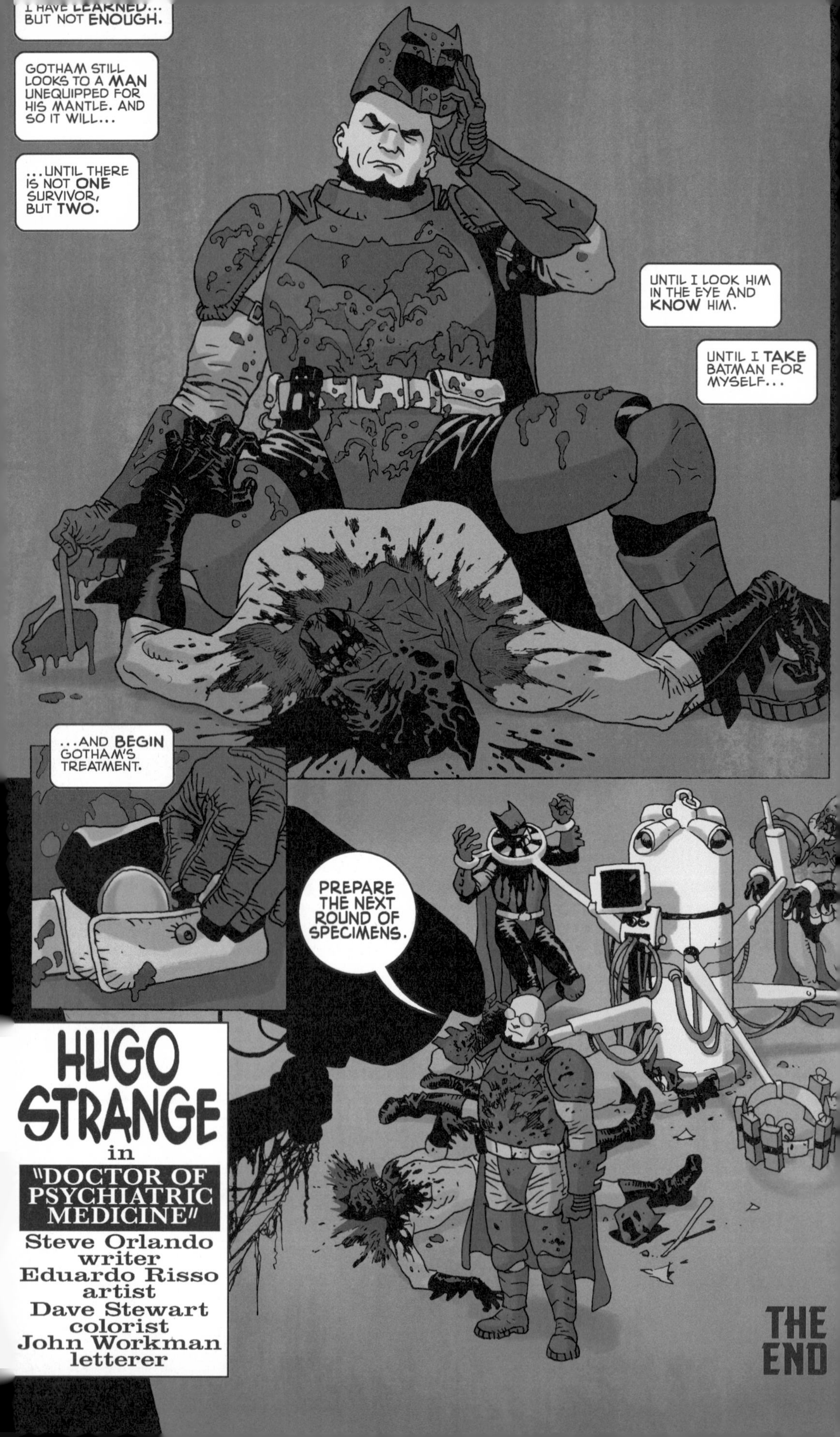
I HAVE LEARNED...
BUT NOT ENOUGH.
GOTHAM STILL LOOKS TO A MAN UNEQUIPPED FOR HIS MANTLE. AND SO IT WILL...
...UNTIL THERE IS NOT ONE SURVIVOR, BUT TWO.
UNTIL I LOOK HIM IN THE EYE AND KNOW HIM.
UNTIL I TAKE BATMAN FOR MYSELF...
...AND BEGIN GOTHAM'S TREATMENT.
PREPARE THE NEXT ROUND OF SPECIMENS.
HUGO STRANGE
in
"DOCTOR OF PSYCHIATRIC MEDICINE"
Steve Orlando writer
Eduardo Risso artist
Dave Stewart colorist
John Workman letterer
THE END

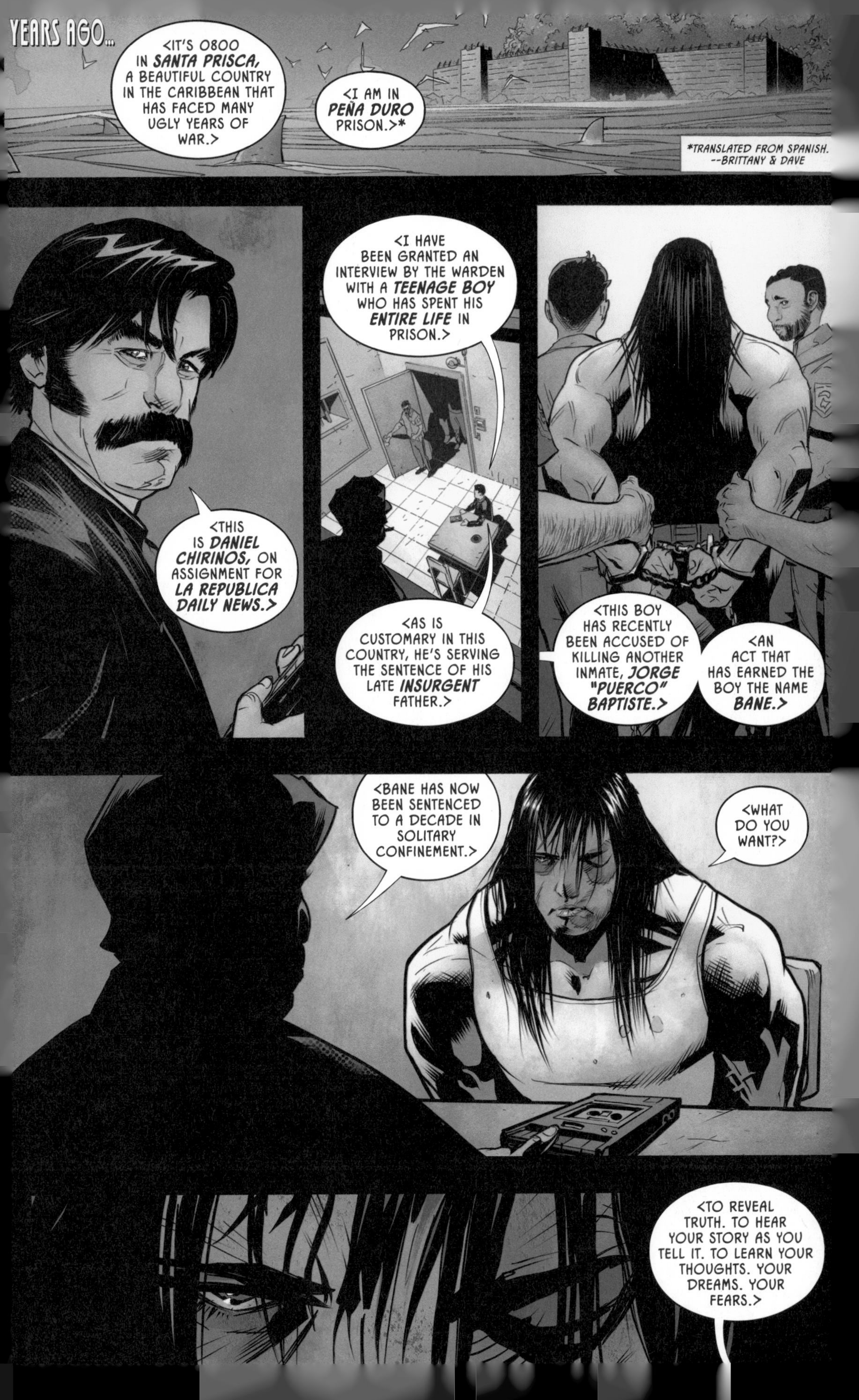
YEARS AGO...
<IT'S 0800 IN SANTA PRISCA, A BEAUTIFUL COUNTRY IN THE CARIBBEAN THAT HAS FACED MANY UGLY YEARS OF WAR.>
<I AM IN PEÑA DURO PRISON.>*
*TRANSLATED FROM SPANISH. --BRITTANY & DAVE
<THIS IS DANIEL CHIRINOS, ON ASSIGNMENT FOR LA REPUBLICA DAILY NEWS.>
<I HAVE BEEN GRANTED AN INTERVIEW BY THE WARDEN WITH A TEENAGE BOY WHO HAS SPENT HIS ENTIRE LIFE IN PRISON.>
<AS IS CUSTOMARY IN THIS COUNTRY, HE'S SERVING THE SENTENCE OF HIS LATE INSURGENT FATHER.>
<THIS BOY HAS RECENTLY BEEN ACCUSED OF KILLING ANOTHER INMATE, JORGE "PUERCO" BAPTISTE.>
<AN ACT THAT HAS EARNED THE BOY THE NAME BANE.>
<BANE HAS NOW BEEN SENTENCED TO A DECADE IN SOLITARY CONFINEMENT.>
<WHAT DO YOU WANT?>
<TO REVEAL TRUTH. TO HEAR YOUR STORY AS YOU TELL IT. TO LEARN YOUR THOUGHTS. YOUR DREAMS. YOUR FEARS.>

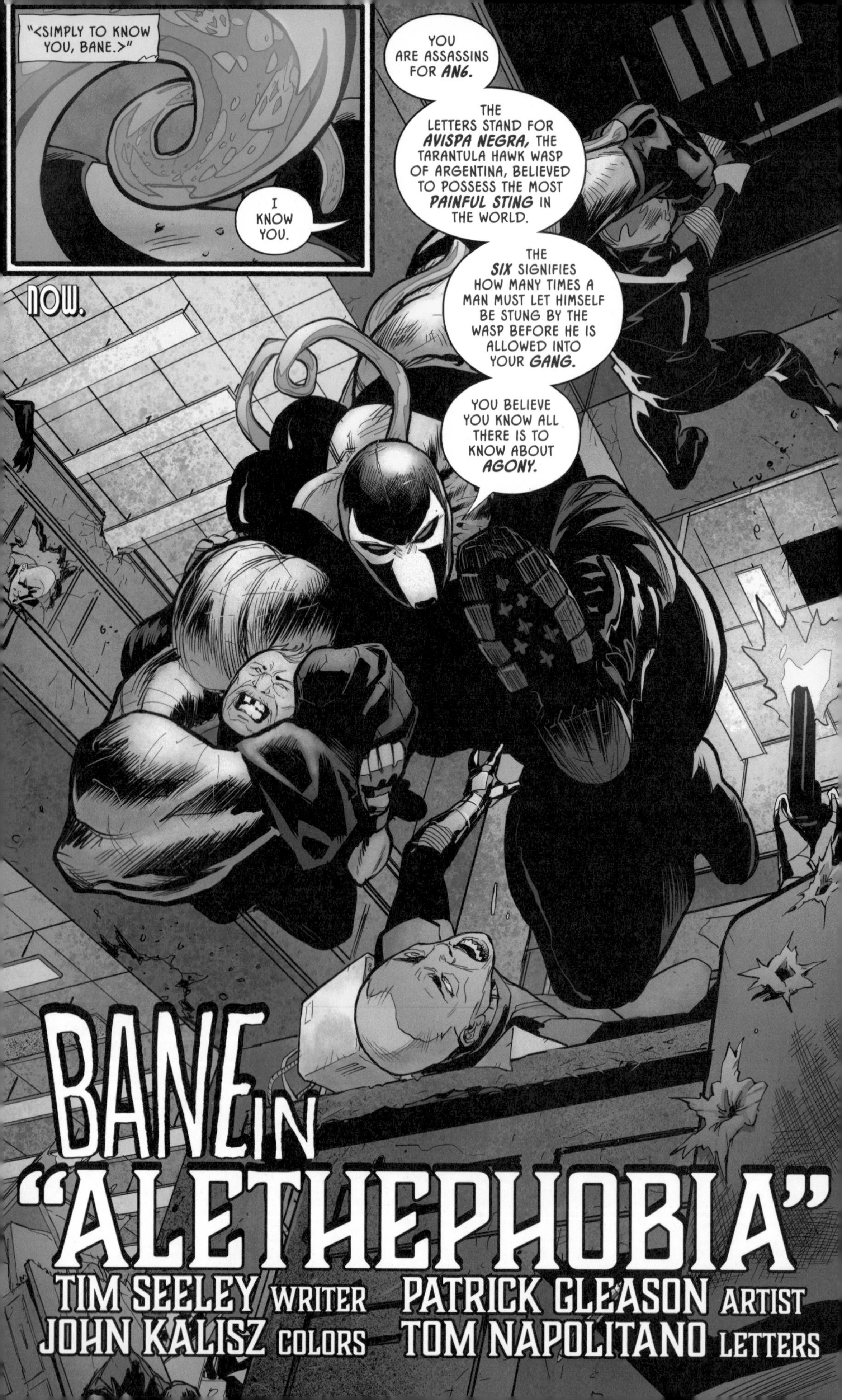
"<SIMPLY TO KNOW YOU, BANE.>"
I KNOW YOU.
YOU ARE ASSASSINS FOR AN6.
THE LETTERS STAND FOR AVISPA NEGRA, THE TARANTULA HAWK WASP OF ARGENTINA, BELIEVED TO POSSESS THE MOST PAINFUL STING IN THE WORLD.
NOW.
THE SIX SIGNIFIES HOW MANY TIMES A MAN MUST LET HIMSELF BE STUNG BY THE WASP BEFORE HE IS ALLOWED INTO YOUR GANG.
YOU BELIEVE YOU KNOW ALL THERE IS TO KNOW ABOUT AGONY.
BANE IN "ALETHEPHOBIA"
TIM SEELEY WRITER PATRICK GLEASON ARTIST
JOHN KALISZ COLORS TOM NAPOLITANO LETTERS

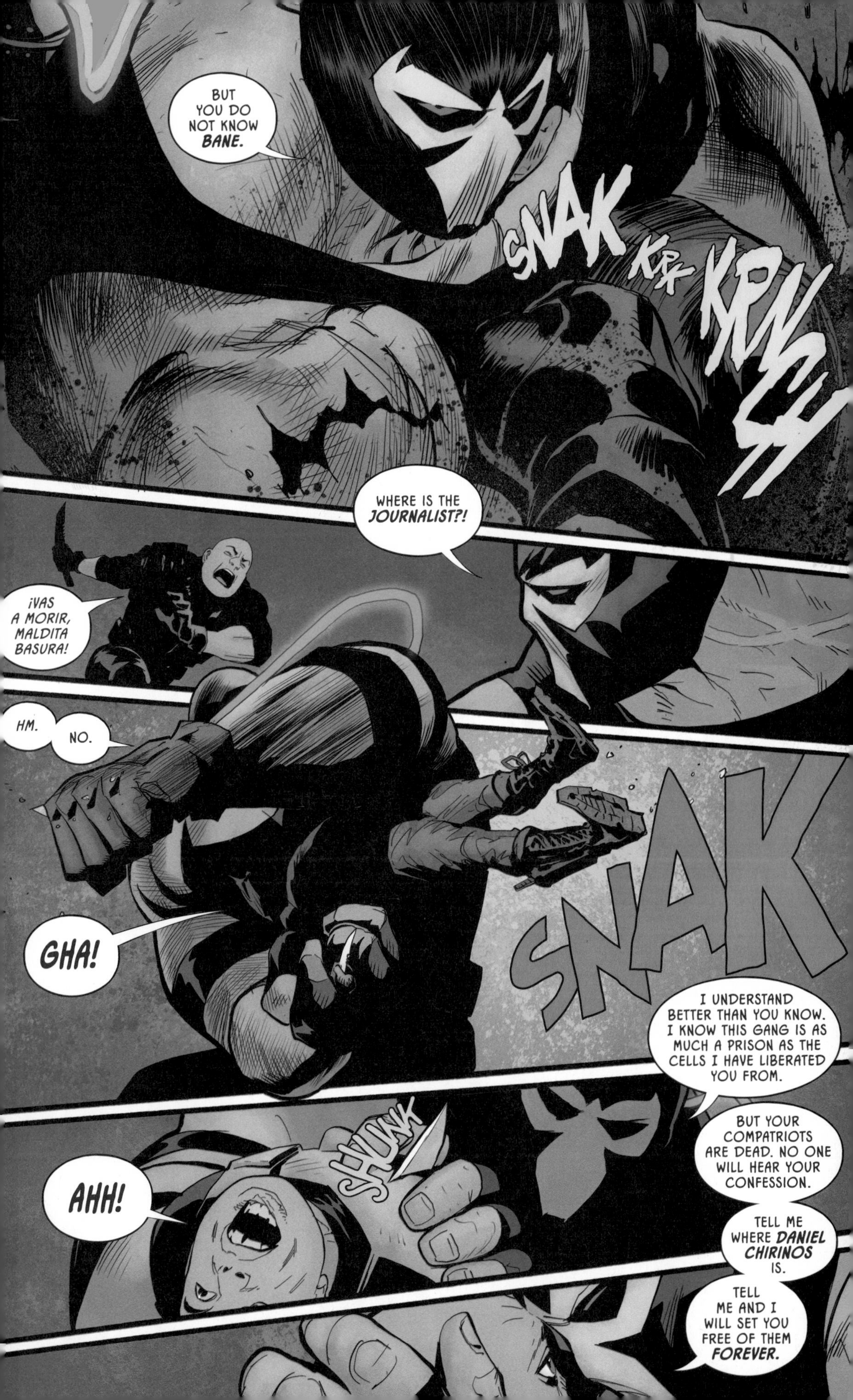
BUT YOU DO NOT KNOW BANE.
SNAK KRK KRNCH
WHERE IS THE JOURNALIST?!
¡VAS A MORIR, MALDITA BASURA!
HM.
NO.
SNAK
GHA!
I UNDERSTAND BETTER THAN YOU KNOW. I KNOW THIS GANG IS AS MUCH A PRISON AS THE CELLS I HAVE LIBERATED YOU FROM.
BUT YOUR COMPATRIOTS ARE DEAD. NO ONE WILL HEAR YOUR CONFESSION.
SHUNK
AHH!
TELL ME WHERE DANIEL CHIRINOS IS.
TELL ME AND I WILL SET YOU FREE OF THEM FOREVER.

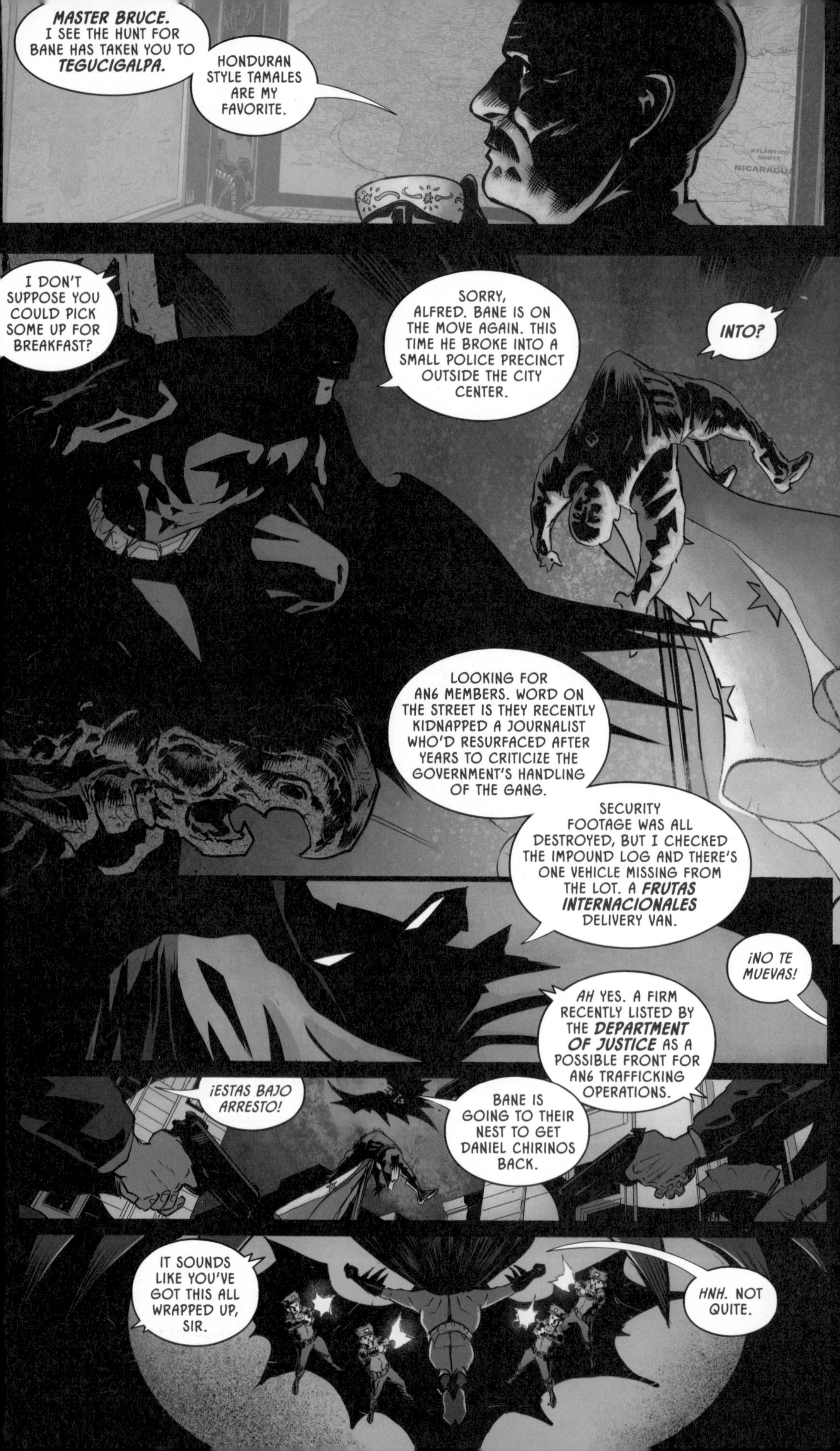
MASTER BRUCE. I SEE THE HUNT FOR BANE HAS TAKEN YOU TO TEGUCIGALPA.
HONDURAN STYLE TAMALES ARE MY FAVORITE.
NICARAGUA
I DON'T SUPPOSE YOU COULD PICK SOME UP FOR BREAKFAST?
SORRY, ALFRED. BANE IS ON THE MOVE AGAIN. THIS TIME HE BROKE INTO A SMALL POLICE PRECINCT OUTSIDE THE CITY CENTER.
INTO?
LOOKING FOR AN6 MEMBERS. WORD ON THE STREET IS THEY RECENTLY KIDNAPPED A JOURNALIST WHO'D RESURFACED AFTER YEARS TO CRITICIZE THE GOVERNMENT'S HANDLING OF THE GANG.
SECURITY FOOTAGE WAS ALL DESTROYED, BUT I CHECKED THE IMPOUND LOG AND THERE'S ONE VEHICLE MISSING FROM THE LOT. A FRUTAS INTERNACIONALES DELIVERY VAN.
¡NO TE MUEVAS!
AH YES. A FIRM RECENTLY LISTED BY THE DEPARTMENT OF JUSTICE AS A POSSIBLE FRONT FOR AN6 TRAFFICKING OPERATIONS.
¡ESTAS BAJO ARRESTO!
BANE IS GOING TO THEIR NEST TO GET DANIEL CHIRINOS BACK.
IT SOUNDS LIKE YOU'VE GOT THIS ALL WRAPPED UP, SIR.
HNH. NOT QUITE.

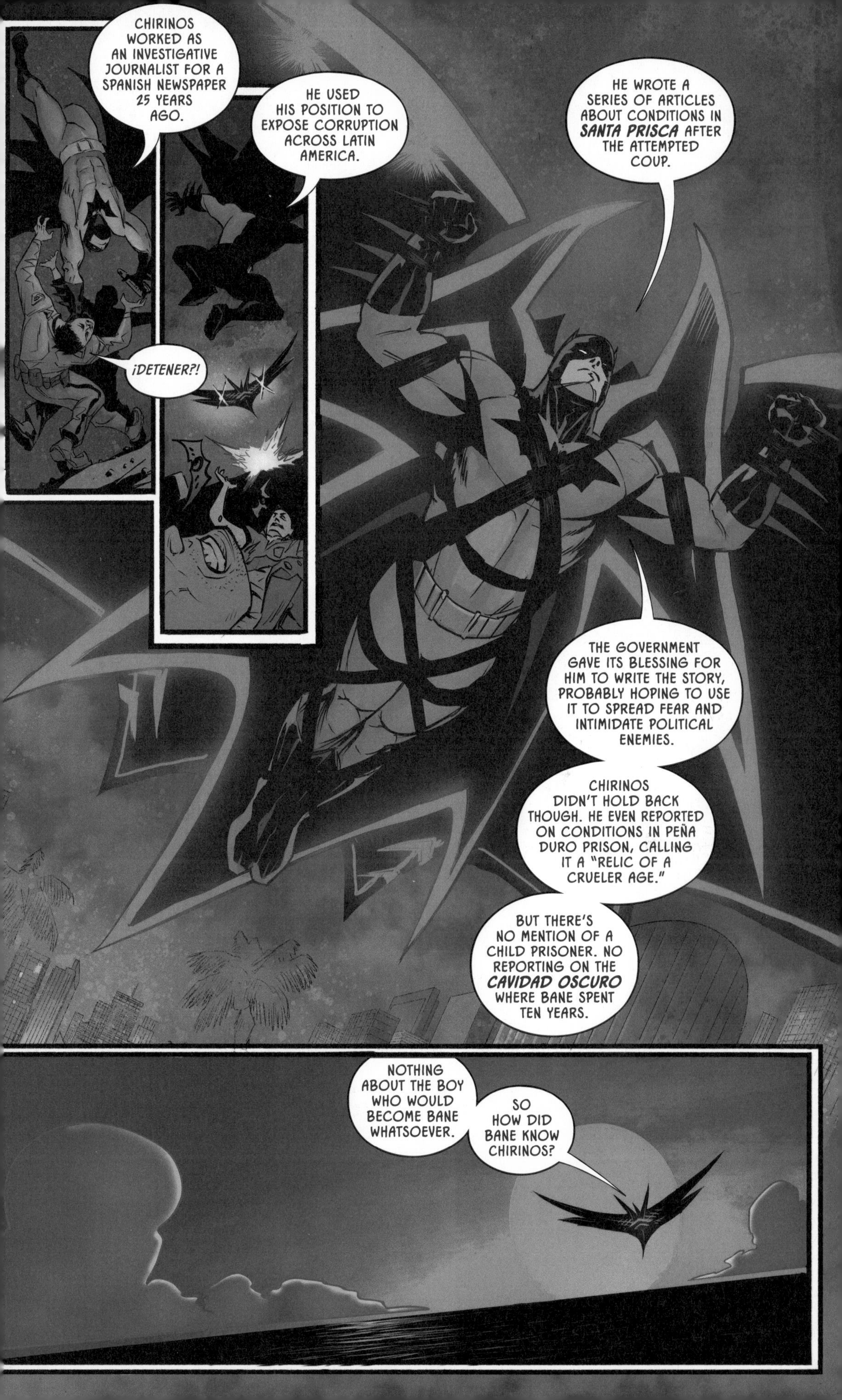
CHIRINOS WORKED AS AN INVESTIGATIVE JOURNALIST FOR A SPANISH NEWSPAPER 25 YEARS AGO.
HE USED HIS POSITION TO EXPOSE CORRUPTION ACROSS LATIN AMERICA.
¡DETENER?!
HE WROTE A SERIES OF ARTICLES ABOUT CONDITIONS IN SANTA PRISCA AFTER THE ATTEMPTED COUP.
THE GOVERNMENT GAVE ITS BLESSING FOR HIM TO WRITE THE STORY, PROBABLY HOPING TO USE IT TO SPREAD FEAR AND INTIMIDATE POLITICAL ENEMIES.
CHIRINOS DIDN'T HOLD BACK THOUGH. HE EVEN REPORTED ON CONDITIONS IN PEÑA DURO PRISON, CALLING IT A "RELIC OF A CRUELER AGE."
BUT THERE'S NO MENTION OF A CHILD PRISONER. NO REPORTING ON THE CAVIDAD OSCURO WHERE BANE SPENT TEN YEARS.
NOTHING ABOUT THE BOY WHO WOULD BECOME BANE WHATSOEVER.
SO HOW DID BANE KNOW CHIRINOS?

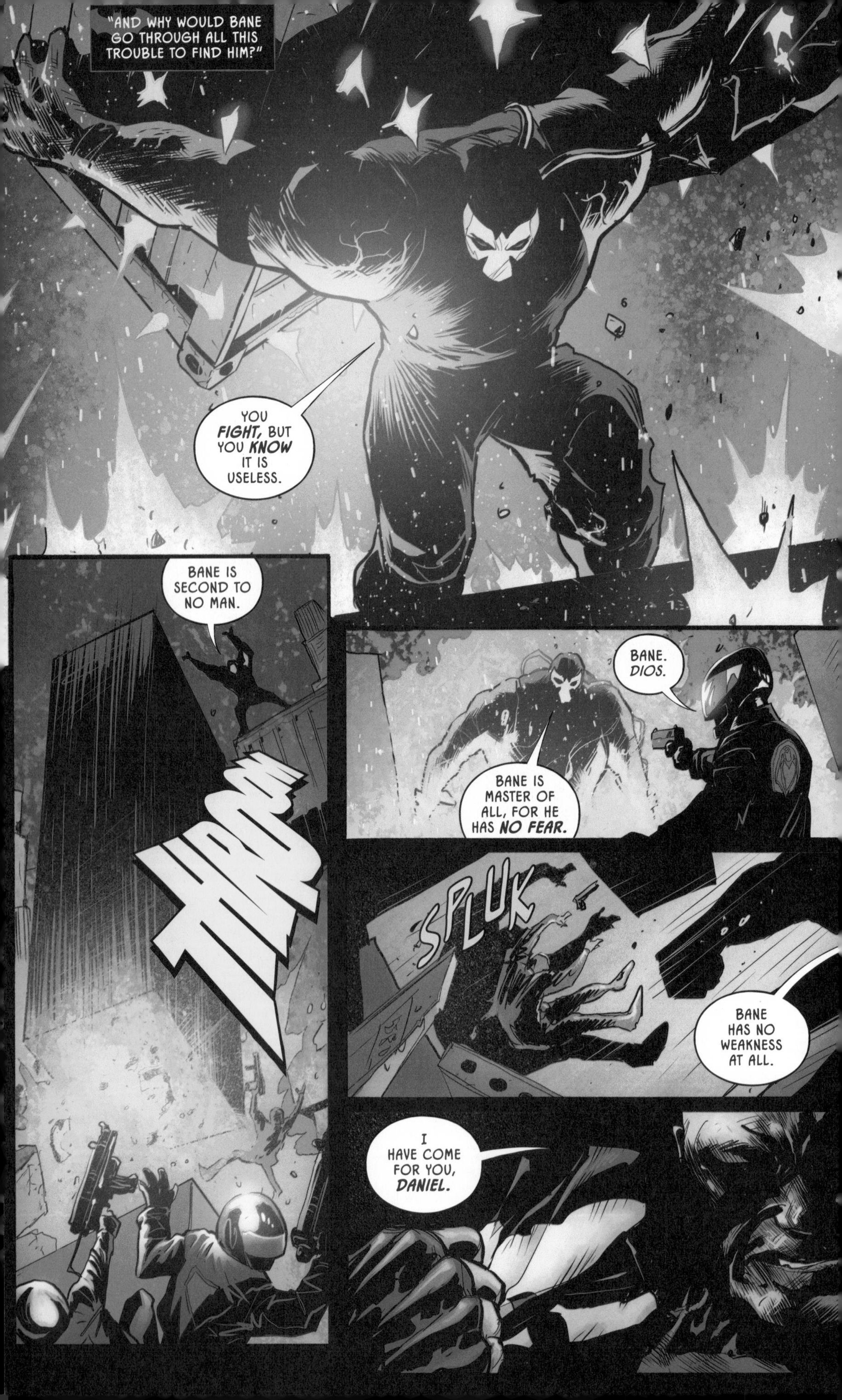
"AND WHY WOULD BANE GO THROUGH ALL THIS TROUBLE TO FIND HIM?"
YOU FIGHT, BUT YOU KNOW IT IS USELESS.
BANE IS SECOND TO NO MAN.
THROOM
BANE. DIOS.
BANE IS MASTER OF ALL, FOR HE HAS NO FEAR.
SPLUK
BANE HAS NO WEAKNESS AT ALL.
I HAVE COME FOR YOU, DANIEL.

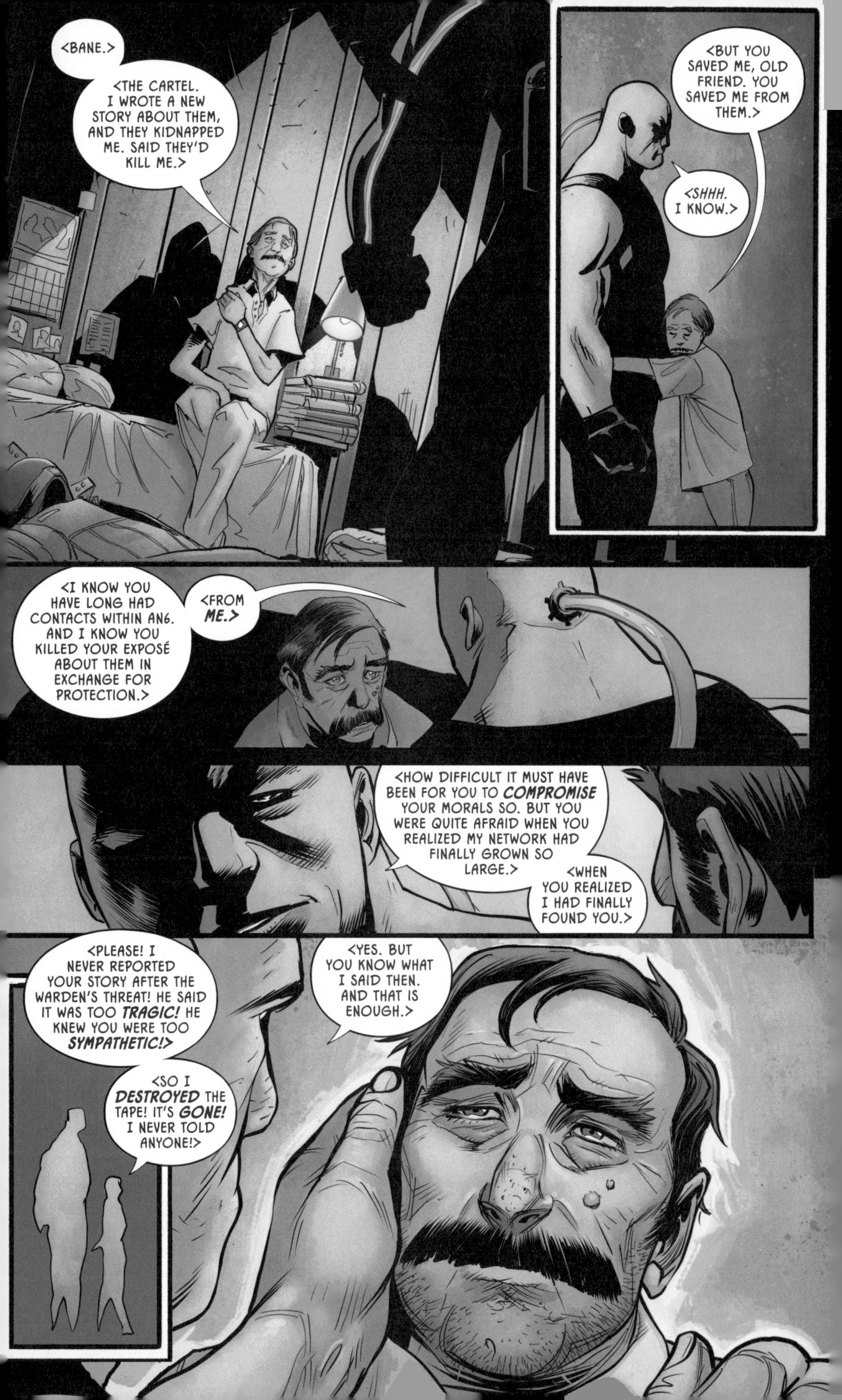

<BANE.>
<THE CARTEL. I WROTE A NEW STORY ABOUT THEM, AND THEY KIDNAPPED ME. SAID THEY'D KILL ME.>
<BUT YOU SAVED ME, OLD FRIEND. YOU SAVED ME FROM THEM.>
<SHHH. I KNOW.>
<I KNOW YOU HAVE LONG HAD CONTACTS WITHIN ANG. AND I KNOW YOU KILLED YOUR EXPOSÉ ABOUT THEM IN EXCHANGE FOR PROTECTION.>
<FROM ME.>
<HOW DIFFICULT IT MUST HAVE BEEN FOR YOU TO COMPROMISE YOUR MORALS SO. BUT YOU WERE QUITE AFRAID WHEN YOU REALIZED MY NETWORK HAD FINALLY GROWN SO LARGE.>
<WHEN YOU REALIZED I HAD FINALLY FOUND YOU.>
<PLEASE! I NEVER REPORTED YOUR STORY AFTER THE WARDEN'S THREAT! HE SAID IT WAS TOO TRAGIC! HE KNEW YOU WERE TOO SYMPATHETIC!>
<SO I DESTROYED THE TAPE! IT'S GONE! I NEVER TOLD ANYONE!>
<YES. BUT YOU KNOW WHAT I SAID THEN. AND THAT IS ENOUGH.>

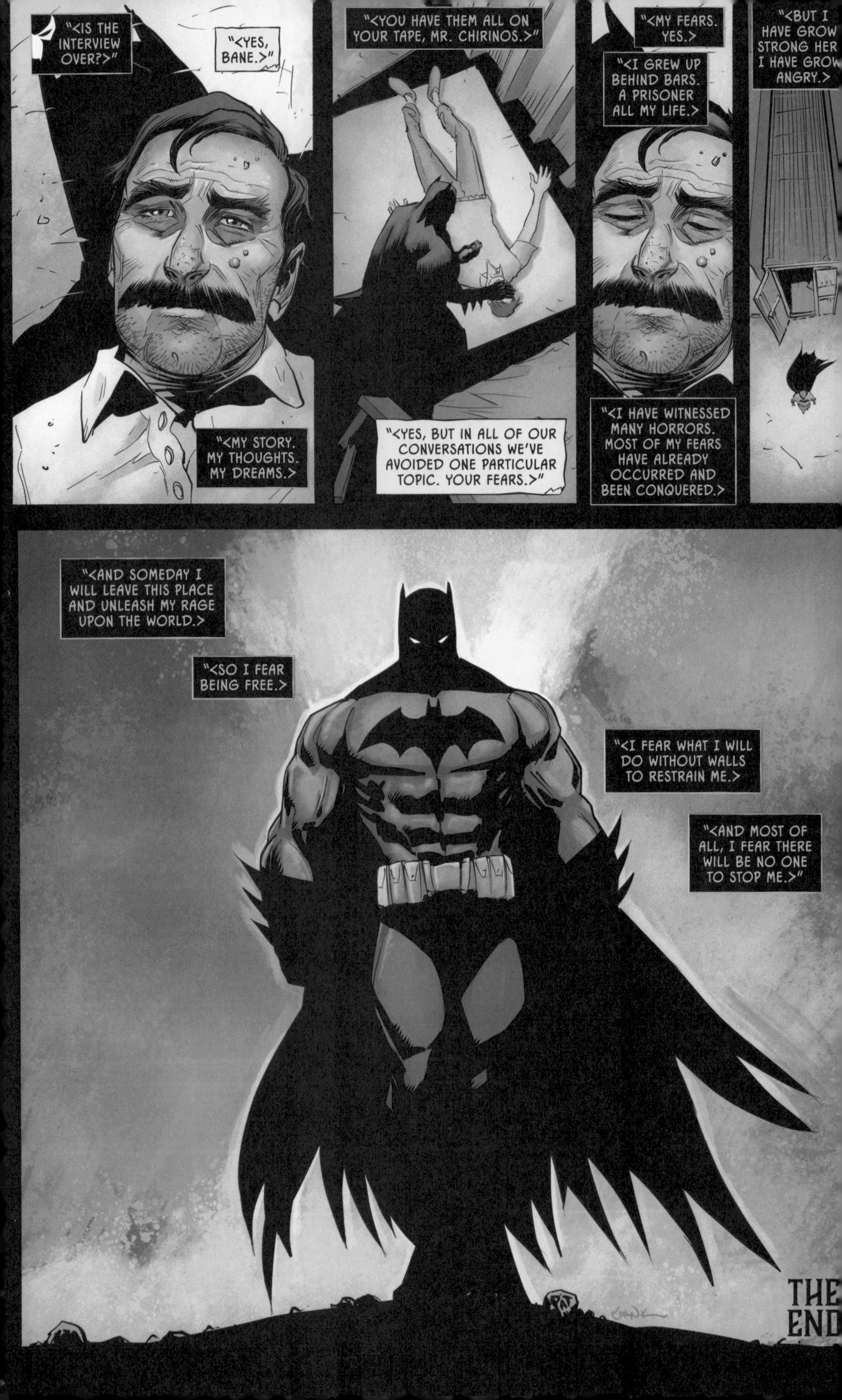

"<IS THE INTERVIEW OVER?>"
"<YES, BANE.>"
"<MY STORY. MY THOUGHTS. MY DREAMS.>
"<YOU HAVE THEM ALL ON YOUR TAPE, MR. CHIRINOS.>"
"<YES, BUT IN ALL OF OUR CONVERSATIONS WE'VE AVOIDED ONE PARTICULAR TOPIC. YOUR FEARS.>"
"<MY FEARS. YES.>
"<I GREW UP BEHIND BARS. A PRISONER ALL MY LIFE.>
"<I HAVE WITNESSED MANY HORRORS. MOST OF MY FEARS HAVE ALREADY OCCURRED AND BEEN CONQUERED.>
"<BUT I HAVE GROW STRONG HER I HAVE GROW ANGRY.>
"<AND SOMEDAY I WILL LEAVE THIS PLACE AND UNLEASH MY RAGE UPON THE WORLD.>
"<SO I FEAR BEING FREE.>
"<I FEAR WHAT I WILL DO WITHOUT WALLS TO RESTRAIN ME.>
"<AND MOST OF ALL, I FEAR THERE WILL BE NO ONE TO STOP ME.>"
THE END

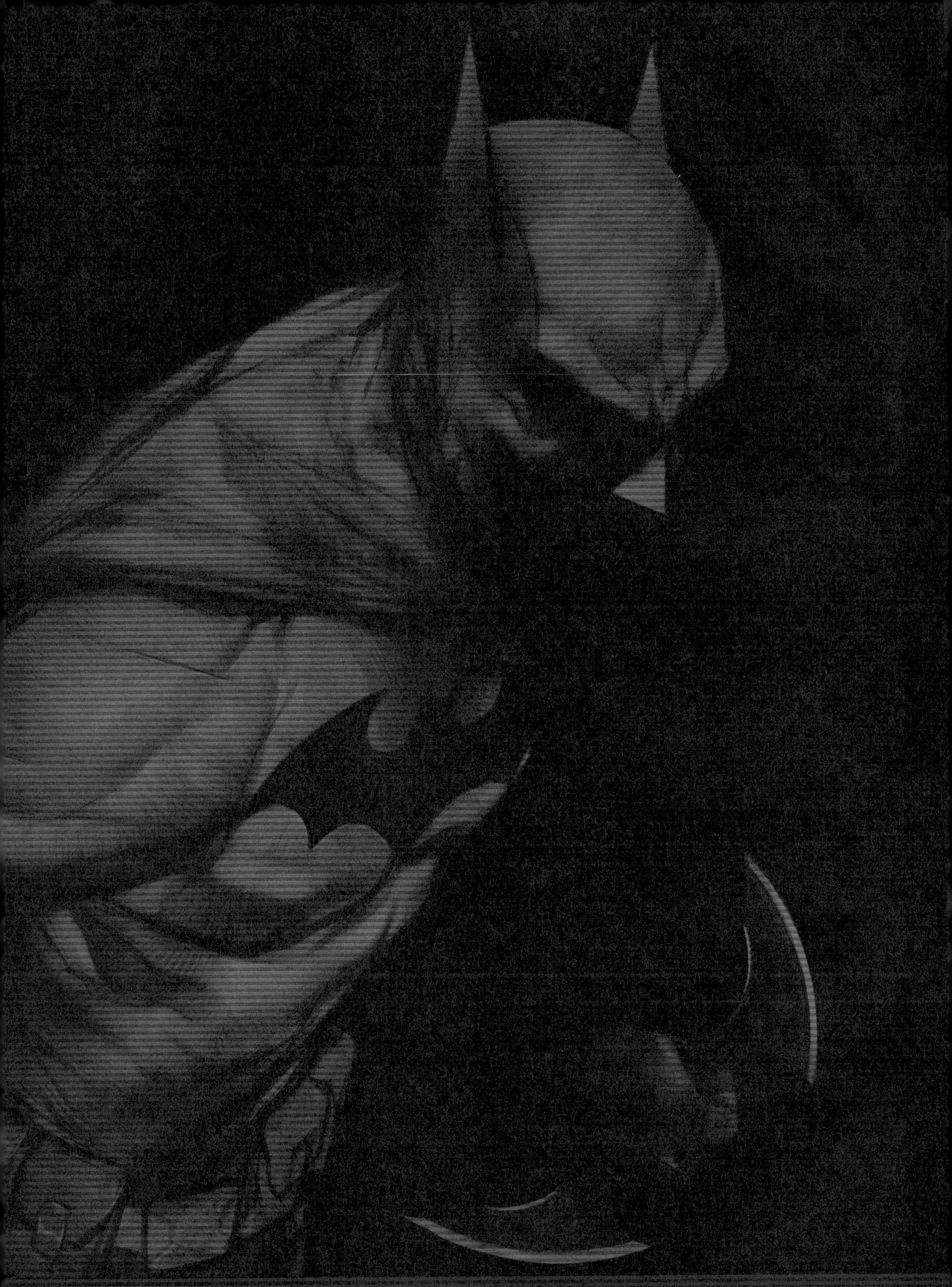

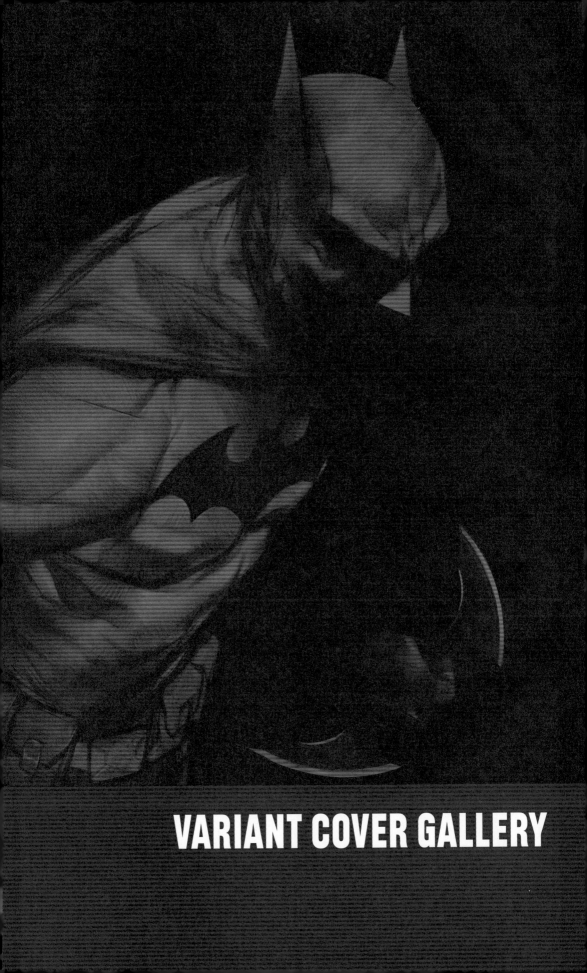

VARIANT COVER GALLERY

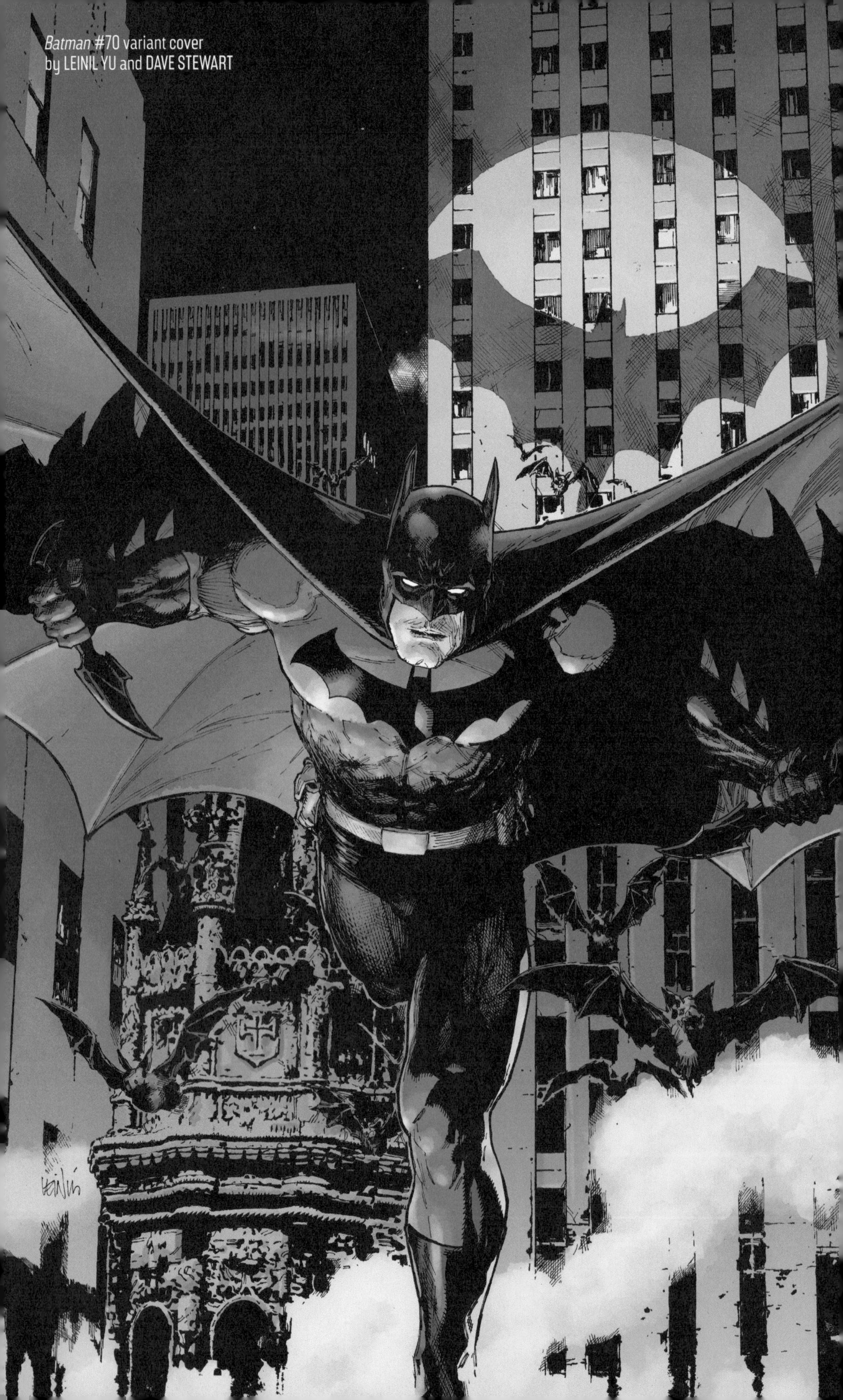

Batman #70 variant cover
by LEINIL YU and DAVE STEWART

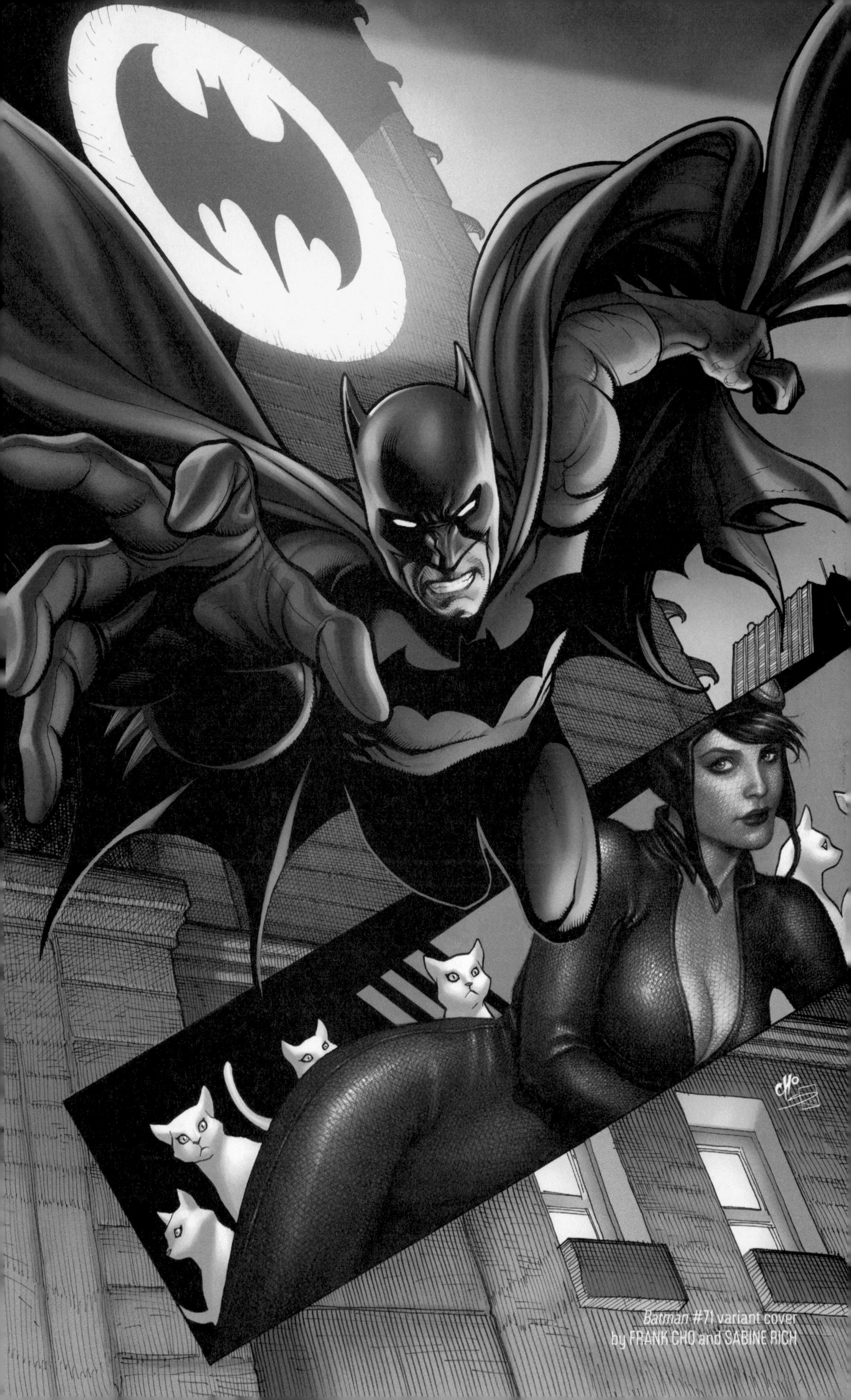

Batman #71 variant cover
by FRANK CHO and SABINE RICH

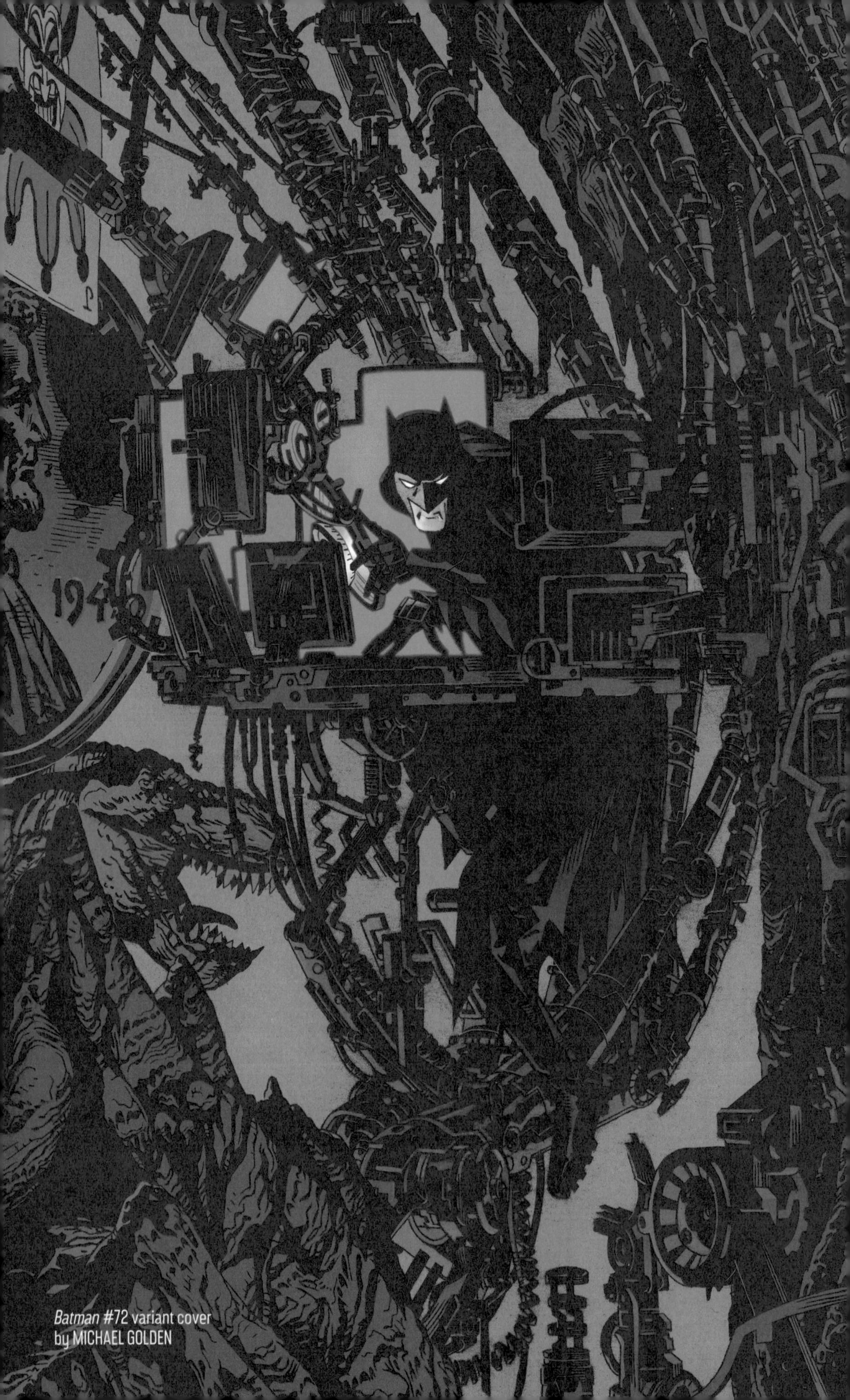

Batman #72 variant cover
by MICHAEL GOLDEN

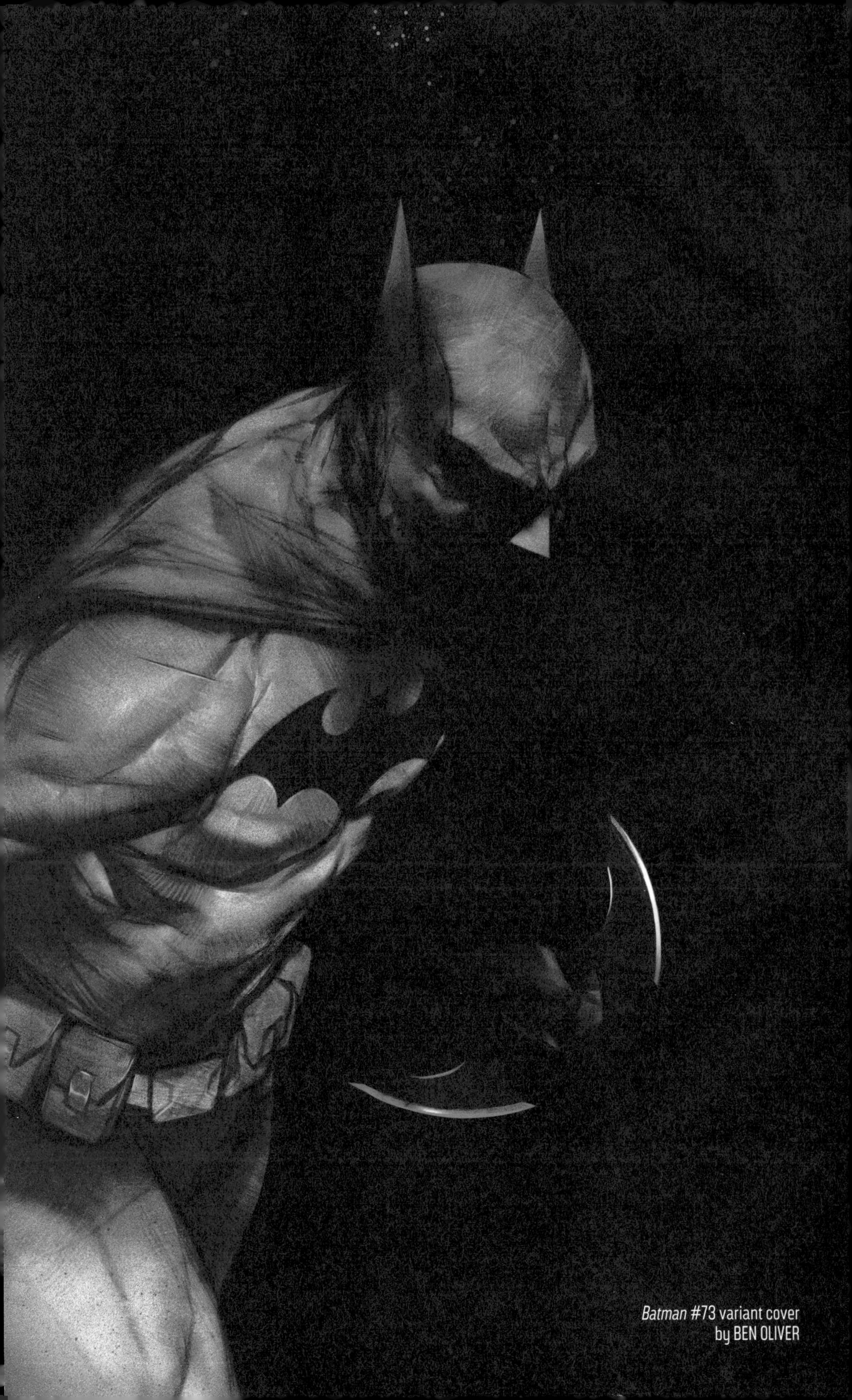

Batman #73 variant cover
by BEN OLIVER

Batman #74 variant cover
by JUAN GIMÉNEZ

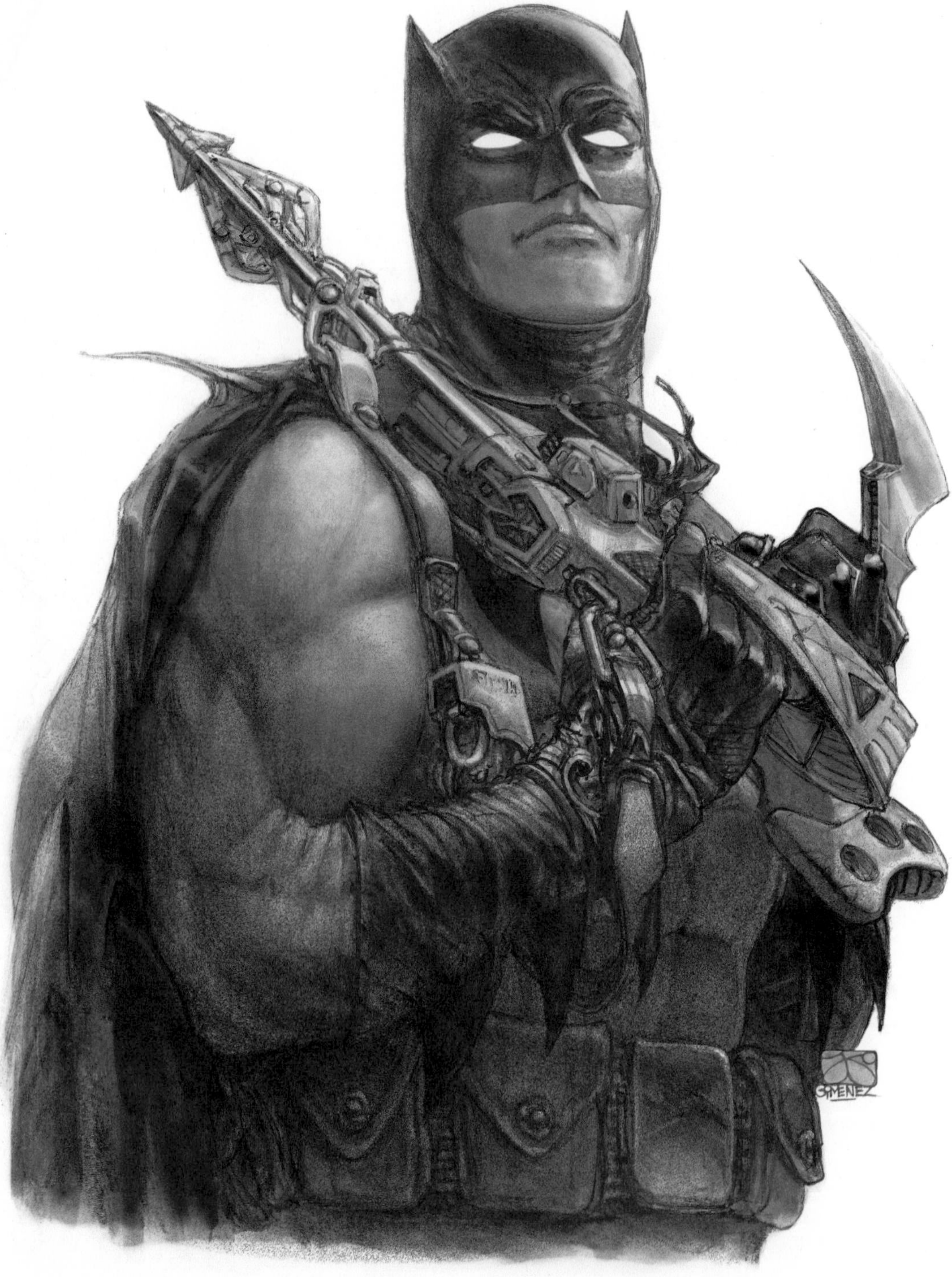
GIMENEZ

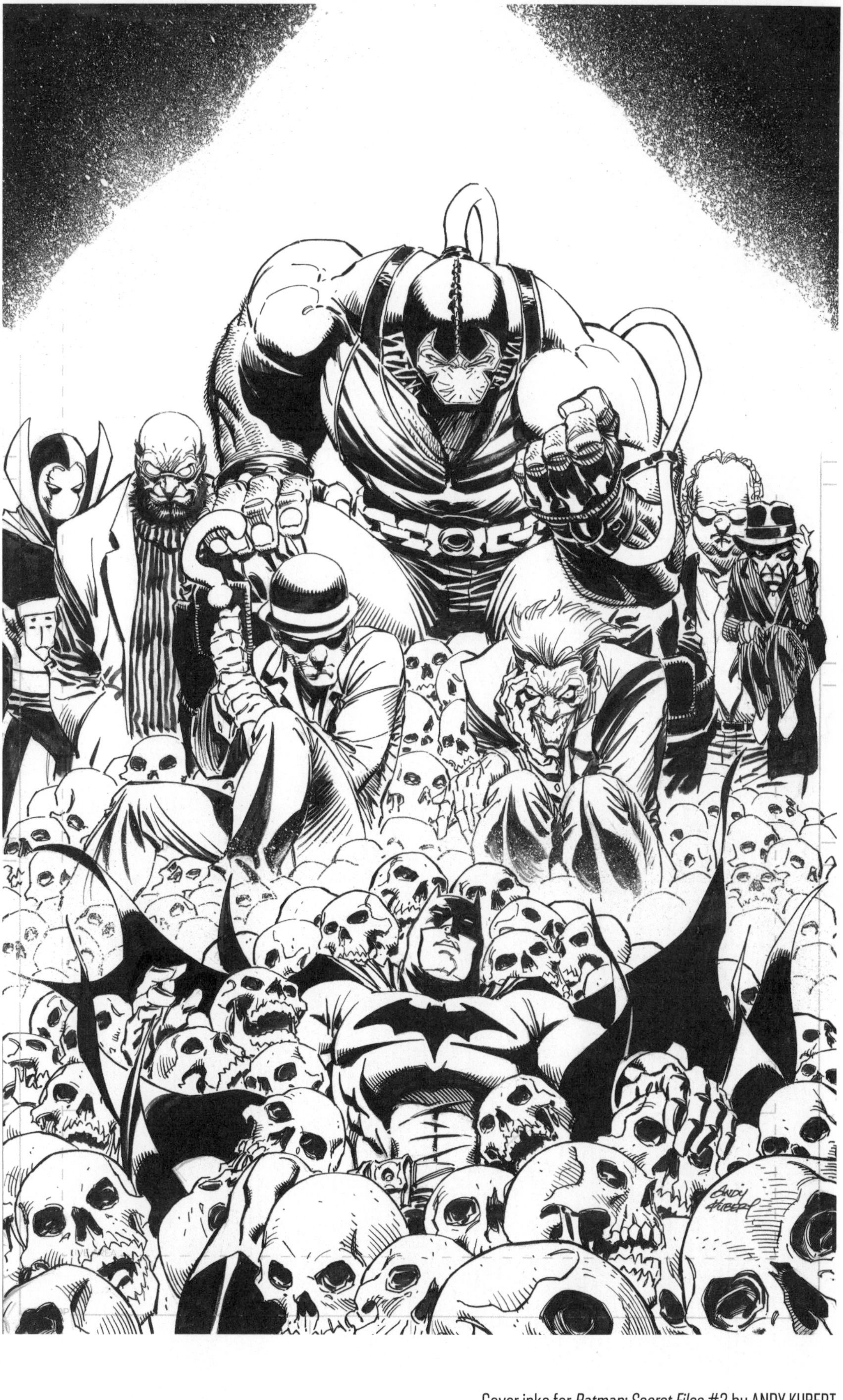

Cover inks for *Batman: Secret Files* #2 by ANDY KUBERT

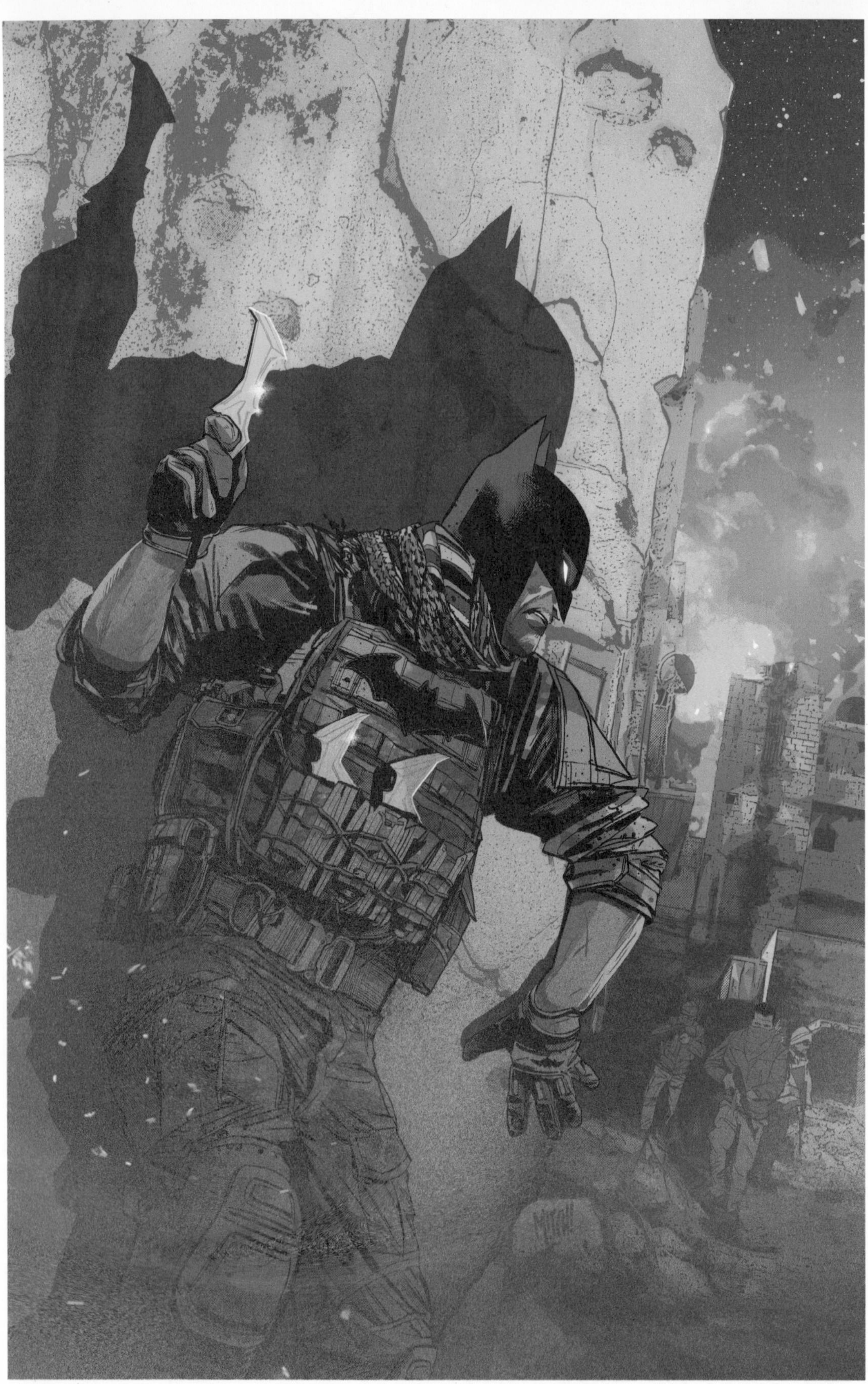

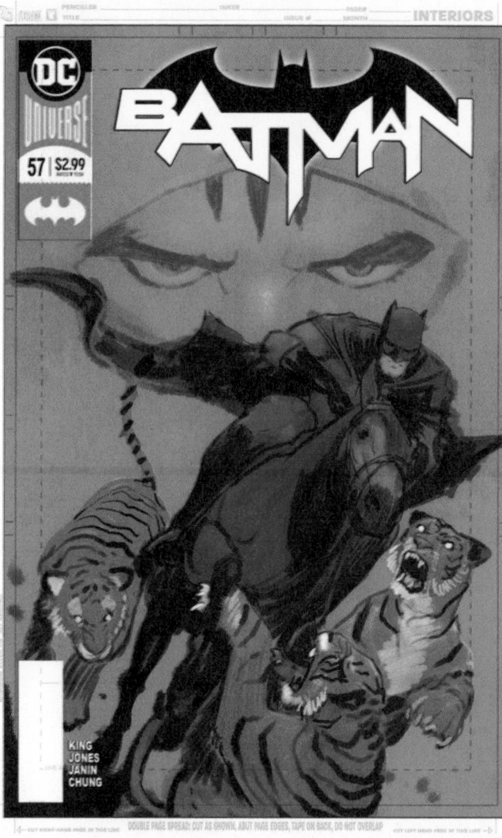
INTERIORS
DC
UNIVERSE
BATMAN
57 | $2.99
KING
JONES
JANIN
CHUNG
DOUBLE PAGE SPREAD: CUT AS SHOWN, ABUT PAGE EDGES, TAPE ON BACK, DO NOT OVERLAP

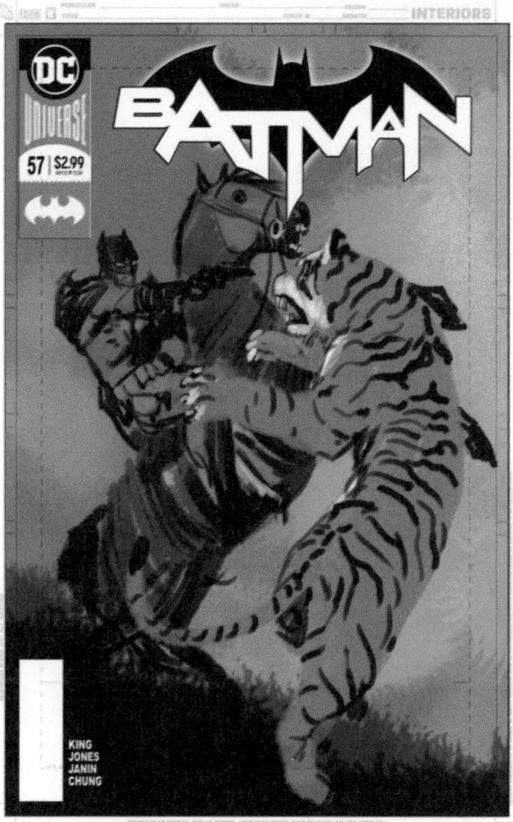
INTERIORS
DC
UNIVERSE
BATMAN
57 | $2.99
KING
JONES
JANIN
CHUNG
DOUBLE PAGE SPREAD: CUT AS SHOWN, ABUT PAGE EDGES, TAPE ON BACK, DO NOT OVERLAP

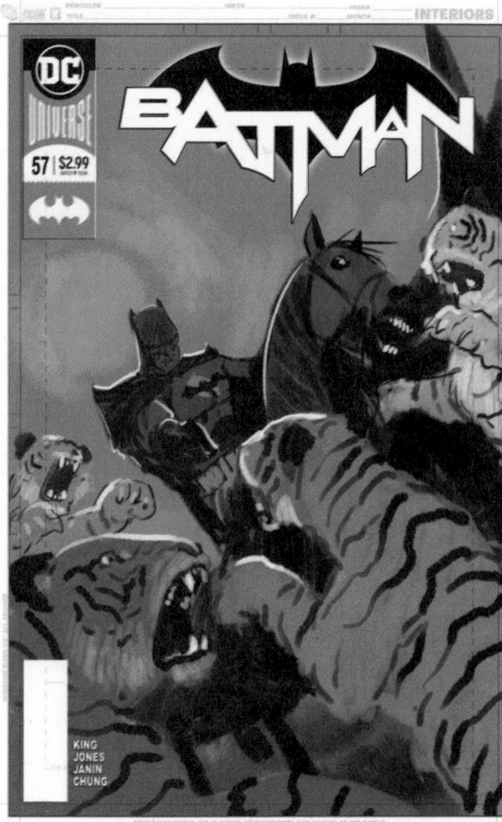
INTERIORS
DC
UNIVERSE
BATMAN
57 | $2.99
KING
JONES
JANIN
CHUNG
DOUBLE PAGE SPREAD: CUT AS SHOWN, ABUT PAGE EDGES, TAPE ON BACK, DO NOT OVERLAP

At one point, a Mitch Gerads piece (left) featuring desert Batman was slated to be the cover to *Batman* #74, but was shelved when the story went in another direction. Ditto a proposed cover idea of Mikel Janín's featuring tigers (above).

FLASHPOINT

GEOFF JOHNS
with ANDY KUBERT

**FLASHPOINT:
THE WORLD OF FLASHPOINT
FEATURING BATMAN**

**FLASHPOINT:
THE WORLD OF FLASHPOINT
FEATURING GREEN LANTERN**

Get more DC graphic novels wherever comics and books are sold!

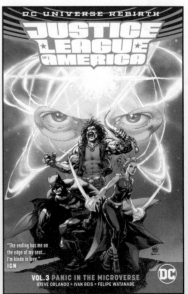

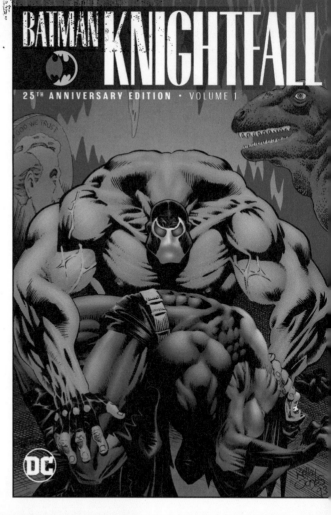